TRIUMPH
IN THE WEST

FIELD-MARSHAL VISCOUNT ALANBROOKE

ARTHUR BRYANT

TRIUMPH IN THE WEST
1943–1946

*Based on the Diaries and
Autobiographical Notes of Field Marshal
The Viscount Alanbrooke*

KG., O.M.

COLLINS
ST JAMES'S PLACE, LONDON

FIRST IMPRESSION   NOVEMBER, 1959
SECOND IMPRESSION   NOVEMBER, 1959

PRINTED IN GREAT BRITAIN
COLLINS CLEAR-TYPE PRESS : LONDON AND GLASGOW

FOREWORD

In one of my diary entries, sandwiched between an account of a C.O.S. Committee and of interviews with Montgomery and the Prime Minister, there is a note that Arthur Bryant came to luncheon and that I " found him very interesting ". He seems to have found me interesting too! If anyone else does so, it will be due to his years of patient labour in presenting my diary record of my war experiences and setting it against the broader picture of the war as a whole. The friendship that inspired that labour has been one of the best things life has brought me.

The work of a C.I.G.S. or a Commander-in-Chief is only possible because he is a member of a team in which thousands of others play their part. For this reason it is impossible to thank as I should all who helped me to play mine. In the course of the autobiographical notes quoted in this volume I have tried to express what I owe to my two colleagues of the C.O.S. Committee and to the distinguished officers—all, like them, trusted and valued friends—who worked with me at Storey's Gate, at the War Office and in the field. I have tried, too, in recording, in July 1945, the end of our long partnership, to express some sense of the obligation which, in common with every Briton, I owe to the great statesman who led us out of the abyss to victory. But for him, as Sir Arthur has written, there " would have been neither turn of the tide nor triumph in the west ". That, in the course of my duty, I had sometimes to oppose him or criticise his strategic projects does not in any way diminish the admiration I feel for him or the debt I owe him for the trust he reposed in me and the leadership he gave me.

Though there are many whom I have no space to thank by name, I should like to take this opportunity of recording my debt to my personal staff. In my Military Assistants, Colonel R. Stanyforth and Colonel Brian Boyle, I had two of the most painstaking and hard-working assistants one could have asked for. Ronnie Stanyforth's efficiency and ability did much towards making life less unpleasant during the first winter of the war and my two evacuations from France in the summer of 1940. Brian Boyle's meticulous attention to the minutest details while I was C.I.G.S. saved me an infinity of trouble, and I could always rely on being provided with all the papers I could possibly need at any meeting arranged in the most systematic order. I was blessed, too, in turn, with two wonderful A.D.C.s in the late Captain A. K. Charlesworth and Colonel H. V. S. Charrington—both of whom gave me not only devoted service but what I valued even more, friendship and companionship. " Barney " Charlesworth was my daily companion for five years and his death was one of the most serious personal losses I suffered in the war. Rollie Charrington, an old friend of many years standing, volunteered out of the kindness of his heart to come to me after Charlesworth's death, and his presence during the last year of my service was like that of a brother.

My tribute of personal gratitude would not be complete without mention of my batman, Corporal L. Lockwood, and my car driver, Sergeant P. G. Parker. Corporal Lockwood was with me for the whole of my period as C.I.G.S., acting as butler in my flat and accompanying me on all my trips with the Prime Minister and the C.O.S. Never once did he fail me. In Sergeant Parker I had a driver of exceptional skill who came to me when I became Commander-in-Chief, Home Forces, and remained till my retirement. He drove the Rolls Royce I had inherited from my predecessor right through the Blitz, with darkened streets, no head lamps and debris and demolitions in the road without once having a serious accident. Considering the many thousands of miles we covered together, I owe him much.

In the last resort all command in war depends on the virtues and sacrifices of those who face the enemy in battle. Without them—the sailor, soldier and airman—all my planning and that of my chief and colleagues would have been in vain.

ALANBROOKE

CONTENTS

MAPS

Our story in this war is a good one, and this will be recognised as time goes on.

WINSTON CHURCHILL
TO ALANBROOKE

Prelude

THE
ALANBROOKE DIARIES

The Turn of the Tide covered the first eighteen months of Lord Alanbrooke's term as Chairman of the Chiefs of Staff Committee. This volume covers the remaining three years, including the last two of the War. It embraces the Cairo, Teheran, Second Quebec, Second Moscow, Malta, Yalta and Potsdam Conferences, the expulsion of the Germans from Italy, the liberation of France and the Low Countries, the Rhineland campaign and the German surrender. It covers, too, the reconquest of Burma and the defeat of Japan, and a Commonwealth tour which Alanbrooke made immediately after the War to report on the military situation in the Middle East, India, Malaya, Australasia and Africa and in the course of which he stayed at Tokyo with General MacArthur.

The theme of *The Turn of the Tide* was how out of defeat a road was taken that led to victory. That of *Triumph in the West* is how, by following that road, victory was won. It is based on a day-by-day diary commentary on the making of the strategy of this country and the Western Alliance as seen through the eyes of one of its principal architects. His diary was begun in September, 1939 as an unsent letter to his wife; it continued until June, 1946 when he laid down his charge as Chief of the Imperial General Staff and Chairman of the Chiefs of Staff Committee.

In this volume even more than in its predecessor I have based my book on the diary, quoting from it, wherever possible, in preference to Alanbrooke's post-war commentary or my own narrative. The latter has been used only to set his daily

15

jottings into the general framework of a global war, many of whose events he took for granted and whose details the ordinary reader has probably forgotten. Apart from providing this framework I have let the diary speak for itself. It has not been possible, of course, to print it in its entirety. Like all diaries it contains much that is repetitive or day-by-day routine of little general interest. It contains, too, as any diary must, material that might hurt personal feelings without adding anything essential to the record. Such passages, however, are less frequent than some reviewers of *The Turn of the Tide* assumed from the omission marks with which, out of a historian's habit, I indicated every omitted passage. I have therefore been less pedantic and have only used omission marks where substantial or important passages are missing.

This book is not a biography, nor is it a history of the war. It rests on a diary compiled in the heat of pressing events. It reveals how the diarist saw himself and those around him, but not how they saw him. The side of Alanbrooke's character which emerges from his journal is one never seen by those who worked with him and that was far from being the whole man. In contrast to the portrait which he paints of himself— impatient, irritable and, at moments of exhaustion, anxious and even querulous—he was, by the testimony of almost all who served with him, habitually self-controlled, calm and imperturbable. " I am feeling very weary and old," he wrote in his diary a few weeks before D-Day, " and wish to God this would finish! " No one near him would have guessed it. To the members of the War Cabinet, to his colleagues of the Chiefs of Staff Committee and to the commanders in the field he seemed a man of iron without nerves or feelings.

The contrast between Alanbrooke's outward bearing and the uninhibited self-revelation of his journal is thus bewildering. As biography the diary is a distorting mirror. It not only presents a personality quite different to the selfless, though stern and reticent soldier who, apparently unmoved by disaster and pressure, directed Britain's armies from the winter of Singapore to the summer of Lüneberg Heath. It reflects the unguarded moods of a deeply sensitive and self-repressed man carrying an almost intolerable burden and releasing feelings that he could not reveal to anyone except the person for whom the diary was kept. It was a safety-valve for irritation and anxiety in a life of constant frustration and strain. Alanbrooke was not, as may at times seem from its pages, a disagreeable man expressing disapproval of his colleagues and contempt for every view but his own, but a sensitive and tired human being, tried and exasperated almost beyond endurance by the burden he was carrying and which, because he bore it so efficiently, he was never allowed to lay down.

In letting his diary tell his story Alanbrooke has allowed a picture of himself to emerge very different from the polished portrait of memoir writers. And in the post-war autobiographical notes which, without altering the original record, he added to his diary, he draws attention to his contemporary misjudgments. Thus he tells us how mistaken he was in supposing that the Prime Minister's powers were failing in the strained months before D-Day or in imagining that Churchill had failed to grasp the fallacy in Eisenhower's strategic arguments before the Ardennes offensive. By doing so he deliberately tilts the record against himself.

In one respect at least Alanbrooke's wartime diary reflects his character justly. Though hypercritical of others and intolerant of what he regarded as inefficiency or stupidity, it reveals him as being without personal ambition. Apart from his resolve to win the war as quickly as possible and with as few mistakes and casualties, his only wish was to live in a world at peace, to be reunited to his wife and family and to pursue his hobbies of bird-watching and fishing. He had no axe to grind, either professional or political. It was this, as much as his unique ability and strength of mind, that gave his counsels such weight, particularly with his political chief. However unpalatable his advice—and it was frequently very unpalatable —the Prime Minister always knew that it was disinterested.

* * * * * * * *

A diary has grave limitations, too, as history. It is not a comprehensive assessment of events calmly and dispassionately seen in retrospect but an account of them written amid the passions and anxieties they evoked. Alanbrooke's nightly entries were not balanced situation-reports on the strategic situation;[1] he had neither time nor occasion for such at the end of crowded days which often continued from daybreak until his release from Churchill's side in the small hours of next morning. As the journal of any man of action must be, his diary is a record of conflict. It portrays him in continual verbal battle with adversaries—albeit colleagues and allies—upon whom, in the pursuit of duty, he was seeking to impress his views of what was the right strategy to pursue in order to defeat the Axis with the smallest possible loss of time and life.

Of these friendly adversaries the foremost, towering above everyone else, was the Prime Minister. From first to last his part in winning the war was greater than any man's—British, American or Russian. Though in the years covered by this volume his direct impact on global strategy was less than in the early part of the conflict, and the control of military operations by the Service chiefs he had chosen correspondingly closer, he still remained an incessant participator in their discussions, fertile in resource and inexhaustible in argument, and a spur and stimulus to bold action of every kind. And while, as Minister of Defence, he supervised and intervened in the debates of the professional trinity who hammered out with him Britain's design for victory, as Prime Minister he oversaw every department of the country's life and moulded it into an instrument for total war.[2] This gigantic man fired the whole nation with his passionate indignation, pugnacity, impatience and refusal to admit defeat, and even his faults, when tempered by advice, contributed as much to its victory as his incom-

[1] The difference between his considered views and his nightly snap-judgments can be seen by comparing the Chiefs of Staff's Recommendations of 11th November, 1943 for the attack on Europe printed on pp. 64-6 with the diary comments of the weeks immediately preceding it.

[2] How wonderfully he did so, and with what a comprehension of the country's minutest needs, can be seen from the Minutes printed at the end of every volume of his *Second World War*.

parable virtues. Without him there would have been neither turn of the tide nor triumph in the west.

In planning strategy Churchill and Brooke were the complement of one another. Churchill's task was to mobilize a whole people, inspire it with his resolve for victory and ensure that its effort was used with maximum force and effect. That of Brooke and his fellow Chiefs of Staff was to bring to the council table first-hand experience of the techniques of modern war and prepared plans which, before they could be translated into action, they had to pit—often for many weeks of argument —against their chief's brilliant, though at times insufficiently thought-out, proposals. That there was controversy between the Prime Minister and his C.I.G.S.—who as Chairman of the C.O.S. Committee bore the brunt of his onslaught—was inevitable; no military adviser would have been of any use to Churchill without. Brooke's supreme service to him, to the nation and to the Allied cause was that he never gave way on essentials or allowed himself to be deflected by eloquence or pressure from what he knew to be militarily right. Once, when his opposition to some cherished project had particularly infuriated him, the Prime Minister told General Ismay that the C.I.G.S. hated him and would have to go. When Ismay, acting as peacemaker, reported this to Brooke the latter replied: " I don't hate him, I love him, but when the day comes that I tell him he is right when I believe him to be wrong, it will be time for him to get rid of me."

Churchill never did. For nearly four years he tolerated Brooke's constant restraint and, where necessary, opposition, because he knew at heart, for all his attempts to beat him down, that if his adviser refused to yield on a professional matter he was probably right. Though a perpetual, and frequently invaluable, critic of every measure which he and his colleagues put forward, Churchill was, *au fond*, their indispensable partner, patron and backer. No War Minister can ever have appeared so formidable to his military advisers; none, in reality, ever interfered with them less. Though he disputed with them every move of the game, in noble contrast to the autocrat who misdirected Germany's strategy, there was no instance, after Brooke became Chairman of the Chiefs of Staff Committee, of Churchill's using his unchallenged political power to overrule them.

This was partly due to their Chairman's skill and firmness in welding them, despite differences of opinion, into a single-minded, decisive Council of War, whose will prevailed because it was unanimous. But it was still more due to Churchill's respect for constitutional forms and, despite all appearances to the contrary, to a deep-seated humility[1]—born of the vicissitudes and set-backs of his stormy career—which caused him to recognise, even though he might never admit it, that his approach to military problems needed the corrective of cooler judgments. Where he differed from Hitler and his own predecessor of the First World War, Lloyd George, was that, though well aware that soldiers could make blunders and for ever on the watch for them, he knew that in a dispute on a purely military question between a civilian, however able, and a soldier, the latter, if master of his profession, was more likely to have the correct answer. Having chosen the best and stoutest Service advisers he could find, though constantly probing and prodding them, he knew he could rely on their resistance if he went too far and always deferred in the end to their considered and united opinion. G. M. Trevelyan touched the heart of the matter when he wrote of *The Turn of The Tide*,

" So far from lowering my estimation of Winston the book, to me, has raised it. Napoleon fell because he would never take counsel; his marshals were only his servants, whereas Winston treated his generals as his advisers. This habit of taking counsel, combined with his own personal qualities, is what won the war."

· · · · · · · ·

[1] The late Lord Waverley, who knew Churchill well and served in his War Cabinet, referred in a speech in February, 1957, to this strain of humility in his chief's formidable character, and spoke of it on more than one occasion to the author.

It was Churchill who chose Brooke, Churchill who used him and who, even when he disagreed with him and passionately believed himself right and Brooke and his fellow Chiefs of Staff wrong, had the wisdom and magnanimity to be guided by them. Yet the constant, inescapable presence of that unresting genius imposed a heavy strain on his advisers. Like a transformer, they had to break down, so that it could serve practical military ends, the high-tension of his dynamic power. It had proved too much for Brooke's predecessor, and most people who had worked under the Prime Minister expected that it would prove too much for Brooke. Outwardly, after eighteen months at his side, there was still little sign of its doing so, and to his associates the C.I.G.S. seemed Prime Minister-proof. But under the surface his diary reveals just how great the strain was.

Brooke's wartime picture of Winston Churchill has been criticised in some quarters as marring the portrait that in his old age has been drawn of the great War Minister by the popular Press and a grateful Public—of a man invariably right and without human imperfections. What Brooke shows, in the mingled exasperation and admiration of his day-by-day entries, is the real Churchill—the man who rallied a defeated nation in storm and disaster: passionate, impetuous, daring, indomitable, terrible in anger and pursuing every expedient—sometimes brilliant, sometimes, for he was prepared to try almost everything, fantastic—that could bring about victory. Inevitably, seeing him so constantly, he portrays his weaknesses as well as his strength. In most of the period covered by this volume both Churchill and Brooke—the one in his seventieth year, the other over sixty—were desperately overstrained and tired. Each was usually too exhausted to realise that the other was in the same state. If Churchill, as Brooke shows, was unaware of the strain he was imposing on his subordinates, Brooke, too, tended to forget that military responsibilities were only one of the Prime Minister's many cares and that he came to the strategic debates he describes in the diary exhausted by parliamentary and political duties. This sometimes makes Brooke appear unjust to him.

Deep down Brooke realised this, for he admired and respected Churchill as much as the other trusted and respected him. Reading through his diary entries a decade later he felt that they conveyed a false impression of his feelings for his chief which had always remained those of deep affection for his human side and " unbounded admiration and gratitude for his genius and what he had done in the early years of the war." Even when most exasperated, as in the interminable debates about Far Eastern strategy before the Second Quebec Conference, he could write of him as " that superhuman being " with whom " England had been on the verge of disaster again and again " but " without whom England was lost for a certainty."[1] Yet right up to the time of the Russian breakthrough in January, 1945, aware of Hitler's frenzied search for new weapons, Brooke believed it to be possible for the Allies to throw away their victory by rash or ill-considered action. His fear of this, of Churchill's overbold, and of the Americans' over-rigid, projects is reflected in the diary, as is his irritation at the Prime Minister's incessant, and as he often felt unnecessary, interference in military detail. After Montgomery's victory in the Rhineland it is noticeable how much calmer the diary becomes and how much more relaxed and tolerant its author. With Churchill's retirement and the simultaneous collapse of Japan, though the diarist was by then a very tired man indeed, the strain and stress of his entries disappear almost completely.

But during the anxious winter and spring before D-Day when the Prime Minister was struggling with the after-effects of the pneumonia that had so nearly killed him on his way back from Teheran, and again that autumn after a recurrence of pneumonia before the Second Quebec Conference, Brooke feared that his chief's powers were failing. ' I began to feel,' he recalled, ' that the stupendous burden that he had been carrying so valiantly throughout the war was gradually crushing him.' " I am afraid he is losing ground rapidly," he

[1] *Diary*, 10 Sept., 1944.

wrote in his diary, " he seems quite incapable of concentrating for a few minutes on end and keeps wandering continuously . . . He has probably done more for this country than any other human being has ever done; his reputation has reached its climax. It would be a tragedy to blemish such a past during an inevitable decline which has set in. I am filled with apprehension as to where he may lead us."

He led us to victory, and his trust in his military advisers was a major factor in winning it. Remaining a leader, he refused to be a dictator. Because of this, despite the Axis's immense initial advantage, the war was not only won, but won with the minimum of error and casualties. Britain's finely tempered mechanism of Defence Minister, War Cabinet and Chiefs of Staff in permanent debate to achieve agreement in decision and action proved a more effective instrument for victory than Germany's political dictatorship and subservient military machine. Brooke's chronicle of verbal battle enables us to hear the dynamo at work and watch its processes. Those who complain that the sound is harsh and grating—whether they complain of Brooke or of Churchill—miss the point. Out of that clash in counsel came, with astonishing smoothness, the ordered movements of the great national effort that won the war.

• • • • • • • • •

At Whitehall, because power rested with a Defence Minister who, though in no awe of his Service advisers and ready to harry them mercilessly, would never in their own sphere override them or allow them to be overridden, Brooke in the end usually had the last word.[1] It was otherwise in the controversies between the British Chiefs of Staff and the Americans. At

---

[1] " In the last four years of the war, partly because of the growing prominence of land operations in the British effort and largely because of his own qualities, Brooke normally represented the (Chiefs of Staff) Committee in questions of grand strategy . . . Possessing a clear and acute mind, great professional integrity, and —a useful attribute on occasions—a strong but controlled temper, his views always commanded the respect of the Army, of his Naval and Air colleagues, and, even when the two men differed, of the Prime Minister . . . And when they were required to act as a corrective to Mr. Churchill, it was he who usually bore, and resolutely, the brunt of what ensued." John Ehrman, *History of the Second World War, Grand Strategy* VI, 327.

Washington, where they sat by proxy on the Combined Chiefs of Staff of the two nations, and in the great Anglo-American Conferences, the British Chiefs of Staff had to contend on equal and, as the United States grew stronger, on less than equal terms with their American opposite numbers who not only had the self-confidence of their great country but could not help unconsciously resenting the superior military experience of their British colleagues. Under these circumstances and in the light of America's prodigious war effort and achievement there was only one course for Britain to adopt: for the sake of Allied unity to allow the titular command in the more important operations to Americans. Eisenhower—who became the embodiment of this principle and whose integrity, sense of justice and unique charm perfectly fitted him to fill it—represented the dominant national contribution to the fighting forces of the West and, as such, possessed the same overriding claim to supreme command as the royal princes and archdukes of the monarchical past. So long as he was prepared to remain a Supreme Commander and leave the direction of campaigns and battles to more experienced subordinates, all was well.

Between the hour when, after the calamitous winter of 1941-2, Churchill called Brooke to his side, and the summer of 1944, when the American fighting contribution to the war against Germany began to surpass Britain's, the Western Allies made no major strategic mistake, though American reluctance to commit forces to the Mediterranean prevented them from reaping their full opportunities in that theatre. From the time when the landing in the South of France was finally agreed until the end of the war they made several— nearly all at Washington's or Eisenhower's instance—which not only delayed victory and exacted a heavy toll in human life but threw away part of its ultimate fruits. The story of how this came about is set out more fully in Alanbrooke's diary than in any other published source. In all these conflicts between the British and American Chiefs of Staff, it is interesting to note, Churchill, however prolonged his preceding arguments with his official military advisers, invariably sided

24

with the latter and presented a united front to what he and they regarded as American error. Indeed, in the early stages of the alliance, before Roosevelt began to fail, it was generally Churchill's influence with the President that enabled the more experienced British view to prevail.

. . . .

Surprise has sometimes been expressed that those responsible for directing the war should have disagreed as to how it should be won. It has even been suggested that the sacrifices of younger men in battle should have awed them into greater unity. This is nonsense. Apart from the fact that generals, admirals and air-marshals have usually had their full share of front-line fighting in youth—and this was never truer than when Britain went to war in 1939—strategic decision, if more than one man is to make it, can only be reached through argument and controversy. The diary of a C.I.G.S. in daily conference with others about the conduct of a war must, by its nature, be a record of disagreement. How else, unless all of them started of the same mind, could agreement and decision ever be reached? To complain that Brooke in his diary is for ever criticising the views of others and expressing disapproval of them is to complain of his doing what he was appointed to do. What matters is that, despite, and indeed because of, such controversy, agreement was reached and, far more often than not, right agreement. The historical value of Brooke's diary is that it affords a first-hand and contemporaneous view of this process. Official histories can record the decisions reached, the reasons for them and their results. But they seldom show the creative clash, not only of opinion, but of human temperament in their making. Strategy, like history, is made by men.

Some have questioned whether a diary so frank and revealing as Lord Alanbrooke's should have been published in the lifetime of its author. It was certainly not intended to be, for after his retirement he persistently refused to write his war memoirs or to allow any book to be written about him until after his death. Had others preserved the same silence the public would have had to wait many more years before his diaries saw the light of day or his part in the war became known. But during the first post-war decade a succession of widely read memoirs by American war leaders and Service chiefs appeared, presenting a very different view to Brooke's of the events which had brought about victory and reflecting on the judgment and competence both of himself and of the British commanders who served under him. During this period the six volumes of Sir Winston Churchill's *Second World War* also appeared, giving in great, though not always complete, detail Sir Winston's version of the events in which he and Alanbrooke were so intimately and, after 1941, inseparably associated. The latter's viewpoint and the extremely important story of what he sought to achieve, and how, were thus in danger of being obscured or forgotten.

When the Alanbrooke diaries can be printed in their entirety and collated with the confidential records of the Chiefs of Staff and War Cabinet meetings on which they form a commentary, it will be possible to present a far more just picture of the man himself and the problems with which he was faced. At present, however, there is no other source for assessing Brooke's contribution to victory than this diary-record of the day-by-day discussions in which he took part. The field commanders who served under him and his colleagues had their triumphs on the battlefield to testify to their skill and judgment; what he wrote at the time in his diary is often the only evidence of how he reached the decisions on which these victories depended and persuaded his colleagues, political chiefs and allies to adopt them.

. . . .

As in *The Turn of the Tide*, to distinguish between Lord Alanbrooke's diary and the Autobiographical Notes which he added ten years after the war, I have used double quotation marks for the former and single quotation marks for the latter, which are also set in a slightly less deep inset than the diary extracts.

Chapter One

AN OPTION OF DIFFICULTIES

Strategy, like politics, is the art of the possible.

JOHN EHRMAN

IN THE first week of September, 1943, a letter reached the Chief of the Imperial General Staff from the victorious general who had been his right-hand man in the retreat to Dunkirk and whom just over a year before he had chosen to command a defeated army in the Western Desert. It was dated September 3rd and written on Italian soil.

" My dear Brookie,

" I attacked across the Straits of Messina this morning at 0430 hours. And at 1030 hours I stepped ashore myself on the mainland of Europe just north of Reggio. It was a great thrill once more to set foot on the continent from which we were pushed off three years ago at Dunkirk! "

" The opposition was slight[1] . . . I now have my tactical Headquarters in Europe. It is a great day and it is the anniversary of the outbreak of the war, and the beginning of the fifth year of the war. . . ."

" There is no doubt some of my chaps are getting tired. Continuous and hard fighting is a great strain. . . . I have a feeling you think I am idle and ought not to go to bed after dinner and read a novel or do some quiet thinking in bed.

---

[1] " The Germans evacuated Reggio before we got into the town so we had no opposition from soldiers. But there is a zoo in the town and our shelling broke open some cages; a puma and a monkey escaped and attacked some men of the H.Q. 3rd Canadian Brigade, and heavy fire was opened by the Canadians. . . . It is a curious war." Gen. Montgomery to C.I.G.S., 3 Sept., 1943. Lord Alanbrooke, *Personal Files.*

But I can assure you that if I did not do this I could not possibly go on with the business at the present tempo and pace. . . .

> Yours ever,
> Monty."

With the end of Britain's fourth year at war the penultimate stage had been reached in the grand design which the British Chiefs of Staff had envisaged as the way to defeat Germany and which General Sir Alan Brooke had been persistently pursuing since he had become their Chairman after the fall of Singapore. During the past ten months the great victories of Alamein, North Africa and Sicily, the bombing of the Ruhr and Rhineland and the dramatic defeat of the U-boats in the Atlantic had not only inflicted on Hitler losses which would have seemed inconceivable a year earlier[1] but, while immeasurably improving the Allies' sea communications, had forced him, as Brooke had intended, to deflect a growing proportion of his resources to defend his hitherto unassailable back-door to the south. Now the sudden conquest of Sicily, the fall of Mussolini and the landing on the Italian mainland marked the culmination of the campaign which was to prepare the way for a concerted attack on Germany's heart from west and east—across the Channel and the Russian and Polish plains.

At the Quebec Conference, from which Brooke had returned to England at the end of August, the decision had been taken to invade Normandy in the early summer of 1944 provided operations on the Mediterranean and Russian fronts should by then have made it impossible for the Germans to oppose the landing with a striking reserve of more than twelve mobile divisions and should have immobilized their air-fighter strength in the West.[2] Accordingly Montgomery's Eighth Army—the first Allied force to gain a foothold on the European mainland

---

[1] " It gives one the creeps to look at the map and compare what we had under our dominion about this time last year with the distance we have now been thrown back." *Goebbels Diary*, 371. (21 Sept. 1943.)

[2] *Cross-Channel Attack*, 77 *et seq.*; *Ehrman* V, 56-7.

—had crossed the Straits of Messina with two divisions on September 3rd, while a British-American force of some four divisions, supported by seven British aircraft-carriers, four battleships and eight cruisers and four American cruisers[1] had sailed from the ports of North Africa and Sicily with the object of landing in Salerno Bay, two hundred miles north of Montgomery's Calabrian landing and only thirty miles from Naples. As a result of secret negotiations with the new Badoglio Government—still formally at war with Britain and America—it had been agreed that this second landing should be immediately preceded by an Italian declaration of war against Germany, the disarming of the German garrisons in Italy and the Mediterranean islands and the landing of an Allied airborne division at Rome.

Everywhere on the Continent at that moment the effects were being felt of Hitler's furious reaction to the British strategy of reopening the Mediterranean and striking across it in order to draw Germany's troops from France and Russia into Europe's mountainous southern perimeter. Since the invasion of Sicily in July more than forty Axis divisions had had to be withdrawn or were in process of being withdrawn from other fronts. Already the number of German divisions in Italy had risen from six to sixteen and in the Balkans from twelve to eighteen, while others were on their way along the inadequate roads and railways that led from the Reich to the Mediterranean. And partly because of these withdrawals and the fact that nearly three-quarters of Germany's air-fighter force was by now concentrated in Western and Southern Europe, so giving the Russians the superiority in the air they had hitherto lacked, the Red Army, though still three hundred miles from the German frontier, had been able to advance along the whole of its central and southern front and was still advancing. " The situation has become so critical," Goebbels wrote on September 8th, " that the Fuehrer may fly there himself to take charge." Two days later he noted that the crisis in the East would never have arisen if the divisions that

---

[1] *U.S. Naval Operations World War II*, Vol. IX, App. II.

Germany was forced to send to Italy could have been assigned to the Russian front. " If we had fifteen or twenty first-class divisions to throw into the East intact we would undoubtedly be in a position to repulse the Russians. Unfortunately we must put these fifteen or twenty divisions into combat in the Italian theatre of war." In the next few weeks the Red Army was able to recapture Smolensk, Briansk and the Black Sea naval port of Novorossisik. Meanwhile in the Balkans the peasant partisans of Yugoslavia, relieved of the Italian garrisons, put more than 200,000 men into the field under the Communist guerrilla, Tito. By the end of the month, having liberated the Dalmatian coast, they were already containing, helped by the threat of an Allied landing, eighteen German and eight Bulgarian and Croat divisions. In Greece and Albania similar risings broke out.

Yet because of the American Chiefs of Staff's rigid adherence to the decisions taken at Quebec and their profound distrust of Britain's Mediterranean strategy, the opportunity offered by Hitler's embarrassments was not grasped. By delaying the decision to invade Italy until Sicily was half conquered, they had allowed seven fateful weeks to be lost after Mussolini's fall and now, in their anxiety not to become too deeply committed in the Mediterranean, they had so limited the resources available for the landing on the west Italian coast as to endanger the expedition's safety. Shortage of aircraft-carriers made it impracticable to land farther north than Salerno bay—the farthest point at which long-range fighters based on Sicily could operate—and lack of assault-craft made it impossible to put more than four divisions at first ashore. With only seven Allied divisions coming to their immediate aid—four at Salerno, two in southern Calabria and one landed by the Royal Navy at Taranto—and with more than twice that number of German divisions in their country, the Italian leaders and their bewildered forces failed to act. And while they hesitated, the Germans struck. Within forty-eight hours they had disarmed the Italian garrison of Rome and gained control of all the principal cities of the north. And, freed from the fear of

Italian resistance and any further major Allied descent from the sea against their long and exposed coastal communications, they had fallen fiercely on the invaders at Salerno. For a week it was touch-and-go whether the British and Americans would be able to hold the bridgehead until reinforcements from the sea and Montgomery's men, hurrying up from the south along mined and bridgeless roads, could relieve the pressure of the German armour.

Having for months been trying to impress on his American colleagues the importance of being ready to take advantage of success with every man and weapon available, Brooke had not been sanguine about the Salerno landing. After his return from the Quebec Conference he had gone to the Durham moors on his first furlough for two years, but three days later had hurriedly flown south again.

" *September 8th.* Went up to the War Office in the morning where I discovered that all plans were made to announce the Armistice with Italy that evening and to invade Naples the next morning, combined with an air-borne landing near Rome. In the middle of the day wire arrived from Eisenhower to the effect that Badoglio was ratting and that he did not consider he could hold the Germans in check; however, decided to continue with the operations except for the airborne landing outside Rome."

For the next four days the C.I.G.S. had remained at his Hampshire home, anxiously watching the course of events for which he had been planning for so long but which he was now powerless to influence. On the day that German counter-attacks against the beachhead all but reached the sea, he returned to the War Office.

" *September 13th.* This date brought to an end the first real spell of leave that I have had since taking over the job of C.I.G.S. Archie Nye took the C.O.S. meeting whilst I read hard to bring myself up to date again. A great deal has been going on, and a great deal of what

31

I saw I did not like. The Salerno build-up is not fast enough, whilst the Taranto-Brindisi forces are not being made sufficient use of. It is hell to have to face the chance of being driven out of Salerno at this juncture. Such a set-up would do us no good."

"*September 14th*. News about Salerno landing is going from bad to worse. It is maddening not to be able to get the Americans to realise that they are going to burn their fingers *before* they do so . . ."

On the day that Brooke made this entry the Supreme Commander in the Mediterranean, General Eisenhower, told his naval A.D.C. that if the Salerno battle ended in disaster, " he would probably be out ".[1]

But by the evening of September 16th, just under a fortnight after his men crossed the Messina Strait and a week after the Salerno landing, Montgomery's advance-guard was only a few miles away and the troops in the bridgehead, continually reinforced from the sea, were able to hit back. Though the means for executing it had been dangerously stinted, the strategy of using sea-power to leap-frog up the Italian coastline had proved itself. While Brooke wrote that night in his diary,

" News of Salerno improving,"

his fellow diarist, Dr. Goebbels, was writing,

" At Salerno there is a race against time. Our General Staff still believes it can master the situation and hurl the English and Americans back into the ocean. In the course of the day, however, the situation changed somewhat in favour of our enemies. Every hour is of irredeemable value."

Before next day, when Brooke recorded a further improvement in the situation, the German Command had decided that the risk of being caught between two fires in the foot of Italy was too great and had given orders for a withdrawal to the north. By the 18th full contact had been established between

[1] *Butcher*, 358-9.

the Eighth Army[1] and the growing American and British Fifth Army in the bridgehead. " Salerno landing," the C.I.G.S. wrote that night, " now seems safe ".

It had been a near-run thing. Transatlantic reluctance to implement Britain's Mediterranean strategy had all but caused a major reverse at the very moment that the ball in Southern Europe seemed at the Allies' feet. Behind the shortage of landing-craft[2] and carriers in the Mediterranean lay the American Chiefs of Staff's insistence on limiting the resources allocated to that theatre in order to make it impossible for the British to jettison a cross-Channel invasion in 1944 in favour of a campaign in the Balkans. For though Britain's allies had adopted the strategy propounded by her Prime Minister and Chiefs of Staff, they had never understood the logic on which it was based. It rested on the history of a sea-based Army which had always had to fight with inadequate resources and which, through many costly failures, had learnt to off-set that handicap by using sea-power to hold the enemy with the minimum of force along the widest possible circumference while concentrating striking-strength at the point where it could be most effectively used. The Americans, on the other hand, with their continental military history and their unbounded confidence in their potential numbers and resources, tended to dissipate force both in space and time. When, in pursuit of the agreed policy of destroying Germany first, the opportunity had come to reap the fruits of the Mediterranean strategy by striking with everything available at the enemy's tottering outposts in Southern Europe, the American Chiefs of Staff, conscious of their growing strength, were advocating simultaneous offensives in the Pacific and South-East Asia and a premature withdrawal from the Mediterranean, not only of troops but of the inadequate landing and assault-craft already there, in order to prepare for a cross-

---

[1] On September 20th, Montgomery wrote to Brooke : " We have advanced over 250 miles since we landed at Reggio and it has not been a bad performance; 250 miles by road that is, in a straight line probably less. The bridging problems have been colossal." Lord Alanbrooke, *Personal Files.*

[2] In particular of tank-landing ships—the Achilles' heel of all the Allies' amphibious operations outside the Pacific.

Channel operation that could not be launched for at least another eight months.

.   .   .   .

Yet the enemy was still immensely strong. He was master of almost all Europe except the British Isles and Russia, vast areas of whose richest territory were in his hands. He controlled nearly all South-Eastern Asia and most of the Western Pacific. In Europe, even after the loss of Italy's sixty-six divisions, the Axis disposed of well over three hundred divisions and nearly 7000 first-line aircraft. During the past year the Germans, who in 1940 had assumed that the war was won, had awoken to their danger and, by placing their economy at last on a full war footing, had doubled their production of armour, artillery and aircraft. Under the direction of Albert Speer, nearly two thousand giant tanks, stronger than any the Western allies yet possessed, had been delivered from the factories in 1943, and, despite growing bombardment from the air, the output of operational aircraft had been raised to 22,000. Though this was far below the aircraft production of the United States and Britain, the emphasis laid on fighters was threatening to make the winning of complete air mastery —the indispensable preliminary to a successful cross-Channel invasion—far harder than had been hoped. When that September, in pursuit of the Combined Chiefs of Staff's decision to concentrate against the German aircraft industry, a daylight attack was made by four hundred Flying Fortresses on the ball-bearing factories of Stuttgart, German fighters were able to prevent every single bomber from reaching its target and destroyed a tenth of the attacking force. A month later, in a similar attack on Schweinfurt, 68 out of the 228 bombers sent over were shot down and 138 damaged. And while two-thirds of Germany's aircraft were concentrated against the R.A.F. and the U.S. Air Forces in the European and North African theatres, preparations were being made to launch against southern England revolutionary air-weapons of a kind that, if successful, might render any cross-Channel attack in 1944 out of the question. Already Allied air-reconnaissance had reported the presence of mysterious launching-sites pointed at London along the shores of Northern France. Meanwhile the battle of the Atlantic, temporarily won in the spring, had begun again with the appearance of ocean-going German submarines with new anti-radar equipment and acoustic torpedoes.

The road to victory had been plotted and the Allies had advanced far along it, but it was still a hard and hazardous one. Six months after Alan Brooke had become Chairman of the Chiefs of Staff Committee the three years' tide of Axis victories had been halted at Alam Halfa. Now for a year it had flowed the other way, yet, if opportunity was not taken when it came, it might turn again. At the back of Brooke's mind lay the realisation that any failure to maintain continuous pressure on the enemy's land and air forces would not only expose next year's cross-Channel venture to a stronger counter-attack than could be resisted but would subsequently enable Hitler, with his swift interior lines, to release forces against Russia that might overwhelm her as she had been overwhelmed in 1917.

Brooke was growing old. He had borne the responsibility of high command for three-and-a-half of the most exacting years in the nation's history without intermission, ever since the day when, after saving his troops from encirclement on the road to Dunkirk, he had been entrusted by Churchill with the task of re-forming and then rescuing the remainder of the British Expeditionary Force and subsequently of defending Britain against invasion. That July, before sailing for the Quebec Conference, he had passed his sixtieth birthday. " I went to work," he wrote after his interrupted furlough in September, " with a desperate disinclination to work! I feel that nothing less than a six months' leave could really restore the necessary drive and vitality to pick up this burden again." The daily strain of conference, of persuading others of what his quick, decisive mind and professional experience convinced him was right, the interminable interviews with callers of every description, to so many of whom he had to propound hard things or break unpalatable truths, the need to keep a constant curb on his temper and tongue showed itself more clearly than ever in his diary, though scarcely ever, according to those who served with him, in his work. " An uninteresting C.O.S.," his entry for October 18th ran, " which I found it hard to pay attention to. A series of interviews, a Cabinet meeting, more work, another Monday gone." " One of those days," he wrote two days later, " when even the sunshine fails to dispel the gloom that lies over one. A desperate feeling of failure, incompetency and incapacity to carry this burden any longer." When his colleague and predecessor in the C.O.S. chair, Sir Dudley Pound, returned from the Quebec Conference a dying man and a few weeks later Brooke attended his funeral at the Abbey, he wrote in his diary:

> " I felt as I sat next to his coffin that amongst the three Chiefs of Staff he had certainly chosen the one road that led at last to peace and an end to these worldly struggles, and in some ways, I envied him."

. . . .

For Brooke's burden was overwhelming. Though few outside the little inner ring who directed the war realised it, in his joint capacity as Chairman of the Chiefs of Staffs Committee and Chief of the Imperial General Staff he had been carrying out with his two colleagues the duties of overall commander of all Britain's forces since the end of 1941, when he had exchanged the post of Commander-in-Chief, Home Forces, for the wider and more onerous responsibilities of C.I.G.S. With the development of modern communications and weapons the nature of war had changed so drastically that it could only now be conducted through central and unified command from start to finish. The so-called Supreme Commanders and their staffs in the different war theatres were the operative media through whom the C.O.S. Committee and its Chairman transmitted orders to the operational commanders in the field.

The latter still directed battles and tactical movements, but the strategy and logistical planning that made their victories possible depended on the men who controlled their campaigns from Storey's Gate. " The difference between a Chief of Staff and a Commander-in-Chief in the field," Churchill wrote of Brooke's American *vis-à-vis*, General Marshall, " is more apparent than real . . . The conditions under which the military art is practised nowadays are not at all similar to those of former generations."[1]

The public never realised this, and the chief director of Britain's armies during the latter and victorious years of the war failed to receive the acclaim that came the way of his more publicised subordinates. Nor, unlike them, did he have the inspiration of personal contact with the fighting men he commanded. He did his work *in camera*, unseen and remote from the battlefield. Brooke once defined the task of himself and his two colleagues as " *pre*vision, *pre*planning and *pro*vision." " It was a case," he wrote, " of maintaining before us our policy for the conduct of the war; then of sustaining that policy by process of prevision by deciding what steps were necessary to put that policy into execution; then of pre-planning the operations entailed by selected steps. Finally we had to provide for these operations and ensure that resources were adequate. These steps were carried out months before the operations took place, and when the appropriate time arrived the plans for the operation were handed over to the appointed commander for him to put the final touches to them." Long before the nation learnt of their successful con- clusion Brooke and his colleagues were busy pre-planning the next campaign.

The instrument through which he worked was the Chiefs of Staff Committee—the supreme operational headquarters of all the Commonwealth's military, naval and air forces in the field. Created after the First World War to provide the Government through the Committee of Imperial Defence with continuous co-ordinated Service advice, it had been constituted at the

[1] *Churchill* V, 615.

beginning of the Second World War a direct Committee of the War Cabinet. When in 1940 Churchill assumed the offices of both Prime Minister and Minister of Defence, this professional triumvirate of the three Service chiefs, though still reporting regularly to the War Cabinet and attending its weekly Monday evening meetings, became for all practical purposes responsible to him alone as Minister of Defence and to the Defence Committee of special Ministers which, with decreasing frequency, he called together to assist him. This close and direct contact between the Prime Minister and the Service chiefs ensured the correlation of political and military authority and prevented the dangerous division of strategic responsibility—so nearly fatal in the First World War—between a War Cabinet of " frocks " or politicians ignorant of the military art and a succession of " brass-hat " or professional Service advisers without regular means of making their advice effective. Resolved to avoid a repetition of such divided councils in the far more dangerous circumstances of 1940, Winston Churchill, while reserving political power to himself and his War Cabinet, made the C.O.S. Committee under his supervision the sole instrument for the military control of all warlike operations.

Without the public realising it this silent revolution of the Prime Minister's ended the separation of military execution and political control. After 1940 almost every major question affecting Britain's war effort—not only the movements, supply and reinforcement of her fleets, armies and air forces, but the control of man-power, industry, shipping, agriculture and at times even of imperial and foreign policy—was, if it had any bearing on military operations, referred to the C.O.S. Committee. Nor, as the world supposed—seeing Churchill's stature and prestige—was the Committee the submissive instrument of the great man who had rallied Britain in 1940 and represented her wartime will. In their corporate capacity its three members—the C.I.G.S., First Sea Lord and Chief of Air Staff —were responsible under the Crown for advising the Government in all military matters and, so long as they spoke with a single voice, their advice could only be disregarded at the expense of a public clash between the Prime Minister and the professional heads of all three Services. The Government could overrule them on a political issue; it could, if it chose, remove them, and they could, if they wished, resign. Their differences, unless resolvable by discussion, could be settled in no other way.

This Chiefs of Staff organization was perfectly adjusted to the unpredictable and constantly changing needs of global warfare and, though evolved by a peace-loving parliamentary democracy after its experiences in the First World War, was probably the most efficient instrument for running a war that this, or perhaps any other, country has ever known. Operating under the authority of the War Cabinet and served by its Secretariat, it was closely linked, not only with the three Fighting Services and their commanders and staff officers on every battlefront, but, through a series of inter-related Departmental committees, with every branch of civil government. By this means there was no facet of the nation's wartime life that was not subject under the War Cabinet to the C.O.S. Committee's scrutiny and indirect control and, when necessary, to its swift, overriding directives. The government of the country by Departmental committee and Ministerial responsibility to Parliament was not superseded but streamlined to the needs of war. And as a result, despite Britain's initial unpreparedness, it proved incomparably more efficient as a long-term instrument for directing war than the authoritarian autocracy against which it was pitted. While the Prime Minister dominated and inspired the entire nation from the bridge, the hand of the professional Service triumvirate he had picked was on the strategic tiller, and the response was instantaneous.

The Secretary to the War Cabinet was Sir Edward Bridges, while his Deputy, Lt.-General Sir Hastings Ismay, was in charge of the military wing of its secretariat and acted also as the Defence Minister's personal Chief of Staff. ' On looking back on my work as Chairman of the C.O.S.,' Brooke wrote after the war, ' I cannot exaggerate the debt of gratitude we owed to ' Pug ' Ismay. Gifted with an immense capacity for work and an uncanny ability for producing clear and definite Minutes from confused and indecisive meetings, he oiled the works and kept the C.O.S. organization running on ball bearings. Acting as intermediary between the C.O.S. Committee and the Defence Minister he was apt at times to get the worst from both sides. Yet, no matter how rough things might be, he invariably shouldered his burden with cheerfulness, efficiency and loyalty.'[1] He and his two very able assistants, Major-General Hollis and Brigadier Ian Jacob,[2] served not only the War Cabinet, the Defence Committee, and the Chiefs of Staff Committee but the latter's many sub-committees, including the Joint Planning Committee and Joint Intelligence Committee. Through these last two Committees and their staffs—comprising respectively the Directors of Plans and of Intelligence of the three Services, with co-opted members from interested Ministries and Departments—the information needed by the C.O.S. was collected and examined and outline plans prepared for prospective operations.

Without this superbly streamlined organization Brooke and his two colleagues could have done nothing in an age in which every military action was dependent on complex logistical calculations and preparations made many months before. They controlled an instrument which, owing to the outstanding character and ability of its Secretariat, operated with astonishing speed and simplicity at every level and, without friction or delay, transmitted their decisions and requests to every Department of State. Not the least of Churchill's services to Britain in 1940 was to ensure, by his adaptation of the Chiefs of Staff and War Cabinet organization, that the supreme wartime supervisory and executive functions should be exercised by the same persons and that action should not be stultified by " that exalted brooding over the work done by others " which so nearly brought the country to disaster in 1917-18.

Because after the summer of 1942 Britain was on the offensive and because the *coup de grâce* to Germany could only be admini-

---

[1] *Notes on My Life* XVIII, 107.
[2] To-day Director-General of the B.B.C.

stered on land, the C.I.G.S.'s share in strategic planning was now far more important than in the early stages of the war when her existence depended mainly on what happened on the sea and in the air. On the purely military side Brooke was assisted by another staff hierarchy, that of the War Office. Here he had as right-hand man the Vice-Chief of Imperial General Staff, Lt.-General Archibald Nye, a brilliant organizer who, though he had risen from the ranks, was still under fifty. Nye deputized for him during his frequent absences from England and represented the Army on the Vice-Chiefs of Staff Committee which relieved the C.O.S. of many routine duties. Between him and Brooke there existed complete confidence; the latter wrote of Nye that he was loyalty and efficiency personified and that because of him he could always leave his post knowing the policies he had laid down would be followed to the minutest detail.[1] After 1942 there was also a Deputy Chief of the Imperial General Staff who dealt mainly with technical and scientific matters and was responsible for the organization and equipment of the Army on a Deputy Chiefs of Staff Committee. This post was filled with high ability by a distinguished industrialist and soldier, Lt.-General Sir Ronald Weeks. He and Major-General Kennedy, the Director of Military Operations,[2] and after 1943, his successor, Major-General Simpson, completed the trinity of Brooke's principal War Office lieutenants. " I could not," he wrote of them and their subordinates, " have asked for a better, more efficient and, above all, more loyal lot."

. . . .

In the middle of September, 1943 the routine of directing the war resumed its normal course with the return of the Prime

[1] *Notes on My Life* X, 885. ' His charming personality made him a joy to work with and I owe him the deepest gratitude for the very heavy load he bore for me.' *Idem* XVIII 106.

[2] ' With Ronny Weeks as D.C.I.G.S. I was unbelievably fortunate; to have a man of his outstanding ability who combined a broad experience on military matters with an extensive experience of Industry left my mind completely at rest. In John Kennedy, as long as his health held out, I had a superb D.M.O. gifted with broad strategic vision and the ability to express his thoughts in the clearest language.' *Notes on My Life* XVIII, 107.

Minister from America after a six weeks' absence. Immediately after the Quebec Conference he had gone to the United States for a much needed holiday. Dill wrote to the C.I.G.S. on September 12th, describing his activities in Washington.

"The P.M. left last night on his way to Hyde Park and so home. He is still talking of going by air, but I doubt if he will. His conduct has been exemplary since he came to Washington. He has been active but never too wild. I was greatly afraid of what he might produce when we had, at his instigation, a meeting with the President and the U.S. Chiefs of Staff and again when he got the President to allow him to preside at a Chiefs of Staff meeting. However, as you will see, no harm was done. We stuck to 'Quadrant' ".[1]

On Sunday, September 19th, Churchill returned to England. Brooke met him at 9 p.m. that night at Euston, with the usual crowd of Cabinet Ministers and staff officers. Next day the old routine of attendance began again. After presiding over the C.O.S. in the morning and lunching with the Polish Commander-in-Chief, the C.I.G.S. spent the afternoon preparing for the Monday evening Cabinet meeting which, under the Prime Minister's eloquent chairmanship, lasted from 5.30 to 8.30 p.m.

"After Cabinet Winston called me up to find out if I had read his speech, which I had not. He said he hoped I would do so as he would probably want to discuss it with me after dinner. As I had Ivan Cobbold dining with me there was not much chance to read through it. Shortly after dinner I was called up and had to go round to 10 Downing Street where I was kept till 2 a.m., discussing and checking the speech. He spent an infinity of work over it and was attending to meticulous details."

'On several occasions,' Brooke added after the war, 'I had to participate in the final stages of Winston's pre-

---

[1] The code name for the Quebec Conference. Field Marshal Dill to C.I.G.S., 12 September, 1943. Lord Alanbrooke. *Personal Files.*

parations for a speech. The whole Cabinet table was usually littered with segments of the speech which had been returned by various people with remarks or criticisms. He worked at a tremendous pressure on these occasions and by the small hours of the morning order began to replace the original chaos.'[1]

A week after this entry the Chiefs of Staff Committee and its Chairman were engaged once more in one of their familiar holding actions against the Prime Minister's attempt or apparent attempt—for it was the essence of his relationship with his military advisers that he expected them to resist him stoutly while he tried to argue them into courses of which they disapproved—to commit the country to major operations in Sumatra and Burma. This was at the moment when it was pledged to throw all its resources into liberating France and, as a necessary preliminary, to maintaining unremitting pressure in Italy.

" *September 28th.* C.O.S. at which we studied P.M.'s Minute about proposed operation in the Indian Ocean. Now in addition to the impossible Sumatra operation he hopes to do Akyab, Ramree (Arakan) and Rangoon operations all in 1944. If Germany is defeated by the end of this year, there may be some hope of doing something out there, but Germany is not yet defeated and his world schemes can have only one result: to detract from the main front."

" Cabinet at 5.30 p.m. which lasted till 7.45 p.m. We then had a C.O.S. meeting from 9 p.m. to 10.30 p.m. to prepare for a meeting with P.M. which lasted from 10.30 to 1 a.m. We did practically nothing, or at any rate nothing that could not have been finished in an hour. He was convinced that we are finding every excuse we can to avoid doing the Sumatra operation."

" *September 29th.* Sent for by the P.M. after the morning's C.O.S. meeting, and found him in a much more

[1] *Notes on My Life* X, 789.

pleasant and co-operative mood. He started by saying that he was just as anxious as I was about our Mediterranean strategy and for not doing anything that might draw forces away from the Mediterranean. I think he felt that he had been in an unpleasant mood the previous evening and wanted to make amends for it . . ."

This penitence did not last. Next day, September 30th, Brooke recorded,

" We again struggled with the North Sumatra operation to see whether it could possibly be done without affecting the Mediterranean operations. Intelligence is inadequate and it is therefore hard to form a true picture . . ."

" *October 1st.* A rushed morning with C.O.S. till 12 noon; then meeting with P.M., Chiefs of Staff, Dickie Mountbatten and Pownall.[1] This resulted in an hour's pitched battle between me and the P.M. on the question of withdrawing troops from the Mediterranean for the Indian Ocean offensive. I was refusing to impair our amphibian potential power in the Mediterranean in order to equip Mountbatten for ventures in Sumatra. P.M., on the other hand, was prepared to scrap our basic policy and put Japan before Germany. However, I defeated most of his intentions in the end! "

Part of the Prime Minister's eagerness to dissipate Britain's resources on this distant venture, Brooke suspected, sprang from a generous wish to make amends for the wrong done his old colleague, Prince Louis of Battenberg, at the Admiralty thirty years before, by giving his brilliant son the chance to win his spurs.

It sprang still more from a political motive outside Brooke's terms of reference, with his soldier's objective of winning the war in the shortest possible time. For Churchill, who like Brooke had spent his early soldiering years in India, the British

[1] Lt.-Gen. (now Gen.) Sir H. R. Pownall, whom Brooke had picked as Chief of Staff to Lord Louis Mountbatten, the newly appointed Supreme Commander in South-East Asia.

Raj exercised an irresistible fascination. With his historic vision he saw its beneficent purpose and achievement in preserving peace and order over a large area of the globe. Before the War he had staked and, as many thought at the time, sacrificed his career in an attempt to oppose the spirit of the age in order to preserve British rule in the sub-continent and maintain the century-old partnership of the Royal Navy and Indian Army in safeguarding the peace of Asia. The succession of disasters suffered by these stabilizing forces at the hands of the Japanese had aroused all his instincts of recoil, and he was resolved at the earliest moment to use the renascent power of Britain to expunge her defeats in the East. For this reason, while wishing to avoid a jungle campaign in the Burmese interior, which he described as " like going into the water to fight a shark ", he was demanding operations in the Indian Ocean and off the Burmese coast, in particular in Northern Sumatra, to cut, as he hoped, the enemy's sea communications with Burma. His sense of the far-reaching effects of such a campaign made him reluctant to recognize either its logistical and strategic impracticability or the drain it would make on the Allies' amphibious resources in Europe.

The American President, pursuing a different ideal—that of the co-operation under American leadership of the awakening nations of Asia—also wished to commit Britain to a major Burmese campaign. But it was to be fought, not on the coast, but in the inaccessible mountains of the interior with a view to re-opening the land supply-route to Chiang Kai-shek's China, in whose future and fighting capacity he had an almost mystical faith. He and his Chief of Army Staff, General Marshall, were strongly supported in this Chinese policy by the other dominant personality of the American Joint Chiefs of Staff, Admiral King, who, combining the offices of Commander-in-Chief and Chief of Naval Staff, wished, like every American naval officer, to avenge the defeat of Pearl Harbour at the earliest possible moment and saw in the Chinese mainland an indispensable base for the destruction of Japan. At the Quebec Conference, after much stubborn opposition by his

British colleagues, he had secured the approval of the Combined Chiefs of Staff for a series of amphibious attacks during the next twelve months on the Japanese-held islands of the Central Pacific—the Gilberts, Marshalls, Carolines, Palaus and Marianas. Nor, fearful lest European commitments should interfere with his offensive, was he wasting any time. At the very moment that the Allies, with their insufficient carriers and landing-craft, were endeavouring to make good their footing at Salerno, King was preparing to fly to Pearl Harbour to launch a campaign that in size and brilliance of execution was to rival that of Trafalgar. Already carrier forces more powerful than any in European waters had struck at Marcus Island and Tarawa Atoll as a warning of what was to come. Meanwhile, thousands of miles to the south, MacArthur's forces, having secured local sea and air superiority, were beginning to leap-frog westwards along the coast of New Guinea. Salamaua was taken on September 11th, Lae on the 16th, Finschhafen on October 2nd. Altogether some nineteen American and Australian divisions and a dozen battleships and nearly forty carriers were committed to these far-flung offensive operations on the other side of the world.

Brooke's view was that without far larger resources in air transport and landing-craft than either the British or Americans could yet assemble in India, neither the amphibious operations in Burma envisaged by the Prime Minister nor the mountain and jungle ones propounded by the Americans had the slightest chance of success. They would merely deflect, and to no purpose, resources which were urgently required in the Mediterranean if the indispensable conditions for a successful invasion of France in 1944 were to be fulfilled. Not until 1945, Brooke argued, would the Allies be in a position to strike in such force as to be able to recapture Rangoon and the mouth of the Irrawaddy—the key to the control of Burma. In what remained of 1943, everything not absolutely essential to building up the necessary strength to strike across the Channel ought to be used to maintain pressure on the Germans in Italy and, from that central strategic jumping-off ground, to keep their reserves spread out along the whole Mediterranean, Adriatic and Aegean littoral, at the furthest possible remove from both the Russian front and the Channel shore.

The Russians could no more grasp the significance of what Brooke was trying to achieve than the Americans. To the Red Star generals, in their ignorance of amphibious operations, the only really worthwhile way in which their Western allies could help them was to throw the largest possible force across the Channel at the earliest possible moment. That such an operation involved any harder problem than a crossing of the Volga or Dnieper never seemed to occur to them. Although relieved by Western pressure of two-thirds of the Luftwaffe and more than a third of the Reichswehr, they continued to blackmail Britain and America by dropping hints that unless a " second front " in France were opened speedily they would be unable to continue the war, demanding a share of the Italian fleet—in whose capture they had played no part—and insisting, in the rudest terms and without the slightest regard for their allies' shipping commitments, on an immediate resumption of the till now almost suicidally sacrificial Arctic convoys.[1] Happily the risks involved in the latter had been reduced at the end of September by an attack by British midget submarines on the battleship *Tirpitz* which, by putting her out of action for several months, made it possible to send ships round the North Cape without a major battle-fleet in support.

Thus, on every hand, despite the summer's spectacular victories, Brooke was encountering obstacles to his plans for exploiting the strategic opportunities offered by Italy's long coastline. Though at the beginning of October when their troops entered Naples, Eisenhower and Alexander were still hoping to capture Rome within the next few weeks, thanks to

[1] Even the Prime Minister's Job-like patience with his allies was temporarily exhausted by these tactics. " I have now received," he wrote to Roosevelt on October 16th, " a telegram from U.J." (Uncle Joe) " which I think you will feel is not exactly all one might hope for from a gentleman for whose sake we are to make an inconvenient, extreme and costly exertion. . . . The Soviet machine is quite convinced it can get everything by bullying, and I am sure it is a matter of some importance to show that this is not necessarily always true." *Churchill* V, 240.

the rigid limitations imposed by Washington on their amphibious power, Kesselring, the German Commander-in-Chief,
was not only able to evacuate his troops from Sardinia and
Corsica without loss but had almost completely recovered from
the fear that had hitherto haunted him of landings in central
and northern Italy to cut off his forces in the South. By the
middle of the month there were signs that, in the absence of
any serious threat to their sea flanks, the Germans were
intending to use the natural succession of strong east-to-west
barriers across the mountain backbone of Italy to hold up the
Allies' advance for the maximum possible period. By that
time, owing to the restricted speed of the latter's build-up
from the sea, there were nineteen German divisions in the
peninsula, though not all of them operational, to only six
British and five American. Though to that extent Brooke's
policy of drawing the enemy's reserves southwards had succeeded, there was a growing danger that, unless Alexander's
forces in Italy could be reinforced more swiftly, the Germans
might stage a counter-offensive that would drive the Allies
back into the sea and wreck all their plans for the coming
year. Yet, in deference to the timetable for the build-up of
Overlord on which the Americans had insisted at Quebec, not
only were the seven best Allied divisions in the Mediterranean
—three of them at that moment fighting in Italy—due to leave
for England before the end of November, but also the bulk of
the special assault vessels and large landing-craft needed both
for the Allied build-up in the peninsula and for any further
seaborne attacks behind the enemy's lines.[1]

.   .   .   .

Unfortunately, for the past month the Prime Minister had
been pressing on the Americans a course of action in the
Mediterranean calculated to make them even more suspicious

---

[1] *Ehrman* V, 70, 73. "We are dismayed by the prospect of a long, tedious, and
costly campaign to take Rome—a situation not unlike that which prevailed in
Tunisia last winter. The going in Italy is painfully slow. General Clark is having
difficulty in getting landing-craft to make end-runs, as they are needed so badly
for our overall build-up in Italy." *Butcher*, 373-4, (30 Oct., 1943.)

than usual of British intentions in that sea. It had been hoped that with the surrender of Italy all the Italian-held islands would pass into Allied hands. But while Sardinia and Corsica went the way of Sicily, in the Dodecanese the Germans quickly overpowered their war-weary ex-allies and gained control before British troops from the Middle East, short both of shipping and carrier-borne aircraft, could arrive. Despite the landing by air of a small British party to stiffen the Italians, Rhodes, the chief island of the Dodecanese, was in German hands within three days of the Badoglio Government's surrender. Only on the small islands of Cos, Leros and Samos were a few hundred British troops put ashore from hastily improvised flotillas of coasting-vessels and sailing ships, unsupported by adequate air power.

To the Prime Minister it had appeared, not unnaturally, that a wonderful opportunity was being missed. This was the area which, ever since Gallipoli, he had regarded as the key to Eastern Europe and Asia Minor. " This is a time," he had signalled to the Commander-in-Chief, Middle East, on September 13th, " to think of Clive and Peterborough and of Rooke's men taking Gibraltar."[1] For, once British air power was established on Rhodes, the Navy would be able to resume control of the Aegean and the sea approaches to Turkey, and that country, freed from the menace of the Luftwaffe, would be able to enter the war on the Allied side. Soon, Churchill argued, the whole Balkans would be ablaze, a safe sea supply-route be open to Russia, and Western troops would be able to operate against the flank and rear of the Germans and satellite forces opposing the advance of the Red Army. " Here," he urged the Chiefs of Staff, " is a business of great consequence to be thrust forward by every means."

But, though they did not lessen the Prime Minister's resolution to attack in the Aegean, the decisions at Quebec to limit offensive operations in the Mediterranean had made it impossible to do so. The only force at that moment available to invade Rhodes consisted of a brigade in Egypt and four long-

[1] *Ehrman* V, 89-93.

range fighter squadrons, and, though General Maitland Wilson, the Commander-in-Chief in the Middle East, expressed his readiness to expel the Germans with this force, there was little hope of getting it to Rhodes without an allocation of landing-craft and transport-aircraft from Eisenhower's Western Mediterranean Command. And, though under pressure from the Prime Minister, who kept insisting on the immense importance of the prize, that officer had reluctantly agreed at the end of September to release a few landing-craft for the expedition—Operation *Accolade*—any hope of its succeeding was destroyed on October 3rd by the capture by German parachutists of Cos and with it of the only airfields from which the landing could be covered.

Even this disaster failed to deter the Prime Minister. As always when faced by an insuperable obstacle, he became almost beside himself in his resolve to find a way round it. Brooke's diary records what happened.

" *October 4th.* Found P.M. in a great flutter owing to the attack on Cos island. Cabinet in the evening at which Cos situation was lengthily discussed . . ."

" *October 6th.* Our C.O.S. meeting was taken up by examining the situation created by the German attack on Cos island and its capture by them, the P.M.'s anxiety to recapture this wonderful trophy, and the effect of its loss on the proposed operations to capture Rhodes. It is quite clear in my mind that with the commitments we have in Italy we should not undertake serious operations in the Aegean."

" At 3.15 p.m. we were summoned to a Staff Conference with the P.M.; Andrew Cunningham and Sholto Douglas were both there. P.M. by now determined to go for Rhodes without looking at the effects on Italy, or at any rate refusing to look the implications square in the face. I had a heated argument with him . . ."

" *October 7th.* Another 3 p.m. conference; another one-and-a-half hours' battle with P.M. to hold on to what I think is right. The same arguments brought up again and again. And then finally sent for at 10.30 p.m. to try and swing me and get me to agree in a *tête-à-tête* interview. However, I arrived in the middle of an air-raid. As I walked in, Winston was dashing out with Mary, who was on leave, to take her back to her A.A. Battery in Hyde Park. I was whisked off with them. By the time we arrived the raid was over. We therefore walked round the battery position for half-an-hour. Winston started reminiscing and told me this was the very spot Mrs. Everest, his nurse, used to take him to when he was a small boy whilst he was longing the whole time to get back to his soldiers. And now it was a battery position in which his daughter was serving. He next broke the news to me that on Saturday (to-day being Thursday evening, 11 p.m.) I was to start with him for a conference in Tunis and that we should come back on Tuesday! This is all to decide whether we should try and take Rhodes."

" *October 8th.* . . . I can now control him no more. He has worked himself into a frenzy of excitement about the Rhodes attack, has magnified its importance so that he can no longer see anything else and has set his heart on capturing this one island even at the expense of endangering his relations with the President and the Americans and the future of the Italian campaign. He refused to listen to any arguments or to see any dangers."

" He wired to the President asking for Marshall to come out to the Mediterranean for a conference in Tunis to settle the matter, hoping in his heart to be able to swing the meeting by his personality. However, the President sent him back a very cold reply, asking him not to influence operations in the Mediterranean. This did not satisfy him and he has wired back again asking President to reconsider the matter. He is placing himself, quite unnecessarily, in a false position. The Americans are already desperately suspicious of him, and this will make matters worse."

" Meanwhile it is now nearly midnight Friday, and we none of us yet know whether we are to start for Tunis to-morrow or not . . ."

No trip to Tunis took place. Conscious of his country's growing military strength, Roosevelt stood firmly by the advice of his Chiefs of Staff. For though the Prime Minister protested that the enemy in Italy was retreating and that there would be ample time to capture Rhodes before reaching his defensive lines in the North,[1] to all his offers to proceed at once to Eisenhower's headquarters the President returned an unvarying " *non possumus* ". And though the next day the British leader, still undismayed, wired General Maitland Wilson that the strategic position for the next month in the Mediterranean was expressed in the two words, " Storm Rhodes ", he was by now confronted, not only by the agreed policy of the Combined Chiefs of Staff, but by the inescapable logic of facts. By October 9th the Allied Command in the Mediterranean was aware that the German land forces in the peninsula were half again as numerous as its own and that, with the build-up of the latter proceeding—for lack of landing-craft—at only about a quarter of the rate that had been hoped for, the danger of a successful enemy counter-attack was very real. Following a conference that day with his three operational Commanders-in-Chief, all of them British, Eisenhower wired the Prime Minister,

" We sincerely regret that current situation in Italy, aggravated by drastic changes of the last forty-eight hours, . . . does not permit at this moment diversion necessary to successful *Accolade*. Every conclusion submitted in our report to Combined Chiefs of Staff was agreed unanimously

[1] " We know that the enemy is withdrawing to the north, fighting rearguard actions and carrying off booty; we cannot yet tell whether it is in October or November that we can occupy Rome, but it is certain that we shall not come in contact with the main German forces at the top of the leg of Italy till December or even later, and we certainly have control of the rate of advance. There is therefore plenty of time to provide a division for the conquest of Rhodes and restore it to the battlefront in Italy before we reach the German fortified line." *Churchill* V, 189.

by all Commanders-in-Chief from both theatres. It is personally distressing to me to have to advise against a project in which you believe so earnestly."[1]

" A quiet day at home," Brooke recorded in his diary on Sunday, October 10th,

> " with continuous telephone calls connected with Roosevelt's last reply to P.M.'s wire. I spent half-an-hour with him on the telephone during which he stated everyone was against him but that the situation was so changed in Italy that we must readjust our thoughts! . . ."

. . . .

Brooke saw as clearly as his political chief the immense advantages to be won by bringing Turkey into the war and the tragedy of abandoning the five thousand British troops who had been sent to the Dodecanese and had to be left to their fate for lack of sea and air forces to support or rescue them. But owing to Hitler's exploitation of the breathing space offered him by the Americans' refusal to grasp their Mediterranean opportunities, everything had to be sacrificed to the primary and all-important end of remaining in Italy and maintaining sufficient pressure there to keep the German reserves concentrated in the South until the cross-Channel attack could be launched. To that problem the Chiefs of Staff now addressed themselves. Unless the Americans could be persuaded to modify the rigid schedules of withdrawals from the Mediterranean agreed two months earlier at Quebec, the very enterprise to which they wished to sacrifice everything—the cross-Channel invasion—would be rendered impossible by a failure of the preliminary operations essential to its success. Unless sufficient German forces could be contained in the South immediately before and during the first three crucial months of *Overlord*—and a successful campaign in the Italian peninsula, with its simultaneous threat to Austria, Southern France and the Balkans, was now the only way by which this

[1] *Ehrman* V, 98-9.

53

could be achieved—the enemy's concentration against the Normandy landings would be faster than the Allied build-up in the bridgehead.

The difficulty was to overcome the suspicion of the American Chiefs of Staff who, as a result of the Prime Minister's over-enthusiastic plea for operations against Rhodes, were now more convinced than ever that the British leader and his lieutenants were trying to evade their D-Day commitments in favour of adventures in the Eastern Mediterranean. The problem was complicated by the fact that, so far as the Prime Minister was concerned, there was an element of truth in the suspicion, for, being both an intensely humane and brilliantly imaginative man, he feared a repetition of the senseless slaughter of the Western Front offensives of the first War, and believed it possible to substitute for them a more subtle and economical attack against the enemy's back-door in South-Eastern Europe.[1] Though after the Italian surrender the C.I.G.S. had pointed out that any attempt by Britain to exploit the situation by landing forces in countries like Greece hitherto held down by Italian troops would involve her in military commitments incompatible with the agreed Anglo-American strategy in the Central Mediterranean,[2] Churchill continued to hope that by an imaginative use of small landing-parties it might be possible to turn the already formidable partisan risings in the Balkans into a major avalanche. This he believed might bring down the Nazi structure in Eastern Europe and obviate the need to storm Hitler's fortress from the West.

[1] " While I was always willing to join with the United States in a direct assault across the Channel on the German sea-front in France, I was not convinced that this was the only way of winning the war, and I knew that it would be a very heavy and hazardous adventure. The fearful price we had had to pay in human life and blood for the great offensives of the First World War was graven in my mind." *Churchill* V, 514.

[2] " At present all discussions concerning the liberation of Greece . . . are based on the assumption that an Allied force will, sooner or later, be invading Greece and that a large number of troops would be available to maintain law and order. While it may be expedient so to tell the Greeks and correct to plan on this assumption, it is in fact contrary to our present strategy. . . . This would involve us in a military commitment of at least two divisions. . . . The provision of these divisions may well prove impossible unless we are to detract from the main effort in the Central Mediterranean." C.I.G.S., 12 Sept., 1943. *Ehrman* V, 86-7.

Though also haunted, like everyone who had experienced the first War, by the nightmare of an unsuccessful landing in the West, Brooke knew that victory could only be won ultimately through *Overlord*. His fear was lest it should fail through American over-confidence and reluctance first to contain and break the German reserves in the South. On October 14th the Chiefs of Staff Committee set on record its "uneasiness . . . that the rigidity imposed by the ' Quadrant ' decisions " was " hampering the proper exploitation of the Allied successes in the Mediterranean ". Five days later the Chiefs of Staff were asked by Churchill to prepare a paper on the current situation in that theatre with special reference to the partisan movement in the Balkans. " C.O.S. at which we received a note from the P.M.," Brooke wrote that night in his diary,

> " wishing to swing the strategy back to the Mediterranean at the expense of the Channel. I am in many ways entirely with him, but God knows where this may lead us as regards clashes with the Americans. This evening another meeting with P.M. at 10.30 p.m., attended by Smuts, Attlee, Cadogan, Lyttelton, Leathers, etc. Here again P.M. worked on the same scheme and advocated another Combined Chiefs of Staff meeting next month and early at that. He suggested first week in November which is quite impossible . . ."

A week later, on October 21st, General Alexander— Eisenhower's operational Commander-in-Chief in Italy—presented a most depressing report on the military situation. Relieved by the now obvious Allied shortage of landing-craft and carriers of any serious risk of a major descent in their rear, the Germans with nineteen divisions in the country to the Allies' eleven were digging in firmly on both the narrow coastal plains and across the mountainous spine of the peninsula. Unless continuous pressure could be brought to bear on them one of two things must happen: either they would achieve a stalemate in Italy and be free to withdraw divisions to France or they would take the offensive and drive the Allies into the

55

sea. It was therefore essential, Alexander argued, to continue to attack throughout the winter. But, having numerical superiority only in the air and being confronted by natural defensive positions of great strength, the Allies' only hope of doing so was by combining frontal attacks on the mountain passes with landings from the sea on the enemy's flanks and rear. To make this possible, assault landing-craft scheduled for immediate return to England would have to be retained in the Mediterranean instead of being put into cold storage, as the Americans wished, until the cross-Channel attacks could be launched in 1944.[1]

The first task, therefore, of the British Chiefs of Staff was to persuade their American colleagues to relax the programme agreed at Quebec. " It is becoming more and more apparent," Brooke wrote in his diary on October 25th,

> " that our operations in Italy are coming to a standstill, and that owing to lack of resources we shall not only come to a standstill, but also find ourselves in a very dangerous position unless the Russians go on from one success to another. Our build-up in Italy is much slower than that of the Germans and far slower than I expected. We shall have to have an almighty row with the Americans who have put us in this position with their insistence to abandon the Mediterranean operations for the very problematical[2] cross-Channel operations. We are now beginning to see the full beauty of the Marshall strategy! It is quite heart-breaking when we see what we might have done this year if our strategy had not been distorted by the Americans."
>
> " *October 26th.* I was sent for by Winston at 10 a.m. to discuss Alexander's last wire which stated that operations

---

[1] *Ehrman* V, 69-70. " The reduction in craft," Alexander reported, " already decreased by wear and tear, has been so serious as to preclude us from taking advantage . . . of the enemy's inherent weakness, which is the exposure of his two flanks to turning movements from the sea."

[2] By " problematical " Brooke meant that the pre-requisite conditions for their success had neither yet been created nor even agreed. At this time the Americans were still insisting that a landing in France could be made on a three-division front —a smaller one than in Sicily—and were refusing to allocate enough assault-craft to it to make a successful assault and build-up practicable.

in Italy were coming to a standstill. Discussed with him the best methods of getting Americans to realise that we must for the present concentrate on the Mediterranean. Then met the C.O.S. and prepared a wire for Washington which we discussed with Winston at 12.15 p.m."

" *October 27th.* In afternoon had a long interview with Lord Rennell who is just back from Alex's H.Q. He was rather depressing about conditions prevailing at Eisenhower's H.Q., and compared it to Cairo at its worst."

" At 6 p.m. a meeting at which the P.M. and Smuts gave a long discourse on relative merits of Mediterranean theatre as opposed to the cross-Channel operations. I believe the whole of it was intended for Beaverbrook with the idea of educating him. Finally P.M. turned to him and asked him what he thought about it. He replied that he had always been an ardent supporter of the cross-Channel operation but now that we were committed to the Mediterranean we should make a job of it."

' We were now firmly established in the lower part of the leg of Italy. We had command of the air and command of the sea. The enemy flanks therefore remained open to combined operations on both sides throughout the length of Italy. The main artery of rail communications consisted of one double line of railway open to air attack throughout its length. Conditions were therefore ideal for hitting the enemy hard and for enforcing on him the use of reserves in the defence of Italy.'

' The attitude of Ike's H.Q. was not encouraging. I knew that he never really appreciated the strategic advantages of Italy. We had certainly arrived at the time when the most active planning and preparation were necessary for next year's cross-Channel operation, but these plans and preparations could not be allowed to slow down operations which were in themselves one of the most important of those preparations. The American outlook was unfortunately one of—" We have already wasted far too much time in the

Mediterranean doing nothing, let us now lose no more time in this secondary theatre. Let us transfer and allot all available resources to the main theatre and finish the war quickly in Germany." '

" *October 28th.* A difficult C.O.S. at which we discussed the desirability or otherwise of vacating Leros. A very nasty problem. Middle East have now got themselves into the difficult situation of being neither able to hold nor to evacuate Leros. Our only hope would be assistance from Turkey and airfields from which the required air cover could be provided."

" News from Russia continues excellent."

' News from Russia continued to be the vital point on which our whole strategy was hinged. If Russia had collapsed all our strategic plans would have gone west. German forces liberated from Russia would have made a cross-Channel operation impossible and endangered our position in Italy and Middle East. Luckily the signs of a turn in the tide were becoming more and more apparent.'

" *October 29th.* A heavy cold. Started with a long C.O.S. which lasted till 12.30 p.m. Then at 3 p.m. the P.M. to discuss South-East Asia operations, and thank God succeeded in getting decisions out of him. Then discussed control of Mediterranean."

" After our meeting I asked him whether he would agree to put Dill up for a peerage in the New Year's Honours' List. I felt doubtful as to how he would react, and was surprised to find that he jumped at it. He only asked whether he might perhaps prefer an O.M. I must now see that he sticks to it."

" *November 1st.* Found my table groaning with telegrams! A rushed briefing period, followed by a fairly long C.O.S. Cabinet meeting at 5.30 p.m. Now I am off to another 10.30 p.m. meeting. We are to discuss plans for another Combined Chiefs of Staff meeting. How I hate those meetings and how weary I am of them! ."

" When I look at the Mediterranean I realise only too well how far I have failed. If only I had had sufficient force of character to swing those American Chiefs of Staff and make them see daylight, how different the war might be. We should have had the whole Balkans ablaze by now, and the war might have been finished in 1943. I blame myself, yet doubt whether it was humanly possible to alter the American point of view more than I succeeded in doing. And what I did I would never have achieved had it not been for Dill's help, his close association with Marshall, his deep knowledge and the implicit confidence I had in him."

' I was suffering from a heavy cold and had not fully recovered from the strain of the Quebec Conference. Reading between the lines I think I cannot have been far off a nervous breakdown. Nevertheless, there is a great deal in what I wrote. Just when there were fruits to be gained, the Americans selected this moment to damp down our efforts; troops, landing-craft and transport were removed and re-allocated. At very little cost Crete and Rhodes could have been rendered possible operations without affecting Italy, whereas as matters stood these were only possible at the expense of Italian operations and were consequently ruled out. Success in Crete and Rhodes might have had the happiest repercussions in Turkey and the Balkans without ever committing a single man in the Balkans.'

" *November 2nd.* A long C.O.S. meeting which started with our weekly interview with the Joint Intelligence Committee. I had to disagree with a report they had submitted as to number of divisions that could concentrate in Northern Italy. . . ."

" Defence Committee meeting with P.M. who kept us up till midnight, mainly discussing our impending journey to the Mediterranean."

· · · · · · · ·

The proposed Combined Chiefs of Staff meeting in the Mediterranean was to be the prelude to a more important conference. Since Quebec the Prime Minister and President had been preparing the ground for a meeting with Stalin. In August, in a letter congratulating them on the success of the Sicilian campaign and the downfall of Mussolini, the Russian leader had so far departed from his usual unco-operative attitude as to agree that a meeting of the heads of the three Governments was desirable, though he added that, as he was unable to relinquish the direction of the Russian front for even a day, he could not go far afield. Though Churchill as usual declared himself ready to go anywhere, at any time and at any risk, the President was equally insistent that his constitutional office prevented him from losing touch with Washington. And as Stalin would not venture further than Teheran or Roosevelt than Cairo, all that could be arranged for the moment was a meeting of the Foreign Ministers of the three Powers at Moscow.

This had opened on October 19th with Molotov, voted by his colleagues into the chair, demanding that the allies should cross the Channel in the spring of 1944 and that immediate steps should be taken to bring Turkey into the war and secure Swedish air bases for bombing Germany. Three days later the Chiefs of Staff Committee, Brooke records, received a wire from Eden " asking for replies as to the lines he was to take concerning Russia's desire to get Turkey and Sweden into the war ". But with the Germans firmly established at Rhodes and the Allies unable, for lack of landing-craft, to expel them, the Turks were in a most unco-operative mood. Goebbels, with his eye on Germany's Balkan neighbours, was jubilant. " There isn't the slightest reason," he wrote in his diary, " for Turkey to abandon her neutral position. The Turkish states-men are far too realistic to enter upon so daring an adventure." Indeed the apparent inability of the Allies to agree delighted the German Propaganda Minister. " As was to be expected," he wrote, " the English and Americans were unable to get anywhere with their demand for fixing Western Soviet boundaries. . . . The neutral countries realise perfectly what went on in Moscow; almost everywhere there is doubt and concern. Despite our military misfortunes our political position has seldom been so strong. . . . London already concedes to the Soviets that the small States of Europe no longer have any right to existence."[1]

Yet though the German position in Southern Europe was far stronger than had seemed possible two months earlier, and Goebbels congratulated himself on the Allies' lack of progress in Italy,[2] the withdrawal of German reserves in the autumn to fill the gap created by the Italian collapse had by now opened wide the floodgates on the Russian plains. Early in November the Red Army recaptured Kiev and farther south reached a point only 200 kilometres from the former Polish frontier, while the German garrison of the Crimea was almost cut off by the rapidity of its advance. "We are waiting," Goebbels wrote on November 3rd, "the arrival of our relief forces in the East"—forces which with forty-nine German divisions now in the Balkans and Italy,[3] were almost impossible to find. Meanwhile the R.A.F., shifting its attack from the Ruhr, had opened its winter offensive against Central Germany. On November 5th Kassel was laid waste. A fortnight later the attack was transferred to Berlin. "A time of universal misfortune," Goebbels wrote, "has fallen on this city of four and a half millions. Hell itself seems to have broken loose upon us."

Meanwhile Brooke and his two colleagues prepared for their meetings with the Americans and Russians. Dudley Pound's place had now been filled by Andrew Cunningham, the great admiral who had held the Eastern Mediterranean in 1941, and who arrived from Washington to take his place on the C.O.S. in the latter part of October. Far more a leader of men than an office administrator, there had been doubts at

---

[1] *Goebbels* 398 (1 Nov., 1943).

[2] "We have achieved great defensive military successes in Italy. The English and Americans are simply not advancing and must pay for every kilometre of ground with rivers of blood. . . . It will put a damper on them and they will be better able to imagine what awaits them if they attempt an invasion of the West at a moment favourable to us." *Goebbels*, 407 (8 Nov., 1943).

[3] Compared with eighteen in July. *Ehrman* V, 69.

first as to how he would shape at the council table, but Brooke's fears were soon resolved. " Andrew Cunningham's arrival in the C.O.S.," he wrote, " was indeed a happy event for me. I found in him first and foremost one of the most attractive of friends, a charming associate to work with and the staunchest of companions when it came to supporting a policy agreed to amongst ourselves, no matter what inclement winds might blow. I carry away with me nothing but the very happiest recollections of all my dealings with him. His personality, charming smile and heart-warming laugh were enough to disperse at once those miasmas of gloom and despondency which occasionally swamped the C.O.S."[1]

This, however, was still in the future. The C.I.G.S.'s diary continued:

" *November 3rd.* This morning's C.O.S. meeting took a nasty turn in the shape of a long discussion between Chief of Air Staff and the new First Sea Lord. Neither would give in and I had a difficult time. I wonder if this is the first of many more of this kind? "

" Dined with P.M. at 10 Downing Street, a dinner for the King attended by Portal, Cunningham and Hollis. P.M. in very good form. He had wanted to send a wire to Eden on his way back from Moscow that it was necessary to remind the Turkey that Christmas was coming! The King was as usual perfectly charming and remained there till 12.30 a.m. We were then kept up for another hour by the P.M. and only returned home shortly after 2 a.m."

" *November 4th.* A long discussion with the Planners to decide best method of presenting the problem of the Mediterranean dilemma to the Combined Chiefs of Staff."

" Call from the P.M. for a 3 p.m. meeting to discuss Eisenhower's last telegram and to frame a new wire to Washington to try to straighten out the situation. Finally

[1] *Notes on My Life* X, 803-4.

Cabinet at 6 p.m. to discuss this development and Winston's wire to President backing up our wire."

" *November 5th.* A Manpower morning. First with a discussion at the C.O.S. and then a Cabinet meeting from 11.30 to 1.30 p.m. We discussed the policy of banking on the defeat of Germany in 1944 and of retaining intensity of war at the maximum whilst allowing for a cessation of hostilities in 1945 except for Japan, and armies of occupation."

" *November 8th.* Arrived at War Office to find table littered with telegrams from Moscow and Washington. One from Washington with a suggestion by Leahy that Marshall should be made Supreme Commander of European theatre, to combine North Africa and cross-Channel! Luckily P.M. was entirely with us and sent back strong telegram to Dill with his views as to the absurdity of the proposal. The trouble is that meanwhile our proposal to combine the control and command of the Mediterranean is being side-tracked . . ."

November 9th. Long discussion at our C.O.S. meeting concerning future Mediterranean strategy. I was not in full accord with plans put forward by Planners. Essential that we should clear our minds as to our recommendations before meeting the American Chiefs."

" *November 10th.* A long C.O.S. again. We were busy formulating our Mediterranean policy for the forthcoming meeting with the American Chiefs of Staff at which we are bound to have a pretty stiff contest."

During the first week in November the joint efforts of the Prime Minister and British Chiefs of Staff succeeded in eliciting from Washington a decision to postpone until December the departure from the Mediterranean of the sixty-eight tank landing-ships scheduled at Quebec for transfer to England in early November. Without this the Italian offensive would have had to have been abandoned altogether. There was now at least a hope that the Americans could be induced to follow up the strategy so successfully launched in the summer and on which, in Brooke's view, all the hopes of an invasion of France depended.

On November 11th—exactly a quarter of a century after the German surrender in the First World War—the Chiefs of Staff Committee presented their recommendations on the strategy that they believed necessary to bring about an early German defeat in the second.

" 1. For some time past it has been clear to us, and doubtless also to the U.S. Chiefs of Staff, that disagreement exists between us as to what we should do now in the Mediterranean, with particular reference to the effect of future action on *Overlord*. The point at issue is how far what might be termed the ' sanctity of *Overlord* ' is to be preserved in its entirety, irrespective of developments in the Mediterranean theatre. This issue is clouding the whole of our future strategic outlook and must be resolved. . . .

2. At the outset we must point out that since the decisions taken at ' Quadrant ' there have been major developments in the situation. The Russian campaign has succeeded beyond all hope or expectations and their victorious advance continues. Italy has been knocked out of the war; and it is certainly not beyond the bounds of possibility that Turkey will come in on our side before the New Year. In these changed conditions we feel that consideration of adjustments of, if not actual departures from, the decisions taken at ' Trident ' and ' Quadrant ' is not only fully justified but positively essential.

3. Nevertheless, we emphasize that we do not in any way recoil from, or wish to side-track, our agreed intention to attack the Germans across the Channel in the late spring or early summer of 1944, or even earlier if *Rankin*[1] conditions were to obtain. We must not, however, regard *Overlord* on a fixed date as the pivot of our whole

---

[1] The Code name for action in France if German morale or resistance suddenly collapsed.

strategy on which all else turns. In actual fact, the German strength in France next spring may, at one end of the scale, be something which makes *Overlord* completely impossible and, at the other end, something which makes *Rankin* not only practicable, but essential. Consequently, to assume that the achievement of a certain strength by a certain date will remove all our difficulties and result in shortening the duration of the war is entirely illusory. This policy, if literally interpreted, will inevitably paralyse action in other theatres without any guarantee of action across the Channel.

4. With the Germans in their present plight the surest way to win the war in the shortest time is to attack them remorselessly and continuously in any and every area where we can do so with superiority. The number of places at which we can thus attack them depends mainly on the extent to which they are stretched. Our policy is therefore clear; we should stretch the German forces to the utmost by threatening as many of their vital interests and areas as possible and, holding them thus, we should attack wherever we can do so in superior force.

5. If we pursue the above policy we firmly believe that *Overlord* (perhaps in the form of *Rankin*) will take place next summer. We do not, however, attach vital importance to any particular date or to any particular number of divisions in the assault and follow-up, though naturally the latter should be made as large as possible consistent with the policy stated above. It is, of course, valuable to have a target date to which all may work, but we are firmly opposed to allowing this date to become our master and to prevent us from taking full advantage of all opportunities that occur to us to follow what we believe to be the correct strategy.

6. In the light of the above argument, we submit the following proposals for action in the Mediterranean:

(1) *Unification of Command*

Unification of Command in the Mediterranean . . .

is an essential and urgent measure which should be put into effect irrespective of any other decisions taken about this theatre.

(2) *The Italian Campaign*

The offensive in Italy should be nourished and maintained until we have secured the Pisa-Rimini Line.

(3) *Yugoslavia, Greece and Albania*

Our policy should be to place on a regular military basis and to intensify our measures to nourish the Partisan and irregular forces in these countries. If necessary, we might form a limited bridgehead on the Dalmatian or Albanian coasts.

(4) *Turkey*

We should bring Turkey into the war this year.

(5) *The Dardanelles*

We should aim to open the Dardanelles as soon as possible.

(6) *The Balkans*

We should undermine resistance in the Balkan States and do everything possible to promote a state of chaos and disruption in the satellite countries.

7. If the above measures necessitate putting back the date upon which the forces agreed to be necessary for *Overlord* will be available in the United Kingdom, this should be accepted, since it does not by any means follow that the date of the invasion of France will be put back to the same extent.

8. To sum up, our policy is to fight and bomb the Germans as hard as possible all through the winter and spring; to build up our forces in the United Kingdom as rapidly as possible consistent with this; and finally to invade the Continent as soon as the German strength in France and the general war situation gives us a good prospect of success."[1]

To this document the Prime Minister next day added his approval with the words, " I cordially agree ". After further

[1] *Ehrman* V, 109-11.

debate, however, the sentence, " If necessary, we might form a limited bridgehead on the Dalmatian or Albanian coasts," was omitted in order to avoid any aggravation of the American suspicion that the British were seeking to commit the West to a Balkan campaign. With this single omission the document—entitled " *Overlord* and the Mediterranean Operations "—was adopted as the official British plan to be submitted to the Combined Chiefs of Staff at their forthcoming conference. On the same night Brooke wrote in his diary:

> " *November 11th.* Long C.O.S. meeting with the Joint Intelligence Committee and Duncan Sandys to reorganize the research organization and necessary action required to meet German rocket. Then interview with Sinclair (Ministry of Supply) concerning production required during 1944, '45 and '46. Not an easy matter to predict for."

> " We are now getting near our departure for Cairo. I feel that we shall have a pretty serious set-to which may strain our relations with the Americans, but I am tired of seeing our strategy warped by their short-sightedness."

Chapter Two

THE
TEHERAN CONFERENCE

*We are still ignorant of what happened at Teheran. Every-
body is tense and full of expectation. . . . The entire world
news machinery is geared to the long-awaited Teheran
communiqué.*

GOEBBELS, *Diary*

ON NOVEMBER 14th, two days before the surrender of the British garrison of Leros, the Prime Minister left for Malta in the battle-cruiser *Revenge*. The President, in high spirits at the thought of meeting Stalin, had sailed from America on the previous morning with his Chiefs of Staff. Their conversation, as they crossed the Atlantic, turned on the trouble they expected from Churchill over alternatives to a second front[1] and the need to secure for General Marshall the supreme command of all operations against Germany from the Channel to the Aegean. Only in this way, they felt, could the British be stopped from evading their promise to invade France in 1944. Their allies' half-heartedness in the matter seemed proved by their refusal—communicated to them during the voyage by the Chiefs of Staff in London—to place their strategic bombing force in England under the commander of *Overlord*.

[1] " It was their experience that, while the Prime Minister invariably gave his most enthusiastic and eloquent approval to *Overlord* in principle, he steadfastly refused to accept it as a scheduled fact, preferring to believe that German power could be worn down by attrition to the point of collapse, whereupon the Anglo-American forces in the United Kingdom could perform a triumphal march from the Channel to Berlin with no more than a few snipers' bullets to annoy them." *White House Papers*, II, 762-3.

The President and his advisers were resolved, too, as at the Quebec Conference three months earlier, to force the British to launch a campaign in Burma to reopen the road to China. " We were prepared," wrote Admiral Leahy, " to hear British objections to the Burma operation, particularly its amphibious phase, but the President seemed determined that we formulate the best possible plans to support the Chinese war-effort." A possible alternative put forward by Admiral King was that their allies should invade the Malay peninsula north of Singapore and capture Bangkok. The only drawback in the American view to these projects seemed, as Leahy put it, " that there would be a demand for more landing-craft than we had available . . . for large-scale amphibious operations."

It was against this background that at 1 a.m. on the morning of November 17th Brooke flew from Northolt for Malta. He had been on the point of starting forty-eight hours earlier but had been delayed by icing conditions; " this is bad," he had written, " as Winston will be off to Italy without me and I want to be there when he sees Alexander and Monty." After refuelling at Gibraltar he had taken off again at 10 a.m.

" I am writing this flying over the Western Mediterranean, having left Gib. about an hour ago. We are travelling in the P.M.'s York, and I am in his state cabin and therefore very comfortable; bed with sheets, small table, chair and lavatory complete. We are now on our way to Malta, hoping to make it before dark. Lovely calm sea and bright blue sky with a few fleecy clouds."

" *Later*. We had a lovely fly along the north coast of Africa, Oran, Algiers, Bougie, Philippeville and Bône. Passed just south of Tunis and saw Pantelleria island in the distance . . . Finally arrived in Malta at 3 p.m., having only left Northolt at 1 a.m. the same day; twelve hours flying to cover 2500 miles."

" I was met on the aerodrome by a guard of honour and Park the Air Officer Commanding, Tedder, and

Oxley the O.C. Troops. Drove up to the Palace where I found Gort and Alexander and also Eisenhower. P.M. has not yet arrived. We passed his battleship and cruiser, escorted by their destroyers, some way out to sea."

" I cannot help feeling what a very different visit this is from my last one to Malta, August, a year ago, when I crept in at night, had eighteen air-raid alarms during the day and crept out again in the dark. The whole island at that time was on short rations and Gort in a very depressed mood, whilst I tried to cheer him up with the prospects of North African operations. Thank God those days are over! "

" P.M. arrived about 7.30 p.m., bringing with him Winant, Mrs. Vic Oliver, ' Pug', Martin and Cunningham. Dined at 8.30 p.m. and afterwards much talking which kept us away from bed till after midnight. Dead tired. I am dropping off to sleep."

" *November 18th. Malta.* It had been decided last night with the P.M. that we should have a meeting with him at 11 a.m., and that at 2 p.m. he should start off with Alex and me for Italy. This morning all plans were changed. First of all, the P.M. had a cold and, therefore, could not go to Italy; secondly he wanted to have a talk with Alexander in the afternoon, therefore Alex and I could not start for Italy; and thirdly the President had wired that, in view of the fact that security had been violated and the Germans had already published the fact that we were all meeting in Cairo, we should have to find another place. He suggested Khartoum. P.M. suggested Malta, and Gort was horrified at the thought of it. Wires flew in all directions, and I think that in the end we shall be going to Cairo."

" Had a talk of about one hour with Alex in the garden which was good value. We then had our conference with the P.M. in bed, Chiefs of Staff, John Cunningham[1] and

---

[1] Admiral, now Admiral of the Fleet, Sir John Cunningham, Commander-in-Chief, Mediterranean.

Tedder. P.M. gave long tirade on evils of Americans and of our losses in the Aegean and Dalmatian coast. He was not at all at his best, and I feel nervous as to the line he may adopt at this Conference. He is inclined to say to the Americans, ' All right, if you won't play with us in the Mediterranean, we won't play with you in the English Channel.' And if they say, ' All right, then we shall direct our main effort in the Pacific,' to reply, ' You are welcome to do so if you wish '. I do not think that such tactics will pay."

" After lunch Alex, Moran and I went for a drive round Malta and went to the northern point from which we could see the islands of Gozo and Comino. P.M. in bed all day, but by way of getting up for dinner."

" *Later*. P.M. got up for dinner, saying he was feeling better. He kept us up only to close on midnight. Alex and I have planned to start for Bari in his plane at 9 a.m. to-morrow. P.M. says he may follow us up in the evening."

" Long military discussion at dinner and after dinner, which filled me with gloom. . . ."

' Since the strength of the American forces was now building up fast and exceeding ours, Winston hated having to give up the position of the predominant partner which he had held at the start. As a result he became inclined at times to put up strategic proposals which in his heart he knew were unsound, purely to spite the Americans. He was in fact aiming at " cutting off his nose to spite his face ". It was usually fairly easy to swing him back on to the right line. There lay, however, in the back of his mind the desire to form a purely British theatre when the laurels would be all ours.'

" *November 19th. Malta and Cairo*. Woke up to find it pouring with rain. Reports from aerodrome were uncertain and undecided. We started for the aerodrome and got half-way there when we were met and informed that there would be no flying to-day, and probably none

71

to-morrow. This knocks my trip to Italy on the head. Meanwhile, no further news from the President as to whether he is prepared to stick to Cairo for our meeting."

" During morning Alex and I went off to visit the Palace and also the Church of St. John, the old Knights Templars' Church; most interesting. In the afternoon I went with Winant, Portal and Alex to see the collection of old books and documents in the library. A most wonderful collection, with letters from Henry VIII, Queen Anne, various Georges, Marie Antoinette, etc. Also a collection of old Bibles and books marvellously painted and illustrated."

" P.M. has now decided to go on by sea to Alexandria. Hope therefore to fly on to Cairo in his York, leaving here about 9 a.m."

" *Later*. When I came down for dinner I was informed that the P.M. had decided that, if no reply came in from Roosevelt before 10 p.m. (and he considered the chances a thousand to one against), he would stop on another night and would require his York aircraft to remain in Malta in case he required it. We had, therefore, arranged for a Dakota to take me on instead. However, during dinner a wire arrived stating President was prepared to go to Cairo, so P.M. decided to sail at 11.30 p.m. in H.M.S. *Renown*, and the York again became available for me. He was in very good form at dinner and finished up with a long dissertation on his post-war reconstruction ideas and his slogan of ' Food, House and Work for everyone.' Also his instructions to Woolton working with Oliver Lyttelton to produce these requirements. After dinner he left to embark and Gort accompanied him."

' The events of this day have always remained very deeply rooted in my mind, as it was the first day that I really got to know and understand Winant. First I had been with him in the library where I had invited him to come with us, and afterwards we went for a drive round the island together.

I had always been taken by him, but had never up till then been able to break through the iron-curtain of reserve that kept out the outer world. What I found behind this curtain was quite enchanting—a man who had made a deep study of life and had not arrived at his convictions easily. What he had arrived at was well worth hearing from his own lips. We were both discussing the wonderful rehabilitation to be acquired through close contacts with nature, and especially so in time of war. He said that, no doubt I must have read Earl Grey's *Fallodon Papers*? I had to confess that I had not. Whereupon he at once said he must rectify this defect and that he would send me a copy immediately on his return. He kept his promise, and this book has remained one of my most cherished possessions. Later he gave me a wonderful folio set of some twelve volumes of Audubon's *Birds of America*. His friendship I always look upon as one of those great blessings which the war occasionally produced as an antidote to all its horrors.'

"*November 20th. Cairo.* At 9 a.m. there was a general exodus and farewell to Gort. Alexander was off to Bari, Portal off to Tunis, and I, accompanied by Bob Laycock, started for Cairo. I am at present writing in the air, flying along the edge of the African coast east of Tripoli. We struck due south on leaving Malta so as to avoid Crete and any possible contacts with Germans from that island. Start of journey was a bit bumpy, but has now smoothed down. We are flying over the edge of that sea of yellow and brown sand looking out over the deep blue of the Mediterranean, which gradually shades off into the light blue of the horizon and leaves the horizon ill-defined. Below us is the black bootlace of the tarmacked desert road. Last time I was over it on the way to Tripoli it was alive with lice-like lorries spaced out every hundred yards, busy building up our forces for the invasion of Tunisia. Now it is desolate and deserted without a vestige of life to be seen on it."

" I wish our Conference was over. I despair of getting our American friends to have any strategic vision. Their drag on us has seriously affected our Mediterranean strategy and the whole conduct of the war. I blame myself for having failed to overcome their short-sighted views and allowed my better judgment to be affected by them. It would have been better to have resigned my appointment than to agree to any form of compromise. And yet I wonder whether such action would have borne any fruit."[1]

" *Later.* At 3.30 p.m. we arrived on the aerodrome beyond Mena. ' Jumbo ' Wilson and Adam were on the aerodrome to meet me and took me on to the villa which I am to live in with Dill, Portal, Cunningham. It is a villa outside Cairo on the way to Mena and belongs to some Egyptian princess. It is quite comfortable except for the plumbing, which is none too good and water seldom hot.[2] Dill turned up shortly after I had arrived, and we both went to dine with ' Jumbo ' Wilson."

" *November 21st.* Went to G.H.Q. to attend the Intelligence conference. Then had a long talk with ' Jumbo ' Wilson. He came to lunch and at 2.30 p.m. we went to meet the P.M. on his arrival by plane from Alexandria. Then to the Mena Hotel which has been taken over as our offices and conference rooms and went through a series of documents which the Americans had produced. Finally dined with P.M., together with Dill, Portal, Wilson, Sholto Douglas, Mountbatten and Casey."

" P.M. kept us up till after 1 a.m. I am not happy at

[1] In a letter from Washington the Head of the British Military Mission, Field Marshal Dill, had written a few weeks earlier: " I do not believe it was ever possible to make the Americans more Mediterranean-minded than they are to-day. The American Chiefs of Staff have given way to our views a thousand times more than we have given way to theirs. Of course, this has led to compromises which are always dangerous, but inevitable when one is dealing with a strong ally. But after all, things have gone well and I still think the defeat of Germany next year is a good bet." Dill to Brooke, 16 Oct., 1943. Lord Alanbrooke, *Personal Files.*

[2] General Arnold, the American Chief of Air Staff, when he visited it, remarked that it was " quite racy in its choice of paintings and other decorations. . . . I wouldn't have swapped the extra hot water we had in our villa for all the pictures and fixtures and fittings in their house." *Arnold,* 220.

the line he proposes to take in approaching this Conference. We decided on the programme and are to start by dealing with Chiang Kai-shek who has arrived with Madame. And then we shall start on our Mediterranean discussion. The whole programme is affected by Stalin's visit to Teheran and the necessity of meeting him there by a given date after concluding our talks here."

'We should never have started our Conference with Chiang; by doing so we were putting the cart before the horse. He had nothing to contribute towards the defeat of the Germans, and for the matter of that uncommonly little towards the defeat of the Japanese. Why the Americans attached such importance to Chiang I have never discovered. All he did for them was to lead them down a garden path to a Communist China.'

" *November 22nd. Cairo.* Started the day with a C.O.S. at 10 a.m. at which we discussed our procedure for the rest of the meeting. After lunch had our first Combined meeting when we again decided on procedure. Martel then came to see me. Dill and I then called on Miles Lampson and on Casey.[1] After dinner meeting with President, P.M., all Chiefs of Staff, Mountbatten, Stilwell, Chennault, Harry Hopkins, to discuss Dickie Mountbatten's plans and to prepare for meetings with Chiang Kai-shek."

" After that P.M. took Dill, Portal and me to his villa. He was very pleased with the results of his talks with the President and thinks we shall not have so very much difficulty. Personally I doubt this. Got home after midnight."

" *November 23rd. Cairo.* We started the day with rather a rushed C.O.S. meeting, as at 11 a.m. we were due to go on to the President's villa for a meeting with Chiang Kai-shek. It was a historical meeting with the President,

[1] Lt.-Gen. Sir Giffard Martel, former Head of Military Mission at Moscow; Sir Miles Lampson, British Ambassador to Egypt, now Lord Killearn; and the Rt. Hon. Richard Casey, resident Minister of State in the Middle East.

P.M., Harry Hopkins, Chiang Kai-shek, Madame, all the Chiefs of Staff, Dickie Mountbatten, Stilwell, Chennault, Carton de Wiart,[1] and a ' full house ' of Chinese generals."

" I was very interested in the Chinese pair. The Generalissimo reminded me of a cross between a pine-martin and a ferret. A shrewd, foxy sort of face. Evidently with no grasp of war in its larger aspects, but determined to get the best of all bargains. Madame was a study in herself; a queer character in which sex and politics seemed to predominate, both being used to achieve her ends. Not good-looking, with a flat Mongolian face with high cheek-bones and a flat turned-up nose with two large circular nostrils looking like two dark holes leading into her head. Jet black hair and sallow complexion. She had certainly made the best of herself and was well turned out. A black satin dress with a yellow chrysanthemum pattern on it, a neat jacket, big black tulle bows at the back of her head and a black veil over her face, light-coloured stockings and black shoes with large brass nails, covering small feet. Tapered fingers playing with a long cigarette-holder in which she smoked continuous cigarettes."

" The meeting was a slow one with everything inter-preted by a Chinese general reinforced by Madame. Dickie Mountbatten explained his whole plan; then a few questions were asked by Chiang. Finally a long dis-cussion in which Chiang seemed to make whole operation dependent on presence of naval forces in the Indian Ocean."

" After lunch a meeting with Combined Chiefs of Staff which became somewhat heated, with King on the subject of the Andaman Islands and the possibility of landing-craft being diverted from this operation to the Aegean. At 3.30 p.m. the Chinese (General, Admiral and Air Marshal) came in, and I had a desperate time with them

---

[1] Lt.-Gen. Sir Adrian Carton de Wiart, V.C., who, having escaped from an Italian prison, had been appointed the Prime Minister's representative at Chiang Kai-shek's headquarters.

to try and get them to speak. All they wanted to do was to listen, and, as we had nothing more to say except to argue with them and answer their questions, the meeting came to a standstill. We had to suggest that they should examine the plan a little deeper and return to-morrow, thus wasting more of our precious time. After the meeting I had an hour with Dickie Mountbatten. Then finished off office work and returned here by 7 p.m."

"We then had Leahy, King and Arnold to dine. Unfortunately Marshall was unable to come. The cook gave us an excellent dinner and things went well. King was as nice as could be and quite transformed from his morning's attitude."

That evening—so pleasantly contrasting with the afternoon's stormy session—is referred to by three of the four American Chiefs of Staff in their memoirs. "We had an excellent dinner", wrote General Arnold, "good food, good wine, splendid service and good conversation. Genghis Khan, Kublai Khan, Knights of Malta, Carthaginians, the Turkish conquest of the Mediterranean—we touched on all of these before we returned to our villa at 10.30." "Sir Alan Brooke," Leahy recalled, "told us the history of the Knights of Malta, of which he obviously had made a study."[1] It was their colleague, Admiral King's, sixty-fifth birthday; the duel between him and Brooke earlier in the day had been even more heated than the latter's diary suggests. For, with the C.I.G.S. as spokesman, the British Chiefs of Staff had strongly opposed the American proposal to discuss the South-East Asia campaign before agreeing on the plans for assailing the Axis fortress in Europe and the overall strategy for the war against Japan. Only when these had been settled, the C.I.G.S. had maintained, would it be practicable to allocate assault shipping for the very minor operation against the Andaman Isles—*Buccaneer*—which the new theatre commander, Mountbatten, was advocating as the best way of harrying the Japanese with

[1] *Arnold*, 220; *Leahy*, 237.

the limited resources available. The Americans had listened with impatience to Brooke's formidable battery of statistical evidence to prove that no assault-craft could be spared for even the smallest operation in the Indian Ocean until after Eisenhower's and Alexander's impending sea attack on the German flank in Italy and then only if *Overlord* were postponed from May till July to give time for the shipping sent from the Mediterranean to the Bay of Bengal to be brought back to Europe.[1] " Before we finished," wrote Arnold, " it became quite an open talk, with everybody throwing his cards on the table, face up." " Brooke got nasty," Stilwell recorded, " and King got good and sore. King almost climbed over the table at Brooke. God, he was mad! I wish he had socked him . . . 3.30 a.m. Chinese came. Terrible performance. They couldn't ask a question. Brooke was insulting. I helped them out . . . Brooke fired questions and I batted them back."[2]

' This very Chinese day,' Brooke recalled after the war, ' has remained rooted in my memory. I have never known whether Madame Chiang gate-crashed into the morning's Plenary Meeting or whether she was actually invited. It makes little difference, for I feel certain she would have turned up, whether invited or not. She was the only woman amongst a very large gathering of men and was determined to bring into action all the charms nature had blessed her with. Although not good-looking, she certainly had a good figure which she knew how to display at its best. Gifted with great charm and gracefulness, every small movement of hers arrested and pleased the eye. For instance, at one critical moment her closely clinging black dress of black satin with golden chrysanthemums displayed a slit which exposed one of the most shapely of legs. This caused a rustle amongst some of those attending the conference, and I even thought I heard a suppressed neigh come from a group of the younger members! '

[1] *Ehrman* V, 158-63.
[2] *Arnold*, 220; *Stilwell Papers*, 245, cit. *Whitehill*, 302.

' The trouble that lay behind all this was that we were left wondering whether we were dealing with Chiang or with Madame. Whenever he was addressed, his Chinese general sitting on his right interpreted for him, but, as soon as he had finished, Madame said, " Excuse me, gentlemen, I do not think that the interpreter has conveyed the full meaning to the Generalissimo." Similarly, whenever Chiang spoke, his general duly interpreted the statement, but Madame rose to say in the most perfect English, " Excuse me, gentlemen, but the general has failed to convey to you the full meaning of the thoughts that the Generalissimo wishes to express. If you will allow me I shall put before you his real thoughts." I certainly felt that she was the leading spirit of the two, and that I would not trust her very far.'

' As for Chiang, I think the description I gave of him fits him well; a shrewd but small man. He was certainly very successful in leading the Americans down the garden path. He and his Chinese forces never did much against the Japs during the war, and he did not even succeed in keeping his country from becoming Communist after the war. And yet the Americans never saw through all his short-comings, pinned their hopes on him and induced us to do the same. I often wonder how Marshall failed to realise what a broken reed Chiang was when he went out to China just after the defeat of Japan.'

' Anyhow, here we were on 23rd November, 1943, sitting in a Plenary Conference with President, P.M., Chiang and Madame to decide how we could meet his wishes for operations in the Indian Ocean to support armies near Chungking. What is more, we were prepared to pander sufficiently to Chiang to affect possible operations in the Aegean against our primary enemy.'

' The second Chinese farce on this day took place in the afternoon when three Chinese Chiefs of Staff attended our meeting to discuss operations in Burma. We had previously provided them with our proposed plans and asked them to read these so as to discuss them with us at our Combined Chiefs of Staff meeting. As the Conference was on British controlled soil I was in the chair and welcomed them as they arrived. I told them how much we had looked forward to this opportunity of discussing our plans in the war against Japan with them. We felt that, with their long contacts with the Japanese both as neighbours and as enemies, they must be in a special position to know how to bring about their ultimate defeat. I told them we had spent many hours in preparing the plans we had given them to examine and that we hoped now to receive their help and assistance in perfecting them. And I finally asked them for their views and criticisms. There ensued the most ghastly silence! The room was packed with some sixty or seventy British and American staff officers and at the end of the table a dozen or so Chinese staff all whispering together in a state of excitement. At last a Chinese spokesman arose and said, " We wish to listen to your deliberations! " This was followed by a silence in which you could have heard a pin drop, whilst I racked my brain as to what to do next. I then explained to them carefully that we had already spent hours of deliberation to arrive at the plans we had submitted. That our deliberations on these plans were now finished, and that it rested with them to express their views on them. Finally I asked them once more to express their own views and criticisms. This was followed by another of those deadly silences, only broken by Chinese whisperings. Just when I could no longer bear the silence, up got the same Chinese spokesman and repeated the very same words: " We wish to listen to your deliberations! " ' '

' I felt all eyes turn on me with suppressed amusement, wondering what I should do next. And for a few seconds I had no idea what I should do next. Then I rose and told them that possibly they had not yet had time enough to study the plans or, perhaps, had not been able entirely to understand them. I suggested we should give them a further twenty-four hours to study the plans and that we should attach to them special staff officers to explain them. As soon as this suggestion had been interpreted there was a real " flutter in the dovecot ", and before we had time to realise it they had all slipped out through the door and disappeared. Mopping my brow, I turned to Marshall and said, " That was a ghastly waste of time! " To which he replied, " You're telling me! " Considering that it was thanks to him and the American outlook that we had had to suffer this depressing interlude, I felt that he might have expressed his regret otherwise.'

' These two episodes on one day went a long way to convince me that there was little to be hoped for from Chiang's China.'

Not till November 24th—only three days before they were due to meet the Russians at Teheran—did the Western Allies turn to the all-important business of co-ordinating their campaign in the Mediterranean with the cross-Channel invasion they had provisionally scheduled for May. First through the mouth of the Prime Minister at the Plenary meeting on the 24th and then, at the military conferences on the 25th and 26th through the Chairman of their Chiefs of Staff, the British presented the case they had been preparing for the past month: that it would be madness, in order to adhere to an invasion date only intended as a general target, to throw away the chance of inflicting on the Germans in Italy and the Mediterranean the losses that had always been envisaged by the British Chiefs of Staff as the indispensable preliminary to a successful invasion of North-Western Europe. The reluctance of their allies to re-align their plans in the light of existing conditions seemed to them inconceivable folly; to the Americans the British wish to do so appeared as one more proof of their unaccountable preference for an Italian or Balkan side-show to the major campaign in France that could alone give decisive victory. The Prime Minister's obsession with the Dodecanese and Turkey increased their suspicions. Unlike the British they did not wish to discuss the Italian campaign, still less the

81

situation in the Ægean, before meeting the Russians, for they hoped that the latter might help them to overrule the arguments of Churchill and his C.I.G.S.[1]

Brooke's diary tells the story of the next three days:

" *November 24th.   Cairo.*   We started with our usual C.O.S. meeting which lasted till 11 a.m. when we all went over to the President's villa for a meeting with him and the Prime Minister.   The President started with a general statement expressing his views as to the conduct of the war.   This did not last very long, and then the P.M. gave a masterly statement on European strategy and the best ways of maintaining pressure on Germany during the winter months and the dangers of spelling the word *Overlord* with the letters *Tyrant*.   It was a good address and should help us in our deliberations."

" After lunch we met the American Chiefs at 2.30 p.m. Marshall was late as he had been lunching with Chiang Kai-shek who had suddenly decided that unless several impossible conditions could be fulfilled he would refuse to play his part in the operations.   Shortly afterwards the Chinese Chiefs arrived and spent an hour asking the most futile questions.   Finally Stilwell, as spokesman for Chiang, repeated what Marshall had said.   We decided to send Mountbatten round to discuss matters with him (Chiang) and to aim at obtaining an agreement . . ."

" After several days' deliberation we have made no progress whatever."

' The return of our Chinese Chiefs to the Combined

1 " The U.S. Chiefs of Staff had no doubt in their own minds as to just what all this signified.   They felt certain that whenever the persistent Prime Minister started talking about Rhodes. or veering towards the ' right ' from Northern Italy, he was resuming the advocacy of strategic diversions in South-Eastern Europe and away from Northern France.   They prepared themselves for battles at Teheran in which the Americans and Russians would form a united front." *White House Papers* II, 770. See also *Leahy* 237-8   It is interesting to note that, according to a contemporary diary entry of Captain Butcher's, Harry Hopkins on November 21st expected the Russians to team up with the British at Teheran in favour of a Balkan rather than a Normandy operation in 1944. *Butcher*, 384. See also *Ehrman* V, 156.

meeting was again a fiasco. When I had them assembled I again asked them if they had any questions or criticisms they wished to put forward. After another one of those devastating silences only filled by Chinese whispers, the spokesman got up and asked:—" What is the proportion of Indian troops as opposed to British troops which will take part in this proposed operation? " I then reminded him that we had provided them with staff officers to answer just such questions and then gave them the figures they had asked for. With the greatest difficulty I extracted a few more questions and then gave up the conflict in despair. It was evident that they understood nothing about strategy or higher tactics and were quite unfit to discuss these questions.'

" *November 25th. Cairo.* We started the morning with our usual C.O.S. meeting at which we decided on the best line of action for the afternoon Combined meeting. At noon we went round to the President's villa when a series of photos were taken, both still and movie. First of all the high and mighty—President, P.M. and Generalissimo. Then the same as above, with Chiefs of Staff and Chinese generals. Finally the above with politicians, diplomats, etc. Not a very attractive lot to look at. But I have no doubt that we had not been much more beautiful in the military groups! "

" At 2.30 p.m. we had an ' off the record ' Combined meeting and made considerable progress. I put forward our counter-proposals for continuing active operations in the Mediterranean at the expense of a postponement of the *Overlord* date. We did not meet with half the reaction we were expecting. On the other hand the Chinese negotiations are not going well and Chiang Kai-shek is busy bargaining to obtain the maximum possible out of us."

" At 6 p.m. we had a service at the Cathedral for the Americans in honour of ' Thanksgiving Day. . . .' "[1]

[1] A cynical American described this British gesture of goodwill as " Lend-Lease in reverse! " *Leahy*, 238.

" *November 26th. Cairo.* A long C.O.S. meeting to decide line on which to work this afternoon. We had Commanders-in-Chief, Middle East, to hear their views about the Ægean operations. At 2.30 p.m. met the Americans and it was not long before Marshall and I had the father and mother of a row! We had to come to an ' off the record ' meeting and then began to make some progress. In the end we had secured most of the points we were after."

" At 5 p.m. attended a tea party given by Chiang Kai-shek and Madame, a dismal show. Very hot and stuffy room. Had some fifteen minutes' talk with him through an interpreter. He did not impress me much, but hard to tell at a meeting like that. Meanwhile Madame holding a court of admirers. The more I see of her, the less I like her."

This was the final afternoon of the Cairo talks. More than half the Conference had been wasted in academic discussions about South-East Asia and China. But though still insisting on the need for a British offensive in the Indian Ocean and Burma, the Americans, when finally forced to discuss the matter, had proved less intransigent about the abandonment of the Italian campaign and the date of D-Day than the British had expected. Though they had refused to commit themselves until the Russians had been heard, they left their Allies with the impression that they no longer regarded the datum-line of May 1st for the invasion of Normandy as sacrosanct.[1] They had agreed, too, to the appointment of a Supreme Commander for the Mediterranean, so accepting, at least in theory, the British view that that sea should be regarded as one, while their proposal that the Supreme Commander of *Overlord* should also command the Mediterranean had been dropped. The British Chiefs of Staff had stressed the impracticability of this suggestion in a Memorandum presented to their allies on the 26th.

[1] *Ehrman* V, 167.

" The Supreme Commander for the war against Germany will have to consult both the United States and the British Governments on almost every important question . . . He will only be able to make a decision without reference to high authority on comparatively minor and strictly military questions . . . He will thus be an extra and unnecessary link in the chain of Command . . . The United States Chiefs of Staff propose . . . that the decisions of the Supreme Commander should ' be subject to reversal by the Combined Chiefs of Staff.' If the main object of this new arrangement is to ensure rapid decisions, it looks as though the above proviso will lead to deplorable consequences. Instances will occur in which the Supreme Commander has issued orders and the troops have marched in accordance with these orders, only to be followed by a reversal of the order by the Combined Chiefs of Staff and consequent confusion. Again, it may happen that the British Chiefs of Staff agree with a decision taken by the Supreme Commander while the United States Chiefs of Staff totally disagree with it. What happens then? Or again, the Combined Chiefs of Staff may whole-heartedly support, on military grounds, a decision taken by the Supreme Commander, only to find that one or other of the Governments concerned is not prepared to ratify it. Then what happens? "

" If the Supreme Commander is going to exercise real control, he will need to assemble the whole paraphernalia of Intelligence, Planning and Administration on an unprecedented scale. This staff will merely be a great pad between the theatre commanders and the Combined Chiefs of Staff. . . . The conclusion to be drawn is that the Supreme Commander of the war against Germany will never have, under the system of Government which now obtains in the United States and the United Kingdom, authority to deal with anything but strictly military, and comparatively minor, problems. He will be boosted by the Press and public opinion as a Superman who is going to lead the two nations to victory. This is a mere delusion. His position will be a sham. In important matters he will not be able to do anything more than is now done by the theatre commanders."

" If the well-tried machinery that has led us safely through the last two years has failed in the smaller problems, it would be better to examine that machinery and see how it could be speeded up and adjusted, rather than to embark upon an entirely novel experiment, which merely makes a cumbrous and unnecessary link in the chain of command and which will surely lead to disillusionment and disappointment."[1]

Yet though the Americans had abandoned their plan to hand over the entire direction of the war against Germany to a single Supreme Commander—in other words, to General Marshall—Brooke and his colleagues were far from happy about the impending conference with the Russians. Instead of the Western Allies meeting Stalin with an agreed plan, they were going to Teheran with unresolved aims. It had been hard enough to agree on a realistic strategic policy with the Americans in the past; it was going to be far harder with the Russians at the conference table urging courses which, however immediately beneficial to themselves, might entail disaster for those who carried them out. Though she was still deploying larger forces against Germany than the United States, Britain after four years of war had nearly reached the end of her reserves of manpower. Henceforward she was bound to grow progressively weaker compared with America and Russia. A week earlier, backed by Spruance's gigantic fleet, American troops and marines had landed at Makin and Tarawa; while in the past month, helped by the deflection of German reserves and the bulk of the *Luftwaffe* to the Mediterranean and the West, the Russians had advanced at one point to within a hundred miles of the old Polish frontier. If the two giants of East and West now joined hands in imposing a strategy of which Britain disapproved, it was going to be almost impossible

[1] *Ehrman* V, 169-72.

to prevent them. And this was precisely what the American President and his military advisers were hoping to do.

.   .   .   .

" *November 27th. Teheran.* 1300 miles. We had an early rise, being called at 4.30 a.m. By 5.45 a.m. we were leaving our villa in the dark and light mist for the aerodrome. When we arrived there we were told that the mist would delay our departure. However, by 7 a.m. we were moving down the runway for our take-off for Teheran. Our party consisted of Dill, Cunningham, Portal, ' Pug ' Ismay and Boyle and secretaries. We were travelling in the new York designed for the Chiefs of Staff. Very comfortable. We crossed the Canal near Suez and could see the Italian battleships in the Bitter Lakes. Then across the Sinai Peninsula until we struck Beersheba; from there on across the top of the Dead Sea, and, as visibility was good, we could see Jerusalem, Bethlehem, Hebron and Jericho."

" We then headed for Habbaniya aerodrome near Baghdad, where we came down and spent an hour looking round and being told the story of the attack on the aerodrome in the early days of the war. After taking off again we were served with the most excellent lunch and with oxygen for those who wanted it. We had to travel at 14,000 feet for a long bit of the way, but I found it did not bother me and that I did not require any oxygen. We arrived at Teheran a few minutes behind the P.M. who had started an hour later but had flown direct."

" We are not yet certain whether Stalin has arrived or not; according to rumours he is here. I am not looking forward to the next few days. The Conference will be difficult and there is no saying where they may lead us to."

' One amusing rumour, which I failed to enter in my

diary, was the local Teheran explanation for this sudden gathering of important people in their capital. Our visit happened almost to coincide with some local election. It was therefore decided that all these V.I.P.s had gathered together here to ensure that the Persian elections were run on impartial lines! '

' The Security arrangements were not of the best, and, as the American Embassy lay some way out of the centre of the town, it was decided to house the President in the Soviet Embassy, where they had room, and to hold our conferences in this Embassy also. As the British Legation buildings were just alongside the Soviet ones, we only had one road to cross to attend meetings and the P.M.'s security was also made easier.'

" *Sunday, November 28th. Teheran.* Had a quiet morning to make up for previous night's loss of sleep. Then spent an hour in the office prior to running a Chiefs of Staff meeting till lunch. We were worried with the whole situation. We have not got agreement with the Americans on the main points for discussion and it was evident that we were heading for chaos."

" P.M. has a throat and has practically lost his voice. He is not fit and consequently not in the best of moods. We tried to get him to agree to going on with the Andaman operation so as to get American agreement in the Mediterranean. He would not do so."[1]

" At 4 p.m. we went over to the Russian Embassy for our first Plenary Meeting. The following were present:— Stalin, Roosevelt, Winston, Anthony Eden, Harry Hopkins, Molotov, Voroshilov, Dill, Portal, Cunningham,

---

[1] Admiral Leahy, who like his colleagues never seemed able to understand the nature of the relationship between Churchill and Brooke, wrote of the British proposal at Cairo two days earlier to abandon amphibious operations in the Indian Ocean: " Carrying out the orders of Churchill, their Commander-in-Chief, the British Staff, headed by Brooke, insisted that the Andaman operation could not be carried out. I informed our British colleagues that the American Chiefs could not recede from their present position on the Andaman attack without orders from the President." *Leahy*, 238.

Leahy and King, 'Pug' Ismay, Boyle, Dean and three interpreters. Stalin turned up in his uniform of Field-Marshal, but to my mind no more attractive than I thought him last time I saw him. Molotov looked almost saturnine."

" We all sat round a large round table. The President started off with an introductory statement which he followed up with a brief review of the war in the Pacific. To which Stalin replied that he much appreciated what we were doing in that theatre and that it was only the fact that the Germans fully engaged him that prevented him from co-operating with us. This was cheering news and implied Russian help as soon as Germany was defeated."

" The President then alluded to the Western Front and made a poor and not very helpful speech. From then onwards the conference went from bad to worse. Stalin replied by advocating cross-Channel operations at the expense of all else. Winston replied and was not at his best. President chipped in and made matters worse. We finished up with a suggestion, partly sponsored by the President, that we should close operations in Italy before taking Rome. That we should land six divisions in Southern France at the beginning of April and carry out *Overlord* on May 1st."

" Turkey, according to Stalin, was beyond hope and nothing would induce her to come into the war on any account. Dardanelles were apparently not worth opening! In fact, after complaining that we were not holding sufficient divisions away from Russia, Stalin's suggestion was that practically no action should take place during the winter months."

" We sat for three-and-a-half hours and finished up the conference by confusing plans more than they ever have been before."

' The meeting had, however, been of intense interest and

a great deal had been made clear which I had not yet realised. This was the first occasion during the war when Stalin, Roosevelt and Winston sat round a table to discuss the war we were waging together. I found it quite enthralling looking at their faces and trying to estimate what lay behind. With Churchill, of course, I knew fairly well, and I was beginning to understand the workings of Roosevelt's brain, as we had had several meetings with him. But Stalin was still very much of an enigma. I had already formed a very high idea of his ability, force of character and shrewdness, but did not know yet whether he was also a strategist. I knew that Voroshilov would provide him with nothing in the shape of strategic vision. My last visit to Moscow had made that quite clear to me, when I had spent several hours with Voroshilov discussing the problem of a Second Front.'

' During this meeting and all the subsequent ones which we had with Stalin, I rapidly grew to appreciate the fact that he had a military brain of the very highest calibre. Never once in any of his statements did he make any strategic error, nor did he ever fail to appreciate all the implications of a situation with a quick and unerring eye. In this respect he stood out compared with his two colleagues. Roosevelt never made any great pretence at being a strategist and left either Marshall or Leahy to talk for him. Winston, on the other hand, was more erratic, brilliant at times, but too impulsive and inclined to favour unsuitable plans without giving them the preliminary deep thought they required.'

' Stalin was now evidently far better satisfied with his defensive position. He was beginning to feel that the Germans had shot their bolt; immediate pressure on the West was no longer so urgently required. What is more, from his point of view the entry of Turkey was no longer so desirable. He no longer had (if he had ever had) any great desire for the opening of the Dardanelles. This would bring in the British and the Americans on his left flank in an advance westward through the Balkans. He had by then pretty definite ideas as to how he wanted the Balkans run after the war; British and American assistance was therefore no longer desirable in the Eastern Mediterranean.'

' His new outlook on Italy was also interesting; there was now no pressure on our forces to push on up the leg of Italy. Such an advance led too directly towards Yugoslavia and Austria, on which no doubt he had by now cast covetous eyes. He approved of Roosevelt's proposal to close down operations in Italy and to transfer six divisions to invade Southern France on April 1st, whilst the main Channel operation would take place on May 1st. I am certain he did not approve such operations for their strategic value, but because they fitted in with his future political plans. He was too good a strategist not to see the weakness of the American plan. To cease operations in Italy before Rome would at once free the required reinforcements to meet six of our divisions under the precarious conditions of a landing and all the subsequent problems connected with their maintenance on this new front. The potential war effort of our divisions on transfer from Italy to Southern France would in the early stages have been reduced by half. Furthermore, this plan allowed the whole of the month of April for the annihilation of these six divisions, whilst fighting in Italy was at a standstill and *Overlord* had not yet started.'

' I feel certain that Stalin saw through these strategical misconceptions, but to him they mattered little; his political and military requirements could now be best met by the greatest squandering of British and American lives in the French theatre. We were reaching a very dangerous point where his shrewdness, assisted by American shortsightedness, might lead us anywhere. It is not surprising that I found this series of meetings so difficult. Here we were with the Americans determined to start Operation *Overlord* on the wrong leg if they possibly could, and Stalin inwardly hoping that they would do so. On the top of it all were promises from the President to Chiang on the Andaman operation given on the first day of our Cairo meetings, and Winston's eyes continually glancing towards the approaches to the Dardanelles and Balkans.'

" *November 29th. Teheran.* Seven hours spent in conferences and six of them through interpreters! We started the morning with a Staff meeting at 10.30, consisting of Leahy, Marshall, Voroshilov, Portal and myself. We spent three hours at it, and at the end were no further advanced. Voroshilov's main theme was that the cross-Channel operation must have preference over all others, and that the date must remain May 1st. In vain I argued that by closing operations in the Mediterranean German forces would be free to proceed to other theatres. Our friend Voroshilov refused to see any of these arguments, having evidently been briefed by Stalin. . . . Anyway Leahy said nothing and Marshall only stressed the importance that the Americans had always attached to cross-Channel operations. By 1.30 p.m. I adjourned the meeting."

" At 2.45 p.m. we held a short C.O.S. meeting to compare notes and frame future action. At 3.30 p.m. we went over to the Russian Embassy to see Winston present the ' Stalingrad Sword ' to Stalin. Bands, guards of honour, national anthems, etc. Speech by Winston after which he handed the sword over in the name of the King to Stalin. Stalin kissed the sword and handed it over to Voroshilov, who promptly dropped it out of its scabbard! However, finally it was handed over to the commander of the Russian guard of honour and marched off securely. Then photographs of the usual groups."

" We then sat down at 4 p.m. for another three hours' conference. Bad from beginning to end. Stalin meticulous with only two arguments—cross-Channel operation on May 1st, also offensive in Southern France. Americans supported this view, quite unaware of the fact that it is already an impossibility. Finally decided that Americans and ourselves should have another meeting to-morrow with a view to arriving at some form of solution for our final Plenary meeting at 4 p.m."

" After listening to the arguments put forward during the last two days I feel like entering a lunatic asylum or nursing-home! . . ."

' My day of seven hours of conference, six of them with interpreters, had got to the bottom of me. I was evidently looking at life with very dark glasses. The Americans had forced us to put the cart before the horse in the early stages by meeting Chiang Kai-shek before having our meetings with them. Now the same was occurring with the Russians.'

Hopkins's " White House Papers " show that Roosevelt went to Teheran believing he could bridge the ideological gulf between the U.S.S.R. and the West by holding himself out as an impartial arbitrator between the British and Russian points of view. In his private talks with Stalin he deliberately gave the latter the impression that, with its egalitarian and forward-looking outlook, America was better able to understand Russian needs than the conservative imperialist Power that had maintained the balance of world affairs in the past. The American-Russian axis he sought to create in the political sphere was to be reflected in the military. " At the first Plenary session of the Conference on the 28th," wrote Admiral Leahy, " the Soviets and Americans seemed to be nearly in agreement as to the fundamental strategic principles that should be followed." Stalin announced that, his policy of neutrality in the Far East notwithstanding, he welcomed every American success against Japan and would join the war against her as soon as Germany was defeated. And he not only upheld the American contention that the date—May 1st—provisionally fixed at Quebec for *Overlord* should be adhered to regardless of its effect on the Italian campaign, but, to the delight of the Americans, championed a suggestion, originally made by Eisenhower but never seriously considered by the Combined Chiefs of Staff, that the Italian campaign should be abandoned in favour of a landing in the spring on the Mediterranean coast of France—an operation which in the view of Brooke and his colleagues would have the very effect of drawing the German reserves westwards which the Italian campaign was intended to prevent. In this atmosphere little heed had been paid to Churchill's passionate protest against abandoning an enterprise in which twenty British, or British-controlled, divisions were committed and which was holding down a large German army, merely in order to adhere exactly to the provisional date originally proposed for *Overlord*. At the subsequent meeting of the Russian, American and British Chiefs of Staff on the 29th, it had fallen to Brooke " to insist stubbornly ", in Leahy's words, " that all available Mediterranean forces should be used in the Italian and Eastern Mediterranean campaigns."[1] During this meeting, according to Hopkins, Voroshilov asked the C.I.G.S. point-blank if he attached the same importance to *Overlord* as General Marshall. Brooke said he did, but added that he knew the strength of the German defences of France and that under certain circumstances *Overlord* could fail. When Voroshilov went on to say that no operation, whether in the Mediterranean or elsewhere, could be regarded as anything but an auxiliary to *Overlord*, Brooke replied that it was exactly in that light that he and his colleagues regarded it, but that, unless some such operation was carried out, the conditions necessary for *Overlord* would not obtain.[2]

When, at the end of the afternoon's Plenary session on the 29th, the correlation of the Mediterranean campaign with the date of *Overlord* was referred to the Combined Chiefs of Staff, Stalin protested at such a matter being left to a mere military committee. But when next day, after a prolonged session with his British and American colleagues, Brooke reported their decisions to the Heads of the three Governments, the Russian dictator, as well as the President and Prime Minister, expressed profound satisfaction at what had been agreed. Brooke's diary, written in the small hours of the following morning, indicates what was achieved.

[1] *Leahy*, 244.
[2] *White House Papers* II, 778. *Ehrman* V, 177-9.

" *November 30th.* Got up with the feeling that we had an unpleasant day in front of us, but it did not turn out to be too bad after all. We began with an ordinary C.O.S. meeting at 8.45 a.m. This was followed by a Combined Chiefs of Staff meeting with the Americans at 9.30 a.m. Here we had a difficult time trying to arrive at some agreement which we could put before our Russian friends in the afternoon."

" After much argument we decided that the cross-Channel operation could be put off to June 1st. This did not meet with all our requirements, but was arranged to fit in with the proposed Russian spring offensive. We also decided to stage what we could in the way of operations in Southern France. I pressed hard again to obtain the abandonment of the Andaman Islands attack so as to render more landing-craft available for the Mediterranean. Still same political difficulty with the President."

" At 12.30 we adjourned to see the P.M. and inform him of the results. Then lunch with our Ambassador in the Legation building. After that out for three-quarters-of-an-hour's shopping in the curio shops near the gate of the Legation."

" Then another talk with Winston before attending another Plenary meeting, at which I gave out the results of our decisions, and President, P.M., and Stalin made pretty speeches. Finished meeting by drafting military communiqué for the Press. This finished up the first of our tripartite meetings with the Russians. One thing is quite clear; the more politicians you put together to settle the prosecution of the war, the longer you postpone its conclusion! "

Yet, though he had to concede much, the C.I.G.S. had achieved far more than he realised. During the three-quarters-of-an-hour that morning in which his fellow Chiefs of Staff had considered the line they should take with their American colleagues, he had secured their agreement to the following.

That, in order to hold the Germans in Italy and prevent their reserves from being transferred to Russia, the Allied armies should continue their winter offensive until they had taken Rome and reached the Pisa-Rimini line, retaining for this purpose until the middle of January the sixty-eight tank-landing-ships scheduled for return to England. That because of this the target date for *Overlord* should be postponed to the end of May. That the time and scope of the suggested landing in the South of France—Operation *Anvil*—should be settled only when the amount of assault shipping available for it was known. That commando forces alone should be used to assist the partisans in Yugoslavia and that no operations should be undertaken in the Eastern Mediterranean unless Turkey was prepared to enter the war; and that, in view of Stalin's announcement that Russia would attack Japan after the defeat of Germany, the Americans should be asked to drop the idea of an amphibious operation in the Indian Ocean in order to release landing-craft for *Anvil*, which could otherwise only be staged on a single division front. To all these propositions, which Brooke now presented to the American Chiefs of Staff, the latter agreed, excepting only those relating to the Indian Ocean and Aegean which it was felt, for political reasons, would have to be referred back to the President and Prime Minister.[1]

The approximate date chosen for D-Day had been dictated by what Brooke saw to be three inescapable essentials: the need to maintain sufficient preliminary pressure in Italy, the impossibility of obtaining and assembling enough assault shipping in the Channel before the summer, and the immediate necessity of enabling the President and Prime Minister to offer an invasion date to Stalin that would satisfy him and secure the conditional promise he had made on the previous day of a simultaneous Russian offensive to contain the Germans in the east—an operation which the experience of the past two Russian summers had shown could not be launched before June. By accepting the first of that month as the latest day

[1] *Ehrman* V, 181-3.

for crossing the Channel and making the date and size of the proposed subsidiary landing in Southern France—which, being American sponsored, might at least serve to deflect landing-craft from the Pacific—dependent on the shipping available for the more important operations in Italy and Normandy, the British C.I.G.S. made it possible for Roosevelt and Churchill, at the expense of only a slight exaggeration, to tell Stalin that *Overlord* would be launched some time during May " in conjunction with a supporting operation against the South of France on the largest scale that is permitted by the landing-craft available at that time."[1]   Under cover of this formula the detailed application of what had been decided could still be left to the arbitrament of circumstances. After his feat at Casablanca in January of securing agreement for his Mediterranean strategy, this adaptation of the rigid and academic dictates of his allies to what was logistically practicable, at the very moment when he and Churchill appeared to have been defeated, was probably the most important achievement of Brooke's career. It was made possible by the stubborn courage with which, despite illness and his apparent betrayal by his closest ally and friend, the Prime Minister fought with Stalin and Roosevelt for the British thesis during three critical days and nights.[2] Together he and Brooke had averted what might well have led to the worst disaster in British—and American—military history.

That night there was a grand dinner to round off the Conference.

> " We finished the day with a banquet in the Legation building to celebrate Winston's 69th birthday.[3]   The guests consisted of President, Stalin, Molotov, Anthony

---

[1] *Ehrman* V, 182-3.

[2] As Harry Hopkins's biographer put it, " Churchill's tireless advocacy of his own strategic concepts had been more than ever taxing to patience." *White House Papers* II, 790.

[3] This had followed a stormy private dinner given on the previous evening by Stalin to the President and Prime Minister at which, horrified by his host's announcement that he proposed to shoot the entire German General Staff after the war, Churchill temporarily left the room in indignation. *Churchill* V, 339-43; *Feis*, 273-4.

Eden, Harry Hopkins, Harriman, Clark Kerr, Bullard, Voroshilov, all American Chiefs of Staff, all British Chiefs of Staff, Winant, Somervell, Randolph and Sarah Churchill, Roosevelt's son and son-in-law. One side Winston sat with President on his right, on the other Anthony, with Molotov on his right and Harry Hopkins on his left. On the centre of the table was a large cake with sixty-nine candles burning."

" We had not long been seated when the P.M. said that it was his birthday party; that we should dine in the Russian manner and that anybody that liked could propose a toast at any time during the meal. He, therefore, started off by proposing the health of the King, the President of the U.S.A. and President of the Union of Soviet Republics. Then speeches ran fast and furious without a stop. The President made a very nice speech alluding to his and my father having known each other when he and I were boys and then proposed my health. Stalin then chipped in and said that, as a result of this meeting and of having come to such unanimous agreement, he hoped that I should no longer look upon Russians with such suspicion, and that if I really got to know them I should find that they were quite good chaps! "

" This was a most unexpected and uncalled-for attack. I could not let this accusation pass, so waited for a propitious moment to get up. It was rather nervous work considering what the audience was."

" I thanked the President for his very kind words which I assured him I had deeply appreciated. I then turned to Stalin and reminded him that in the afternoon's conference (when we had been discussing cover plans and secret measures) the Prime Minister had said that ' in war the truth must be accompanied by an escort of lies to ensure its security.' I reminded him that he himself had described how in all big offensives he produced masses of dummy tanks and aeroplanes on the fronts he was not going to attack, whilst he moved up forces quietly and under cover of darkness on the front of real attack. After four years of war and the continual cultivation of false appearances for the enemy, was it not possible that one's outward appearances might even deceive one's friends? I felt convinced that he must have been looking at the dummy aeroplanes and guns and had failed to observe the real and true friendship and comradeship which I felt towards him and all the Soviet forces."

" This went very well and met with some success. After dinner I returned to the attack and we finished the best of friends with a long hand-shake, and almost with our arms round each other's necks! He said that he liked the bold and soldier-like way in which I had spoken and the military strength of my voice. These were true military qualities that he liked and admired,[1] and that we were now on the best of terms; furthermore, that it must be remembered that some of the best friendships of this world were founded on original misunderstandings."

" It was a wonderful evening. On one occasion, when Winston was referring to political tendencies in England, he said that the whole political world was now a matter of ' tints ' and that England could be said to have now quite a ' pink ' look. Without a moment's hesitation Stalin snapped back, ' a sign of good health '. The President finished up by returning to the tint theme and said that the effect of this war would be to blend all those multitudinous tints, shades and colours into a rainbow where their individuality would be lost in the whole, and that this whole rainbow represented the emblem of hope. . . . Finally by 1.30 a.m. I was able to escape to bed."

[1] " During dinner . . . Stalin spoke about General Brooke. He thought that he did not like the Russians. He had been very abrupt and rough with them at our first Moscow meeting in August, 1942. I reassured him, remarking that military men were apt to be blunt and hard-cut when dealing with war problems with their professional colleagues. Stalin said that he liked them all the better for that. He gazed at Brooke intently across the room." *Churchill*, V, 340.

' I found it a very nervous test getting up to reply to Stalin's toast in front of that audience. I had a very trying quarter of an hour preparing my reply during which I would have given almost anything to go on remaining seated. I had, however, by then seen enough of Stalin during our Moscow visit to know that, if I sat under his insults, I was finished in his eyes for good and all and written off as spineless. Luckily by the time I made my speech he had consumed a fair share of champagne, which he was not so well used to as vodka! '

' There was one other episode which at the time may have seemed of little importance and, therefore, escaped being included in my diary. It still lives clearly in my mind, and I might at this moment still be sitting in the Legation dining-room—a room which I believe had originally been built by the Royal Engineers in Persian style. One might almost have been inside a Persian temple. The whole of the walls were covered with a mosaic of small pieces of looking-glass set at every conceivable angle, the windows with heavy deep-red curtains, and the walls had on them the pictures of the Royal Family which one expects in an Embassy or Legation. The Persian waiters were in blue and red liveries with white cotton gloves, the tips of the fingers of which hung limply and flapped about as they handed plates round.'

' When we came to the sweet course, the Chef of the Legation cuisine produced his trump card. It consisted of a base of ice a foot square and some four inches deep. The centre, a round hole of some three inches diameter, had been bored, and in this hole a religious night-light had been inserted. Over the lamp and hole a perforated iron tube stood erect some ten inches over the ice. On the top of the tube a large plate had been secured with icing-sugar. On the plate rested a vast cream ice, whilst a small frieze of icing-sugar decorated the edge of the plate. When lit up and carried in by white-gloved hands with long finger tips, the total effect was beyond description.'

' Two such edifices entered and proceeded solemnly round the table whilst each guest dug into the ice. I watched the tower approaching us carefully and noticed that the heat of the lamp had affected the block of ice that it rested in; the perforated iron tower had been affected by the melting away of its base. It was no longer perpendicular and by now looked more like the Tower of Pisa. The plate on top had assumed a rakish tilt; an accident was now inevitable. The ice by then was practically over Martin's head but sloping rapidly towards mine. I seized Somervell, my right-hand neighbour, and shouted to him to duck. We both buried our faces in our empty plates and only just in time. With the noise of an avalanche the whole wonderful construction slid over our heads and exploded in a clatter on the table between me and Berejkov. The unfortunate Berejkov was at that moment standing up interpreting a speech for Stalin and he came in for the full blast. He was splashed from his head to his feet, but I suppose it was as much as his life was worth to stop interpreting. In any case he carried on manfully whilst I sent for towels and, with the help of the Persian waiters, proceeded to mop him down. To this day I can still see large lumps of white ice-cream sitting on his shoes and melting over the edges and through the lace holes.'[1]

[1] *Notes on My Life* XIII, 7-10.

Chapter Three

CAIRO AND ITALY

THE CONFERENCE with the Russians was over, and it remained for the Western Allies to return to Cairo to finish their unfinished debates on the plans for the campaigns to which they had committed themselves. Leaving the President and Prime Minister to spend a final day discussing the political future with Stalin, the British and American Chiefs of Staff left Teheran early on December 1st.

" We left the Legation at 7.30 a.m. and by 8 a.m. we were roaring down the run-way, taking off for Jerusalem. We had a very good journey and landed on an aerodrome some thirty-five miles from Jerusalem. There we were joined by Marshall, King, Arnold and Somervell. We then drove to the King David Hotel where we are being done quite exceptionally well. This was intended as a way of returning the Williamsburg hospitality of the American Chiefs."

" After lunch we did a tour of Jerusalem with a monk guide and were shown all the usual sights. I was very interested in it all, but cannot help feeling that it is all so far detached from the real events that I would sooner retain my own conceptions of these. However, from the historical point of view of all the events that have occurred since the Crucifixion and their vast influence on the whole destiny of Europe, it is quite enthralling."

" We finished up the day with a banquet for the American Chiefs, a band and a dance in the hall. On the whole, this show has been a success. We presented all the Chiefs of Staff with a small olive-wood cigarette box, with silver plate on it with their names inscribed."

"*December 2nd. Cairo.* We left the hotel at 8.30 a.m. and returned to Jerusalem city to visit the Dome of Omar. From there we went on to the Garden of Gethsemane which finished our tour. We returned to the hotel, said good-bye to the Franciscan monk who had acted as our guide and then motored back to Lydda aerodrome. There we took off for Cairo where we arrived in time for a late lunch. On arrival on the aerodrome we were informed that the P.M. and the President were expected in a few minutes, having changed their plans."

The chief business remaining to be settled was the appointment of a Supreme Commander for *Overlord*—a decision which, as he was to be an American, rested with Roosevelt; the measures necessary to sustain Turkey and reopen the Aegean in the now, it was felt, unlikely event of that country being persuaded to enter the war—a point, about which Churchill, however, remained doggedly optimistic, much to the Americans' suspicion; and the allocation of sufficient assault shipping for, successively, the campaign in Italy, the operations promised to Chiang Kai-shek in the Indian Ocean, and for *Overlord* and the landing in the South of France which was either to precede or accompany it.

"*December 3rd. Cairo.* Started with a C.O.S. to try and sort matters out. Then at 12.30 p.m. went round for a meeting with the P.M. Found that he had been queering our pitch by suggesting to Leahy that if we did not attack Rhodes we might at any rate starve the place out."[1]

"We then lunched with the P.M. and at 2.30 p.m.

---

[1] "In the course of these discussions the Prime Minister's constant preoccupation with an attack upon the so-called soft underbelly of Europe rather than upon Southern France came into consideration. Clearly, Mr. Churchill much preferred the idea of squeezing the Germans by proceeding through North Italy and crossing into Northern Yugoslavia to landing on the southern French coast. At the same time he constantly reverted to Rhodes and the Dodecanese Islands in the Aegean Sea." Whitehill and King, *Life of Admiral King*, 315.

went back for our meeting with the American Chiefs of Staff. We were dumbfounded by being informed that the meeting must finish on Sunday at the latest (in forty-eight hours) as the President was off. No apologies—nothing! They have completely upset the whole meeting by wasting all our time with Chiang Kai-shek and Stalin before we had settled any points with them. And now, with nothing settled, they propose to disappear into the blue and leave all the main points connected with this Conference unsettled. It all looks like some of the worst sharp practice that I have seen for some time. The rest of the meeting was quite hopeless and we settled little else."

' I am afraid I was unnecessarily bitter with the American Chiefs of Staff. I withdraw every word connected with " sharp practice " and am quite certain that the one thing that Marshall would never have tolerated was anything connected with " sharp practice ". I have seldom met a straighter or more reliable man in my life.'

" *December 4th.* First a Chiefs of Staff meeting to try and decide how best to tackle our American friends. This lasted from 9.45 to 10.15 a.m. when we went to the P.M. He was upset by Dickie Mountbatten's latest telegram asking for more forces for the capture of the Andaman Isles. . . ."[1]

" Then at 11 a.m. went round for an interview with President, Americans and P.M. P.M. gave a long discourse and then called on me to express my views. I said that this Conference had been most unsatisfactory. Usually at all these meetings we discussed matters till we arrived at a policy which we put before the P.M. and the President for approval and amendment. And that we subsequently examined whether ways and means admitted

[1] During the past week, since his return to India, Mountbatten had discovered that the proposed operation against the Andamans, *Buccaneer*, would require as many as 50,000 men—instead of the mere 14,000 the President had optimistically hoped—and 120 carrier-borne fighters, a force which would involve an even larger call on the Allies' inadequate amphibious assault resources than had originally been contemplated. *Ehrman* V, 184-7; *Churchill* V, 364.

of this policy being carried out, finally putting up a paper for approval which formed our policy for the future conduct of the war. This time such a procedure had been impossible. We had straight away been thrown into high-level conferences with the Chinese. These had hardly been finished when we were rushed off to Teheran for similar conferences with Stalin, and now that we were back we were only given two days to arrive at any concerted policy."

" We then proceeded with the desirability of giving up the Andaman Islands operation in order to concentrate on the European front. Here we at once came up against political difficulties. The President had made promises to the Generalissimo of an amphibious operation and did not like to go back on his word. We made no progress."

" Dashed back to the house where I had Sosnkowski and Anders lunching with me. Then back for 2.30 p.m. conference with the Americans where we did not get very much further. Finally asked to dine alone with Winston to discuss questions of Command. The President had to-day decided that Eisenhower was to command *Overlord* whilst Marshall remained as Chief of Staff. I suggested ' Jumbo ' Wilson as Supreme Commander for the Mediterranean, Alexander as Commander-in-Chief Italian Land Forces, Paget for Middle East Command, Montgomery *vice* Paget and Oliver Leese *vice* Monty.[1] He was inclined to agree but said he had at one time thought of me as Supreme Commander Mediterranean and Wilson as Chief of Imperial General Staff, but that it would be better if I remained where I was."

" I agreed that it would be best. ' Jumbo ' Wilson would have a great deal to pick up to become C.I.G.S., whereas he knew half the Mediterranean intimately. I hope he does not change his mind again."

' I found the Prime Minister very tired that evening, and

[1] As Commander-in-Chief 21 Army Group and Eighth Army respectively.

it was with difficulty that I could get him to absorb all the intricate points connected with it. I had devoted a great deal of thought to this problem, had found it hard to solve, but was now perfectly clear in my own mind. First of all, the selection of Eisenhower instead of Marshall was a good one. Eisenhower had now had a certain amount of experience as a commander and was beginning to find his feet. The combination of Eisenhower and Bedell Smith had much to be said for it. On the other hand, Marshall had never commanded anything in war except, I believe, a company in the First World War.'

'The removal of Ike from the Mediterranean left a difficult gap to fill. I did not want to touch either Alex or Monty for this job, as I required them for the Italian campaign and for the British contingent of *Overlord*. Had I had my own way I would have selected Monty for *Overlord* and Alex for Italy, but I knew I might well have difficulties over this preference of mine, first with Winston and secondly with Eisenhower. I, therefore, introduced 'Jumbo' Wilson for Supreme Command Mediterranean, and to take over from Ike.'

"*December 5th. Cairo.* A very difficult day filled with a series of meetings from Chiefs of Staff and Combined Chiefs of Staff to Plenary meetings, but negotiations remained at a deadlock, as we were holding out for a cancellation of the Andaman Islands attack which the President, having made promises to Chiang Kai-shek, would not cancel. It all proved too clearly that we had been quite right in insisting (without success) that Chiang Kai-shek should come at the end instead of the start of the meeting."

"In the afternoon another Combined Chiefs of Staff meeting at which we called in Stopford and Troubridge[1] to discuss the Andaman Islands and to see whether any

[1] Maj.-Gen. (now Gen. Sir) Montague Stopford and Rear-Adm. (later Vice-Adm. Sir) Thomas Troubridge.

smaller alternative operation could not be formed to
' save face ' with Chiang."

" Finally dined with American Chiefs of Staff."

During that day Brooke and his British colleagues with some
difficulty secured the agreement of the American Chiefs of
Staff to six propositions which they then together submitted
to the President and Prime Minister at a Plenary meeting of
the Conference. These were

" 1. *Overlord* and *Anvil* are the Supreme operations for
1944. They must be carried out during May, 1944.
Nothing must be undertaken in any other part of the
world which hazards the success of these two operations.

2. *Overlord*, as at present planned, is on a too narrow
margin. Everything practicable should be done to
increase its strength.[1]

3. The examination of *Anvil* on the basis of a not less than
a two-division assault should be pressed forward as
fast as possible. If the examination " (by the Combined Staff Planners) " reveals that it requires
strengthening, consideration will have to be given to
the provision of additional resources.

4. Operations in the Aegean, including in particular the
capture of Rhodes, are desirable provided that they
can be fitted in without detriment to *Overlord* and *Anvil*.

5. Every effort must be made by accelerated building and
conversion to provide the essential additional landing-
craft for the European theatre.

6. The decision(s) made by the Combined Chiefs of Staff
at the ' Quadrant ' Conference " (Quebec) " covering
the bombing of German industrial targets and the
destruction of the German air force . . . are reaffirmed."[2]

Over the proposed operations in the Indian Ocean and

[1] At that time, according to General Morgan's COSSAC plan—based on the
amount of assault-craft available—on only a three-division basis, little more than
had been put ashore in Sicily on the first day against infinitely less formidable
defences. *Churchill* V, 516-17.

[2] *Ehrman* V, 188-90.

Burma the Chiefs of Staff of the two nations had still failed to agree. The British put forward their own, and separate, view.

" We fully realise that there are political and military implications in the postponement of *Buccaneer*. As regards the political implications we must leave these to be taken into consideration by the President and Prime Minister. As regards the military disadvantages, these are overridden by the far greater advantages to be derived from a successful invasion of the Continent and the collapse of Germany."

The American Chiefs of Staff, on the other hand, considered

" political and military considerations and commitments make it essential that Operation *Tarzan* " (a land offensive in Northern Burma) " and an amphibious operation in conjunction therewith should take place. Apart from political considerations, there will be serious military repercussions if this is not done, not only in Burma and China, but also in the South-West Pacific."[1]

Paradoxically, it was the British Chiefs of Staff, whom the Americans had so long suspected of being half-hearted about an invasion of France, who were now pressing their allies to concentrate their forces for it and eschew diversions elsewhere.

Yet, though the American Chiefs, particularly Admiral King, still persisted in treating the promises made by their President to the Chinese Generalissimo as sacrosanct and urged that Mountbatten should be told to launch the attack on the Andamans in the spring with such resources as he possessed, the President, with his greater sense of realism, reluctantly saw the force of Brooke's and Churchill's arguments. That evening, before dinner, overruling his Chief of Naval Staff, he sent the Prime Minister the welcome message, " *Buccaneer* is off ". Subsequently he drafted with him the terms of a telegram to be sent to Chiang Kai-shek, telling him that the European commitments entered into with the Russians at Teheran left no

[1] *Idem*, 190.

resources available for an operation in the Bay of Bengal in 1944.

> " *December 6th.* To our joy this morning we discovered that the President had at last agreed to cancel the Andaman Islands attack. He had sent a wire to that effect to the Generalissimo. This may lead to the latter's refusing to carry out his part of the Burma campaign. If he does so, it will be no very great loss. At any rate we can now concentrate all our resources on the European theatre."

> " Again a series of meetings ending up with a Plenary meeting at 6 p.m. at which we handed in our final report to the President and Prime Minister, who expressed their full satisfaction. Old Smuts had turned up for the final meeting."

> " I shall rest very well to-night and feel very satisfied at the final results."

' The satisfaction over the final success was all the greater owing to the struggle it had required. I had got the date of *Overlord* pushed on to June 1st so that it would not cripple the Italian campaign, and the South France offensive turned into something more elastic which could be adjusted without affecting Italy too seriously. Then the Andaman attack had been put off, thus allowing landing equipment to be assembled in the Mediterranean and not diverted to the war against Japan before Germany was defeated . . .'

Next morning, at the final Combined Staffs meeting of the " Sextant " Conference, the C.I.G.S. as Chairman voiced this satisfaction. In the words of the official record, " Sir Alan Brooke said he would like to express on behalf of the British Chiefs of Staff their deep gratitude for the way in which the United States Chiefs had met their views . . . General Marshall said that he very much appreciated Sir Alan Brooke's gracious tributes. He felt that it was most important that during the next month or so the British and United States Chiefs of Staff should both study how best the magnitude of future Conferences could be reduced."[1]

. . . .

" *December 7th*. We started the day with another C.O.S. meeting, followed by a Combined Chiefs of Staff meeting to settle a few additional points. The President had left early in the morning, and later Inonu, President of Turkey, also left."[2]

" After lunch we went round to the P.M.'s villa to listen to MacArthur's Chief of Staff, Sutherland, explain the future plans and views of General MacArthur. At 7.30 p.m. we met at our house for a brief Chiefs of Staff meeting to consider a Minute written by P.M. concerning operations in Turkey in anticipation of her entry into the war."

" Finally dined with the P.M., Smuts, Dill, Portal, Cunningham, Marshall, King, Arnold, Leathers and Hollis. Eden came in as dinner was finishing. . . . P.M. in tremendous form, and Smuts charming as ever."

" During the dinner the P.M. asked us all to express our views as to when Germany would be defeated. Marshall predicted March and, if not then, November. Dill gave even money on March. I gave six to four on March; remainder favoured March or November."[3]

" *December 8th*. *Cairo*. Portal and Cunningham left early in the morning, and Dill went off immediately after breakfast. I had a long talk with ' Jumbo ' Wilson at his H.Q., explaining to him possibilities of the future. Then he and I went off with Smuts to inspect the march past of the South African Division; a very impressive show. After

---

[1] *Ehrman* V, 201-2.

[2] The Turkish President and delegation, who, at the Prime Minister's invitation had arrived at Cairo on December 4th, had shown no enthusiasm for the latter's thesis that they should enter the war. It was a joke among the Americans who, fearing Eastern Mediterranean commitments, no more wanted Turkish intervention than the Turks themselves, " that all the Turks wore hearing devices so perfectly attuned to one another that they all went out of order at the same instant whenever mention was made of the possibility of Turkey's entering the war." *White House Papers* II, 790-1. See also *Churchill* V, 370-1.

[3] 1945. The war in Europe ended at the beginning of May of that year.

lunching out there we motored home and I went on to the Mena offices for an hour's work. Then visited ' Pug ' Ismay, who is unwell, and on to my house for an interview with Sosnkowski. From there on to the Embassy to dine; P.M., Smuts, Eden, Cadogan, Casey and his wife, young Jellicoe, Maclean[1] back from Yugoslavia, Randolph, Sarah, ' Jumbo ' Wilson were there. Kept up late and finally had to drive back here with the P.M. All my good work of my dinner with him is gone. He is now back again wanting Alexander as Supreme Commander for Mediterranean and has pushed old ' Jumbo ' Wilson aside. I shall have heavy work ahead. The trouble has been caused by Macmillan,[2] who has had a long talk with the P.M. suggesting Alex as the man for the job and that he, Macmillan, can take the political load off him. He, Macmillan, came round to see me for an hour this evening and evidently does not understand what the functions of a Supreme Commander should be."

" *December 9th. Cairo.* Started the day by seeing Smuts off. Smuts was as charming as ever. Last night at the Embassy dinner he pulled me aside to tell me that he was not at all happy about the condition of the P.M. He considered that he worked far too hard and exhausted himself. . . . He said he was beginning to doubt whether he would stay the course; that he was noticing changes in him. He then said that he fully realised my task was getting more and more difficult with the P.M., but that I must stick to it and do my best to keep him on the right track. He said that he had been saying things to the P.M. to try and assist me in my task. He fully realised that I had been correct in sticking to my job when he and the P.M. had tried to get me to replace Auchinleck; he also fully appreciated what a heavy responsibility it entailed and what a heavy task it was."

[1] Lt.-Col. Fitzroy Maclean, Brig. Commanding British Military Mission to Yugoslav partisans.
[2] The Rt. Hon. Harold Macmillan, Minister Resident at Allied Headquarters in North-West Africa and Mediterranean.

" I was very sorry to see him disappear in his silver aeroplane over the horizon. Then drove back and went on to discuss Yugoslavia and Greece with ' Jumbo ' Wilson. From there I was ordered for *tête-à-tête* lunch with the P.M. We lunched in the garden; he was looking very tired and said he felt very flat, tired and pains across his loins. However he swatted flies with his flap throughout the lunch and counted their corpses. We discussed Command in the Mediterranean. He kept on harping back and repeating details which were of no consequence, and I saw that it was useless in his tired state to discuss large issues."

" Half-way through lunch he asked me whether I did not think I had better be made a Field-Marshal in view of all the responsibility I was carrying! I told him there was nothing I would appreciate more when he considered I deserved it. He then said that Portal was to be made a Marshal of the R.A.F. and he considered I should be a Field-Marshal. He said he would speak to the King about it."

' I shall always remember that lunch as a bad nightmare. He was dressed in his grey zip-suit, with zip-shoes, and his vast Mexican hat. We sat amongst the flower beds at a small card-table and were served with an excellent lunch by two Egyptian liveried waiters. He held a fly-whisk in his hand. After two spoonfuls of soup he started discussing the question of the Command of the Mediterranean and said, " It is all quite simple, there are . . ." then down came the fly-whisk with a crash, and a fly corpse was collected and placed in a fly mortuary near the corner of the table. He then had two more spoonfuls of soup and said: " This is the most *dee*licious soup ", followed by another spoonful. He then started again: " As I was saying, it is all quite simple, there are just three areas . . ." Crash, down came the fly-whisk and another corpse was conveyed to the mortuary! '

' This procedure went on through most of the lunch, but we never got beyond the " three areas " before having to convey another fly to the mortuary. The interesting part was that there were not " three areas " in this problem of Command, and yet I knew well that in his present worn-out condition it was quite impossible to make him grasp this fact. I let him go on killing flies, knowing well that there was no possibility of doing any work. I felt desperately anxious about him at that lunch. I had just been listening on the previous evening to Smuts's fears about him, and I began to wonder how near he was to a crash and how serious that crash would be.'

" *December 10th. Cairo* (650 miles). Got up at 5.15 a.m. and by 6.15 was off for Luxor. I had borrowed Sholto Douglas's plane and fixed up with Emery to come with me. We had an excellent journey and arrived on the small aerodrome near Luxor at 9 a.m. Here we were met by a shaky old car which took us to the office where we secured the necessary tickets and then went to the river bank to cross over to the west bank. Here an old Ford in the last stages of decay met us and we started a precarious journey to the Valley of the Kings. The car repeatedly stopped in spite of one attendant spending his whole time inside the bonnet whilst the car was running! "

" Emery was quite invaluable as he knew just what to take us to in the very limited time. We began with Tut-ankh-amen's tomb which thrilled me. We then did two more of the Kings' tombs, after which Emery took us to see a tomb which he had discovered himself."

" We then went to visit the large temple and palace on the west bank, finally motoring back past the two Colossus figures. Here the inevitable happened and one of the front tyres burst. No spare wheel, a jack that did not work, but nothing stopped our mechanics. The car was lifted by hand, the tyre removed, and we rumbled on on the rim. We recrossed the Nile and went to the Desert

Palace Hotel for lunch. After lunch we visited the Luxor temple and the old large temple farther north on the way back to the aerodrome. We took off at 4.30 p.m. and flew back in the moonlight. A full moon shining on the desert and reflected in the Nile—a glorious sight."

" ' Jumbo ' Wilson and Sholto Douglas came to dinner, after which we discussed the prospects and timing of the Rhodes attack. At 11 p.m. we drove round to the Embassy where the P.M. was dining. At midnight we started off. I drove with the P.M. to the aerodrome and he went on discussing a reorganization of Command all the way. Finally at 1 a.m. we took took off in the York."

" *December 11th. Carthage.* (1550 miles.) At 9.30 a.m. we arrived over Tunis after a very good journey, but not much sleep as plane was overheated. Owing to a mistake arrived at a wrong aerodrome first and had to take off again. Finally we arrived at the right place, and there we found Eisenhower and Tedder waiting for us. P.M. very tired and flat. He seemed to be in a bad way; the Conference has tired him out and he will not rest properly and insists on working. I cannot think that it is wise for him to go to Italy in this condition. After breakfast he went and rested till lunch."

" Meanwhile I had a very useful conference with Eisenhower and Tedder on various points connected with operations in the Mediterranean, but mainly on the question of the selection of his successor and of the organization of the Command. I warned him of the attitude the P.M. was taking and asked him to assist me in making it quite clear to the P.M. what the organization should be. I told him that I had been at the P.M. for some time now trying to get him to understand, but that he always returned to his own faulty conception. Ike's suggested solution was to put Wilson in Supreme Command, replace Alex by Monty, and take Alex home to command the land forces for *Overlord*. This almost fits in with my idea except that I would invert Alex and Monty."

' It was very useful being able to have this talk with Ike in which I discovered, as I had expected, that he would sooner have Alex with him for *Overlord* than Monty. He also knew that he could handle Alex, but was not fond of Monty and certainly did not know how to handle him.'

" P.M. rather more rested at lunch. I tried to induce him not to go to Italy, but so far have failed. He has spent most of the afternoon resting."

' I was getting very worried about Winston's health. He seemed to be going from bad to worse. It was most unfortunate that morning that we had come down on the wrong aerodrome, as they took him out of the plane and he sat on his suit-case in a very cold morning wind, looking like nothing on earth. We were there about an hour before we moved on and he was chilled through by then. I felt that a trip to Italy in December with snow and seas of mud, living in cold caravans, would finish him off. I discussed the matter with Moran who entirely agreed. I therefore tackled Winston in the evening and told him that he was wrong in wanting to go to Italy. I granted that the troops would be delighted to see him and that he would enjoy the trip, but said that I did not think he had any right to risk his health in this way when he had such far more important matters in front of him connected with the war. I was beginning to make a little progress, and then I foolishly said: " And what is more, Moran[1] entirely agrees with me." He rose up on his elbow in the bed, shook his fist in my face and said: " Don't you get in league with that bloody old man! " '

' After that there was no alternative but to leave the matter alone for a bit. As we shall see, thank Heaven, God

[1] Sir Charles Wilson, who had been raised to the peerage as Lord Moran— Sir Winston's devoted and ever-watchful physician.

took a hand in the matter, and the next day he was running a temperature.'

"*December 12th. Carthage*. I was dog-tired last night and sleeping like a log at 4 a.m. when I was woken by a raucous voice re-echoing through the room with a series of mournful, 'Hulloo, Hulloo, Hulloo!' When I had woken sufficiently I said, 'Who the hell is that?' and switched on my torch. To my dismay I found the P.M. in his dragon dressing-gown, with a brown bandage wrapped round his head, wandering about in my room. He said he was looking for Lord Moran and that he had a bad headache. I led him to Moran's room and retired back to bed. But for the next hour the whole house resounded with the noise of people waking up and running round. This morning on getting up I discovered that the P.M. had a temperature of about 102°, and is not in a good way at all. Moran is uncertain as to what the trouble is but is anxious to get him home as quickly as possible. The visit to Italy must be definitely off as far as he is concerned, and I am rather doubtful whether I shall be able to make it or shall have to accompany him back."

'After this bad night of Winston's, and in view of the temperature he was running, I asked Moran what he diagnosed the trouble was. He said that as far as he could judge at present it might be another go of pneumonia or it might just be a case of 'flu. I asked him what he would require if it was a case of pneumonia and he replied that in that case he would have to have a pathologist, two nurses and a portable X-ray set. I asked him where these would have to come from and he said the two former from Cairo and the latter probably from Algiers. I told him these would take some time to get and that we should wire at once for them; if it was pneumonia we should never forgive ourselves for having wasted twenty-four hours.'

' It was fortunate those wires were sent to Cairo. I think that by then Clemmie had also been wired for.'

" *Later*. Alexander turned up during the morning and we had a long talk, after which he went for a talk with the P.M. As might be expected, Alex is ready to do just what he is told and does not show any great sign of disappointment at the possibility of not being appointed Supreme Commander."

" P.M.'s temperature went down considerably during the day, but Moran did not think he was so well again in the evening. Eisenhower came round in the afternoon and we had a long talk with him and Alex. Tedder came to dine. Settled that Alex should go back to Italy to-morrow and that I should accompany him."

' In my talk with Alexander about Command I found him, as always, quite charming to deal with, always ready to do what was requested of him, never scheming or pulling strings. A soldier of the very highest principles.'

" *December 13th*. *Bari* (600 miles). P.M. not too well during early part of night, and Moran was up with him for a long time. We wired for pathologist and two nurses yesterday, who are due at 2.30 p.m. to-day."

" I am by way of starting at 11.30 a.m. with Alex for Italy, but am still rather doubtful about leaving the P.M. in his present state. However, I do not feel that there is much that I can do here now by my presence."

" Have just sent a wire to Algiers for a portable X-ray set as Moran wants to take a photograph of his lungs to make certain that they are not effected."

" *Later*. I went to see P.M. and found him looking more cheerful and he was all for my going off. I have therefore put Tedder in touch with Moran, so that Moran should have someone to appeal to for help if necessary."

.   .   .   .

ITALY

" *December 13th.* At 11.30 a.m. left with Alex for the aerodrome where we took off in his plane at 12 noon for Bari. We had a lovely flight, first over the Bon peninsula, then close to Pantelleria, and struck Sicily on the southern coast about the centre. I had an excellent view of the landing places of American, Canadian and British forces. We then crossed over the south-east corner of the island to the Catania Plain where we did a good circle round to look at it properly. Mount Etna looked glorious with its lovely snow-covered top looking through a blanket of

118

low clouds which ringed the mountain half-way up. We then worked along the east coast of the island towards Messina. I had no idea that this coast was so lovely. We then crossed over to the Italian coast and skirted along the sole and the ball of the foot of Italy, crossing the bay under the instep and striking Taranto harbour. From there we crossed the heel and landed at Bari after a four hours' most interesting flight. It gave me a great thrill setting foot on European soil again, a full four years[1] after I had stepped off at St. Nazaire. Little did I know at St. Nazaire that after four years I should step back at Bari."

" Went with Alex to his office and listened to the latest news. Then came back to my room to sort out my kit for to-morrow's move on to Montgomery's H.Q. While I was doing so the Germans arrived over Bari port for a raid, and I spent half an hour in watching the most beautiful fireworks as all the A.A. let loose on them. I was quite safe, being some five miles out of Bari, so was able to watch and enjoy at my leisure. This is the second heavy raid on this place. In the last one they destroyed some seventeen ships by fire owing to an ammunition ship blowing up."[2]

" *December 14th. Monty's H.Q. Sangro River.* I started the day by attending Alex's Intelligence conference at his H.Q. We then had an early lunch shortly after 12 noon and by 1.30 p.m. left Bari aerodrome in Alex's plane to fly to Termoli, about 130 miles up the east coast."

" On the aerodrome we were met by the Eighth Army Air Officer Commanding (Broadhurst) who took us up in a Stork, a German one which had been flown over from Yugoslavia—a most wonderful machine in which we flipped along amongst the tree tops and chimney stacks.

[1] Brooke was wrong; it was three and a half years.
[2] On December 2nd—" the greatest single loss from air action inflicted upon us during the entire period of Allied campaigning in the Mediterranean and in Europe." *Eisenhower,* 224.

We had an excellent view of all the battlefront on the way up and finished with a special reconnaissance of the Sangro River and all its difficult crossings."

"We landed on a small strip near the mouth of the river and were there met by Montgomery. He took us in his open car along the Sangro River, explaining all his plans and difficulties. We then returned to his Camp in a field on the high ground just south of the river and I was shown my caravan for the night. We then had tea followed by a long talk with Monty."

"Off to bed early. Weather not as cold as I had expected. Monty strikes me as looking tired and definitely wants a rest and a change. I can see that he does not feel that Clark is running the Fifth Army right nor that Alex is gripping the show sufficiently. He called me into his caravan just before dinner and asked me how much importance we attached to an early capture of Rome, as he saw little hope of capturing it before March."

"To my mind it is quite clear that there is no real plan for the capture of Rome beyond a thrust up the coast by Monty, and no longer any talk of a turn to the left by his forces towards Rome. The mountain roads are considered too difficult for any real chance of success based on such a swinging movement. I must now see during the next few days what hopes rest in the plans for the Fifth Army. Frankly I am rather depressed from what I have heard and seen to-day . . ."

The Allied offensive in Italy had been resumed in the last week of November, when Montgomery's Eighth Army on the Adriatic coast began to force the Sangro River and tried, in mud and rain, to outflank the German winter line from the east.[1] On December 1st, the day on which Brooke and his

---

[1] "I am preparing," he had written to Brooke on November 18th, "to deal the Germans a heavy blow on the Adriatic side. All I want is good weather. I have gone all out for surprise and have concentrated such strength on my right flank that, given fine weather and dry ground under foot, I will hit the Boche a crack that will be heard all over Italy . . . I fear, however, the Fifth Army is absolutely whacked. So long as you fight an Army in combat teams and the big

colleagues left Teheran, Mark Clark's Fifth Army had struck on the other side of the mountainous peninsula in the Mignano gap where the Naples-Rome highway ran through the hills. But without sufficient assault-craft to land in strength in the enemy's rear, the Allies could make little use of the trump-card which sea-command had given them, and, instead of proving a death-trap to the defenders, as Brooke had designed, Italian geography became, under climatic conditions that neutralized the Western Powers' air ascendancy, an insuperable obstacle to the offensive.

" *December 15th.   Alex's Forward Camp near Vasto.*   Left Monty's camp at 9 a.m. and dropped down into the valley of the Sangro which we followed till we crossed it and its tributary and arrived at Freyberg's divisional H.Q.   He was on the road to meet us and had formed up for our inspection a batch of some thirty prisoners caught that night.   They were a very poor lot of humanity of all ages, sizes and shapes."

" We then drove on to the 8th Indian Division H.Q. On the way we passed the badly bombed and shelled villages which the Germans had held whilst defending the northern bank of the Sangro.   We went on to the Canadian Div. H.Q. and talked to their Commander. Then back to the mouth of the Sangro River when we had lunch, after which we were flown back here where Alex has an advanced H.Q. alongside of Eighth Army H.Q.   We had tea with Eighth Army officers[1] and then came back here for dinner."

---

idea is that everyone should ' combat ' somebody all the time, then you don't get very far.   My own observation leads me to the conclusion that Clark would be only too delighted to be given quiet advice as to how to fight his Army.   I think he is a very decent chap and most co-operative;   if he received good and clear guidance he would do very well."   Montgomery to C.I.G.S., 18 Nov., 1943. Lord Alanbrooke, *Personal Files.*

[1] There is a reference to this visit in the memoirs of General de Guingand, Montgomery's Chief of Staff, which shows incidentally how unreliable on minor points of detail even the most authoritative memoirs can be compared with contemporary diaries and letters.   De Guingand writes: " When everyone was speculating who would be the commanders for the ' Second Front ' we were

" My impression of the day is that we are stuck in our offensive here and shall make no real progress till the ground dries, unless we make greater use of our amphibious power . . . I have an impression that Monty is tired and that Alex has not fully recovered from his jaundice. The offensive is stagnating badly, and something must be done about it as soon as I get back."

" *December 16th. Alex's Camp at 5th Army H.Q., Caserta.* Left camp at 8 a.m. and motored to a brand new landing-strip just south of Vasto. There we took off at 9 a.m. with an escort of fighters to fly to Naples. It was a lovely morning. We headed for Foggia first, and then turned west over the hills. The scenery was quite lovely. After three-quarters of an hour flying we began to drop again and Mount Vesuvius came into sight with quite a large feather of smoke coming out of its summit."

" We landed at 10 a.m. on the Naples landing-ground and proceeded to the American H.Q. commanding the town. We then did a detailed tour of the port to see the marvels that had been accomplished in the way of clearing up all the debris of the German destruction. Ships had been raised from the bottom; others left on their side were used as new quays, whilst the sunken ones had superstructures built on them to allow of their use as landing-stages. A real fine performance."

" After lunch we motored out to the American Fifth Army H.Q. Camp, where Alex has a small camp also. We dined with Clark in his Mess. I had a long talk with him about the offensive on his front and do not feel very cheered up as to the prospects of the future from what I

---

visited by the Prime Minister, the C.I.G.S. and Eisenhower. They were flown up to Montgomery's Headquarters near the Sangro river and had lunch." In fact, both the Prime Minister and Eisenhower were in North Africa. In one memory of the C.I.G.S.'s teatime visit on December 15th, de Guingand is almost certainly correct. " We were naturally very interested in our Army Commander's future. . . . Every possible combination was worked out, but still nothing official was heard. The C.I.G.S. had tea with us in my mess on his way back to Bari and no fly that we dropped produced any reaction. But then he is a keen fisherman and knew the game." *de Guingand*, 335.

heard from him. He seems to be planning nothing but penny-packet attacks and nothing sufficiently substantial."

" *December 17th. Caserta.* Got up early and left camp by 8 a.m. in a jeep. A very cold morning, and a jeep is not a warm conveyance in which to drive. We motored up through Capua to Dick McCreery's Corps H.Q. Then I had a talk to various officers of his staff and then went on in his jeep to the front. We motored within 2500 yards of the Boche, and in full view of him, without being fired at. Hawkesworth then gave us a description of the attack on Mount Camino from our old front line. We then motored up the slopes as far as the jeeps would go, and then took to horses to go up a perpendicular mule-track to a small plateau below Monastery Hill. Here Brigadier Lyne gave us an excellent description of how his brigade of Queen's battalions stormed this frightful height. It was all most interesting and very vivid as the old Boche trenches and equipment were still lying about, and they were even burying Boche still while we were there."

" We then rode down at the risk of breaking our necks and had lunch at the bottom. We visited the rest of the front in a jeep and, after having tea with McCreery, got back to camp at 8 p.m. Very weary after twelve hours' hard work. Before coming home we looked up Templer[1] (Commander of 56th Division) who was in hospital. We also went to say good-bye to Clark."

' The great value of that day was to have been given such excellent accounts of the fighting that had been taking place. I was able to make a very good mental picture of the types of operations that were required and was consequently far better able to visualize the fighting when back in London. From the top of Mount Camino I had been able to see quite clearly Mount Cassino and the country round, and had discussed with Alex the very nasty nut we should have to crack there. All this experience proved invaluable at a

[1] Now Field-Marshal Sir Gerald Templer.

later date when I had difficult times with Winston concerning
Alex's attacks on Mount Cassino.

" *December 18th.* *Carthage* (650 miles). Left Caserta at
8 a.m. and motored to Naples airport. There we emplaned
for Bari. We then flew over Salerno Bay and had a good
look at operations connected with the landing. We
reached Bari at 10.30 a.m., when I said good-bye to Alex,
and at 10.45 started off again in his plane for Tunis. We
flew back across Italy, coming out at southern end of
Salerno Bay and then cut straight across the sea to the
corner of Sicily just west of Palermo. Very bumpy for a
bit; by 1.45 p.m. we were landing in Tunis."

" I went to see the P.M., after having a long talk with
Moran about his health. Winston started by telling me
that the King was very pleased to make me a Field-
Marshal and that it would be announced on January 1st,
He then told me that his temperature was now normal.
but that his heart was the trouble. I told him all about
my trip to Italy and he wanted to hear all details. We
settled up final details about Command. He has now
settled definitely for ' Jumbo ' Wilson as Supreme Commander of Mediterranean. He instructed me to get
Martin[1] to draft the wire to President Roosevelt to that
effect. He was rather upset when I told him I was off
to-morrow morning, and I had to be firm, as he was
suggesting my stopping on for several days."

" *Later.* After his afternoon rest I went back again to
see him and to discuss draft Martin had prepared of a
telegram to the President about Command. It is now
decided that Wilson becomes Supreme Commander
Mediterranean, that Alexander stays in Italy, and that
Monty comes home to command land forces for *Overlord*,
whilst Oliver Leese takes over Eighth Army, and Paget
relieves ' Jumbo ' in the Middle East. It is a great relief
having those various points settled."

[1] John (now Sir John) Martin, Private Secretary to the Prime Minister.

" After dinner I had to go back again to say good-bye to the P.M. Clemmie was sitting on the bed with him, and Randolph was also there. He was in very good form, but objecting to having to spend a week in bed before going on to Marrakesh for his fortnight's recuperation."

' In my talk with Winston I said nothing to him about the depressing impressions I had gained whilst in Italy. I knew from experience that he would only want to rush into some solution which would probably make matters worse. I had to keep these misgivings to myself and look for a cure.'

' I did not mention in my diary that on that day my Military Assistant (Brian Boyle) had acquired a turkey, alive and on the hoof, for his Christmas at home. From now onwards this turkey became one of the passengers and was allowed to walk about the plane, and was occasionally held up to look out of the window.'

" *December 19th. Gibraltar* (1000 miles). I slept in Eisenhower's villa and went to the P.M.'s house for breakfast. Then I met Lord Moran who said P.M. had had a very good night and that he was still normal, that he could now be considered as safe from the pneumonia, but that his heart was the only danger. He had had during the last few days two goes of heart flutter with a pulse of 130, and that, as a result of such a flutter, a clot might form that would affect his brain. He must therefore be kept quiet, but was proving troublesome."

" Went to the aerodrome at 9 a.m. to get into the Liberator Mrs. Churchill had flown out in. At 10 a.m. we took off. A very wild blustery day, but as soon as we were up it was quite smooth. We flew round Bizerta and then along the African coast. We had a strong head wind and it took us five-and-a-half hours' flying, only arriving at 3.30 p.m."

" We came up to Government House where we are to have dinner, waiting for a verdict as to whether the weather conditions will be good enough for us to fly on to England to-night. The chances are not too good as the weather has been very bad in England lately."

" It is very hard to believe that I have not been away quite five weeks; it feels more like five years. So much has been done during that period, so much ground covered, so many conferences, so many decisions, so many visits and so many impressions. My brain is feeling tired and confused, with a desperate longing for a long rest. I suppose I might as well long for the moon! "

" *Later.* After dinner we were told that the weather was good enough for us to fly and that we were to embark between midnight and 1 a.m., ready to fly by 1 a.m. We came down to the aerodrome shortly after midnight and made ourselves as comfortable as we could in the plane. Poor Boyle had started a go of jaundice, so we gave him the only bed available. By 1.30 a.m. we were off."

" *December 20th. London* (1500 miles). We had a very good journey, made an excellent landfall, and by 9.30 a.m. were running down the runway at Northolt aerodrome. By 10.30 we were back again in London, having covered some 13,000 miles by air."

" After a bath and breakfast I went up to the War Office where I had an hour's interview with the Secretary of State. The afternoon was spent in getting myself up to date again and in going through recent papers, together with interviews with Vice-Chief of Imperial General Staff, Quartermaster General, Humfrey Gale, Director of Military Intelligence, and Military Secretary. Am feeling very sleepy and dog-tired as I did not get much sleep in the plane last night."

' When my poor Boyle was taken off to hospital I found myself landed with his turkey which we had named " Macaroni ". In the morning I had left the turkey in a basket at the flat. Suddenly in the evening on returning to the flat I remembered the poor bird. I asked the batman what he had done with it. He replied, " There was no bird, sir, only some fish! " I went round to see the " fish " and was greeted by a chirrup from my old friend still in its bag. It was quickly liberated, given food and drink and remained at large in the flat till I went down to Ferney Close and took it with me. There it lived for many happy days and even contributed eleven lovely eggs to our sparse rations! '

Chapter Four

CONFLICTING STRATEGIES

In war you don't have to be nice: you only have to be right.
Attributed to SIR WINSTON CHURCHILL

O N THE last day of 1943, Brooke took the chair at his first Chiefs of Staff meeting in London since his departure for Teheran. " It was not," he wrote, " a very arduous one; mainly concerned with putting straight telegrams from P.M. who is now becoming very active. In the afternoon had interviews with Duff Cooper, Laycock,[1] and with Captain Power, R.N., concerning Rome amphibious operation. Then Army Council meeting and an interview with Bedell Smith concerning the setting up of H.Q. for cross-Channel operations. He and Eisenhower are anxious to take all heads of Staff departments out of the Mediterranean. This will want watching."

Next day the C.I.G.S. received the highest award of his profession.

> " *January 1st, 1944.* Heard on the 8 a.m. wireless that I had been promoted to Field-Marshal. It gave me a curiously peaceful feeling that I had at last, and unexpectedly, succeeded in reaching the top of the ladder. I certainly never set out to reach this position nor did I ever hope to do so even in my wildest moments. When I look back over my life no one could be more surprised to find where I have got than I am."

No British Field-Marshal had ever borne wider responsibilities than Brooke at that moment. As Chairman of the Chiefs of

[1] Maj. Gen. (now Sir Robert) Laycock, Chief of Combined Operations.

Staff Committee he and his two colleagues had on their hands a military offensive in Italy whose continuance, in the face of immense logistical difficulties and the growing opposition of an ally with superior resources, he believed to be essential for immobilizing Germany's strategic reserves; a naval blockade of Europe on whose success the cohesiveness and striking-power of the Grand Alliance depended, and a round-the-clock bombardment of Germany's industrial cities, communications and airfields to secure control of the skies over Hitler's continental fortress; and at the far side of the world a campaign in Burma, conducted with inadequate forces, largely out of deference to American illusions about China. Most important of all, in less than six months' time, he and they had to launch their over-strained country's remaining striking-force in an amphibious operation of unparalleled hazard whose failure would enable the enemy both to regain the initiative in the east and destroy Britain's capital with the revolutionary weapons now being assembled on the other side of the Channel. Though the detailed planning of *Overlord* was the task of the Supreme Commander and his staff, ultimate responsibility for it still rested with the Combined Chiefs of Staff, who had to issue general Directives for it and correlate it with operations in other parts of the world, while the executive burden of assembling the vast Anglo-American host for the impending assault fell mainly on the British War Office and the C.I.G.S. as its head. Its command, offered to Brooke six months earlier, had for political reasons been given to the militarily inexperienced Eisenhower, but the operational direction of the ground forces had been entrusted to his chosen lieutenant Montgomery. Three days before the end of the year, hearing of his appointment, the latter had written from Italy,

" My dear Brookie,

" I must thank you for promoting me to command the armies in England. It is a big job and I will do my best to prove worthy of your selection. There is a terrible lot to do and not much time in which to do it. Immediately I arrive

I will come and see you and get your orders about taking over from Paget. . . ."[1]

This Montgomery did, as Brooke's diary records, as soon as he reached London.

"*January 3rd.* After lunch meeting with Monty to discuss his ideas for plans for invasion."

"*January 4th.* A long Chiefs of Staff meeting at which we did our weekly review of the threat of the rocket and pilotless plane. Evidence goes on accumulating. Also had a talk with 'Jumbo' Wilson and discussed attack on Rome. In the afternoon Paget[2] came to say goodbye. He is evidently upset and sad at being superseded by Monty but is taking it all very well. Now I have to work out all the other incumbent changes."

"*January 5th.* A C.O.S. meeting at which we were employed trying to sort out a tangle existing in the Mediterranean. Most of the difficulties are caused by the P.M. at Marrakesh convalescing and trying to run the war from there. The latest suggestion arrived to-night is that I should fly out to Marrakesh for a conference this week-end with Alexander, Bedell Smith, etc."

For with his usual pluck the Prime Minister was making light of his convalescence. " I never remember," he wrote, " such extreme fatigue and weakness in body. . . . Every temptation, inducement, exhortation and to some extent compulsion to relax and lie down presented itself in the most seductive form.

---

[1] Montgomery to Brooke, 28 Dec., 1943. Lord Alanbrooke, *Personal Files.*

[2] General Sir Bernard Paget, Commander-in-Chief 21 Army Group since the previous summer and of Home Forces since 1941. ' It was with deep grief that I was replacing Paget with Montgomery. I was very fond of Paget; he had done me wonderfully as Chief of Staff when I took over Home Forces, and he had done extremely well in all the early stages of the training and toughening of troops in Home Forces for their eventual role as a Liberation Army. But I am certain that my selection of Monty was a correct one, for, besides his own exceptional qualities as a leader in battle, he also had by now a great deal of experience. I found it nevertheless a difficult decision to make and one that gave me many a pang. Paget, of course, took it all in a wonderful way and continued giving of his best.' *Notes on My Life,* XXI, 47.

... However, events continued to offer irresistible distraction."[1] This took the form of a whirlwind campaign to gather resources for the landing on the Roman coast with which, during his recent visit to Italy, Brooke had proposed to break the dead-lock.[2] The enthusiasm with which the irrepressible patient bombarded the Americans and everyone within reach with requests for the essential additional landing-craft, though it contributed materially to producing them, did nothing to diminish the American Chiefs of Staff's suspicion of Britain's Mediterranean strategy.

"*January 6th.* Discussed the desirability of my flying out to Marrakesh with C.O.S. Both Portal and Cunning-ham not in favour owing to the fact that, unless Marshall is also present, Americans may well accuse us of exercising unilateral control of operations in the Mediterranean...."

"*January 7th.* A difficult C.O.S. meeting as Winston sitting in Marrakesh is now full of beans. As a result a three-cornered flow of telegrams in all directions is gradually resulting in utter confusion. I wish to God that he would come home and get under control."

"After lunch went to see Amery[3] who, having just been appointed President of the Alpine Club, has become more mountain-warfare minded than ever. He would almost convert the whole Army in Italy into mountaineers! How-ever, there is a great deal in what he says...."

"*January 10th.* Usual early start. Found a mass of telegrams in as a result of the P.M.'s conference at Marrakesh. The operation for the attack just south of Rome is now all settled for the 22nd of this month. Pray God that the weather may be fine for it, otherwise it might well end in a bad disaster. Unfortunately weather is none too certain at this time of the year."

[1] *Churchill* V, 398.
[2] "My recommendations for strong amphibious operations in the Rome area are being acted on, which is good." An earlier plan for a landing near Rome had been abandoned for lack of shipping and landing-craft, but Brooke had revived it.
[3] Secretary of State for India.

" Also telegram from P.M. about handing over Italian ships to Russia. This evening small War Cabinet at 5 p.m. at which I had to explain the outline of the Italian Rome amphibious operation. At 5.30 p.m. the usual Cabinet."

" *January 11th.* We had our weekly examination at the C.O.S. of the prospects of the pilotless plane and of the counter-measures. The bombing of the launching emplacements in Northern France is not going well."

" We next considered handing over of Italian naval ships to the Russians. Militarily there are nothing but disadvantages in such a procedure. Unfortunately, during moments of special friendship, promises were made by the powerful ones to Stalin in Teheran."[1]

" After lunch we had a long Selection Board, the first one attended by Monty. We have now, I think, settled all the various appointments incumbent on the major changes and on the preparations for the cross-Channel Operation."

Brooke spent the next two days in Norfolk with the King.

" *January 13th.* Ran the usual C.O.S. meeting during the morning, and after lunch left the War Office at 3 p.m. for Sandringham. I took Lockwood and Parker[2] with me. Reached Sandringham just about 6 p.m. We found, however, Sandringham empty as the King is using a smaller house close by."

" At the gate we were stopped by a policeman who, after examining our identities, turned on a series of little magic blue lights on either side of the avenue up to the house. On arrival there I was met by Piers Legh who took me round to the drawing-room. There I found the Queen alone with the two princesses. She said she had some tea for me, which she rang for and then poured out for me.

---

[1] Owing to the prejudice these promises seemed likely to have on Allied relations with the now collaborating Italian authorities, Churchill with his usual generosity had substituted the offer of a British battleship and other naval vessels. *Churchill* V, 402-6.

[2] His batman and chauffeur. The former had been valet to the Duke of Kent.

The older of the two princesses also came along to assist in entertaining me, whilst the younger one remained on the sofa reading *Punches* and emitting ripples of laughter at the jokes. The King came in a little later and also sat at the small table whilst I drank my tea."

" After tea the King asked me to come to his study and I had about an hour with him discussing the war, various appointments, the Prime Minister, the new medals, etc. In every subject he displays intense interest and is evidently taking the greatest trouble to keep himself abreast of everything."

" I then went up to dress for dinner which was not till 8.45 p.m. We assembled in the drawing-room—Lady Delia Peel, Lascelles, Piers Legh and Arthur Penn who had arrived just before dinner. After a bit the King, Queen and eldest princess came in and we all did the necessary bowing and curtsying. We went in to dinner when I sat on the Queen's right. An exceptional charm and natural-ness, backed by a good sense of humour and complete lack of pomposity, made her exceptionally attractive."

" After the Queen had left, the King got me to sit next to him, and we sat on for another half-hour. When we came to the drawing-room the Queen offered us tea which she poured out, and we talked till about 11.30 p.m., when we all went off to bed."

" *January 14th. Sandringham.* Breakfast was at nine, and was not attended by any of the Royal family. After break-fast Harry Cator and Oliver Birbeck came as the two additional guns, which made us six in all, as Lascelles did not shoot."

" We started at 10 a.m. and walked to the first beat. The King throughout the day took complete charge and posted all guns himself. It was all very informal and pleasant. The Queen and family turned up during the morning and kept with the King most of the time. A very happy little family group, full of jokes and laughter. We had a very good day and shot 348 pheasants (all wild birds)

65 partridges, etc. The day was quite glorious, a lovely sunny day with no wind and ideal temperature."

" We returned about 4.30 p.m. and, after changing, assembled in the drawing-room for a sit-down tea at a long table with the Queen pouring out at our end. After tea I attended to an envelope of papers sent up from the War Office, and shortly afterwards the King came to fetch me for another talk with him in his study. This was followed by dinner on the same lines as the former evening except that I sat on the Queen's left this time."

' Lockwood was quite familiar with all the Sandringham habits. While loading for me he suddenly asked me:—" Do you like Cox's Orange Pippin apples, because they grow a very good brand here. If you like them we could bring some home with us." When I told him he must certainly not take any, he said: " Oh, I would not dream of doing that! They send them to market from here and I can pay the gardener." I agreed that as long as they were legitimately paid for that there would be no harm in taking a few.'

" *January 15th. Sandringham.* The two outside guns to-day were Lord Coke and a local farmer, A. Keith. The weather was not quite so good during the morning owing to mist, but this cleared up and the latter part of the day was again glorious. The Queen and family again came out during the morning. This time we lunched out in a sort of tin School House."

" We had another very good day with 312 pheasants and 23 partridges, etc. During the afternoon we saw some woodcock and shot 9 of them. The evening was again filled up with the same routine as on the previous days. Before going to bed the Queen said good-bye, but the King said he would be down before I left."

' During that day's shooting the Queen had recognized Lockwood who was loading for me, and came over with the two princesses to talk to him. He was of course overjoyed at being recognized.'

" *Sunday, January 16th.* This morning at 10 a.m. the car was all loaded up and ready. The King had been down talking to me for about a quarter of an hour. He then very kindly asked whether he could talk to Parker as he had driven him when he visited Gort (whose chauffeur he was) when he visited France. Parker beamed all over. The King had also had a talk with Lockwood while we were shooting. Finally I said good-bye to the King, thanked him profusely and drove off."

" It had been a most interesting experience. The main impression that I have carried away is that the King, Queen and their two daughters provide one of the very best of examples of English family life. A thoroughly closely knit and happy family all wrapped up in each other. Secondly, I was greatly impressed by the natural atmosphere, entirely devoid of all pomposity, stiffness or awkwardness. They both have a gift of making one feel entirely at home. The Queen, I think, grows on one the more one sees her and realises the wonderful qualities she possesses."

" I had a bad journey back owing to fog which got thicker as we approached London. I had a lot of work to do and a large bag to go through which kept me busy the whole afternoon."

' I forgot to mention in my diary that in the morning when the King came out to speak to Parker I had one ghastly moment that he would find the whole of the back of the car packed with his best Cox's Orange Pippin apples. But Lockwood was too clever to be caught out like that; there were lots of them all cleverly hidden, and all had been paid for.'

· · · · · · · ·

While Brooke had been at Sandringham the Supreme Commander had arrived in England. A fortnight earlier there had been a passage of arms between the latter's Chief of Staff and the C.I.G.S. when, according to Eisenhower's A.D.C.'s diary, Bedell Smith had demanded a wholesale transfer of British senior officers from Eisenhower's old headquarters in the Mediterranean and, on being refused, had declared that Sir Alan was not being ' helpful ' and had started for the door. " This provoked," he added, " a bit of frank talk." Brooke's comment on the incident was:

> ' I had to put Bedell in his place and inform him that I was responsible for the distribution of the Staff on all fronts and could be relied on to take their various requirements into account. I told him I would have no string-pulling.'

There is no further mention of the matter in Brooke's account of his meeting with Eisenhower on January 17th, but he must have raised it, for the same American diarist records,

> " After his meeting with the C.I.G.S., Ike said he had been amazed over a complaint voiced by Sir Alan against Bedell. . . . Ike did not fail to bring up the personal complaint of the C.I.G.S. and Bedell expressed regret he had been abrupt. Thought perhaps the war was getting on his nerves, or his stomach, or both."[1]

Brooke's diary continues:

> " *January 17th.* This morning's Chiefs of Staff meeting consisted of nothing but dealing with a mass of various telegrams on subjects such as parachutists for South-East Asia, arguments concerning landing-craft to be withdrawn from South-East Asia to Mediterranean, Chiang Kai-shek's refusal to use his Yunnan Forces, latest reports on German pilotless planes, desirability of infiltrating Spitfires into Turkey, difficulties with Portuguese concerning American attempts to share use of Azores with us, etc., etc."

> " After lunch Eisenhower came round to see me, in very good form. He is apparently quite prepared to face the question of curtailing South of France operations depending on its merits."

[1] *Butcher*, 404 (20 Jan., 1944).

" Finally Cabinet—the last to be run without Winston who is due back to-morrow."

"*January 18th.* The morning was somewhat upset by the return of the P.M. who arrived at Paddington at 10 a.m., when we all proceeded to meet him. Then C.O.S. meeting, with Cherwell attending to consider the latest reports of progress made by the German pilotless aeroplane and on the bombing of the launching-points in France. At 12.15 Cabinet meeting to listen to P.M."

" After lunch I had an hour with Alan Hartley,[1] just back from India to hear all the latest news. Then a sad interview with Kenneth Anderson to tell him he would not be commanding the Second Army in the forthcoming offensive, as Dempsey is to replace him. He took it very well."

" *January 19th.* The P.M. is starting off in his usual style. We had a Staff meeting with him at 5.30 p.m. for two hours and a Defence Committee from 10.30 p.m. for another two hours. And we accomplished nothing. In all his plans he lives from hand to mouth; he can never grasp a whole plan either in its width (i.e. all its fronts) or its depth (long-term projects) . . ."

' Winston's lack of " width " and " depth " in the examination of problems was a factor I never got over. He would select individual pieces of the vast jigsaw puzzle which we had in front of us and concentrate on it at the expense of all others. When I used to say, " But can't you see that if we concentrate on B, plans A and C will be affected? " he would reply, " I do not want to see A and C. Can't you see that B is the vital point? " I used to reply that B was certainly important at the time, but reminded him that last week A had been of major importance and that probably next week C would require most attention. These arguments were useless, and he would continue examining B as if A and C did not exist.'

[1] General Sir Alan Hartley.

' Similarly as regards depth—when I said to him, " You are now putting your left foot down here, but where do you propose to put your right foot and where are we going? " he would reply by shaking his fist in my face and saying, " I do not want any of your long-term policies, they only cripple initiative! " '

.　　.　　.　　.　　.　　.　　.　　.

The Prime Minister, now in his seventieth year, had just emerged from a dangerous illness. At Malta and at Teheran, in each case after an exhausting journey, he had continued to work with a high temperature, and now, driven by the same single-minded resolve that had sustained him—and his country —during every waking minute of the past four years, he had returned to duty before he was fully recovered. It is not surprising that he found difficulty in concentrating and making up his mind. What upset Brooke and his colleagues was that, on his being asked to approve the plans they had prepared for implementing the agreement made with the Americans at Cairo for future strategy against Japan, he had denied all knowledge of such an agreement. When they reminded him that he and the President had initialled it, he replied that he did not consider his doing so binding. Instead he reverted to his old project, rejected by both the British and American Chiefs of Staff, for a landing in Sumatra which he believed, entirely contrary to their opinion, would cut Japan's seaborne communications with Burma.[1]

Both Churchill and Brooke—himself now over sixty—were feeling the strain of prolonged responsibility. As in the previous winter before Alamein and the North African landings, they were awaiting the outcome of operations on which they had staked their country's all. The first preliminary to these was to be launched at that very moment. On January 17th, Alexander had begun a new offensive to force the Germans from their positions on the Garigliano and Rapido, to be followed, as soon as it had drawn enemy reserves south, by a landing at Anzio—

[1] *Ehrman* V, 424-7.

the Operation *Shingle* which Brooke had recommended in December and the Prime Minister had so enthusiastically pressed on the Americans. " Operations in Italy going better," the C.I.G.S. noted on January 20th,

> " Oh! how I hope that the Rome amphibious operation will be a success. I feel a special responsibility for it as I resuscitated it after my visit to Italy. It may fail, but I know it was the right thing to do, to double the amphibious operation and carry on with the out-flanking plan."

In the early hours of the 22nd the landing took place. It was the fifth seaborne invasion Brooke had helped to launch in little more than a year. Soon after noon he learnt that it had achieved complete surprise. By evening 36,000 troops and 3000 vehicles were ashore within thirty miles of Rome and sixty miles behind the German lines on the Rapido. The enemy reaction was the same as in North Africa and at Salerno. Hitler ordered the Gustav Line to be held at all costs and every available reserve to be rushed south to throw the Allies into the sea. But though this was the reaction the C.I.G.S. had wanted —for the more German divisions committed in Italy, the better for *Overlord*—owing to the American refusal to reinforce Alexander the latter's forces were dangerously weak. " News of Rome landing continued to be good," Brooke wrote on the 25th, "but I am not happy about our relative strength in Italy. We have not got a sufficient margin to be able to guarantee making a success of our attacks. And the ground unfortunately favours the defence."

It was the nature of the Chiefs of Staff's work that, by the time the plans they had devised were being tested on the battlefield, they were already engaged on others whose implementation lay in the future. On the Monday after the Anzio landing Brooke returned to Storey's Gate to discuss, not the course of Operation *Shingle*—whose success he could now do little to further—but that other Mediterranean landing in Southern France which Eisenhower and Marshall had urged should precede *Overlord* and to which, under American and

Russian pressure, the British had been forced to agree at Teheran as the price of a continued offensive in Italy. Thanks largely to Montgomery it had now become clear to Eisenhower and Bedell Smith—though not yet to Marshall—not only that the three-division assault front in Normandy allowed for at the Quebec Conference was too narrow, as the British and C.O.S.S.A.C. had always held, but that it could only be strengthened if the assault-craft scheduled for the preliminary landing on the French Mediterranean coast were allocated instead to *Overlord*.

" *January 24th.* Left home 8 a.m. Had a long C.O.S. meeting at which Eisenhower turned up to discuss his paper proposing increase of cross-Channel operations at expense of South France operations. I entirely agree with the proposal, but it is certainly not his idea and is one of Monty's. Eisenhower has got absolutely no strategical outlook. He makes up, however, by the way he works for good co-operation between allies."

" After lunch Monty came to see me and I had to tell him off for falling foul of both the King and the Secretary of State in a very short time! He took it well as usual."[1]

" Long Cabinet from 6 to 8.15 p.m. with Winston in great form. He was discussing Stalin's latest iniquities in allowing *Pravda* to publish the bogus information that England was negotiating with Germany for a peace. He said, "Trying to maintain good relations with a Communist is like wooing a crocodile. You do not know whether to tickle it under the chin or to beat it over the head. When it opens its mouth you cannot tell whether it is trying to smile or preparing to eat you up! ' "

[1] ' I cannot quite remember now what iniquities Monty had committed this time. I think that the King had taken exception to the kit he wore and had instructed me to draw his attention to dress regulations.' *Notes on My Life*, XII, 61. Montgomery, who had wasted no time in applying to his new Command in England the confidence-building techniques he had successfully practised in Africa, was also in trouble with the Prime Minister. " It would seem to be about time," the latter had minuted on January 19th, " that the circular sent to generals and other high commanders about making speeches should be renewed. . . . There seem to have been a lot of speeches and interviews lately." *Churchill, V*, 601.

" After dinner another meeting from ten to midnight to discuss artificial harbours for the invasion. Here again he was in very good form."

" *January 25th.* A long meeting this morning. First of all Cherwell and Duncan Sandys were with us whilst we discussed the situation concerning the pilotless plane and the rocket. Then representatives from the Foreign Office and Special Operations Executive to discuss various aspects of S.O.E. activity in Greece, Yugoslavia, Poland and Czechoslovakia . . ."

" *January 26th.* Have just dined and am now off in my train for a day with ' Hobo '[1] and his swimming tanks, and wire-destroyers."

" *January 27th.* Eisenhower met me at the station last night and we travelled up by special train through the night. Hobart collected us at 9 a.m. and took us first to his H.Q. where he showed us his models and his proposed assault organization. We then went on to see various exhibits such as the Sherman tank for destroying tank mines with chains on a drum driven by the engine, various methods of climbing walls with tanks, blowing up of mine-fields and walls, flame-throwing Churchill tanks, wall-destroying engineer parties, floating tanks, teaching men how to escape from sunken tanks, etc. A most interesting day, and one which Eisenhower seemed to enjoy thoroughly. Hobart has been doing wonders in his present job and I am delighted that we put him into it."

" *January 28th.* At 4.30 p.m. Winston suddenly convened a meeting as he had misread some of the telegrams and thought that an additional division was being sent to oppose the Rome landing. He was also full of doubts as to whether Lucas was handling this landing efficiently. I had some job quietening him down again. Unfortunately this time I feel there are reasons for uneasiness."

[1] Maj.-Gen. (Sir) P. Hobart, Montgomery's brother-in-law, whom early in 1943 Brooke had appointed to command the Experimental (79th) Armoured Division to test and develop specialized armoured equipment for storming the D-Day beaches.

" *January 29th*. Called up by Winston on the 'scrambler' after midnight. . . ."

" *January 31st*. Usual early start and rush of Monday. First a C.O.S. meeting during the morning. Then a Cabinet in the afternoon, and finally a C.O.S. meeting after dinner with the P.M. to discuss preparation of improvised ports for cross-Channel operations. P.M. in great form and full of chaff and leg-pulling."

" News from Italy bad and the landing south of Rome is making little progress, mainly due to lack of initiative in the early stages. I am at present rather doubtful as to how we are to disentangle the situation. Hitler has reacted very strongly and is sending reinforcements fast."[1]

' The Anzio bridgehead was in any case proving one point clearly, namely the German determination to try to hold on to Italy down to Rome. We were doing just what we wanted and were drawing and holding reinforcements in Italy and thus keeping them away from Northern France.'

" *February 1st*. News continues to be poor from Italy. . . ."

" *February 2nd*. Usual C.O.S. meeting with some difficult problems. Then office work, followed by a lunch for the Chinese. Then interview with ' Budget ' Loyd telling him he was for Command of London District, and Arthur Smith that he was for Iraq-Persia Command. Finally dinner at 10 Downing Street when the guests were the King, Eisenhower, Bedell Smith, Monty, Lascelles and the three Chiefs of Staff. P.M. brought out many gems. Amongst others:—' Politics are very much like war, we may even have to use poison gas at times.' ' In politics, if you have something good to give, give a little at a time, but, if you have something bad to get rid of, give it all together and brace the recipients to receive it.' "

" Referring to the American desire to sack the King of

---

[1] By that day there were five German divisions opposing the three and a half divisions in the bridgehead. *Ehrman* V, 227.

Italy and Badoglio:—' Why break the handle of the coffee-pot at this stage and burn your fingers trying to hold it? Why not wait till we get to Rome and let it cool off? ' "

" The King remained till 1 a.m. Ike stopped on a little longer, and it was 1.30 a.m. when I reached home."

" *February 3rd.* We had a long C.O.S. meeting over the wire to send back to American Chiefs of Staff to convince them that, with the turn operations have taken in the Mediterranean, the only thing to do is to go on fighting the war in Italy and give up any idea of a weak landing in Southern France."

" *February 4th.* ' Pug ' has been having a row with the P.M. in defending a document we had produced yesterday. Winston had asked us to consider the advisability of pressing De Valera to sack the German Ambassador in Dublin for security's sake. . . . Winston apparently wished for another answer and was angry because he could not get it."

' " Pug " Ismay in his work as intermediary between the C.O.S. Committee and the P.M. bore all the brunt of the first storms which some of our papers created and was able next morning to warn us as to what the reactions were. He was kept up practically every night by Winston and seldom received any word of encouragement, and yet went on serving Winston with the utmost devotion.'

" Meeting with the P.M. at 3 p.m. to discuss our cable to the Americans which he approved. This is a wire connected with our intention to concentrate on the Italian campaign and to give up the idea of a subsidiary landing in the South of France."

. . . .

The cable sent that day to Washington followed an earlier one of January 26th in which the British Chiefs of Staff had recommended that the initial *Overlord* assault should be increased from a three- to a five-division front and, in order to find additional landing-craft, that it should be postponed until June and the preliminary landing on the Riviera be either limited to a single division or reduced to a mere threat, which, because of Allied command of the sea, would as effectively tie down German forces in Southern France. But though the Americans now agreed that the *Overlord* assault should be strengthened and offered to provide sixty more landing-craft, they still refused to accept any later date for *Overlord* than May 31st or reduce the scale of *Anvil*.

By the beginning of February, however, the Allies' continued failure either to break out of the Anzio bridgehead or through the German mountain defences around Cassino had shown that the enemy was resolved to fight it out in Southern Italy. To the British Chiefs of Staff the corollary seemed obvious: that the one way to contain the German reserves and prevent them from reinforcing Normandy was to maintain the offensive in Italy and not abandon it in order to stage an amphibious operation which was no longer necessary. But their cable to Washington on February 4th made no impression on their American colleagues who still refused, despite changed circumstances, to depart from the letter of the Teheran programme. At that moment they had just launched an assault on the Marshall Islands and were in the throes of debating their future Pacific strategy.[1] They, therefore, replied that the British must discuss any technical difficulties presented by *Overlord* with Eisenhower, whom they empowered to act as their agent.

Thus, with the cross-Channel attack only three months away, Brooke and his colleagues were faced by a deadlock. When the Combined Chiefs of Staff's formal directive for *Overlord* was

---

[1] *Ehrman* V, 238-40; *Churchill* V, 451-2. " In watching the flow of requests for material for *Overlord* particularly landing-craft, and the responses from the War Department," wrote Eisenhower's A.D.C. on February 6th, " I am more and more impressed that the good old U.S.A. really is fighting two major wars at once. The fighting in the Pacific is absorbing many landing-craft during this critical phase of the European war; no telling how much our demands interfere with the prosecution of our effort in the Pacific. Whoever has the task, and I suppose it's the Combined Chiefs, in deciding between the Pacific and European wars must be in a terrible dilemma; but, from our standpoint we feel that, since we are committed to winning the European war first, we should have the primary call on landing-craft." *Butcher*, 417 (6 Feb., 1944).

issued to Eisenhower early in February, he had to be instructed that the date for entering Northern Europe was May, though both he and the British Chiefs of Staff knew this to be now impossible. Brooke's diary tells what happened.

"*Monday, February 7th.* Usual early start, and found my table full of telegrams including some from American Chiefs of Staff disagreeing with us as regards cancelling the South of France operation. Nothing left but to ask them to come over to discuss. Time now too short for any other course."

"After lunch —— came as I had asked him to call and discuss a letter of his opened by the Censor on its way to Ireland. In it he had criticized the selection of Montgomery versus Paget and I had to explain to him how we stood. While he was there the P.M. sent for me and kept me for three-quarters of an hour discussing with him the situation in Italy. He was in the depths of gloom and I had a hard time cheering him up. At 5.30 p.m. Cabinet, by which time he was more cheerful."

"*February 8th.* A day spent almost continuously with the P.M. Started with a call to go and see him at 9.15 a.m. That was put off to 12 noon instead, when he kept me till 1.15 p.m. At 6 p.m. we met again till 7.45 and finally from 10 p.m. to 12 midnight. A great deal of this was concerned with a proposed venture of his to land two armoured divisions in Bordeaux twenty days after the cross-Channel operations. I think we have ridden him off this for the present."

"*February 9th.* . . . At 5.15 p.m. I was handed a five-page telegram which P.M. had drafted to the President covering the whole strategy of the war, and most of it wrong! He asked for it to be discussed with him at 10.30 p.m. Unfortunately there was a Cabinet at 5.30 p.m. There I had a battle with him concerning the imposition of a ban on visitors to the South Coast in anticipation of our proposed operation. For some unaccountable reason he was against the ban. We had a royal scrap and I think I had the best of it."

" At 7.30 p.m. we came out and had a hurried C.O.S. meeting to examine the P.M.'s wire which required drastic amending. At 8.15 I had Eisenhower, P. J. Grigg, and Andrew Cunningham to dine. At 10.30 p.m. back again for our meeting with the P.M. to get him to alter his wire. We expected a holy row! Luckily another wire from Roosevelt came in which cut right across the one we were considering and saved most of the trouble. Now midnight."

" *February 10th.* We had a long C.O.S. meeting which Eisenhower and Bedell Smith attended at 12 noon. They had prepared a paper showing the requirements for the cross-Channel operation which coincided with our views. Marshall had also wired that he left it to Eisenhower to take a final decision. Therefore all seems to be going well at present. . . ."

That week-end Brooke received a letter from John Dill in Washington describing the cross-currents that were making it so difficult for the British Chiefs of Staff to reach agreement with their American colleagues.

" I have been in and out of Marshall's room lately trying to get him to see your point of view regarding *Anvil-Overlord* and trying to get his point of view. I take it that now that the U.S. Chiefs of Staff have delegated their powers to Eisenhower on this question, you will be satisfied."

" The U.S. Chiefs of Staff are engaged in a fresh battle regarding Pacific strategy. It really is the Navy, and King in particular, *v.* the rest. The result of the attack in the Marshalls has given them all great encouragement to go farther and faster. Risks can now be taken which they would not look at a month ago. The fact is, I think that, the Japanese air forces are now not up to much and can be crushed locally. No-one expected that the Americans could so flatten the Japanese air forces in the Marshalls that huge naval task forces could sail about unmolested. But that is what happened."

" King does not get any easier as time goes on. I am ashamed of a rather sneaking regard for him. He has built up a great Navy but he does not trust us a yard. . . . I believe his war with the U.S. Army is as bitter as his war with us. But he has his admirals well in hand."[1]

These transatlantic differences reacted on Britain's strategy not only in Europe but in the Far East. During the week-end of February 12th/13th two visitors from the other side of the world reached London. One was Lieutenant-General Lumsden, the British military representative at MacArthur's headquarters in Australia; the other Major-General Wedemeyer, Mountbatten's American Deputy Chief of Staff, who had been sent from Delhi by the latter to expound in London and Washington a plan for capturing Sumatra as soon as amphibious resources could be released from Europe. This project, however, was strongly opposed by Mountbatten's Deputy Supreme Commander, General Stilwell, who, unknown to his chief, had simultaneously dispatched a rival mission of his own to Washington to denounce it.[2]

Brooke's diary for Monday the 14th mentions these visitors.

" *February 14th.* News of Italy still none too good, but I feel the bridgehead south of Rome should hold all right and that ultimately we may score by not having had an early easy success. Hitler has determined to fight for Rome and may give us a better chance of inflicting heavy blows under the new conditions."

" In the afternoon Lumsden came to see me and was most interesting concerning the Pacific. Apparently Admiral Nimitz and MacArthur have never even yet met, although working side by side. King and MacArthur are totally

---

[1] Field-Marshal Sir John Dill to Field-Marshal Sir Alan Brooke, 9 Feb., 1944. Lord Alanbrooke, *Personal Files.*
[2] *Ehrman* V, 431-5.

opposed in their plans. Marshall and King are frightened of MacArthur standing for Presidency. General opinion is that King has finished serving his useful period, etc., etc. All military plans shadowed by political backgrounds. God knows how this will straighten itself out! "[1]

" At 5.45 p.m. usual Cabinet meeting which lasted till 7.50 p.m. Then 10 p.m. meeting with the P.M. to listen to Wedemeyer's plan which he had brought back from Dickie Mountbatten. I had long and difficult arguments with P.M. He was again set on carrying out an attack on north tip of Sumatra and refusing to look at any long-term projects or master plans for the defeat of Japan. . . ."

" The arguments were difficult, as Wedemeyer and his party were of course trying to sell their goods, namely operations through the Malacca Straits, and these entailed the capture of Sumatra which the P.M. wanted. But he refused to argue the relative merits of opening the Malacca Straits as opposed to working via Australia. After much hard work I began to make him see that we must have an overall plan for the defeat of Japan and then fit in the details."

" *February 15th.* Our C.O.S. meeting finished about noon and I then went round to listen to Admiral Cooke give an hour's lecture on the fighting for the Marshall Islands. After lunch Harrison, one of Mountbatten's staff officers, came to see me. We discussed Dickie's plan and his requirements for his offensive. Then Charles Allfrey back from Italy. Finally Arthur Smith to say goodbye before departure for Iraq-Persia Command. There is no doubt that he is a very fine man, entirely selfless and with only one thought—that of serving his country."

" Received a telegram from Alex that he was not

---

[1] ' Lumsden was our liaison officer with MacArthur and did excellent work as such. He gained MacArthur's entire confidence, sat next to him at meals, and kept us wonderfully well informed. On this occasion his reports were not up to their usual standard and he seems to have accumulated a lot of gossip.' *Notes on My Life*, XII, 72.

satisfied with Lucas[1] as commander of the Corps in the bridgehead south of Rome and asking me to consult Eisenhower. This resulted in a long series of telephone calls to Eisenhower and to P.M. and I only got to bed by 1 a.m."

" *February 16th.* I had hardly arrived in the office when I was sent for by the P.M. who wanted to send Alexander to command the troops in the bridgehead, and Wilson to command the main front. I am afraid I rather lost my temper with him over this and asked him if he could not for once trust his commanders to organize the Command for themselves without interfering and upsetting all the chain and sequence of Command. He gave up his idea for the present but may well return to the attack. . . ."

" *February 17th.* Bitterly cold and feels like snow. A long C.O.S. and mostly concerned with post-hostility matters; it is not yet easy to concentrate one's thoughts on after-war matters! We were at it hard from 10.30 to 1.15 p.m. and even then had only skimmed the surface."

" After lunch I had an interview with Brocas Burrows who is off to Moscow (to replace Martel), and found that the Foreign Office had been briefing him on such a completely conciliatory basis that he did not imagine he was to get anything back out of the Russians."

' Our attitude to Russia was of always giving and never bargaining to get something back. We were doing all we could for them in supplying them with equipment which we delivered in spite of terrific losses at sea. And yet we never even obtained an order of battle from the Russians. . . .'

---

[1] General Lucas's successor—Lt.-Gen. Lucien Truscott, a fine and forceful commander who took part in the initial landings—held that Lucas was unfairly blamed by Churchill and other distant critics for failing to drive on Rome. L. K. Truscott, *Command Missions.* Mr. Majdalany who cites Truscott's opinion in his book, *Cassino,* feels that Lucas was too cautious and that a more dynamic commander was needed. F. Majdalany, *Cassino,* 73-4, 77. Field-Marshal Alexander, in his Dispatches written after the war, says that at the time he thought Lucas was wrong, yet, looking back, he feels he was right to wait and consolidate.

" *February 18th.* . . . . Monty to dinner quietly with me which was very good value and most helpful."

" *February 19th.* A very long C.O.S. meeting. First of all Eisenhower, Bedell Smith, Tedder and Cooke, representing American Chiefs of Staff, all came in to discuss the desirability of having an amphibious attack against South of France to coincide with cross-Channel operation. Luckily I had discovered last night from Monty that he and Bertie Ramsay had agreed to curtail the cross-Channel operation to provide for a South of France operation. They should have realised that the situation in Italy now made such an operation impossible. They had agreed to please Eisenhower, who was pressing for it to please Marshall! "

" I had a little difficulty with Eisenhower, but not much, to make him see sense, as all he required was a little pressure to go back to the plans he really liked best now that he had at least shown some attempt to support Marshall's idea. I think the matter is now all right."

Eisenhower's proposals, to which he had obtained Montgomery's and Ramsay's reluctant agreement, had been based on a compromise shipping plan to make possible both *Overlord* and *Anvil* but at the price of a dangerous loss of flexibility at the crucial moment in both landings just when the assaulting troops would be at their most vulnerable. The crux of this particular problem was the overall shortage of tank landing-ships which the British had originally invented and the Americans had undertaken to make but which, faced by the needs of the Pacific war, they had as yet failed to provide in sufficient numbers for Europe. With the same optimism that had caused him to urge a cross-Channel attack in 1942, the Supreme Commander had tried to ignore this inescapable objection to his hope of two invasions. As the American official historian put it, " By increasing the personnel lift on the first tide of the assault without any corresponding vehicle lift increase, the

S.H.A.E.F. proposal either would land men who could not proceed with their task until their vehicles had arrived, thus causing congestion on the beaches, or would compel half-loaded personnel ships to wait offshore thus exposing both ships and men to unjustifiable risks. The validity of these objections was fully considered by General Eisenhower, but he considered the sacrifices and risks worth accepting in order to permit the simultaneous diversionary attack on Southern France. Although at first strongly opposed, General Montgomery at last agreed and the proposals were submitted to the British Chiefs of Staff. The Chiefs of Staff disapproved the compromise on the grounds, first, that it skimped both *Anvil* and *Overlord*, and, second, that the slow progress of the Italian campaign made the possibility of providing the necessary built-up forces for *Anvil*[1] so remote as to be negligible.' Employment, as planned, of ten divisions in Southern France, General (*sic*) Brooke pointed out, would leave only twenty divisions to fight the critical battle in Italy and to meet ' other commitments which might arise in the Mediterranean.' Eisenhower left the meeting at which this discussion took place, feeling that the chances of carrying out *Anvil* were slim."[1]

The diary continues:

" *February 21st.* Returned to London to find considerable damage done by bombs during previous night. One bomb in the middle of Whitehall opposite the Treasury had done much harm and had blown in all windows of the War Office except mine. Two bombs in the middle of the Horse Guards had blown in all 10 Downing Street, Admiralty and Horse Guards windows, etc. Guards

---

[1] *Cross-Channel Attack*, 171-3. Of this meeting Eisenhower's A.D.C. wrote, " Ike, representing the U.S. Chiefs of Staff, went into the ' ifs ' and ' ands ' of *Overlord* and *Anvil* to the British Chiefs of Staff this morning. The fact that he represents the U.S. Chiefs of Staff in dealing with the British Chiefs of Staff throws a tremendous weight on his shoulders. It makes him the recipient of all the arguments and pressures which the British, particularly the Prime Minister, may wish to advance for or against any particular project involving the U.S. Joint Chiefs and affecting the European Theatre. The Supreme Commander has wrestled continually to keep *Anvil* alive, but to-day it had a bad sinking spell." *Butcher*, 422. (19 Feb., 1944.)

Memorial badly chipped. One bomb at end of St. James's."

" Long C.O.S. meeting with planners discussing Pacific strategy and deciding on plan of action to tackle the P.M. with to convince him that we cannot take the tip of Sumatra for him. We shall have very serious trouble with him over this. But we have definitely decided that our strategy should be to operate from Australia with the Americans and not from India through the Malacca Straits."

" Cabinet at 6 p.m."

" *February 22nd.* A very long and difficult C.O.S. Eisenhower came again to represent American Chiefs of Staff and to argue their point concerning the Mediterranean. It is quite clear to me from Marshall's wire that he does not begin to understand the Italian campaign. He cannot realise that to maintain an offensive a proportion of reserve divisions is required. He considers that this reserve can be withdrawn for a new offensive in the South of France and that the momentum in Italy can still be maintained. Eisenhower sees the situation a little more clearly, but he is too frightened of disagreeing with Marshall to be able to express his views freely."

" After Eisenhower, Wedemeyer came next to argue out and explain the Burma campaign. I am not a bit happy about the final plans; there is no definite objective and large forces of Long Range Penetration Groups are being launched for no definite purpose. If ever there was a campaign that has been mishandled it is the Burma one, and mainly due to the influence exercised by Chiang Kaishek, through the President, on the American Chiefs of Staff."

" *February 23rd.* Another long C.O.S. First interview with Joint Intelligence Committee, then visit by Duncan Sandys whilst we discussed German progress with rocket and pilotless plane and results of our attacks on them."

" Then checking off telegram to American C.O.S. as a

result of our meeting with Eisenhower yesterday. We have got all we want, but must word the wire to let the Americans ' save face ' as much as possible. . . ."

On this day Brooke gained his main point over the war in Europe. By appointing Eisenhower to act as their representative while their attention was engaged in the Pacific, the American Chiefs of Staff had enabled their British colleagues to resolve the deadlock over the Italian campaign. They had already agreed to postpone *Overlord* to May 31st—the latest date that conformed to the letter of the Teheran decisions—with an understanding that the Supreme Commander should be allowed a few days' latitude either way to meet the requirements of tide and moon. Now, pressed by Montgomery and the British Prime Minister and Chiefs of Staff, Eisenhower promised to recommend to Washington that the Italian campaign should for the present take precedence over all other Mediterranean operations, including *Anvil*. Convinced by the failure of a further attack on Monte Cassino in mid-February and an all-out, though unsuccessful, German assault against the Anzio bridgehead, the British Chiefs of Staff were more sure than ever that the key to *Overlord* lay, as they put it, in " bleeding and burning " the Germans where they had resolved to fight. In a letter written on February 21st, Montgomery had urged Eisenhower to " throw the whole weight of our opinion into the scales against *Anvil*." Next day Churchill proclaimed the British thesis in Parliament. " Hitler's decision," he said, " to send into the South of Italy as many as eighteen divisions, involving, with their maintenance troops, probably something like half a million Germans, and to make a large secondary front in Italy is not unwelcome to the Allies. We must fight the Germans somewhere, unless we are to stand still and watch the Russians. This wearing battle in Italy occupies troops who could not be employed in other greater operations, and it is an effective prelude to them."[1]

The deciding factor in persuading Washington to concentrate

[1] *Churchill* V, 434-5. See *Ehrman* V, 241; *Eisenhower*, 254-5.

for the present on two, instead of three, campaigns in Europe was a report from the Supreme Commander Mediterranean. In it General Wilson stressed that any withdrawal from Italy of forces for *Anvil* would make it permanently impossible to link the Anzio bridgehead with the main Allied armies facing the Gustav line. On February 25th the President and American Chiefs of Staff accepted the London recommendations, with a proviso that the situation should be reviewed again on March 20th—a concession to Eisenhower who, like Marshall, was determined that his brain child, *Anvil*, should not be abandoned altogether. Until then Brooke was free to apply his mind to the equally difficult problem of persuading the Prime Minister to accept a strategic plan for the war against Japan compatible with the resources available for it.

"*February 24th.* A short C.O.S. for a change with no difficult problems, but to-morrow promises badly, as we then discuss the Pacific strategy with the P.M. and he will wish to fasten on to the tip of Sumatra like a limpet."

"During the afternoon went for a walk to look at last night's air-raid damage. Corner of St. James's and Pall Mall badly smashed up by a stick of bombs. All windows in St. James's Palace and the clock are gone, Hardy's fishing shop and all adjoining shops. Conservative Club windows all blown in, Spinks' completely gone and also picture shop alongside poor old Orleans Club. German bombs seem to be much more powerful than they were."

"In the evening went to study plans for artificial ports. After dinner another German air-raid lasting an hour-and-a-half and very noisy."[1]

"*February 25th.* I am quite exhausted after seven-and-a-half hours with Winston to-day, and most of that time engaged in heavy argument. First of all we discovered at the C.O.S. that the P.M. had never been informed that

[1] One of the nine night raids on London—" the little Blitz "—which the Germans made in February and March 1944 as a reprisal for the R.A.F.'s giant raids on Berlin.

the Japanese main fleet had moved to Singapore, although we had known this fact for the last two days. This had to be rectified at once and entailed——getting ticked off."

" At 12 noon the Chiefs of Staff met the P.M. and were kept till 1.45 p.m. He was still insisting on doing the North Sumatra operation and would not discuss any other. I had a series of heated discussions with him."

" Then a hurried lunch and at 3 p.m. we met again. This time he had packed the house against us, and was accompanied by Anthony Eden, Oliver Lyttelton and Attlee, in addition the whole of Dickie Mountbatten's Army, Naval and Air officers. The whole party were against the Chiefs of Staff. Thank God I have now got Andrew Cunningham to support me. It just makes all the difference from the days of poor old Dudley Pound."

" We argued from 3 p.m. to 5.30 p.m. I got very heated at times. Winston pretended that this was all a frame-up against his pet Sumatra operation and almost took it as a personal matter. . . ."

" I then rushed to the War Office for a talk with Wedemeyer before his return to America. Then an interview with Swayne to break the news to him that he is to go to India as Chief of Staff. Then Strang just back from Australia, followed by Military Secretary, Director of Military Operations and Director of Military Intelligence. Meanwhile P.M. called up and asked me to dine. I thought it was to tell me that he couldn't stick my disagreements any longer and proposed to sack me. On the contrary, we had a *tête-à-tête* dinner at which he was quite charming, as if he meant to make up for some of the rough passages of the day. He has astonishing sides to his character. We discussed Randolph, my son Tom, his daughters, my daughters, the President's unpleasant attitude lately, the fact that we may have to go to America soon, the Italian front, the air-raids, etc."

" At 10 p.m. another C.O.S. meeting which lasted till 12 midnight. P.M. in much more reasonable mood, and I

think that a great deal of what we have been doing has
soaked in. I hope so at least."

.   .   .   .

Though, like the Chiefs of Staff, Churchill had agreed at
Cairo to sending the Fleet to the Pacific, he had the strongest
reasons now for wishing to use it instead in the Indian Ocean.
Since then Admiral King's Pacific offensive against the
Marshalls and Gilberts had opened with brilliant success, while
MacArthur's forces, leapfrogging to the west of Rabaul, had
undermined the whole Japanese position in the South-West
Pacific. Not only was it becoming clear that the American
admirals would have little need for the Royal Navy's help, but
the contrast presented by these successes with Britain's plight
in Southern Asia was humiliating in the extreme. From Hong
Kong to the Indian frontier the whole of her Eastern possessions
were in enemy hands, while the Japanese Army in Burma,
which was known to have been heavily reinforced, was preparing to strike at Assam. Only by concentrating the full
available might of Britain in India and the Indian Ocean, the
Prime Minister held, could the disgrace to British arms in Asia
be wiped out and the power of her *Raj* be re-established.

Both Cabinet and Foreign Office tended to support Churchill.
The Chiefs of Staff, however, were concerned with the military
problem of first defeating Germany and then of winning the
Eastern war as soon as possible after her defeat. They contended
that the way to do so was to cut the tentacles of Japanese naval
power at its terminal points near Japan—the ultimate objective
of the American advance across the Pacific, now gathering
momentum with the establishment of bases in the Gilberts and
Marshalls. The First Sea Lord and Chief of Air Staff wanted
the Navy and Air Force to share in this attack, and Brooke,
most sea-minded of soldiers, agreed with them. And he and
they were all three convinced that the possession of a base in
Sumatra would not have the strategic or tactical results the
Prime Minister envisaged.

There were other reasons for their opposition to amphibious

156

operations in the Bay of Bengal. To both Churchill's plan and the more detailed one put forward by Admiral Mountbatten and General Wedemeyer, there was a fatal objection: that they needed forces and resources which Great Britain could not make available until at least six months after Germany's defeat. With her dwindling reserves of man-power and her economy desperately strained to meet the demands of *Overlord* and the Mediterranean, she had for the present to fight the war in the East, as far as the Army and Air were concerned, with what she already had there. Nor could she look for any help from America, whose vision was focused on the far more important fighting on the Pacific. Her sole interest in South-East Asia— —uncompromisingly championed by General Marshall's protégé, " Vinegar Joe " Stilwell—lay in a campaign which that single-minded officer had just launched, with the help of Wingate's airborne " Chindits," in the mountains and jungles of Northern Burma to reopen the land supply-route to China, the only alternative to the inadequate airlift over the Himalayan " hump " to which the American air forces in India were committed.[1]

If, therefore, Britain was to take any part in the defeat of Japan, now to be achieved with Russian aid within a year or eighteen months of Germany's defeat, she must embark on measures which were within her means and which could be set in train with the forces now available. Since the only substantial reinforcements she could send to the East were naval and any large-scale amphibious operations against the Burmese or Malayan coasts were for the present impossible, it seemed better to concentrate her Far Eastern Fleet in the Pacific where it could either operate with the main American naval forces against Japan or, as was suggested later as a compromise

---

[1] Roosevelt had made this plain in a telegram to Churchill on February 25th, reinforcing the view of the American Chiefs of Staff. " I fail to see how an operation against Sumatra and Malaya, requiring tremendous resources and forces, can possibly be mounted until after the conclusion of the war in Europe. . . . There appears much more to be gained by employing all the resources we now have available in an all-out drive into Upper Burma so that we can build up all our air strength in China and ensure the essential support for our westward advance to the Formosa-China-Luzon area." *Ehrman* V, 454-6.

to meet Churchill's wish to employ British forces in British waters, towards the Celebes and Borneo in conjunction with MacArthur's advance from New Guinea on the Philippines.[1] Either course would necessitate an Australian base and close co-operation with the Governments of Australia and New Zealand, both of which were eager to join in a general offensive against Japan. And though the shipping problem involved in providing a fleet-train in the vast spaces of the Pacific naturally alarmed the Cabinet and the hard-pressed Minister of War Transport, Lord Leathers, Australia was a far more practicable base for such a campaign than India. Not only was the latter deficient in modern port facilities and overland communications,[2] but it was facing grave internal problems. Though the Indian Army, recruited from hereditary fighting races, had been little affected by the Congress leaders' Civil Disobedience campaign, the urban population was seriously disaffected, while four years of war had had disastrous effects on the country's primitive economy. A few months earlier a failure of the rice crop, coupled with the world shipping shortage, had caused more than half a million deaths in Bengal. Now a new disaster threatened from a failure of the wheat crop—a calamity which later that year, after the Prime Minister had appealed in vain to Roosevelt for an allocation of shipping to avert famine, was to cause the British Chiefs of Staff to cut their military shipping programme in order to import Australian wheat to India.

What was certain was that, if Britain was to share in the defeat of Japan—a point in which Prime Minister and Chiefs of Staff were at one—a decision on future strategy would have to be made soon. Otherwise the necessary bases, installations and stores could not be got ready in time. But this decision, since he could not persuade the Chiefs of Staff to agree to his Indian Ocean project, the Prime Minister stubbornly refused

[1] An admirable account of the successive proposals and arguments of the British Chiefs of Staff and Prime Minister, and of the reasons for them, will be found in John Ehrman's Volume V of *Grand Strategy* (Official History of the Second World War), 405-50.

[2] In April 1944 the number of locomotives in India, an area roughly the size of Europe, was less than that operated by the L.M.S. Company in Britain. *Ehrman* V, 465.

to make. The burden of overcoming his opposition, and that of the War Cabinet, fell mainly on Brooke. It was this that made him see in every hesitation of his still ailing chief signs of impending collapse and which gave to many of his diary entries that spring a note almost of despair. His irritation, however, at the Prime Minister's procrastination found expression only in his diary and scarcely ever in his speech or manner. As always, he gave his views clearly and unequivocally but no indication of how angry he was.

"*February 28th.* . . . Usual briefing for the Cabinet at 6 p.m. where Winston was in an impossible mood with nothing but abuse about everything the Army was doing. Every commander from 'Jumbo' Wilson to last Company commander was useless, the organization was useless, the Americans hopeless, etc., etc. It was all I could do to contain my temper. . . ."

"Just before going to bed I received a disturbing wire from Alexander. He evidently is not very happy about the Anzio bridgehead, proposes to relieve 56th Division by 5th Division and to add an extra division. This at once reacts on number of landing-craft available for cross-Channel operations, as, if we begin returning those that should go home, the bridgehead will be affected. He also proposes to reorganize defence by bringing Eighth Army over to the Cassino front; in that I think he is right."

"*February 29th.* Sent Alex's cable on to the P.M., knowing it would cause trouble during the day.[1] Then

[1] That night Brooke replied to Alexander's cable.
" 1. I agree with your proposal to side-step Eighth Army to cover Cassino and Liri Valley fronts. I feel however that in these circumstances Eighth Army could not still remain responsible for its present front on North-East coast, and presumably you have a plan for control of a latter front, possibly by detachment directly under your own H.Q. Please let me know your proposed arrangements.
" 2. I am not quite clear about how you propose to effect your comprehensive regrouping programme. For instance, although you propose it will result in 'all American and French divisions remaining in Fifth Army,' it seems . . . that 88 U.S. Div. has commenced relieving 36 U.S. Div. west of Cassino. This is presumably only a temporary measure, but I would be grateful to know very early your full programme of proposed reliefs and how you see all formations disposed on completion regrouping." Lord Alanbrooke, *Personal Files.*

went to C.O.S. and from there on to see model ports. After lunch P.M. called up and, after a discussion with him, suggested we should meet at 4 p.m. We remained till 5.30 p.m. At 10 p.m. had another meeting with P.M. This time Ike and Bedell Smith attended. We worded a wire to send to American Chiefs of Staff. Referring to the Anzio bridgehead, Winston said:—' We hoped to land a wild cat that would tear out the bowels of the Boche. Instead we have stranded a vast whale with its tail flopping about in the water! ' "

" *March 1st.* A fairly short C.O.S. You came up at lunch time after which I went to receive my baton from the King. Then back to War Office for a rush, followed by a Cabinet at 6 p.m., lasting till 8 p.m. We again discussed the security measures under which we wish to impose a ban on visitors to the coast.[1]"

" Whilst receiving my baton the King said that he understood that there was some idea about continuing our Pacific operations from Australia instead of India. Had I any maps or Appreciation that would explain what was intended. I told him we had just prepared an Appreciation. He then said he would like to see it. I then found myself in a difficult position; if I went any further I might well be considered as trying to rope in the King's support against the P.M. As I was going out, the King again asked for a copy of this Appreciation."

" *March 2nd.* A short C.O.S. after which I asked to see the P.M. and went round at 12.45. I wanted to discuss the King's request; I told him I wanted his advice and he started talking about quite a different subject! I then returned to my point and told him my trouble about the

---

[1] ' The ban on visitors to the South coast during the preparations for *Overlord* was a very natural request. There were no end of preparations to be made, assembly of landing-craft and ships, loading ramps, concentration of material, and in addition many deceptive preparations to keep the enemy expecting crossings on the Calais-Dover front. It was difficult enough to maintain secrecy in any case, but if a large number of visitors were to be allowed to come to the South Coast it would become impossible. Yet Winston would not give a decision and put all sorts of difficulties in the way.' *Notes on My Life*, XII, 85-6.

King's request, and that I did not want to go behind his (the P.M.'s) back about it. He then said he had written a new paper about it, rang the bell to get it and started reading it. I returned to my point and reminded him I had come to ask his advice. He replied that he must just read this bit of his new paper to me. And so we went on fencing. Finally I said that his paper would certainly be considered later by the C.O.S., but what I wanted was a definite decision as to what action I was to take. I said I proposed to inform the King that the P.M. had not yet had time to see our paper and that I thought that owing to our differences of opinion he should be given some more time to consider it and prepare his remarks. He agreed to this procedure."

" *March 3rd*. A very long C.O.S., for as soon as we had finished our ordinary discussion Portal asked for the meeting to be cleared of secretaries and then explained his difficulties of Command of the Air Force under Eisenhower. Apparently Tedder who was Deputy Chief is now to assume more direct command. Then I had to discuss the very difficult problem which is brewing up and in which the P.M. is trying at present to frame up the War Cabinet against the Chiefs of Staff Committee. It is all about the future Pacific strategy; it looks very serious and may well lead to the resignation of the Chiefs of Staff Committee. . . ."

At this point—for the Chiefs of Staff were growing desperate at the lack of decision—the Military Secretary of the War Cabinet intervened with a note to the Prime Minister proposing that, as the difference between him and his official advisers could not be resolved on military grounds, he should resolve it on political. " It seems absolutely certain," Ismay wrote, " that you and your Ministerial colleagues will not agree to the Pacific Strategy. On the other hand, the Chiefs of Staff . . . are extremely unlikely to retract the military opinions they have expressed. . . . Nor can we exclude the possibility of resignation

on the part of the latter. A breach of this kind, undesirable at
any time, would be little short of catastrophic at the present
juncture. *Overlord* is, in all conscience, a sufficiently hazardous
operation. It must be given every chance.

" I suggest that you should call a meeting . . . of the Defence
Committee next week to go exhaustively into the Indian Ocean
and Pacific strategies. . . . It is just possible that agreement can
be reached. If so, well and good. If not, would it not be
possible and right for you to take the line that the issue cannot
be decided on military grounds alone and that, apart from the
military merits of the respective strategies, political considerations must be overriding? I cannot but think that the Chiefs of
Staff would accept this decision with complete loyalty and
would set to work at once to make the best possible plans for
implementing it. Their position vis-à-vis their American
colleagues would then be perfectly clear. They could say: ' We
are not authorized to discuss any plans for moving British land,
sea and air forces into the Pacific. We should like to concert
with you how best to implement the Indian Ocean strategy.'
If the U.S. Chiefs of Staff disagree, it would then become a
matter for the Heads of Government."[1]

Yet, though he summoned the Defence Committee to try to
overcome his military advisers' resistance, the Prime Minister
did not take Ismay's advice. Brooke's diary continues:

" *March 6th.* An early start. During the C.O.S. meeting
we discussed how to handle the P.M. We are replying to
the paper he has produced, and on Wednesday after
dinner we are to have a meeting with him. . . ."

" *March 7th.* Most of our C.O.S. meeting was devoted
to preparing notes for to-morrow evening's meeting with
the P.M. He has produced the worst paper I have
seen him write yet, trying to make a case for an attack
on the tip of the island of Sumatra. He compared his
plan to our outline plan for the defeat of Japan operating with Americans and Australians from Australia

[1] Gen. Ismay to Prime Minister, 4 March, 1944. *Ehrman* V, 448-9.

through New Guinea towards Philippines and Formosa, etc."

" In the afternoon Macmillan came to see me and we concerted as to how we could best save ' Jumbo ' Wilson from the P.M.'s wrath. He is angry with him as he does not feel he is having sufficient control over him and will not recognize his inter-Allied position."[1]

" *March 8th.* C.O.S. meeting when we discussed papers prepared to counter the P.M.'s statements about Pacific strategy. Then a long meeting with Secretary of State. At 3.30 p.m. interview with Lord Moran who is worried about Winston's latest attempts to start off wandering again whilst he does not think that his health is up to it; wanted my assistance to stop him."

" At 4 p.m. interview with the King of Greece who wishes Greek Brigade to be moved to Italy as soon as possible, and who is worried by various guerrilla political factions in Greece. Back for meeting with Quartermaster-General and Director of Military Operations to discuss relative merits of India as opposed to Australia from an administrative point of view as a base for operations in South Pacific."

" At 6 p.m. Cabinet meeting to discuss security arrangements for *Overlord.* . . . We finished by leaving the two main difficulties, the Diplomatic channels and the Coastal Belt ban, unsettled. Back to dinner for more work immediately after it, and finally at 10 p.m. off for our meeting with the P.M. on the Pacific strategy. Our party consisted of Chiefs of Staff, Portal not too anxious to argue against the P.M., and dear old Cunningham so wild with rage that he hardly dared to let himself speak! I, therefore, had to do most of the arguing with the P.M. and Four Ministers. It was only too evident that they did not know their subject and had not read the various

[1] ' The whole trouble was due to the fact that old ' Jumbo ' Wilson was not as pliable in Winston's hands as Alex would have been. Wilson was a tough old specimen and he just let Winston's abuse run over him like water off a duck's back.' *Notes on My Life,* XIII, 2.

papers connected with it and had purely been brought along to support Winston. And damned badly they did it too! I had little difficulty in dealing with any of the arguments they put forward.[1] Finally we succeeded in getting the P.M. to agree to reconnaissances of Australia being carried out as a possible base for future action."

"*March 10th.* I was sent for before our C.O.S. meeting by the P.M. who told me that he had decided, after all, to allow the ' Visitors' Ban ' to be imposed on South Coast. A triumph after the long battle I had had."

"In the evening a very useful visit by Monty to tell me how he was getting on with his preparations for the attack. He is making good headway in making plans and equally successful in making enemies, as far as I can see! I have to spend a great deal of my time smoothing off some of these troubles."

"*March 13th.* Faced again with the P.M.'s restlessness. He now wants to go to Bermuda to meet the President on the 25th of this month. There is nothing special that we want to discuss as Chiefs of Staff; in fact we do not want to meet American Chiefs until we have arrived at some form of agreement with the P.M. about the Pacific strategy. Medically it is all wrong that he should go."

"Cabinet at 6 p.m. P.M. has now got the Joint Planners with him to discuss the Pacific strategy. Heaven knows what he is up to and what trouble he is brewing for us for to-morrow."

' This was a new departure on the part of the P.M. He had never before laid his hands on the Planners and announced that they were really his staff and not that of the C.O.S.! Without the Joint Planning Committee or Planners and the Joint Intelligence Committee it would have been

---

[1] For the paper in which Brooke and his colleagues answered the Prime Minister's Memorandum see *Ehrman* V, 445-8.

quite impossible for the C.O.S. Committee to function. Through these two branches all the information and intelligence was collected and all plans were prepared for future offensives, whilst events of current operations were kept under review. To suggest, as the P.M. was doing, that the Planners were part of his staff and not that of the C.O.S. Committee was the equivalent of depriving the Headquarters of command of its operational branch. Even if he did complete a plan with the Planners, the plan would still have to come before the C.O.S. Committee.'

" *March 14th*. Apparently P.M. is now prepared to put off the date of departure to 31st March, but still hopes to go to Bermuda. I had another interview with Moran yesterday to try and stop the P.M. on medical grounds. He tells me he is writing to the P.M. to tell him that there are three good reasons why he should not go:—

(*a*) He may become a permanent invalid if he does.

(*b*) Owing to his very recent go of pneumonia he is quite likely to get another if he exposes himself to the hardships and fatigues of a journey, and

(*c*) he is liable to bring on a heart-attack. . . ."

" Just heard from Alexander that Freyberg's attack on Mt. Cassino is to be launched to-night."

" Sirens have just been blown for another air-raid."

" *March 15th*. The Germans are in a bad way in South Russia. I have said all along that there could be no military reason to justify their strategy in South Russia. I could only account for their actions by attributing them either to Hitler's orders or to political reasons connected with Rumania. Well, it looks now as if the Germans are about to pay the penalty for their faulty strategy."[1]

" *March 16th* We had the Planners in at our meeting this morning and discussed with them the instructions the P.M. gave them on Monday night concerning planning for the capture of Sumatra. He sent me and the Director

[1] On Hitler's orders they had tried to retain territory by defending dangerously extended salients which they lacked the man-power to hold. As a result they had been forced back with heavy loss along almost the entire front.

of Military Intelligence separate Minutes drawing our attention that Freyberg's name had been spelt Freyburg in this morning's intelligence reports."

" *March 17th*. On conclusion of our C.O.S. meeting we were sent for by the P.M. to discuss latest American forecast of their moves through the Pacific, which have been speeded up by several months in view of their recent successes in the Marshall and Admiralty Islands. He then informed us that he had discovered a new island just north-west of Sumatra called Simalur. He had worked out that the capture of this island would answer as well as the tip of Sumatra and would require far less strength. However, by the time he had asked Portal for his view, he found out that from the point of view of the air he had little hope of building up his aerodromes and strength before being bumped off. From Cunningham he found out that from a naval point of view, with the Jap fleet at Singapore, he was courting disaster. I began to wonder whether I was in Alice in Wonderland or qualifying for a lunatic asylum! . . ."

" *March 18th*. Just as we were finishing our C.O.S. meeting we were told that the P.M. wanted to see us. This was to inform us that he proposed to wire to the President that we should go to Bermuda for Easter and that we were to have a Combined Chiefs of Staff meeting there. As there is nothing for us to meet about and on the Pacific strategy we have up to now failed to arrive at an arrangement with the P.M., I do not see what we can do. He insists, however, on going and proposes from there to fly to Gibraltar and on to Italy, which will probably be the end of him. . . ."

" *March 20th*. One of the worst of Cabinet meetings . . . Winston has now produced an impossible document on the Pacific strategy in which he overrides our opinions and our advice."

This document had been addressed to each of the Chiefs of

Staff separately in the hope of breaking their corporate resistance. It had resulted from a telegram which, unknown to them, the Prime Minister had sent Roosevelt on March 10th asking whether any American operation in the Pacific in the next twelve months would be handicapped by the absence of the British naval contingent promised at Cairo. This had reached Washington at the very moment that the American Chiefs of Staff had decided to give priority to Admiral Nimitz's drive through the Central Pacific towards Formosa at the expense of the more southerly Philippine advance advocated by General MacArthur, who was believed to welcome the idea of naval aid from Britain. The President had replied saying that, so far as could be foreseen, no British detachment would be needed in the Pacific before the summer of 1945. Armed with this answer the Prime Minister circularized the Chiefs of Staff, stating that the question of Far Eastern strategy need now only be considered from the point of view of British interests and virtually ordering them, not as a Committee but as individuals, to adopt the military policy he favoured. " The Ministers on the Defence Committee are convinced," he wrote,

" and I am sure that the War Cabinet would agree if the matter were brought before them, that it is in the interest of Britain to pursue what may be termed the ' Bay of Bengal strategy,' at any rate for the next twelve months. I, therefore, feel it my duty, as Prime Minister and Minister of Defence, to give the following rulings:

(*a*) Unless unforeseen events occur, the Indian theatre and the Bay of Bengal will remain, until the summer of 1945, the centre of gravity for the British and Imperial war effort against Japan.

(*b*) All preparations will be made for amphibious action across the Bay of Bengal against the Malay peninsula and the various island outposts by which it is defended, the ultimate objective being the reconquest of Singapore.

(*c*) A powerful British fleet will be built up, based on

Ceylon, Addu Attol and East Indian posts, under the shield of our strong shore-based aircraft. . . .

' I should be very ready to discuss the above rulings with the Chiefs of Staff in order that we may be clear in our minds as to the line we are going to take in discussions with our American friends. Meanwhile, with this difference on long-term plans settled, we may bend ourselves to the tremendous and urgent tasks which are now so near, and in which we shall have need of all our comradeship and mutual confidence.'[1]

The Chiefs of Staff refused to be brow-beaten.

" *March 21st.* We discussed at the C.O.S. meeting how best to deal with Winston's last document. We cannot accept it as it stands, and it would be better if we all three resigned sooner than accept his solution. We are telling him that it will be essential for us to put in a written reply, but that we can, if he likes, discuss with him his paper before we put in our reply. . . ."

In other words, the professional Heads of the three Fighting Services met the Defence Minister's attempt to dictate to them by acting together in their corporate capacity through the accepted constitutional channels, refusing either to agree to his solution or to adopt an attitude which would leave him with no alternative but a loss of face or their joint resignation. The situation was delicate in the extreme and any false or hasty move could have had disastrous repercussions. D-Day was little more than two months away, the deadlock in Italy was still unresolved, and the Japanese, after an unsuccessful probe in the Arakan peninsula, had just struck at the British forces guarding the North-Eastern frontier of India. Sustained by the support of his political colleagues, Churchill was convinced he was right; his military advisers were not only convinced he was wrong but that he was asking the impossible. On the very day that they discussed his memorandum the American Chiefs of

[1] *Churchill* V, 512.

Staff, alarmed by the reference to a Bay of Bengal strategy in his telegram to Roosevelt, informed London that under no circumstances would they support amphibious operations there, which in their view would be rendered completely unnecessary by their projected advance across the Pacific. The only operation in South-East-Asia they were prepared to supply was General Stilwell's campaign in Northern Burma to open the overland route to China.

The Chiefs of Staff, therefore, proceeded with the utmost care, debating for several days the exact form of their reply and repeatedly returning for revision the drafts which General Ismay, as Military Secretary of the War Cabinet, submitted to them. Their final memorandum, dated March 28th, submitted more than a week after the Prime Minister's letter, began by assuring him that they believed, from the communication he had addressed to them individually, that he still misunderstood their views and proposals and that they would welcome the opportunity of further discussion. But they categorically rejected his charge that they had committed the Government to any line of policy without consulting him, and reaffirmed their belief that the Pacific strategy, if found to be practicable, was far more likely to shorten the war against Japan than the Bay of Bengal strategy demanded by the Prime Minister which was subject to two inescapable disadvantages: that it would leave the major part of the British Fleet idle in the Indian Ocean until the European situation allowed the necessary complementary land, air and amphibious resources to be re-deployed in South-East Asia; and that, if Germany should still be fighting at the end of the year, Culverin[1] could not be mounted unless the Americans were prepared to lend considerable resources for it. Vital though it was to reach an early decision, only three weeks had passed, they recalled, since the Prime Minister had agreed that the door should remain open until the necessary data had been collected as to the relative capacities of Australia and India as bases and the shipping possibilities of both. " It is not until these have been cleared up

---

[1] Code name for the proposed operation against Northern Sumatra.

in accordance with the authority which you have given us that it will be possible for us to make a final recommendation as to which of the two policies offers the greater military advantages."

With this it was clear the Prime Minister had either to content himself or receive the resignation of the three Chiefs of Staff. He tacitly chose the former. To his old friend and ally, Sir John Dill in Washington, who had written to Brooke sympathizing with his difficulties,[1] the C.I.G.S. wrote on March 30th:

" I have just about reached the end of my tether and can see no way of clearing up the frightful tangle that our Pacific strategy has got into. . . . We cannot arrive at any agreement with the Prime Minister. We are adhering to the ' Sextant ' agreement and are carrying on with the examination and study of the policy we adopted as the ' basis for further study.' . . . We feel that the Indian Ocean Policy will result in our walking round with the basket picking up the apples whilst the Americans climb up into the tree and shake the apples off by cutting their lines of communication. The Prime Minister, on the other hand, remains as determined as ever to do *Culverin* and has got very little else as a plan to defeat Japan. It is almost impossible to get him to appreciate that by the time he is in a position to do *Culverin* at the present rate of advance the Americans may well be near Formosa or Luzon. The limitations of India as a base for large-scale operations he refuses to accept, and at the same time refuses Archie Wavell's requests for grain to avoid impending famine which might seriously affect India as a base. . . ."

" I am quite clear in my own mind that strategically it is right for us to use all our forces in close co-operation from Australia across the Pacific in the general direction of Formosa. By operating our forces alongside of MacArthur

---

[1] " What the hell of a time you must be having. It is a thousand pities that Winston should be so confident that his knowledge of the military art is profound when in fact he is so lacking in strategical judgment. The worst of it is that in the Pacific war the Americans are playing right into his hands." Field-Marshal Dill to C.I.G.S., 20 March, 1944. Lord Alanbrooke, *Personal Files.*

we can pool resources at sea and in the air for various closely connected steps. Whereas by retaining our forces in the Indian Ocean we operate independently, incapable of close co-operation, with the result that operations will be more protracted."[1]

[1] C.I.G.S. to Field-Marshal Dill, 30 March, 1944. Lord Alanbrooke, *Personal Files.*

Chapter Five

THE EVE OF D-DAY

The history of war knows no other like undertaking from the point of view of its scale, its vast conception and its masterly execution.

STALIN TO CHURCHILL, *11 June, 1944*

THOUGH THE Prime Minister continued to cling to his dream of amphibious operations in the Bay of Bengal, and though in the secrecy of his diary Brooke continued to express exasperation at what he regarded as his chief's unrealistic views, the attention of Prime Minister and Chiefs of Staff now became increasingly focused on Europe. By the third week in March the time had come for the reassessment of *Anvil*. On the 14th the Chiefs of Staff had asked the Supreme Commander Mediterranean to report on the position in Italy and its effect on future operations. General Wilson had waited to see the results of the renewed offensive which Alexander launched in the Cassino mountains on March 15th; then a week later, when, partly for want of replacements in the depots to make good the casualties, it petered out once more in the face of strong German counter-attacks and terrible weather, he reported that it would be unwise to expect any link-up with the Anzio bridgehead before the middle of May. As he calculated that *Anvil* could not be launched for at least ten weeks after that—that is, until July—he recommended that the Allies should continue to concentrate their main Mediterranean effort in Italy, capturing Rome and, if possible, destroying the twenty-three or twenty-four German divisions in the peninsula, and only land in the South of France at some later date or in the event of a general enemy collapse.

Though it meant abandoning his original conception of *Anvil* as a prelude to Normandy, Eisenhower accepted this recommendation for the sake of the additional assault shipping which its postponement would release for *Overlord*.[1] For Brooke this was a great triumph and relief.

"*March 22nd.* C.O.S. meeting from 10.30 to 1.15 p.m. with a long discussion with the Planners concerning the latest Appreciation by Wilson for the abolition of *Anvil*. Then Eisenhower and Bedell Smith came up to discuss their report which agreed with what we wanted. I now hope that at last all may be well and that the American Chiefs of Staff will see wisdom."

"After lunch I had a series of interviews. And finally we had a meeting with the P.M. to tell him what we had settled. He was in a good mood, and all went well beyond wasting an hour with interruptions of every description. Had we seen the last wire to Stalin? What was happening in Hungary? Why would we use the word 'intensive' when the correct word was 'intense'? He had had a lovely view of last night's raid from the roof. He was going to broadcast on Sunday night. What a strain we had been having for the last three years. Why could not Wilson be more intelligent? etc.? etc.? All these were sandwiched in between each paragraph of the Minutes he was looking through."

"Thank Heaven Roosevelt cannot meet him in Bermuda so our trip next week is off."

"*March 23rd.* . . . Wingate (of Chindit fame) is now wiring direct to the P.M. through Mountbatten, who expresses no definite opinions on the proposals put forward by Wingate. Meanwhile American wire stating that we should push on in Burma and give up all thoughts of Sumatra. P.M.'s reaction was to wire direct to Mountbatten saying, ' If you will conform to American requirements in Burma I shall back you in Sumatra and see that

---

[1] *Ehrman* V, 245-7.

you are allowed to carry out the operation.' We stopped the wire. . . ."

" *Saturday, March 25th.* Started with the usual C.O.S. meeting, then rushed back to War Office and at 11.45 a.m. left with a sixty Dispatch-rider escort for Trafalgar Square! There I was met by the Mayor of Westminster who introduced me to the Lord Mayor. We then started the ceremony and the Mayor of Westminster introduced the Lord Mayor who then introduced me. I then made my ' Salute the Soldier ' speech. I had to lunch at the Savoy with both Mayors, and again more speeches. Finally escaped at 3 p.m."

' Trafalgar Square is certainly not an attractive place to speak in. We had a large platform from which we looked down on some three or four hundred people immediately below us, but the life of London went on all round. Buses rumbling round, taxis and cars hooting, children playing, women gossiping, etc., etc.; not a very inspiring audience to talk to. I cannot believe that either my speech or my sixty dispatch riders did much towards promoting national economy! '

" *March 27th.* Early start. Table crammed with telegrams. News not too good. Wingate reported killed. Manipur threatened by the Japs. Alexander stuck against Cassino.[1] Marshall insisting on doing *Anvil* operation etc."

" Left at 12 noon to lunch with Eisenhower at Bushey Park where he was lunching the War Cabinet. After lunch conference with Ike concerning Marshall's last telegram. Back to London to rush for Cabinet which lasted till 8.30 p.m. Then Monty to dinner. He was in very good

---

[1] Alexander had written to the C.I.G.S. on the 22nd, " Unfortunately we are fighting the best soldiers in the world—what men! You should have seen the bombardment of Cassino by the air and then by the best part of 800 guns . . . from 8.30 a.m.-2 p.m., and then when the New Zealanders advanced to the attack they were met by a lot—no, not a lot, but what remained of these wild animals. I spoke to several of them afterwards—fine, husky-looking fellows and well-mannered. . . . I do not think any other troops could have stood up to it perhaps except these para. boys." General Sir Harold Alexander to C.I.G.S., 22 March, 1944. Lord Alanbrooke, *Personal Files.*

form and brought all maps of his proposed plans for the offensive—I liked his plans."

" *March 28th.* After the morning's C.O.S. meeting we were sent for by the P.M. to discuss the latest American wire about Mediterranean operations and our proposed reply. We found him in a desperately tired mood. I am afraid that he is losing ground rapidly. He seems quite incapable of concentrating for a few minutes on end, and keeps wandering continuously. He kept yawning and said he was feeling desperately tired."

' I had certainly failed to judge the stamina of that unique old man.'[1]

" *March 29th.* A very difficult C.O.S. meeting when we discussed the production of landing-craft for the Pacific in 1945. Third Sea Lord, Hurcomb (Transportation) and Sinclair, all attended. It is one of those awful jigsaw problems when it becomes very difficult to fit in the various pieces."

" I then had Jack Collins to lunch and also Crerar. The latter is just back from Italy and is taking over the Canadian Army. It has been a difficult move to accomplish. I have had to get rid of Andy McNaughton, give Crerar sufficient war experience in Italy and get Monty to accept him with very limited active experience. All has now been accomplished with much anguish and many difficulties, but I have full confidence that Crerar will not let me down. I have, however, I am afraid, lost a very good friend in the shape of Andy McNaughton; I only hope he may be able to realise the true situation to rise high enough for me not to lose his friendship."

" *March 30th.* Telegram from Dill showing that the American Chiefs of Staff are again going to fail to realise what the real strategic situation is in Italy. . . ."[2]

---

[1] *Notes on My Life,* XIII, 15.
[2] " As far as *Anvil* is concerned," Brooke wrote to Dill that night. " I am giving up hope of getting Marshall to understand what the situation is in Italy. It has taken two months arguing for him to see that the situation in Italy now is

For, though Marshall and his colleagues had accepted Eisenhower's recommendation that *Anvil* should not be staged before or at the same time as *Overlord*, they had again refused to abandon it altogether. They were now insisting that it should be put on in early July, so rendering any major exploitation of victory in Italy impossible. They maintained that nothing was to be gained by capturing Rome,[1] that the Italian campaign was a side-show remote from the main theatre of war, and that, once the Anzio bridgehead had been relieved, the Allies' striking forces in the Mediterranean ought to be transferred as quickly as possible to Southern France to assist the break-out in Normandy and provide deep-water ports for American reinforcements and supplies for the future invasion of Germany. To this the British replied that the combination of a summer offensive in Italy and the continuing threat of Mediterranean landings would tie down the German reserves far more effectively than any actual descent on the Riviera, which would merely relieve the enemy of the fear of further landings and enable him to transfer troops to Normandy.[2] Holding that it would be folly to reduce pressure in the one area where they were engaging large German forces for the sake of a dubious operation which could not be staged now for several months, they based their policy not only on the need to prevent a transfer of enemy reserves to France but on the effect of the German concentration in Italy on the Eastern Front, where Hitler's attempts to stem the Russian advance, which had continued throughout the winter, had been repeatedly thwarted for lack of the divisions he had so

---

what could be predicted some time ago and one which renders an *Anvil* on *Overlord* date impossible. The later date will also fail to achieve what he wants, as once ten divisions are taken for *Anvil* the residue in Infantry divisions is not sufficient for the offensive operation required if you want to *hold* forces opposite us in Central Italy. If on the other hand, the Germans start retiring, which is highly unlikely, then *Anvil* at a later date is the correct strategy, and one we have agreed to." C.I.G.S. to Field-Marshal Dill, 30 March, 1944. Lord Alanbrooke, *Personal Files.*

[1] A view which, according to his naval A.D.C.'s diary, Eisenhower shared. " Ike," he wrote on March 27th, " is delighted with the U.S. Chiefs of Staffs' decision to forget Rome. He has never been keen for taking the place, particularly as we have the principal airfields at Foggia." *Butcher*, 435.

[2] *Ehrman* V, 245-54.

impetuously sent into Brooke's strategic trap beyond the Alpine ranges.[1]

" *March 31st*. Telegram from American Chiefs of Staff came in, quite impossible to accept. Again arguing that after uniting Anzio bridgehead and main front we should go on the defensive in Italy, and start a new front in Southern France. They fail to realise that the forces available do not admit of two fronts in the Mediterranean."

" *April 1st*. Had hoped to get off without a C.O.S. meeting, but found it necessary to meet in order to form our new reply to the last American note about the South of France invasion. Marshall quite hopeless. . . . The strategy he advocates can only result in two months without any operations in the Mediterranean, just at the very moment when we require them most owing to the date of the cross-Channel operation."

" *April 3rd*. Nasty rush of telegrams to deal with on my arrival at War Office. Then busy C.O.S. meeting finishing our wire back to the Americans. Cabinet from 5.30 to 8 p.m. After dinner another meeting at 10.30 p.m. We discussed the construction of tank landing-ships and the provision of a Fleet Train for the Navy in the war against Japan. We again beat round and round the bush."

" *April 5th*. Difficulties again with our American friends who still persist in wanting to close down operations in Italy and open new ones in South of France, just at the most critical moment. . . ."

---

[1] For confirmation of this view, see the records of Hitler's military conferences. On December 20th, dealing with the situation on the Eastern Front where a major Russian counter-offensive against the overstretched German lines had begun a week earlier, he said, " I see the situation in the East every day, and it is terrible. With five or six divisions we might still force the decision, or at least a great victory." At another conference on December 27th, General Zeitzler, Chief of the General Staff, repeatedly stressed the difficulty of finding reserves to halt the Russians: " We will have to look around for new forces. . . . If we could just straighten them out a little and get some fresh troops, we could get going again." P. Gilbert, *Hitler Directs His War*, 79, 89, 93.

" Bertie Ramsay came to dine and was interesting concerning the naval preparations for cross-Channel operations."

" At 10.30 p.m. had to attend one of those awful evening meetings of the P.M. We were kept up till 12.45 a.m. discussing use of heavy bombers in support of invasion of France. He is opposed to Tedder's plan to use them on the railways, because he does not think that the results to be achieved will be much, and secondly owing to casualties amongst French civilians."

The use of the Allies' air forces, first to paralyse the enemy's communications and then to win command of the air over the battlefield, had been a chief factor in the invasion of Sicily. It was even more vital for that of France, where the landing was to be made on fortified beaches whose defenders—Germans not Italians—enjoyed the use of the finest rail and road system in Europe, linking them with their factories in the Ruhr. After prolonged discussion between the Combined Chiefs of Staff the British had agreed to place their principal long-range striking weapon, Bomber Command, under the temporary direction of the Supreme Commander of *Overlord*, who was to exercise it through his Deputy, Air Chief Marshal Tedder—a compromise to meet the American wish to throw everything into the cross-Channel operation and the British Air Staff's unchanging view that the end of all air activity was command of the air, from which, they held, every other blessing would flow. The question was whether it was better, as their Commanders-in-Chief contended, for the British and American heavy bombing forces to continue to attack the objectives set them at the beginning of the year—the German aircraft and petroleum industries—or to join until D-Day with the *Overlord* tactical air forces in an all-out attack on the railways and communication centres of Northern France to prevent the concentration of German reserves against the Normandy bridgehead.

It had been left to Tedder, as Deputy to the Supreme

Commander, to report on the rival plans. On March 25th, at a meeting presided over by Portal and attended by Eisenhower, Leigh-Mallory and the Commanders-in-Chief of the British and American strategical bombing forces, it was decided that, while the overall mission of the latter should remain the destruction of the enemy's military and industrial system and of his air combat strength in particular, this should be combined for the next two months with direct assistance to the ground forces.[1]

. . . .

The chain of Command for the invasion was now complete. While Eisenhower was immediately responsible to the Combined Chiefs of Staff for the supreme co-ordination of the whole, his three operational Commanders-in-Chief—Admiral Ramsay, General Montgomery and Air Chief Marshal Leigh-Mallory—were to direct the assaulting naval, military and air forces. Though it was agreed that after the final break-out from the bridgehead the American troops, who would by then outnumber the British, should operate under a separate American Commander-in-Chief, until then Montgomery was to direct the four armies taking part in the invasion—the American First Army under Bradley and the British Second Army under Dempsey, who were to make the initial assault, and two follow-up armies—the one Canadian and the other American—under Crerar and Patton. It was consequently at Montgomery's Headquarters at St. Paul's School that the first briefing or Presentation of Plans took place. Both Brooke and the Prime Minister were present.

" *April 7th.* A long day with Monty. At 9 a.m. I paraded at St. Paul's School to attend a wonderful day that Monty ran to go over the plans for the coming offensive. He started with some very good opening remarks. Then we had Ramsay to explain naval plans and Leigh-Mallory to explain air plans. Lunch followed and after that Bradley

[1] *Ehrman* V, 295-7.

and his two Corps commanders, followed by Dempsey, Bucknall and Crocker. . . ."

" After that Monty produced a ' Summing up,' and the P.M. turned up and addressed a few remarks to the meeting. He was looking old and lacking a great deal of his usual vitality."

" After the meeting P. J. Grigg, Monty and I had an interview with the P.M. to get him to face the reduction of formations in the Guards Division, as they can no longer find reinforcements. We had the usual difficulty. He has been got at by M.P.s and produced every sort of argument against what is an inevitable necessity."

On the day after the St. Paul's meeting the Anglo-American argument over *Anvil* reached a new climax. Both sides had remained stubborn. Nothing, Dill reported, would make Marshall abandon *Anvil*; nothing would make Churchill and Brooke relinquish the prize the approach of summer promised —the capture of Rome and the defeat of the forces Hitler had committed to Central Italy. Unless both campaigns were to be abandoned, a compromise was inevitable. The Americans, to make their unpalatable insistence on *Anvil* acceptable, offered —for the first time—to transfer naval assault-craft from the Pacific to the Mediterranean, promising to place twenty-six tank landing-ships and forty landing-craft at Wilson's disposal. The British reluctantly agreed to the American target date for the Riviera landing—July 10th—but insisted that the Combined Chiefs of Staff should have the right to postpone or cancel it in the light of circumstances and that preparations for it should not be allowed to prejudice either the offensive to relieve the bridgehead or the exploitation of victory in Italy. As the issue of a Directive to General Wilson could no longer be postponed if the operation was to take place at all, the Americans thereupon left it at that.[1]

" *April 8th*. Another difficult C.O.S. meeting dealing with the last reply from American C.O.S. on Mediter-

[1] *Ehrman* V, 253-5.

ranean strategy. They have at last agreed to our policy but withdrawn their offer of landing-craft from Pacific. This is typical of their methods of running strategy. Although we have agreed that the European theatre must take precedence over the Pacific, yet they use some of their available landing-craft as bargaining counters in trying to get their false strategy followed. . . ."

" *April 11th.* Series of telegrams from P.M. to go through. He wishes to wire to Marshall to make one further attempt to obtain landing-craft from the Pacific."

" In the afternoon Alexander turned up to see me, back from Italy. Discussed plan of attack with him; it is not ideal, but he is very handicapped by all the nationalities he has to deal with."[1]

" At 10 p.m. we had a meeting with the P.M. attended by Alex; it lasted till 1 a.m. Our time was spent in going through his telegram to Marshall. I feel certain the reply will be in the negative."[2]

" *April 13th.* A long C.O.S. meeting at which the Lethbridge Committee attended. They have just been touring the world: Washington, Canada, Honolulu, Fiji, New Zealand, Australia, New Guinea, India, Burma, etc., studying the requirements of war against Japan. Their report is very good and provides much food for thought and for progress."

" After lunch series of interviews; Symes back from Burma having been second in command to Wingate, discussed Burma fully with him. Then Sir A. Rowlands from India, sent back by Viceroy. Had long discussion with him on Indian internal situation, grain situation, transportation. He was followed by MacNarney " (Marshall's

[1] In Field-Marshal Alexander's Dispatches a list of these is given: viz. *Imperial:* British, Canadians, New Zealanders, South Africans, Newfoundlanders, Indians, Ceylonese, Basutos, Swazi, Bechuanas, Seychelles, Mauritians, Caribbeans, Cypriot; *Americans,* including Negro Division and Japanese-American Combat Regiment; *Allies,* including Algerians, Moroccans, Tunisians and Senegalese; Poles, Nepalese, Belgians, Greeks, Brazilians, Syro-Lebanese, Palestinians, Jugoslavs; *Co-belligerent,* Italians.

[2] It was. Churchill's telegram was sent on April 12th after revision by the Chiefs of Staff. *Ehrman* V, 257.

Deputy) " and MacCloy " (U.S. Under Sec. for War). " Spent an hour with them discussing all fronts and mostly the existing differences of outlook between the British and U.S. Chiefs of Staff concerning our strategy in the Mediterranean."

" At 6.30 p.m. Cabinet to discuss distribution of man-power, after defeat of Germany, between industry and home development, Occupation of Germany and Japanese war. This lasted till 8.15 p.m. At 10.30 p.m. went on to Defence Committee to discuss air strategy of bombing railway communications in France prior to attack. Am far from convinced that we would not be better employed spending that effort on German aircraft industry. P.M. scared of casualties to the French entailed by this policy. Meeting lasted till midnight and P.M. then called me in for a private talk till 12.30 p.m."

' In the light of after events I consider that my criticism of Tedder's policy was wrong and that he had selected the right policy in attacking railways and bridges. The trouble of the railways was that it meant inflicting casualties on the French.'

" *April 14th.* We had a long C.O.S. meeting attended by the Planners at which we discussed the future Pacific strategy and examined the possibility and advantages of a line of advance on an axis from Darwin towards Borneo. This might give us a chance of running an entirely British Imperial campaign instead of furnishing reinforcements for American operations."

" After lunch Davidson[1] came for an interview prior to his departure, and a Major Wilkinson just back from Yugoslavia who was very interesting. Unfortunately, while he was with me we were sent for by the P.M. He had been drafting a reply to the wire he had received from Marshall about the Mediterranean strategy. I had a hard set-to

[1] Maj.-Gen. F. H. N. Davidson, Director of Military Intelligence.

with him and I hope convinced him that it would be a fatal error. He agreed to redraft the wire on our advised line. I only hope that he does so."

" *April 17th*. Arrived back early in office to find myself swamped with telegrams. After C.O.S. lunched with P.M. at 10 Downing Street; Eisenhower, Bedell Smith and Alexander were there. The conversation at once again turned to the Mediterranean strategy and to the American Chiefs of Staff failure to agree with us as to the necessity to press on with operations in Italy without impairing the prospects by preparations for an operation against Southern France. Eisenhower produced all the arguments we heard the other day. . . ."

Meanwhile, though nothing had come of the Prime Minister's attempts to make the Americans reconsider their decision to withdraw their offer of additional landing-craft from the Pacific, the time won by his persistence coupled with the course of events had, as so often before, accrued to Britain's advantage. During his visit to London Alexander had made it clear that the offensive in Italy could not be launched before the middle of May and the hoped-for junction between the main attacking forces and the bridgehead before the first week in June. This made a landing in the South of France on July 10th out of the question, and on April 19th, with the grudging assent of Washington, the Combined Chiefs of Staff's long-disputed Directive to Wilson was issued in the form which Brooke had wanted. Its object was

" to give the greatest possible assistance to *Overlord* by destroying or containing the maximum number of German formations in the Mediterranean."

The means to be pursued were to

" (*a*) launch, as early as possible, an all-out offensive in Italy;
(*b*) develop the greatest possible threat to contain German forces in Southern France . . .
(*c*) make plans for the best possible use of the amphibious

lift remaining to you, either in support of operations in Italy, or in order to take advantage of opportunities arising in the South of France or elsewhere for the furtherance of your object and to press forward vigorously and wholeheartedly with all preparations which do not prejudice the achievement of the fullest success in (*a*) above."

Alexander's offensive was to be launched on May 11th, just over three weeks before the Normandy landings.[1]

"*April 19th*. At last all our troubles about *Anvil* are over. We have got the Americans to agree, but have lost the additional landing-craft they were prepared to provide. History will never forgive them for bargaining equipment against strategy and for trying to blackmail us into agreeing with them by holding the pistol of withdrawing craft at our heads. . . ."

"*Later*. A meeting from 10.30 p.m. to 1 a.m. First as regards the bombing of railways; the matter put back for another week's consideration, at a time when we are within five weeks of the attack and definite decisions are required. Secondly, Egypt,[2] where may gain a week by delay so as to clear the Greek situation. The P.M.'s best remark of the evening was that:— ' King Farouk was wallowing like a sow in the trough of luxury ! ' "

"*April 21st*. Our C.O.S. was mainly concerned with arranging for subversive operations in Hungary and pressing on with the building of all the harbour equipment for the landings in France."

For the next week Brooke was on leave.

---

[1] *Ehrman* V, 259. See *Feis*, 307.

[2] " Where the political quarrels between the exiled Greeks had now culminated in almost open civil war. During the second week in April the Greek brigade in Egypt had mutinied. The Commander-in-Chief, Middle East, was ordered to disarm them. This General Paget did on April 23rd, with the loss of one British officer and without casualties to the Greeks." *Churchill* V, 482, 485-6.

" *April 30th.* On the 22nd I flew up to Dundee in the morning early, taking Ronnie Weeks with me. We spent the day visiting the 52nd Division and finally finished up at Cairnton where I found Ivan Cobbold. I had a heavenly week there, fishing all day, leaving the house at 9.30 a.m. in the morning and not returning till 11 p.m., except for about an hour at lunch and at dinner. I caught twelve salmon, but lost nine and was fishing badly. I now feel infinitely better."

" This morning took off from Dyce aerodrome (near Aberdeen) at 10 a.m. and landed at Hendon 12.15 p.m. Came back to the flat for work so as to start square to-morrow."

" *May 1st.* Very reluctantly I started work again! First a Chiefs of Staff meeting at 10.30. Then at 12 noon the opening meeting of the Conference of Empire Prime Ministers. Met Fraser at the door, who was very friendly and nice. Mackenzie King also very friendly. But by far the most attractive of the lot was dear old Smuts, just the same as ever and with the same clear refreshing outlook on life. A meeting with various polite speeches, and then photographs in the garden of 10 Downing Street. After lunch I had an hour with ' Jumbo ' Wilson who had just flown home for discussions on future strategy in the Mediterranean."

" At 5.30 p.m. another Dominion Prime Ministers' Conference. Winston spoke for one-and-a-half hours on the strategic situation in Europe. . . . He looked very old and tired, and in my opinion is failing fast."

' " My opinion " was proved to be entirely wrong. He was far from " failing fast." But then he is no ordinary human being and cannot be judged by normal standards.'

" *May 2nd.* C.O.S. meeting at 10.30 at which we had to rush work to finish before 11.30 a.m. when we again met the Dominion P.M.s. I had to give them a survey of the European theatre. It took me about an hour but seemed to keep them quiet and dealt with their questions. We did not finish the meeting till 1.30 p.m."

" Then went through the briefs for the Cabinet and at 4 p.m. ' Jumbo ' Wilson came to propound his various plans. He remained till 5.30 when I dashed off to the Cabinet. This was attended by Dominion P.M.s. My usual statement on the military situation was drawn out to an hour by continuous interruptions. The Cabinet finished with another long discussion on the bombing strategy of an attack on French railways and of killing Frenchmen. . . . Cabinet lasted till 8.30 p.m."

" Then dashed home to dine with ' Jumbo ' Wilson and take him on to a meeting with the P.M. to explain all his various alternative plans. We finished up by again getting on to the bombing of the French railways and were kept up till 1.30 a.m. Shall not get to bed before 2 a.m."

" *May 3rd.* C.O.S. at 10.30 a.m. at which ' Jumbo ' Wilson attended to discuss future plans for Mediterranean. Then Imperial meeting with Dominion P.M.s. Smuts opened with long statement expressing his doubts as to advisability of departing from Mediterranean strategy for a cross-Channel operation. Meeting broke up at 1.15 p.m."

" Dashed off to Franklyn's Home Forces H.Q. to give a talk on the world situation. Back to War Office for a rush of work followed by another Imperial conference from 5.30 to 7.30 p.m. At 10.30 p.m. another meeting with P.M. on bombing of railways which lasted till 1.15 a.m. Winston gradually coming round to the policy."

" *May 4th.* After dinner another of Winston's meetings. P.M. quite exhausted; the meeting meandered on, lasting till midnight."

" *May 6th.* The day was spent in trying to get level with some of the work I had been unable to get through during the week. In the evening motored to Chequers with you for the week-end. The party consisted of Mackenzie King, Godfrey Huggins,[1] Lord Cherwell, Winston's brother,

---

[1] Prime Ministers of Canada and Southern Rhodesia.

Mary and Sarah. We had a walk with Clemmie before dinner, and a film after dinner. Got to bed by midnight."

' The earliest hour I had ever been to bed at Chequers.'

" *May 7th. Chequers.* In the morning we went to church with Clemmie and Mary. After lunch did some work and after tea we went for a walk. Dinner was followed by the usual film, after which Winston took me down to the little study where the secretaries work. There he sat by the fire and drank soup. He looked very old and very tired. He said Roosevelt was not well and that he was no longer the man he had been;[1] this, he said, also applied to himself. He said he could still always sleep well, eat well and especially drink well, but that he no longer jumped out of bed the way he used to, and felt as if he would be quite content to spend the whole day in bed. I have never yet heard him admit that he was beginning to fail."

" He then said some very nice things about the excellent opinion that the whole Defence Committee and War Cabinet had of me, and that they had said that we could not have a better C.I.G.S. Got to bed by 1 a.m."

' Considering the difficult times I had had recently with Winston, I appreciated tremendously his kindness in passing on these remarks to me at the end of our talk. I did not often get any form of appreciation of my work from him and therefore treasured it all the more on these rare occasions. He was an astounding mixture, could drive you to complete desperation and to the brink of despair for weeks on end, and then he would ask you to spend a couple of hours or so alone with him and would produce the most homely and attractive personality. All that unrelenting tension was temporarily relaxed, he ceased to work himself into one fury

---

[1] Three weeks earlier on April 14th, Edward Stettinius, the Lease-Lend administrator, told Captain Butcher that Roosevelt was " becoming increasingly difficult to deal with because he changed his mind so often." *Butcher*, 443.

or another, and you left him with the feeling that you would do anything within your power to help him to carry the stupendous burden he had shouldered.'

" *May 8th.* Made an early start and back in War Office by 9.30 a.m. Portal and Cunningham away on leave and absent from C.O.S. Very busy afternoon, followed by a dinner at Greenwich attended by Curtin, Fraser, Smuts, Attlee, Amery, Bruce, Leathers, P. J. Grigg, etc. Cunningham and I had to rush back to attend a meeting with P.M. at 11 p.m. to discuss our Directive to Mountbatten. Winston terribly tired; required great patience to handle him, but got what we wanted through. Now 1.30 a.m. sleepy and off to bed."

" *May 9th.* Our C.O.S. meeting was mainly concerned with working out strength of force that could be deployed from Australia after Germany had been defeated. In the evening attended dinner at 10 Downing Street for Dominion P.M.s. Smuts as usual made a first-class speech."

" *May 10th.* A day of continuous rush and little to show for it. At 10.45 C.O.S. meeting till 11.30 and then a rush to the Guildhall to arrive in time for Freedom of the City ceremony for Curtin and Fraser. Then lunch at Mansion House with two more speeches by Fraser and Curtin. The latter made two excellent speeches."

" Back to War Office to interview Sosnkowski, who wanted to know why Polish evacuees were being held up in Gibraltar, why we would not enlist in British Forces Polish Jews who left Polish Forces, why casualties from Italy could not be reported home quicker, why he could not be allowed out of this country to visit Italy in spite of the special rule barring all movement out till after invasion of France, etc. He was followed by Blamey " ('Australian C. in C.') " who remained a full hour-and-a-half. We discussed many of the Pacific problems. I found him easy to get on with."

" After that dined at Ritz to entertain Dominion Military, Naval and Air representatives. I suppose this all serves some purpose in welding Imperial bonds, but I doubt it at times. All these speeches strike me as being so much hot air or alcoholic vapour which goes to everybody's head, produces a beatific and complacent attitude of wonderful Imperial understanding. But how much of all this remains there in the cold bleak reality of the morning after? "

" *May 11th.* . . . To-night at 11 p.m. the Italian attack starts. I pray to God that it may be successful. A great deal depends on it."[1]

" *May 12th.* Attack started up to time, but no news all day. I am now (11.30 p.m.) awaiting a message which is being deciphered. It is very trying having to wait for this information."

" Preparation for cross-Channel operations going on full blast, and date drawing very near."

" *May 13th and 14th.* A very short C.O.S. meeting, after which I escaped and returned home for lunch. Spent Sunday at home photographing a Marsh Tit."

' Those two hours in a hide close to a Marsh Tit at its nest made Winston and the war disappear in a cloud of smoke. It was like rubbing Aladdin's lamp. I was transplanted to a fairyland and returned infinitely refreshed and re-created.'

" *May 15th.* Went straight from home to St. Paul's School to attend Eisenhower's final run-over plans for cross-Channel operations. The King, P.M., Smuts and all Chiefs of Staff were present. The main impression I gathered was that Eisenhower was no real director of thought, plans, energy or direction. Just a co-ordinator,

[1] " The great offensive began at 11 p.m. that night, when the artillery of both our armies, 2000 guns, opened a violent fire, reinforced at dawn by the full weight of the tactical airforce." *Churchill* V, 529. Earlier in the day Brooke had wired Alexander, " On the threshold of your great offensive I send to you personally and to the Allied Armies in Italy my best wishes for the future and my appreciation of all you have already achieved. Good luck." Lord Alanbrooke, *Personal Files.*

a good mixer, a champion of inter-Allied co-operation, and in those respects few can hold the candle to him. But is that enough? Or can we not find all qualities of a commander in one man? May be I am getting too hard to please, but I doubt it."[1]

" Monty made excellent speech. Bertie Ramsay indifferent and overwhelmed by all his own difficulties. Spaatz[2] read every word. Bert Harris told us how well he might have won the war if it had not been for the handicap imposed by the existence of the two other Services. Leigh-Mallory gave very clear description. Sholto Douglas seemed disappointed at the smallness of his task, and so was I. Then Humfrey Gale and Graham on Administration, followed by Grasset on Civil Controls of France. A useful run-through. The King made a few well-chosen remarks. After lunch he presented the C.B. to Bradley and two other decorations."

" Back to War Office and finished up with Monty dining quietly with me. He was in very good form and bearing his reponsibilities well."

' If I was asked to review the opinion I expressed that evening of Eisenhower, I should, in the light of all later experience, repeat every word of it. A past-master in the handling of allies, entirely impartial and consequently trusted by all. A charming personality and good co-ordinator. But no real commander. I have seen many similar reviews of impending operations, and especially those run by Monty. Ike might have been a showman calling on various actors to perform their various turns, but he was not the commander of the show who controlled and directed all the actors. A very different performance from Monty's show a few days

[1] This view of Eisenhower's military, as opposed to administrative, capacities ran directly counter to that held by nearly all American and many British officers at the time. " General Patton," Captain Butcher wrote in his diary that February, " has just been in my office and . . . re-emphasized that Ike is on the threshold of becoming ' the greatest general of all time—including Napoleon.' " *Butcher*, 419 (11 Feb., 1944). And see *Morison*, XI 70.
[2] Lt.-Gen. Carl Spaatz, Commander U.S. Strategic Air Forces in Europe.

previously. Fortunately, as happens so often, Ike had a counterpart in the shape of Bedell Smith. A great deal that Ike was deficient in, his Chief of Staff provided for him. Ike was wise enough to realise this, and whatever job Ike got he took his Bedell Smith with him.'

'Bertie Ramsay disappointed me that morning; in his talk he fell so very far short of doing himself justice. Had I not known all his brilliant qualities well, I might have easily misjudged him that day. In his determination not to skim over the difficulties he emphasised them to such an extent as to give one the impression that he was lacking in confidence in himself—a failing from which he was most certainly not suffering. I have met very few naval officers of whom I had a higher opinion.'

'I think I was somewhat unkind to Bomber Harris, who had shown brilliant skill in the handling of the forces under his command and provided wonderful support during the operation. He had, however, such a conviction that bombers alone could win the war, if given a proper chance, that this conviction was always to the fore.'

"*May 16th.* A fairly full C.O.S. at which we considered most recent evidence of German rocket bomber and pilot-less plane, together with results of our counter-measures. At 12.45 p.m. a final meeting of the Imperial Conference to hear speeches of all the various Prime Ministers and to see the final document signed. To the Russian Embassy to receive the Order of Suvorov. Then back to War Office to be briefed for Cabinet at 5.30 which was attended by Dominion P.M.s. Luckily the Italian news continues to be good. Finally Crerar came to dine and we talked shop the whole evening."

"*May 17th.* Started with usual C.O.S. meeting, then P.M. sent for me. He was in bed, obviously very tired, having been up till 3 a.m. at a dinner with Anthony Eden. He was very disturbed at statements made by Humfrey Gale and Graham at the Monday meeting at St. Paul's

School connected with a thousand clerks of the 3rd Echelon and the fact that the invasion catered for one lorry for every five men.[1] It took me three-quarters of an hour to pacify him, and I cursed Humfrey Gale and Graham and all their ancestors before I had finished."

" *May 18th*. Another day of continuous work. First a long C.O.S. when we had a meeting with the Planners in order to try and settle a final Pacific strategy to put up to the P.M. The problem is full of difficulties, although the strategy is quite clear. Unfortunately the right course to follow is troubled by personalities, questions of command, vested interests, inter-allied jealousies, etc. Curtin and MacArthur are determined to stand together, support each other and allow no outside interference. Winston is determined Mountbatten must be given some operation to carry out; Andrew Cunningham is equally determined that Mountbatten should not control the Eastern Fleet; Americans wish to gather all laurels connected with Pacific fighting, and Winston is equally determined that we should not be tied to the apron strings of the Americans! How on earth are we ever to steer a straight course between all these snags and difficulties? "

" From 3 to 4 p.m. meeting with P.M., Eden, Bedell Smith and Chiefs of Staff to decide how to handle de Gaulle before the invasion, whilst still retaining secrecy. Another Cabinet meeting from 7 p.m. to 8.30 p.m. . . ."

" *May 19th*. Thank Heaven the Italian attack is going well, and it should play its part in holding formations in Italy and keeping them away from the Channel. At any rate we have proved that Marshall and the American Chiefs of Staff were all wrong arguing that the Germans would retire before we could attack and leave only some six divisions to cover their rear, leaving us with large

---

[1] " The amount of paraphernalia sounded staggering . . . I was told . . . that two thousand officers and clerks were being taken across the sea to keep records, and . . . that twenty days after the landing there would be one vehicle ashore for every 4.77 men." *Churchill* V, 543.

forces stranded in Italy which we could not engage.[1] Such a withdrawal may be forced on them later, but not I hope until we have knocked the stuffing out of them."

" *May 20th.* Alexander's news of the Italian fighting continues to be excellent.[2] Thank Heaven for it! I have staked a great deal on the Italian campaign in all our arguments with the Americans. I felt throughout that we had wonderful opportunities of inflicting a real telling defeat on the Germans which would be worth anything in connection with the cross-Channel operations. The only danger was that the Americans should have their way and plan to withdraw forces from Italy at the critical moment. They nearly succeeded in ruining our strategy, and now I pray God we may be allowed to reap the full benefits of it."

' One of Marshall's arguments for going on the defensive in Italy and for withdrawing troops from this theatre was that the enemy would now start withdrawing forces from this front and leave rear-guard forces covering this move-ment. Had this happened we should have been left with redundant forces in Italy. This was quite a sound argument strategically, but it failed entirely to take Hitler's mentality into account. Nowhere yet had he retired voluntarily on any front; in not doing so he had committed grave strategic blunders which led to his ultimate defeat. First Stalingrad which resulted in the loss of von Paulus's army and countless casualties; secondly Tunisia with the loss of 250,000 men and much equipment, shipping and material; thirdly the Dnieper River bend when he might have materially increased his reserves by shortening his front. It was not in Hitler's character to retire.'

" *May 23rd.* Meeting with Joint Intelligence Committee and long discussion with them on situation in France as

---

[1] " Ike said the battle so far was consoling because it indicated that Germans had elected to stand and fight rather than to disengage." *Butcher* 463, (16 May. 1944).
[2] Monte Cassino had fallen on the 18th.

regards accumulation of German divisions to meet invasion. Close on sixty divisions are accumulated."

" Alex's offensive from Anzio bridgehead started this morning, together with offensive in Liri valley. I am rather afraid that he has launched the bridgehead offensive too soon and that he may not reap full benefits of the favourable situation confronting him. However, he alone can judge, being on the spot."

" At 1.30 p.m. flew from Hendon to Oxford to inspect the Glider Pilot Regiment of which I am Colonel. They are a wonderful lot of men. They gave a demonstration of twenty Hanso gliders taking off in fourteen minutes and subsequently the gliders landing in eight minutes. Then flew back to London and finished office work."

" *May 24th.* C.O.S. meeting was a long one. To War Office to see a film of Lethbridge's tour in the Pacific. A good film giving good idea of fighting conditions. Then Sam Hoare came and gave me a general picture of conditions in Spain. Then rushed off to Cabinet meeting on transfer of R.A.F. Regiment personnel to the Army. P.M. appointed a committee under John Anderson to go into the matter."

" Then solitary dinner with Winston. He was very upset by the President's proposed broadcast to Germany to coincide with invasion. We also discussed Pacific strategy, and I found him in a very good mood. At 10 p.m. we had a Chiefs of Staff meeting with him to discuss progress made in pumping out of ' Phoenixes ' and Pacific strategy. I think we have at last got him swung towards an Australian-based strategy as opposed to his old love, the Sumatra tip."

" *May 25th.* Long C.O.S. with meetings with Planners, Lord Leathers, and Henry Pownall. Then hurried lunch and dash to Portsmouth where motor launch took me to vicinity of Isle of Wight to see the ' Whales ', new piers for the invasion. A wonderful sight. From there to Selsea Bill to see the ' Phoenixes ', the large concrete caissons for the breakwaters for the artificial harbours.[1] A wonderful piece of engineering."

" From there to Monty's H.Q. to dine with him. I had to tell him off and ask him not to meddle himself in everybody else's affairs. Such as wanting to advise Alex on his battle or War Office as to how to obtain reinforcements! As usual he took it well. He then motored back to London with me."

" Just heard Anzio bridgehead and main front are joined up together. Thank Heaven for it! "

" *May 26th.* The Italian offensive is going well, enemy reserves are being drawn in, and it is performing just the function we wanted with reference to the cross-Channel operations."

" Another very full day which started with a C.O.S. meeting from 10.30 to 11.30 a.m. Then a meeting with P.M., Eden, Attlee, Oliver Lyttelton, Leathers, Curtin, Blamey and Chiefs of Staff to consider our future strategy. . . . In the end we obtained all we wanted for the present: namely Darwin and Fremantle to be developed for future operations by us, and representatives of our staff to be accepted to work with the Australian General Staff. Meeting lasted till 1.30 p.m."

" Then a rush home for lunch with Martin[2] of the Daily Telegraph. Interview with Blamey with whom I made good progress. After Blamey, Ted Morris back from being Chief of Staff in Delhi, and from whom I had a lot to gather. He was followed by Admiral Noble from Washington who tells me Dill is showing signs of age and is tired. Then a long talk with Pownall just back from Mountbatten's H.Q. in Ceylon. . . . Finally a visit from

---

[1] ' They had been towed round to this spot and then sunk in rows, so that they stuck out of the water like a row of houses. I went on board one of them to examine it and found that it had small platforms for erecting A.A. guns if necessary. When required the water was pumped out of them and they were towed across. Similarly the piers, consisting of flexible roadway mounted on large pontoons, were in sections ready to tow across and assemble on selected site.' *Notes on My Life*, XIII, 48.
[3] Lt.-Gen. Hugh Martin.

Weeks with answers to a series of Minutes from the P.M."

' The news of Dill had been bad of late. He had never really recovered properly from the infection he suffered from after his operation for the hernia he had contracted whilst riding Archie Wavell's horses on a visit to Delhi. He had a sort of anaemia which he could not shake off. I was more and more distressed every time I saw him. For all that he continued to do the most invaluable work in Washington.'

" *May 27th*. A very full C.O.S. programme which I got through all right by going fast and keeping the ball rolling. By 12 noon I was off for Whit Monday week-end and just longing for a rest of a few hours from continual war responsibility. The hardest part of bearing such responsibility is pretending that you are absolutely confident of success when you are really torn to shreds with doubts and misgivings. But when once decisions are taken the time for doubts is gone, and what is required is to breathe the confidence of success into all those around."

" I never want again to go through a time like the present one. The cross-Channel operation is just eating into my heart. I wish to God we could start and have done with it."

Chapter Six

BATTLE FOR THE
BRIDGEHEAD

*The attack will come; there's no doubt about that any more.
. . . If they attack in the West, that attack will decide the War.
If this attack is repulsed the whole business is over. Then
we can withdraw troops right away.*

HITLER, *23 December, 1943*

THE BEGINNING of June, 1944 marked the culmination of the
Mediterranean strategy which the C.I.G.S. had forecast
in his diary on taking office two-and-a-half years before.
Its purpose was not, as many supposed and have since argued,
to invade Hitler's Europe through its "soft under-belly" but,
by drawing and keeping his strategic reserves south of the
Alpine ranges, to make possible a simultaneous attack from
across the Channel and from Russia on a Reich, unable, for
lack of reserves, to use its swift east-to-west communications to
crush both assaults in turn. It was the final military answer—
as Chamberlain's forlorn guarantee to Poland had been the first
political one—to Hitler's declared resolve to conquer Europe
without exposing Germany to another war on two fronts. On
June 2nd, as a portent of what was to come, the first American
heavy bombers, flying from Italy, landed on Russian soil on a
shuttle-bombing mission that was to bring every corner of the
Reich within reach of Allied air attack.

Two days later Alexander's victorious forces entered Rome.
On the same day, June 4th, on Hitler's urgent orders a German
division was withdrawn from Northern France to reinforce his
crumbling Italian front. At that moment the Allies were about to

strike at Normandy. Of Germany's 307 field divisions 165 were holding the Russians, 18 were in Scandinavia, 41 in Northern France and the Low Countries, and no less than 74 in Southern Europe, including 18 in France south of the Loire.[1] In the Reich itself there were only 9 divisions. Germany's Army was stretched to the utmost, and she had no central strategic reserve. It was the justification of the policy for which the British Chiefs of Staff had so long contended and of which, as their Chairman and military member, Brooke had been the arch-exponent.

Everything now depended on whether the forces waiting in England to take advantage of this moment could force a landing in the teeth of the tremendous obstacles facing them, consolidate their bridgehead and break out before the winter. A few months earlier, in Brooke's view, none of these things had been possible. There had not been enough assault-craft to land on a front sufficiently wide to be held; the railway system between France and Germany had still to be smashed; the *Luftwaffe* had not been driven from the skies; and the means were almost totally lacking for building up the invaders' resources fast enough to contain the enemy's counter-attack. The first indispensable step—defined by Brooke at the Casablanca Conference in January, 1943—had been to win the Battle of the Atlantic and remove the U-boat threat to the Allies' sea-lanes. The second had been to gain unchallenged command of the air, not only over the Channel and landing-beaches but over the rail and road communications of Northern France. During April and May the great Allied air sweep against the French railways for which Portal, Tedder and Leigh-Mallory had contended so stubbornly succeeded beyond all expectation. Fifteen hundred of the two thousand engines of the *Région Nord* were immobilised and all but four of the eighty selected transport targets wrecked or destroyed. In a few weeks

[1] In the winter, five months earlier, when cross-Channel operations had been an impossibility, the figures had been 179 on the Russian front, 16 in Norway and Denmark, 48 in South-East Europe of which 22 were in Italy, and 53 in France and the Low Countries, 35 of these being north of the Loire. *Ehrman* V, 279-80; *Cross-Channel Attack*, 259-60.

the whole of Northern France was made a " railway desert ". And it was done with such skill that no indication was given of the direction of the impending attack, which the German Command, fearing for the Belgian plain and the Ruhr, believed would fall on the Pas de Calais, where it continued to keep its best divisions. During May and the first days of June the Allies turned their attention to the Seine bridges, destroying eighteen of the twenty-four between Paris and the sea and damaging three more, so ensuring that there should be no quick reinforcement of the German forces west of that river. During the same period the enemy's radar warning system was almost completely paralysed. By June 5th only one in six of the coastal installations between Calais and Brittany was working.

While this great air victory was being won, the concentration of men, ships and material in England's ports was protected from German air observation. " No one," wrote an American officer serving in the Liberation armies, " who had had a dose of enemy air action against one of our ports in the Mediterranean could believe that the invasion fleet would ever put to sea intact. . . . We saw the tiny harbours along the south coast and the big sprawling harbour of Southampton packed like miniature Pearl Harbours, with ships stacked gunwale to gunwale. They had to crawl so close to one another that it did not seem as if a bomber could drop a pea and miss one."[1] All this assembly of maritime and military strength—so long planned and debated—had taken shape since Brooke's return to England in December and the appointment of the Supreme Commander and his operational Commanders-in-Chief. At the beginning of the year there had not been enough ships to meet even the requirements of the narrow front, three-division landing allowed for by the C.O.S.S.A.C. planners. By June the thousand craft allocated to the operation by the United States had risen to nearly two thousand five hundred, manned by more than 100,000 seamen, including three battleships and three cruisers which at the eleventh hour a reluctant Admiral

[1] Ralph Ingersoll, *Top Secret*, 82. See *Morison* IX 67.

King had released to join the four British battleships and twenty-one cruisers scheduled for the preliminary bombardment. In all more than five thousand ships and eleven thousand aircraft were engaged and over a million picked troops, organized in 37 divisions, half of them American and half British and Canadian.

Yet the assembly, training and equipment of this vast force had been only the beginning. The Allies had now to do what no one had done since William the Conqueror, and that Philip of Spain, Louis XIV, Napoleon and Hitler had all attempted in vain. In two days they had to transport across the stormy tidal waters of the Channel, without hurt from U-boat, mine, E-boat or *Luftwaffe*, nearly 200,000 armed men and land them with 20,000 mechanical vehicles on open beaches along a fifty-miles stretch of fortified coast, negotiating a complex network of undersea obstacles and immobilizing shore defences of immense strength. Ever since November, when Germany's most original-minded commander, Field-Marshal Rommel, had been sent to organize the Channel defences under von Rundstedt, Supreme Commander in the West, half a million troops and conscript workers had been toiling to strengthen the " Atlantic Wall ". The tidal stretches before the beaches had been strewn with steel and concrete wrecking devices, the sands and roads into the interior had been mined and barred by fortifications and tank traps, while every accessible landing-place was enfiladed by the fire of hidden batteries and the level spaces behind the coastline studded with wooden posts to prevent airborne landings. And though, thanks to Alexander's persistent attack, in the south, the Germans had been unable to transfer troops from Italy to the Channel coast and had been even forced to send half-a-dozen more divisions to that country, since the halting of the Russian winter offensive by the spring thaw they had been steadily reinforcing Northern France. In January twenty-four of their thirty-two Panzer divisions had been in Russia and only eight on other fronts; by June there were only eighteen facing the Red Army, while twelve were either in France or on their way there, three of them within striking distance of the Normandy coast and three more just beyond the Seine and Loire.

Early in May, when D-Day was only four weeks away, alarming reports began to reach S.H.A.E.F. that the Germans were reinforcing Normandy. Three months earlier Montgomery's Intelligence had reckoned that the Allies would have not more than six divisions to meet in the sector; by the middle of May it seemed certain there would be at least eight, with another four by the morning of D plus 2. It was known that the " desert fox " meant to defeat the invasion on the beaches; " Rommel," his old adversary declared, " has made a world of difference since he took over. . . . He will do his level best to ' Dunkirk ' us." And, though the enemy had not, as the Allies feared, found out their plans, from his remote East Prussian headquarters Hitler, acting on intuition, ordered a reinforcement of the crucial sector between the Seine and Cherbourg. Fortunately, advised by the naval authorities that a landing on this coast was almost impossible and deceived by British feints in the Straits of Dover, von Rundstedt and Rommel continued to believe that the blow would fall north of the Somme.

Storming the beaches was the least of the invaders' tasks. Anzio and Salerno, like Gallipoli before them, had driven home the lesson of all contested landings that, once ashore, there must be no halt until the deepest and widest possible bridgehead had been won. Montgomery had impressed this in his briefing on May 15th. " Armoured columns must penetrate deep inland and quickly on D-Day; this will upset the enemy's plans and tend to hold him off while we build up strength. We must gain space rapidly and peg claims well inland." " Best way to stop counter-attacks," he had written, " is to be offensive ourselves; must not let initiative pass to the enemy; we must *crack about* and force the battle to swing our way."[1] For the Allies' difficulty was to hold off the enemy's armoured counter-attacks while they were struggling to get their supplies and reinforcements ashore and build up strength. Within a week, the planners reckoned, the Germans would be able to concentrate

[1] *Wilmot* 216; Alanbrooke, *Personal Files*, 20 March, 1944.

eighteen divisions, six of them armoured, against the bridge-head; by the end of the first month between thirty and forty. Not for seven weeks after D-Day could the invaders hope to bring the whole of their own 37 divisions into battle against the 59 German divisions in France and the Low Countries.

The hard core of their problem was logistical. It lay in the fact that a single division in the battleline needed at least 600 tons of supplies a day and that, until Cherbourg could be reached and captured, everything for the invading forces would have to be landed on open beaches. So would their reinforcements. Even with the two artificial harbours, secretly pre-fabricated in Britain during the winter, it was going to be a race against time to build up strength fast enough to hold off and ultimately break the defenders.

With so much to achieve and at stake it was inevitable that those responsible should have fears for the issue. Even the Americans, who two years earlier had wished to embark on it before their forces had been trained and equipped and before almost any of the logistical wherewithal to make it possible were available, were now assailed by doubts. Three weeks before the convoys were due to sail, Eisenhower's naval A.D.C. was told by Bedell Smith that the chances of being able to hold the bridgehead were no more than fifty-fifty. " Will the Channel run red with blood? " he asked in his diary. During those tense days of spring he noted how his chief, whose cheerful confidence sustained everyone, looked increasingly worn and tired.[1]

The boldest of the Allied leaders—the apostle of attack and victory—had always believed that a cross-Channel invasion would be attended by appalling casualties. " The possibility of Hitler's gaining a victory in France cannot be excluded," the Prime Minister had written at the beginning of the year; " the

---

[1] *Butcher*, 462 (12 May, 1944). See *idem*, 18 March, 18, 28 April. Some months later after the invasion had succeeded, Eisenhower gave Butcher the draft of a communiqué he had written on the eve of D-Day. It ran, " Our landings in the Cherbourg-Havre area have failed to gain a satisfactory foothold and I have withdrawn the troops. My decision to attack at this time and place was based upon the best information available. The troops, the Air and the Navy did all that bravery and devotion to duty could do. If any blame or fault attaches to the attempt, it is mine alone." *Butcher*, 525.

hazards of battle are very great."[1] Haunted by the massacres of the great frontal attacks of the First World War, he had never ceased to hope that their repetition could be avoided by a less costly approach through Southern Europe, unlike Brooke, who, for all his insistence on a Mediterranean strategy as the indispensable preliminary to *Overlord*, believed that only through the latter could the fighting power of the *Wehrmacht* be broken. As late as May 3rd, only a month before D-Day, Churchill had confided to the assembled Dominions' Prime Ministers that, if he had had his own way, the lay-out of the war would have been different and he would have rolled up Europe from the southeast to join hands with the Russians.[2] Yet, as always he accepted, and rose to, the challenge. At the first presentation of invasion plans on April 7th, General de Guingand noticed that when he spoke he at first appeared grave and tired but that " he finished with great strength." Five days later the Prime Minister wrote to Dill in Washington that he had " hardened very much upon *Overlord* and was further fortified by the evident confidence of Eisenhower, Brooke and Montgomery." " I am in this thing with you to the end," he told Eisenhower on May 8th, his eyes filling with tears, " and, if it fails, we will go down together."[3]

On May 30th—five days before the night fixed for the airborne landings and the invasion armada's approach to the beaches—the Allied Air Commander-in-Chief, Sir Trafford Leigh-Mallory, wrote to warn General Eisenhower that the American airborne divisions, which under Montgomery's plan were to be flown in full moonlight at only a thousand feet across the Cherbourg peninsula, would probably be annihilated by anti-aircraft fire. He had already represented the danger of the plan to Montgomery but, having failed to shake his conviction, felt it his duty to warn the Supreme Commander. The latter, whose moral stature grew as the hour for attack approached, replied that the operation was so essential that it must be carried out at whatever cost. For unless the airborne divisions

[1] Prime Minister to Dominions Secretary, 25 Jan., 1944. *Churchill* V, 602.
[2] *Ehrman* V, 555.
[3] *Ehrman* V, 574-5; *Butcher*, 458.

could secure the causeways through the inundations that the Germans had made behind their coastal defences, the American forces landing on the Allies' right would be penned in a narrow strip between the floods and the sea and be unable to strike across the peninsula to cut off Cherbourg—the deep-water port on whose capture the future break-out depended.

Grave as were the risks of battle, there was another factor even less predictable. The three airborne divisions that were to drop behind the coast on the night before invasion required darkness for their approach and a moon to identify their targets. Since only a tide that reached half-flood forty minutes after first light—the minimum period needed by the bombarding naval and air forces to immobilize the coast defences—could bring the assault-craft and swimming tanks ashore short of the underwater obstructions without exposing the infantry and the engineers who were to demolish these to a fatally long advance across fire-swept beaches, there were only three days in each lunar month when the exact combination of moon and tide made it practicable to land at all. And unless advantage could be taken of the first of these periods—from June 5th to 7th—it was doubtful whether there would be time either to build up strength enough to break out of the bridgehead before the winter or to forestall the now imminent attack on London and the invasion ports that the enemy was known to be about to launch with his secret weapons.

Throughout May the weather had been perfect, with almost continuous sunshine and calm seas and skies. But on the last day of the month there were disquieting signs over the Azores and on the morning of June 1st a slight drizzle in the Channel. By the evening of the 3rd—thirty-six hours before the landing-hour—three depressions were approaching from the Atlantic, and high winds with continuous low cloud were predicted for the 5th, 6th and 7th. Postponement seemed inevitable and on the morning of Sunday the 4th, when the troops were already embarked, the operation was put off for twenty-four hours. But that night, when Eisenhower and the three Commanders-in-Chief again met the meteorologists, though a storm was raging in the Channel there seemed a hope that by the 6th the wind would have abated sufficiently to make a landing possible. When the likelihood of this unexpected let-up was confirmed at four next morning the Supreme Commander, backed by Ramsay and Montgomery, ordered the invasion fleet to sea. Brooke's diary refers only briefly to this episode.

" *Sunday, June 4th.* Cross-Channel operation was to have started on the night 4/5th, but the weather was too bad, strong wind and low clouds. The operation therefore had to be put off, which is most regrettable. I had intended returning on Sunday evening, but stopped on as the operation was put off. Winston meanwhile has taken to his train and is touring the Portsmouth area. . . ."[1]

' This prolonged waiting period before the operation was shattering. I remember having all the same feelings as I used to get before starting a point-to-point race, an empty feeling at the pit of one's stomach and a continual desire to yawn.'

" *June 5th.* Left early, news having been received on previous evening that we were in Rome."

" Winston had returned on Sunday evening in a very highly-strung condition. He invited the Chiefs of Staff to lunch. I found him over-optimistic as regards prospects of the cross-Channel operation and tried to damp him down a bit. Similarly in Italy he now believes that Alex will wipe out the whole of the German forces."

" A long Cabinet at which it was explained how troublesome de Gaulle was being now that he had been fetched back from Algiers. He is refusing to broadcast unless Eisenhower alters the wording of his own broadcast. . . ."

" It is very hard to believe that in a few hours the cross-Channel invasion starts. I am very uneasy about the whole operation. At the best it will fall so very far short of the

---

[1] ' He had done his best to be on board a cruiser that night to participate in the operations. He never breathed a word about this plan to me, knowing full well that I would not encourage it. Thank Heaven the King used his authority to stop him.' *Notes on My Life* XIII, 54.

expectation of the bulk of the people, namely all those who know nothing about its difficulties. At the worst it may well be the most ghastly disaster of the whole war. I wish to God it were safely over."

' I knew too well all the weak points in the plan of operations. First of all the weather on which we were entirely dependent; a sudden storm might wreck it all. Then the complexity of an amphibious operation of this kind, when confusion may degenerate into chaos in such a short time, the difficulty of controlling the operation once launched, lack of elasticity in the handling of reserves, danger of leakage of information with consequent loss of essential secrecy.'

' Perhaps one of the most nerve-racking experiences when watching an operation like this unroll itself is the intimate knowledge of the various commanders engaged. Too good a knowledge of their various weaknesses makes one wonder whether in the moments of crisis facing them they will not shatter one's hopes.'

' To realise what it was like living through those agonizing hours, the background of the last three years must be remembered. All those early setbacks, the gradual checking of the onrush, the very gradual turn of the defensive to the offensive, then that series of Mediterranean offensives alternately leading up to this final all-important operation which started in the early hours of next morning.'

That night Brooke received a letter from Montgomery. " I would like to thank you personally," he wrote,

" for your kindly help and guidance during the past five months. It has not been an easy time—for anyone. My great desire throughout has been to justify your confidence in me and not to let you down and I hope I have been able to do this to your satisfaction."

" I cross over to France to-morrow night—if all goes well —and may not see you again."

" So good-bye and good luck."

The die had been cast and a few hours later the operation on which the fate of the war depended had started.

" *June 6th*. By 7.30 a.m., I began to receive first news of the invasion. The airborne landings had been successful, the first waves were reported as going in, opposition not too serious, batteries firing from flanks, etc."

" Throughout the day information has come in. On the British front the landing has gone well and the whole of three divisions are ashore. On the American front the western landing was a success, but the eastern Corps has failed practically along its whole front. They are now asking to land on our western beaches. This will probably have to be done, but must inevitably lead to confusion on the beaches."

" It has been very hard to realise all day that whilst London went on calmly with its job, a fierce conflict was being fought at a close distance on the French coast."

At the end of that first critical day the news was better than had seemed possible when the weather closed in on the Channel at the week-end, though it was less good than had been hoped. Complete surprise had been achieved, partly because the gale that had postponed the landing had given the German Command a false sense of security. The preliminary sea and air bombardment and the specialized armour and swimming tanks that had landed with the infantry had been brilliantly successful, while the *Luftwaffe* had been swept from the skies, and at sea enemy interference had been negligible. The British had made firm lodgments in all their three sectors, penetrating inland at some points for five or six miles. Their airborne division had achieved nearly all its objectives, including the capture of the Orne bridges and of a precarious bridgehead beyond, thus giving protection to the vulnerable eastern flank where the German armoured counter-attack was expected. But it had still to be relieved by the seaborne infantry and had had to fight grimly all day to hold its positions, while an attempt

NORMANDY

to seize Caen—the all-important road centre through which the Panzers would have to move in for the kill—and the airfields beyond had failed. And though, despite delays, the British had taken most of their D-Day objectives, the Americans on the western flank had been less fortunate. One of their two landings had nearly ended in disaster, and for several hours the troops had been pinned down on the beaches. At the end of the day the beachhead here was still little more than a thousand yards deep and cut off both from the British to the east and the rest of the Americans to the west. With unloading everywhere from eight to twelve hours behind schedule because of the weather, everything turned on the speed and strength of the enemy's counter-attack and the weight of armour he could throw against the still confused forces in the isolated bridge-heads.[1]

" *June 7th*. The invasion is a day older. I am not very happy about it. The American V Corps seems to be stuck. We are not gaining enough ground and German forces are assembling fast. I do wish to Heaven that we were landing on a wider front."

" News from Alexander continues to be excellent, he is all for dashing off to the Pisa-Rimini line. And I have been trying to induce him to send something to Ancona as he moves up."

" *June 8th*. From 7.30 to 12 noon we had our usual C.O.S. meeting and a meeting with the Planners. We then went to meet Winston to discuss future plans. He had put forward a paper with much too early plans for operations on the west coast of France with troops from Italy. But

---

[1] Of that critical day Montgomery wrote afterwards: " The first vital moment in the battle was, I think, on the afternoon and evening of D-Day when the left American Corps had a beachhead of only 1000 yards after fighting all day. Other parts of the lodgment area were not linked up, and we were liable to defeat in detail. The answer to invasion across the sea is a strong counter-attack on the afternoon of D-Day when the invading force has not proper communications and has lost certain cohesion. That was Rommel's chance. It was not taken, and we were given time to recover—thank goodness! If you saw Omaha beach you would wonder how the Americans ever got ashore." Gen. Montgomery to C.I.G.S., 13 June, 1944. Lord Alanbrooke, *Personal Files*.

we *must* first see what happens to our cross-Channel operation and what the final stage of Alex's offensive leads to. In any case we must go on smashing up the German forces in Italy up to the Pisa-Rimini line."

By that night the advance guard in Normandy had completed the first phase of its operation. By the junction of the British right with the American left the Allies, with nearly a quarter of a million men already ashore, controlled a continuous thirty-mile stretch of coast to a depth of from five to ten miles. Caen and the airfields beyond were still uncaptured and there was a solid enemy bloc between the two halves of Bradley's American army, whose first objective, the isolation of the Cherbourg peninsula and the capture of Cherbourg, depended on their junction. But owing to the vigour with which the British and Canadians were pressing their southward offensive towards Caen and into the wooded hinterland across the Caen-Bayeux road, the Germans—prevented from concentrating by continuous air attack on their communications—were being forced, as Montgomery intended, to commit their reserves piecemeal in order to hold his left thrust and so were unable either to interfere with the Americans to the west or to mount the major armoured counter-attack the invaders feared. Nor, because Hitler and the High Command believed that a further landing was imminent north of the Seine, had any move been made as yet by the powerful German forces in the Pas de Calais.

" *June 9th.* The news from France is better. The XXX British and V American Corps have now joined up together. However, I am not yet entirely satisfied with the situation and wish the American front would join up and become a connected whole."

" At 7.30 went to Euston station to meet Marshall, King and Arnold who had flown over from Washington. Then back to flat where Crerar had come to dine with me. We had an excellent talk prior to his going over to France with his Army H.Q."

" *June 10th.* American Chiefs of Staff came to meet us at 11.30 a.m. and stopped till 1.30 p.m. We had a general review of the whole front."

" Before that the P.M. had called me up, stating he proposed to visit Monty on Monday and wanted me to come with him. Smuts also coming. We are to leave by train on Sunday night and make an early start by destroyer on Monday."[1]

" *Sunday, June 11th.* Left home at 12 noon to lunch with American Chiefs of Staff at Stanwell Place, near Staines. After lunch we had a combined conference lasting till 5.30 p.m. Decided Italian campaign to stop at Apennines or Pisa-Rimini line, and an amphibious operation to be prepared to land either in Southern France or in Bay of Biscay, depending on situation prevailing at that time. It was interesting to listen to Marshall explaining *now* why the Germans fought in Central Italy! He seemed to forget that I had given him all these arguments several months ago as a prediction of what I was convinced would happen. . . ."

' Now at last we had put the South France operation in its right strategic position. By the time we reached the Pisa-Rimini line, the Italian theatre should have played its part in holding German reserves away from Northern France. We could then contemplate the landing in Southern France to provide a front for French forces from North Africa and to co-operate on southern flank of *Overlord* operations. The Bay of Biscay landings did not attract me.'

That Sunday morning's meeting between the British and American Chiefs of Staff was more amicable than would have

[1] On receipt of this information Montgomery sent a telegram to Brooke: " Note that you and P.M. coming over Monday 12th June. Will meet you and give you full picture. Roads not — repeat not — 100% safe owing to enemy snipers, including women. Much enemy bombing between dusk and dawn. Essential P.M. should go only where I take him, and you must get away from here in early evening. Am very satisfied with progress of operations." Gen. Montgomery to C.I.G.S., 10 June, 1944. Lord Alanbrooke, *Personal Files.*

seemed possible two months earlier when, disgusted by their Allies' refusal to bind themselves to a firm date for *Anvil*, the Americans had withdrawn their offer of additional landing-craft for the Mediterranean. Not only had the latter's suspicions of British half-heartedness over the liberation of Western Europe been disproved by events, but in the last week of April, while Brooke was on leave, the Prime Minister had succeeded in his persistent attempts to get Washington to reconsider its decision in the light of the changed conditions brought about by the postponement of Alexander's offensive. By advancing as an alternative to a belated *Anvil* his earlier project of a landing on the South-west coast of France—Operation *Caliph*—to aid the break-out from the Normandy bridgehead, he had caused Admiral King, who liked bold amphibious operations, to renew his offer of assault shipping from the Pacific provided London agreed to an invasion of either Southern or South-Western France in the latter part of the summer. As a result of talks between General Wilson and the British Chiefs of Staff early in May, detailed plans had been approved for mounting one or other of four alternative landings—the destination to be decided in the light of the Italian campaign—on the coasts either of Southern France or Italy. With this King and his colleagues had declared themselves satisfied and promised to make available, before July 20th, nineteen tank landing-ships and an equal number of tank landing-craft.

.   .   .   .

With Rome now in Allied hands and the German forces in Italy in full retreat and, as was hoped, in danger of annihilation, there seemed nothing that Sunday to prevent agreement between the Allies as to the utilization of their Mediterranean resources after the end of Alexander's victorious campaign. Four days earlier the latter had reported to the C.I.G.S. that of the twenty German divisions formerly standing south of Rome only six remained and that Kesselring's forces would be unable to hold the Pisa-Rimini line—which Alexander expected to attack in another fortnight—without at least ten fresh divisions.[1] The only question to decide was where, after victory in Italy was complete, the Allied force in the South could be best employed. In this mood of hope and concord the Combined Chiefs rose from their conference at Stanwell Place that evening and prepared for their visit to Normandy, where the situation, especially on the American front, was improving fast, with 326,000 men, 54,000 vehicles and 100,000 tons of stores already ashore.

"*June 12th. I set foot in France again.* At 10.15 p.m. last night I left the flat and drove to Ascot station where I picked up the P.M.'s train. I found him with Smuts and the American Chiefs of Staff finishing dinner. We got off to bed at a fairly reasonable time as we had to leave the train at 7.30 a.m. to catch the destroyer *Kelvin* and leave Portsmouth at 8 a.m. Americans had already started in a separate party."

"We had a very comfortable journey over and most interesting. We continually passed convoys of landing-craft, mine-sweepers, bits of floating breakwater (Phoenixes) being towed out, parts of the floating piers (Whales), etc., and, overhead, a continuous flow of aeroplanes going to and coming from France. About 11 a.m. we approached the French coast and the scene was beyond description. Everywhere the sea was covered with ships of all sizes and shapes, and a scene of continuous activity. We passed through rows and rows of anchored tank landing-ships and finally came to a ' Gooseberry', namely a row of ships sunk in a half crescent to form a sort of harbour and provide protection from the sea. Here we were met by Admiral Vian, who took us in his Admiral's barge from which we changed into a ' DUKW'. This ran us straight on to the beach and up another road. It was a wonderful moment to find myself re-entering France almost exactly four years after being thrown out, for the second time, at

[1] *Ehrman* V, 266-7. Of his own troops Alexander wrote: " Neither the Apennines nor even the Alps should prove a serious obstacle to their enthusiasm and skill." See also *idem* 345.

St. Nazaire. Floods of memories came back of my last trip of despair, and those long four years of work and anxiety at last crowned by the success of a re-entry into France."

" Monty met us on the beach with a team of jeeps which we got into and drove off on the Courseulles-Bayeux road to about half-way to the latter place. There we found Monty's H.Q. and he gave us an explanation on the map of his dispositions and plans. All, as usual, wonderfully clear and concise. We then had lunch with him and my thoughts wandered off to four years ago when I was at Le Mans and Laval waiting for Monty and his 3rd Division to join me. I knew then that it would not be long before I was kicked out of France if I was not killed or taken prisoner, but if anybody had told me then that in four years I should return with Winston and Smuts to lunch with Monty commanding a new invasion force, I should have found it hard to believe."

" After lunch we drove round to ' Bimbo ' Dempsey's H.Q. I was astonished to see how little affected the country had been by the German occupation and five years of war. All the crops were good, the country fairly clear of weeds, and plenty of fat cattle, horses, chickens, etc. As usual, Winston described the situation in his inimitable way when driving with me. He said:—' We are surrounded by fat cattle lying in luscious pastures with their paws crossed! ' This is just the impression they gave one. And the French population did not seem in any way pleased to see us arrive as a victorious army to liberate France. They had been quite content as they were, and we were bringing war and desolation to the country."

" We then returned to Courseulles, having watched a raid by Hun bombers on the harbour, which did no harm. We re-embarked in Admiral Vian's barge and did a trip right along the sea-front, watching the various activities. We saw tank landing-craft unloading lorries, tanks, guns, etc., on to the beaches in a remarkably short time. We then went to the new harbour being prepared west of

Hamel. There we saw some of the large ' Phoenixes ' being sunk into place and working admirably. Also ' Bombardons' to damp down waves, ' Whales ' representing wonderful floating piers, all growing up fast."

" Close by was a monitor with 14″ gun firing away into France. Winston said he had never been on one of His Majesty's ships engaging the enemy and insisted on going aboard. Luckily we could not climb up owing to seaweed on the bulges, as it would have been a very noisy entertainment had we succeeded. Then we returned to our destroyer and went right back to the east end of the beach where several ships were bombarding the Germans. Winston wanted to take part in the war and was longing to draw some retaliation. However, the Boche refused to take any notice of any of the rounds we fired. We therefore started back about 6.15 p.m. and by 9.15 p.m. were back in Portsmouth after having spent a wonderfully interesting day. We got on board the P.M.'s train where we found Marshall and King. We dined on the way back to London, where we arrived shortly after 1 a.m., dog-tired and very sleepy."

" *June 13th.* Last night the Germans used their pilotless planes for the first time, but did little damage. Cherwell and Duncan Sandys came to the C.O.S. meeting when we discussed action to take, and we decided that we must not let defence interfere with the French battle."[1]

" At 11.30 a.m. American Chiefs came and we had a Combined meeting when we drew up Directives for Wilson and Eisenhower. We settled to limit advance in Italy to the Apennines and to prepare for amphibious operations of a three-division lift for either Bay of Biscay, Western Mediterranean or Adriatic. Decision as to which to do to depend on course of events."

[1] On the previous day, depressed by the Allies' expansion of their bridgehead, Keitel, Jodl and Doenitz in conference at Berchtesgaden had expressed the hope that the bombardment of London by flying bombs would cause them to attempt a second and unsuccessful landing in the Pas de Calais and so relieve the pressure in Normandy. *Wilmot*, 316-17.

" In afternoon Cabinet at 6 p.m. to discuss relaxation of various security measures which had been brought into force during the period prior to cross-Channel operations."

The Directive which, as a result of that morning's meeting, the Combined Chiefs of Staff sent to the Supreme Commander Mediterranean, read:

". . . The overriding necessity is to apply all our forces to the enemy, at the earliest possible moment, in the best way calculated to assist the success of Operation *Overlord*.

" We must complete the destruction of the German Armoured Forces in Italy south of the Pisa-Rimini line. No Allied forces should be withdrawn from the battle that are necessary for this purpose.

" When we have reached the Pisa-Rimini line, three possible courses of action will be open to us:

  (*a*) an amphibious operation against the South of France;
  (*b*) an amphibious operation against the West of France;
  (*c*) an amphibious operation at the head of the Adriatic;

" We cannot make the final choice from among these three courses at the moment. Which will pay us best depends on several factors, at present unknown, such as:

  (*a*) the progress of Operation *Overlord* with the forces now assigned to it.
  (*b*) The direction and degree of success of the forthcoming Russian offensive.[1]
  (*c*) the German reactions to (*a*) and (*b*) above.

" The one factor common to all three courses is an amphibious operation, and the Combined Chiefs of Staff have decided to go forward forthwith with preparations on the greatest scale for which these resources can be provided and at the earliest date. . . . The Combined Chiefs of Staff would

[1] Promised by Stalin at Teheran and confirmed on April 25th and, in a congratulatory telegram to the Prime Minister, on D-Day. A subsidiary offensive in the Leningrad area had begun on June 11th, but the main attack in the centre was delayed by weather till the 23rd.

observe on the choice of a plan that they are not inclined to favour landing in the area of Marseilles because of the strength of the coastal defences and the unprofitable line of advance up the Rhône valley. The operation in France most likely to help Operation *Overlord* appears to them to be either a landing initially at Sète designed to lead to the early capture of Bordeaux and to the support of the guerrillas in Southern France or a direct descent on the west coast of France so as either to open a port through which to achieve a direct build-up from the U.S.A. or if necessary to afford direct support to the *Overlord* forces should they not be making sufficient progress."[1]

This Directive, a copy of which was sent to Eisenhower, made provision both for the Mediterranean landing which the Americans wished to make as soon as possible after mid-summer and for the prior destruction of the German forces now retreating up the leg of Italy, and for that freedom of action which was the essence of Alan Brooke's—and Britain's—strategy.

" *June 14th.* . . . A meeting with the American Chiefs of Staff in the afternoon which started at 2.30 and went on till 5 p.m. We discussed the Pacific and found that they were in agreement with a proposed strategy based on North-Western Australia and directed through Amboina towards Borneo."

" Dashed back to War Office to finish off work there; then on to 10 Downing Street for a dinner with P.M. attended by the King, Attlee, Lascelles, Marshall, King, Arnold, Cunningham, Portal, Ismay and self. The King, I think, enjoyed himself thoroughly and did not leave till 1.45 a.m."

" Winston began one of his long harangues stating that the Army was certain to crowd in ' dental chairs ' and Y.M.C.A. institutions instead of bayonets into the landing

---

[1] Combined Chiefs of Staff to Supreme Commander, Mediterranean, 13 June, 1944. *Ehrman* V, 268-9.

in France.[1] What we wanted, he said, were combatants and fighting men instead of a mass of non-combatants. We argued with him that fighting men without food, ammunition and petrol were useless, but he was not open to conviction. . . ."

"*June 15th.* Started C.O.S. meeting at 10.30 a.m. with the Planners discussing difficult man-power problems. Then at 11.30 Mr. Fraser came to discuss the future of the New Zealand force. He is all for joining with us in the offensive from North Australia."

"After lunch the American Chiefs of Staff again, this time to discuss Burma. It is quite clear in listening to Marshall's arguments and questions that he has not even now grasped the true aspects of the Burma campaign. After the meeting I approached him about the present Stilwell set-up, suggesting that it was quite impossible for him to continue to fill three jobs at the same time necessitating his being in three different locations, namely Deputy Supreme Commander to Mountbatten, Commander China Corps, and Chief of Staff to Chiang Kai-shek! Marshall flared up and said that Stilwell was a ' fighter ' and that is why he wanted him there, as we had a set of commanders who had no fighting instincts. . . . I found it quite useless to argue with him."

' Marshall had originally asked us to accept this Stilwell set-up to do him a favour, apparently as he had no one else suitable to fill the gaps. I was so enraged by his attitude that I had to break off the conversation to save myself from rounding on him and irreparably damaging our relations.'[2]

"Home to write up diary, and, whilst writing, a series

[1] " Mr. Churchill . . . complained about a new word that everyone was using that he did not understand. It was ' logistics,' which he rather preferred to call supplies, but the Combined Chiefs insisted that there was more to logistics than just supplies, for you had to plan what to have and when and where to have it and how to move it." *Whitehill*, 343.

[2] " It is odd," Dill wrote from Washington, " how that charming person Marshall can fly off the handle and be so infernally rude. Also he gets fixed ideas about things and people which it is almost impossible to alter." Field-Marshal Dill to C.I.G.S., 7 July, 1944. Lord Alanbrooke, *Personal Files.*

of German pilotless planes have come over. The second time we have had this form of entertainment."

" Monty seems to be meeting with more serious opposition and to have been suffering a series of heavy counterattacks, which so far he appears to have resisted."

That day Brooke had received a long letter from Montgomery. It had been written at intervals during the fighting on June 13th and 14th, and described his operations towards Caen and to the west of it, where the Germans, using ideal defensive country, were fiercely resisting the British and Canadians. At that time the Americans, by taking Carentan, had effected a link between the two halves of their army, only to lose it again on the 13th, before finally recapturing it on the 14th. " We are in a very reasonable position in Second British Army," Montgomery wrote:

" 12,000 tons came in through the beaches yesterday. The American situation is not so good. They are roughly 50% behind in all unloading, i.e. they have only on shore half the maintenance stores they should have. There are a great many ships off the beaches, but no one knows what is in them; the Americans have no Movement Staff, which is a weak point in their organization. . . . They are back again in Carentan, thank God! I see S.H.A.E.F. communiqué said yesterday that the town had been liberated. Actually it has been completely flattened and there is hardly a house intact; all the civilians have fled. It is a queer sort of liberation."

Later in the day he had written again,

". . . When 2nd Panzer Division suddenly appeared in the Villers-Bocage-Caumont area, it plugged the hole through which I had broken. I think it had been meant for offensive action against I Corps in the Caen area. So long as Rommel uses his strategic reserves to plug holes, that is good. Anyhow, I had to think again, and I have got to be careful not to get off balance."[1]

[1] Gen. Montgomery to C.I.G.S. 14 June, 1944. Lord Alanbrooke, *Personal Files.*

Brooke's diary continued:

" *June 16th.* Chief of Naval Staff and Chief of Air Staff were away from C.O.S. meeting, having gone to France. Main topic was pilotless planes which have at last started their attacks on this country. At 11.45 Cabinet meeting to discuss the same subject. This resulted in a staff meeting with P.M. at 5 p.m. attended by Tedder, Hill, Pile, three Chiefs of Staff. Again very few real decisions were arrived at. In my mind three essentials stand out:—

(*a*) attacks by what can be spared from *Overlord* on launching-sites.

(*b*) barriers of fighters, guns and balloons in succession south of London.

(*c*) no sirens and no guns in London!

" We shall, I hope, eventually get these but it will take time. . . ."

" *June 19th.* Arrived up early to find that a pilotless plane had struck the Guards' Chapel, Wellington Barracks, during Sunday Service and had killed about sixty people. Amongst them to my great grief was Ivan Cobbold. And on my writing-table was a letter from him written on Saturday. I cannot get him and poor Blanche out of my mind."

" Hungerford Bridge had also been hit, and most of the windows of the War Office blown in again."

" News from France is good. The Cherbourg peninsula has been cut off by the Americans."

" This afternoon at 5 p.m. conference with the P.M., attended by most of the Air Defence of Great Britain, to decide how to attack the problem of pilotless planes which are from now on to be called flying-bombs. After that, long Cabinet at which Winston was in very good form, quite ten years younger, all due to the fact that the flying-bombs have again put us into the front line."

" *June 20th.* A careful review of the flying-bombs at the C.O.S. meeting. We are fitting up a row of butts for A.A.

guns south of London, with balloons behind them, and fighter aircraft in front. I think we shall be able to build up some form of protection."

" Fighting in Cherbourg goes on well."

" *June 21st.* . . . A large bunch of flying-bombs last night. I did not miss one by more than some twenty minutes on Constitution Hill."

" At 2.45 p.m. a meeting with the P.M. and Smuts. P.M. wanted Smuts to put before us his ideas for the prosecution of the war after clearing the Pisa-Rimini line in Italy. Were we to head for Vienna according to Alexander or were we to launch another expedition into France? Although Smuts liked the idea of Vienna, he considered it would be better to remove a force from Italy and launch a new cross-Channel expedition across the Calais Narrows. He was evidently oblivious of the fact that the port capacity of this country will not support another expedition, that the shipping could not be found, and that, if both these difficulties could be overcome, we should arrive too late in the year to count on suitable weather. . . . We were kept till 4.45 p.m."

" As soon as I sat down to dinner, P.M. called up asking me to come round to meet him and Eden and Macmillan to discuss plans for the war in Italy."

.   .   .   .

After his argument with Brooke over Burma on June 15th, General Marshall, accompanied by the American Chief of Army Air Staff, Arnold, had left England for North Africa and Italy. Here he had become involved in a new dispute with the Supreme Commander, Mediterranean, General Maitland Wilson. Conscious that Kesselring's defeated army, hastily reinforced by eight divisions from Northern Europe and Russia, was putting up a much stiffer resistance to Alexander's pursuing forces than the latter had expected, Wilson was now in favour of the third of the three options proposed by the Combined Chiefs of Staff—a landing at the head of the

Adriatic to threaten the German flank and rear. This and Alexander's hopes of breaking through the Ljubljana Gap into the Hungarian plain aroused all Marshall's old suspicions of Britain's Balkan designs. Prompted by Eisenhower, who was growing increasingly afraid of a stalemate in France, he insisted that a successful invasion of Germany must depend on the capture of deep-water ports in the South of France to supply the forty or fifty divisions now waiting in the United States to sail for Europe. The conflict between the British and American views of the Mediterranean war was thus resumed. On the 19th Wilson informed the Chiefs of Staff that Alexander's forces could not maintain the momentum of their attack if seven divisions were withdrawn for *Anvil* and that, in his opinion, Marshall's preoccupation with the logistics of invading Germany in 1945 was endangering the chance of bringing her down in 1944.

This view received the enthusiastic support of the Prime Minister. What, however, most concerned the C.I.G.S., who did not believe that an advance through the Ljubljana Gap was at present practicable, was the effect that an intensification of the fighting in Italy was likely to have on the summer campaign in France and in Russia, where the Red Army had just opened a major offensive against the already depleted and overstrained German lines. For he was certain, as he had always been, that so long as he was subjected to pressure in Italy, Hitler would reinforce his troops there, even at the expense of more important fronts nearer the heart of the Reich. It was the American Chiefs of Staff's inability to see what a trap, given Hitler's congenital inability to yield ground, Italy constituted to the German Army that, as always, baffled Brooke. Marshall, on the other hand, continued to maintain that the Germans, if strongly attacked in the Apennines, would " withdraw to the Alps without contesting the Po Valley ", and so leave Alexander " beating at the air ".

" *June 22nd*. Gammell, Wilson's Chief of Staff, attended our C.O.S. meeting together with the planners, and we examined Alexander's hopes of an advance on Vienna and all the other alternatives. . . ."

" Am now off for one of the P.M.'s 10.30 p.m. meetings. Eden and Macmillan are to be present. We are to discuss Italian strategy."

" *June 23rd*. We had a long evening of it listening to Winston's strategic arguments. In the main he was for supporting Alexander's advance on Vienna. I pointed out that, even on Alex's optimistic reckoning, the advance beyond the Pisa-Rimini line would not start till after September; namely, we should embark on a campaign through the Alps in winter. It was hard to make him realise that, if we took the season of the year and the topography of the country in league against us, we should have three enemies instead of one. We were kept up till close on 1 a.m. and accomplished nothing."

" As soon as I got to bed flying-bombs came over in a constant stream for the next two hours. Finally the remnants of the night were spoilt by an early telephone call."

" Cherbourg going rather slowly; Alex's advance also slowed up."

" *June 24th*. . . . Winston called me up after dinner to tell me that he had written a new paper on the policy to pursue in North Italy; he was very excited about it."

" *Sunday, June 25th*. Spent quietly at home except for another long talk (on the scrambler) with Winston all about our future policy in Italy and of not depriving Alex of the troops required for his victory. Had to sit up till 12.30 a.m. awaiting Winston's new paper."

" *June 26th*. Arrived up at 9.15 a.m. Masses of telegrams and Minutes in spite of having had a dispatch-rider on the previous evening. Then C.O.S. meeting at which we had to draft a reply to Americans and deal with P.M.'s paper. We are up against the same trouble again, namely saving Alexander from being robbed of troops in order to land in

Southern France. We shall have great difficulty with Americans, especially as Alex keeps on talking about going to Vienna."

" We all had to lunch with Winston and talked shop all the time. Then again had another meeting with him at 6 p.m., which lasted till 8 p.m., to get him to pass our reply to the Americans. All went well, and the reply has now gone but will lead to lots of trouble with our American friends."

" *June 27th*. Rather a troublesome night with a series of flying-bombs coming over between midnight and 3 a.m. One close one made me get out of bed and prepare to get under."

" We had a long C.O.S. meeting, with Lord Cherwell and Duncan Sandys there, discussing how to handle the flying-bomb trouble. The danger really lies in the rocket with the five-ton war-head starting."

" Cabinet at 6 p.m. which lasted to just on 9 p.m. . . ."

" *June 28th*. This morning the American reply to our wire arrived, a rude one at that! They still adhere to *Anvil* being carried out and want it at once. They argue that we have derived benefit out of the Italian campaign in spite of the fact that they were always opposed to it, but state that the reason for its success is attributable to Hitler's error in deciding to fight for Southern Italy. They forget that this is exactly what we kept on telling them would happen."

" And now we have the most marvellous information indicating clearly the importance that Hitler attaches to Northern Italy, his determination to fight for it and his orders to hold a line south of the Pisa-Rimini line whilst this line is being developed. Kesselring's Army is now a hostage to political interference with military direction of operations. It would be madness to fail to take advantage of it and would delay the conclusion of the war."

" We spent most of the day drafting a reply, refusing

to withdraw forces at present for a landing in Southern France with the opportunities that lie in front of us. Winston is also sending a wire to the President backing up our message."

"Meanwhile the war goes well. Cherbourg has definitely fallen, the attack for Caen has started well, the Russian attacks are a great success, and the Imphal-Kohima road is open again."[1]

"*June 29th*. The P.M. has backed our telegram to the American Chiefs by one of his own to the President, which crossed one from the President and necessitated a further one to the P.M.! We are in for an all-in struggle with our American colleagues and I am frankly doubtful of the outcome of it all."

"This evening I collected Rollie at the Cavalry Club at 6 p.m. and we went to Kew Gardens. It was lovely and peaceful there; I felt it was just what I wanted. Work, troubles, difficulties, differences of opinion, etc., had begun to make life jangle badly. Kew Gardens and contact with God through nature put all at rest again."

"*June 30th*. The President's reply had arrived in the night. It is an interesting document, as it is not till you get to the last paragraph that you get to the basic reason for the opinions expressed; owing to the coming Presidential Election it is impossible to contemplate any action with a Balkan flavour on its strategic merits. The situation is full of difficulties; the Americans now begin to own the major strength on land, in the air and on the sea.[2] They, therefore, consider that they are entitled to dictate how their forces are to be employed. We shall be forced into carrying

---

[1] Since the early spring the British forces guarding the Assam frontier had been engaged in a desperate struggle to repel a Japanese invasion of India. The defence of Kohima and a long ding-dong fight on the Imphal plain, in which the defenders were supplied and reinforced from the air, had proved too much for the invaders, and by the beginning of the last week of June the latter were in full retreat, leaving thousands of dead. It had been a wonderful month of triumph for the British Army, with victories in Italy, Normandy and India.

[2] By July 1944 the Americans had between eleven and twelve million men in arms; the British, with a third of their population, only five million. *Ehrman* VI, 18.

out an invasion of Southern France, but I am not certain that this need cripple Alexander's power to finish crushing Kesselring. I am just off now to a 10 p.m. meeting with Winston to try and arrive at a final decision. He has ordered the ' Clipper ' and the ' York ' to stand by, so we may be flying off to Washington before we are much older, but I doubt it. I think Winston will realise there is nothing more to be gained by argument."

" It is very unfortunate that Alex and Winston ever started their scheme about going to Vienna. This has made our task with the Americans an impossible one. . . ."

" *Later*. Just back from meeting with Winston. I thought at first we might have trouble with him; he looked like wanting to fight the President. However, in the end we got him to agree with our outlook, which is:— ' All right, if you insist on being damned fools, sooner than fall out with you, which would be fatal, we shall be damned fools with you, and we shall see that we perform the role of damned fools damned well! ' "

" We left Winston with ' Pug ' drafting a telegram which we are to see to-morrow morning and discuss with him at 11 a.m."

" *July 1st*. C.O.S. met at 10.30 a.m. to discuss P.M.'s proposed wire to President deciding to accept their decision to do *Anvil*. At 11 a.m. we met the P.M. and told him of the minor amendments which were wanted. He was in a good mood and they all went through easily."

" *Sunday, July 2nd*. Wire came back from President agreeing and asking for a Directive to be sent to Wilson. Also sent wire to Alex yesterday to come home."

" *July 3rd*. Americans started attack from Cherbourg southward. Flying-bombs becoming more serious danger and likely to encroach on our war effort if we are not careful. At 5.30 p.m. the record longest Cabinet meeting which lasted till 9.15 p.m. Winston wasted hours, and when we got on to flying-bombs subject he ran short of time. However, the threat is assuming dimensions which will require more drastic action."[1]

" *July 4th.* A long C.O.S. meeting attended by Duncan Sandys and Cherwell at which we discussed all the various measures for defeating flying-bombs. The fighter aircraft are not proving fast enough, the guns are not hitting them, the balloons may have their cables cut, the launching sites are not worth attacking with bombers, etc., etc. In fact, rather a gloomy and unsatisfactory meeting."

" Alexander had turned up early in the morning and I had two interviews with him. I told him that I felt he was missing his chances of smashing up Kesselring *before* he got back to the Pisa-Rimini line, and also that Oliver Leese was not providing the necessary hinge for the Eighth Army which remained continually behind the Americans and French. I am afraid Alex did not like this much, but it is desirable to make him face the facts confronting him instead of his dreams of an advance on Vienna."

" P.M. sent for me at 6.30 p.m., with all his spirit aroused, wishing to continue his arguments with the President and longing to have a good row with him. He has prepared a telegram and I only hope we succeed in stopping him from sending it."

" *July 5th.* Considerable excitement to-day preparing for details for Winston's speech on flying-bombs. We had to consider advisability of reprisals on small towns in Germany as a deterrent. Personally, I am dead against it. The Germans realise fully that we are at present devoting nearly 50% of our air effort in trying to stop these beastly bombs, added to which about 25% of London's production is lost through the results of the bombs. They won't throw away these advantages easily."

.   .   .   .

[1] 'There were no signs of London not being able to stand it, and, if there had been, it would only have been necessary to tell them that for the first time in history they could share the dangers their sons were running in France and that what fell on London was, at any rate, not falling on them.' *Notes on My Life*, XIII, 73.

On June 18th, in a Directive to his British and American Army commanders, Dempsey and Bradley, Montgomery had expressed the belief that Caen and Cherbourg would be captured by the 24th. " Once we can capture Caen and Cherbourg and all face in the same direction," he wrote, " we have a mighty chance—to make the German Army come to our threat and to defeat it between the Seine and the Loire." On the 26th Cherbourg had fallen. With the port in their hands the Americans were free to turn south towards St. Lô and their ultimate objective—the break-out down the western side of the Cotentin peninsula towards the Brittany ports to the south-west and Chartres and Paris to the east. But Caen—the nodal point on which the Allies' eastward wheel was to pivot—still remained untaken at the beginning of July, despite repeated British attempts to capture it both by frontal assault and by penetrating the difficult wooded hill country to the west and south-west of it. To this two things had contributed. One was the great storm, the worst June gale for forty years, which had swept the Channel on June 19th, stopping supplies and reinforcements for four days and leaving the Allies dangerously short of ammunition. The other was the policy of the German High Command—still convinced that the real threat was against the Falaise plain and the flying-bomb launching-sites to the north—of concentrating its armour against the British sector. Owing to Hitler's insistence on controlling even tactical movements from his remote East Prussian headquarters and his hysterical refusal to yield ground, every British advance had been followed by an instantaneous counter-attack and the use of strategic reserves to seal off penetrations. The result was that by the end of June nearly eight Panzer divisions—two-thirds of the enemy's armour in Western Europe—were concentrated on a twenty-mile front, almost entirely against the British.[1]

Though this involved a slight modification of his original plan, Montgomery remained confident. " If," he wrote to

[1] " My general broad plan is maturing. . . . All the decent enemy stuff, and his Pz. and Pz. S.S. divisions are coming in on the Second Army front—according to plan. That has made it much easier for the First U.S. Army to do its task." Gen. Montgomery to C.I.G.S., 27 June, 1944. Lord Alanbrooke, *Personal Files.*

Brooke, " we don't let go and avoid mistakes, we ought to be in a very good position in another week or two." He continued to keep the battle balanced and the initiative in his hands, and, as at Alamein and Mareth, to use the enemy's excessive resistance at one point to stretch and break his lines at another. Others watching the battle from England regarded Montgomery's failure to keep to his time-table as a sign that the offensive was flagging and that his plans had gone wrong. Haunted by the fear that the German wall of iron and fire round the still narrow bridgehead would harden until it became impregnable and that the autumn would see, not a break-out, but the resumption of the terrible static trench warfare that had cost the Western Allies so dear in the First World War, both the Supreme Commander and the Prime Minister, as well as many high-ranking British and American Army and Air Force officers at S.H.A.E.F., increasingly tended to attribute the slowness of the advance to Montgomery's caution and insistence on over-preparation and, in the case of some American observers, to Britain's reluctance to expose her dwindling man-power to casualties.[1]

" *July 6th.* At 10 p.m. we had a meeting with Winston which lasted till 2 a.m. He was very tired as a result of his speech in the House concerning the flying-bombs. As a result he was ready to take offence at anything. He began to abuse Monty because operations were not going faster, and apparently Eisenhower had said that he was over-cautious. I flared up and asked him if he could not trust his generals for five minutes instead of belittling them. He said that he never did such a thing. I then reminded him that in front of a large gathering of Ministers, he had torn Alexander to pieces for lack of imagination and leadership in continually attacking at Cassino. He was furious with me, but I hope it may do some good in the future."

---

[1] During the first six weeks of the invasion the Allies suffered more than a hundred thousand casualties, two-thirds of them American. *Figures brought back by C.I.G.S. from Normandy, 19th July,* 1944. Lord Alanbrooke, *Personal Files.*

" He then put forward a series of proposals, such as raising a Home Guard in Egypt to provide a force to deal with disturbances in the Middle East. It was not till after midnight that we got on to the subject we had come to discuss—the war in the Far East. Here we came up against all the old arguments that we have had put up by him over and over again. Attlee, Eden and Lyttelton were there. Fortunately they were at last siding with us against him. This infuriated him more than ever and he became ruder and ruder. He finished by falling out with Attlee and having a real good row with him concerning the future of India. We withdrew under cover of this smoke-screen just on 2 a.m., having accomplished nothing beyond losing our tempers and valuable sleep."

' I remember that evening as if it was yesterday. Winston had driven me to the verge of losing my temper in several meetings when he had poured abuse on Alex's head in front of Ministers. Although I had explained to him the whole of the topography of the front on a raised model, he kept on attacking Alex's plans of attack, his lack of ideas, his continuing to bump his head on the same spot, the incurring of casualties for no results, his lack of vision and many more failings. As most of the Ministers had little opportunity of judging for themselves and took all he said for gospel, there was every danger of their opinion of Alex being seriously affected.'

' When the whole process was starting again this evening with reference to Monty, although there were only three Ministers it was more than I could stand. I think what infuriated me most was that there had not been a single word of approval or gratitude for the excellent work Monty had done. I lost my temper and started one of the heaviest thunderstorms that we had had. He was infuriated, and throughout the evening kept shoving his chin out, looking at me and fuming at the accusation that he ran down his generals.'

'At one moment he turned to Eden to ask him if there was any foundation for such an accusation. I am glad to say that Eden agreed with me and said that he thought that what worried the C.I.G.S. was that Winston expressed views about generals that might be misinterpreted by Ministers who were not fully acquainted with the facts. This did not calm Winston much, and the lightning and thunder continued to crash, and fortunately from my point of view finally settled on the unfortunate Attlee.'

" *July 7th.* Started C.O.S. at 10 a.m. so as to attend Cabinet at 11 a.m. when Alexander gave an account of the operations in Italy. He did it very well."

" *July 8th.* Had rather a longer C.O.S. meeting than usual for a Saturday. After finishing office work drove Alexander down to Virginia Water which gave us a good chance for a talk. He is the most delightful person and most attractive, but I am afraid entirely innocent of any understanding of the politicians' methods. . . ."

" *July 9th.* A quiet but wet Sunday at home. Received news that Monty had taken Caen."[1]

" *July 10th.* A C.O.S. meeting again seriously preoccupied with flying-bombs. Also probable entry into the war of Turkey. Cabinet at 5.30 p.m. with P.M. in good and affable mood. And now we are faced with another of those 10.30 p.m. meetings! I only hope I shall not lose my temper this time."

" *Later.* 1 a.m. We have now finished our meeting. He was in a pleasant mood. We wandered like a swarm of bees from flower to flower, but never remained long enough at any flower to admit of any honey being produced. It was a blank evening as far as the formulating of plans went."

" *July 11th.* We had a long C.O.S. meeting with

[1] "9 July, 1944. Personal for C.I.G.S. from Gen. Montgomery. Leading troops of Second Army now in outskirts of Caen and pushing on to-night towards centre of city and the river lines." Lord Alanbrooke, *Personal Files.*

Cherwell and Duncan Sandys attending to discuss flying-bombs and rockets. The defence measures are making slow but steady progress. You came to lunch and we saw our first flying-bomb together."

" *July 12th.* The morning as usual filled with C.O.S. meeting, this time settling zones of occupation of Germany after the Armistice. The country to be divided into three zones, Eastern, North-Western and South-Western. The Russians take the Eastern, but we have a difference of opinion with the Americans as to the allocation of the two remaining ones."

' The difference lay in the fact that we wanted the North-Western zone, being the one nearest this country with all ports facing us. The Americans also wanted this zone, and it took us some time before we discovered that this choice was due to the President refusing to let American lines of communication run through a France ruled by de Gaulle. We solved this matter by offering the Americans lines of communication running through the North-Western sector.'

" *July 13th.* The capture of Amboina Island in the Pacific, and the military backing of Foreign Office policy in Greece, were the two topics of discussion at our C.O.S. meeting this morning. The Foreign Office, as I see it, is preparing to force on Greece a Government of their own selection and to support this Government with military power. I can foresee a very serious military commitment very rapidly increasing."

" At 6 p.m. one of Winston's conferences to stimulate construction of synthetic ports in Normandy."

" *July 14th.* We had a rushed C.O.S. meeting in order to meet the P.M. at 11.30 a.m. to discuss Pacific strategy with a view of arriving at a final solution. Attlee, Eden, Lyttelton were there as usual. We were there from 11.30 a.m. to 2 p.m. and settled nothing. We listened to all the P.M.'s arguments which we had listened to again and again. Both Attlee and Eden were against him."

" In the end I said to him:—' We have examined the two alternatives in great detail, we have repeatedly examined them for you, we have provided you with all possible information, and we are unanimous on our advice to you as to which course to select. They both have certain advantages, but in our minds we are quite clear as to which course we should select. However, we are clearer still that one or other course must be selected at once and that we cannot go on with this indecision. If the Government does not wish to accept our advice let them say so, but for Heaven's sake let us have a decision.' "

" He then said that he must go on thinking about it and would give us a decision within a week. I doubt it."

" In the evening motored out to Chequers for the night to meet Mr. Stimson (U.S. Secretary for War). Stafford Cripps also there; I like him more each time I meet him. Stimson quite finished and hardly able to take notice of what is going on round him. After dinner we had a film and a talk, and bed by 2 a.m."

" *July 17th.* A long C.O.S. meeting attended by Woodhouse[1] back from Greece. We were trying to decide policy as regards E.L.A.S. and whether time had come to denounce this organization. The whole future Greek policy is full of danger. . . ."

' I entirely shared the Foreign Office desire to avoid Greece falling into Communist hands. It would have been a great danger in the future for the Eastern Mediterranean. What frightened me was their light-hearted outlook on the affair. They talked of a couple of battalions being all that would be necessary to maintain law and order, whilst I knew that those two battalions would very soon grow into two divisions, and every division we had was required in Italy.'

" A Cabinet this evening lasting from 5.30 p.m. to 9 p.m. . . ."

[1] Col. the Hon. C. M. Woodhouse, commanding Allied Military Mission to Greek Communist organization, E.L.A.S., and its organized guerrillas—E.A.M.

" *July 18th*. We had a long meeting with Cherwell and Duncan Sandys at the C.O.S. meeting to discuss flying-bombs and measures to meet them. The rocket is becoming a more likely starter. The tendency is, of course, to try and affect our strategy in France and to direct it definitely against rocket sites. This will want watching carefully."

" *July 19th*. A nasty disturbed night with about a dozen flying-bombs in the vicinity. The nearest landed about 150 yards away at about 3 a.m. It displaced the window-frame of our sitting-room, and blew a lot of glass out of the surrounding houses."

" Got up intending to fly to see Monty, but could not make early start I had intended owing to heavy fog. Meanwhile at 9.30 P.M. sent for me. I found him in bed in a new blue and gold dressing-gown, but in an unholy rage! ' What was Monty doing dictating to him; he had every right to visit France when he wanted? Who was Monty to stop him? As Defence Minister he had full right to visit any front he wanted! Haig had always allowed him in the last war when he was Minister of Munitions. He would not stand it. He would make it a matter of confidence, etc., etc.' I found it hard to discover what the trouble was, or to put in a word edgeways. At last I discovered that Eisenhower had told him that Monty has asked not to have any visitors during the next few days, and the P.M. had argued out that Monty had aimed this restriction mainly at him. Nothing that I could say would make him believe otherwise. . . ."

" I assured him that I could put the whole matter right in five minutes with Monty and left him. I then went to C.O.S. meeting till 11.30 when I left for Northolt; there Tedder had very kindly lent me his plane in which I had an excellent crossing to an improvised landing-strip near Monty's H.Q. We arrived about 2 p.m."

" I had a long talk with Monty. First I put matter of P.M.'s visit right by getting Monty to write a note to P.M., telling him he did not know that he wanted to come and inviting him. Then warned him of tendency of P.M. to listen to suggestions that Monty played for safety and was not prepared to take risks. . . . I think these backgrounds may assist Monty. I found him in grand form and delighted with his success east of Caen."

" Left at 6.30 p.m.; back in Northolt aerodrome by 7.30 p.m. Drove round to leave Monty's letter with the P.M.; could not see him as he was asleep."

" Got back to flat to find a letter from Secretary of State showing that P.M. had been unbearable all day on the question of Monty trying to dictate to him. He (P.M.) had finally drafted a letter which he wanted S. of S. to send to Eisenhower notifying him of the intended visit of the P.M. and of the fact that he would not see Monty. S. of S. called me up on the telephone. I told him what I had done, and while we were talking he received a message from the P.M. stating that the letter to Eisenhower was not to be sent."

" Shortly afterwards P.M. called me up and said that he was delighted with Monty's letter and felt rather ashamed of himself for all he had said."

' Winston had never been very fond of Monty; when things went well he put up with him, when they did not he at once became " your Monty ". Just at this time Eisenhower had been expressing displeasure and accusing Monty of being sticky, of not pushing sufficiently on the Caen front with the British whilst he made the Americans do the attacking on the right. Winston was inclined to listen to these complaints.'

' When I saw Monty I asked him what he was doing stopping the P.M. from coming to France. He assured me that he was doing nothing of the kind. I then told him that whether he was or not did not matter, but the important thing was that the P.M. was certain he was.'

' Monty then told me that Stimson had visited Bradley's H.Q. and had remained with him so long that orders for an attack could not be got out, and the attack had to be postponed for twenty-four hours. Monty had therefore asked Ike to stop visitors for the present. This message had been passed on to the P.M. by Ike.'

' I, therefore, told Monty to go into his caravan and to write a letter to the P.M. on the following lines:—" The C.I.G.S. has just informed me that you are under the impression that I am trying to stop you from coming to France. This is the very last thing I should do, and I will always welcome your visits. I shall always have a caravan available for you, and if my duties prevent me from coming round with you personally, I shall always have a staff officer at your disposal. I only hope you will pay me a visit soon." '

' The letter worked like magic. I think Winston had forgotten that I had gone to France when he called up and said:—" I have had such a nice letter from Monty; he wants me to come to France whenever I like, he will meet me himself when he can, if not he will have a staff officer at my disposal, and he will also always have a caravan at my disposal." '

" *July 21st.* This morning when I turned on the 8 a.m. news I was astounded to hear of the attempt on Hitler's life, although this was exactly what I had been expecting for some time. It is hard at present to tell how serious the business may be and how it will ultimately turn out."

" A bad night with buzz-bombs, finishing off with one well within the quarter-mile radius of this flat."

" Maccready came to C.O.S. meeting and gave us latest Washington news, which included Marshall's reactions to our wire trying to cancel the Southern France invasion. Apparently he put it all down to Winston."

" A quiet interview with a long discussion with our Professor Ellis[1] about the impending rocket attacks. He is pretty certain they are coming and works the rocket out at some fifteen tons weight with a range of 160 miles. Not a pleasant prospect! "

[1] Sir Charles Ellis, Scientific Adviser to the Army Council.

" *July 23rd.* My birthday at which I became 61 years and almost felt like 71, as I started a heavy cold."

" *July 24th.* Poisonous cold with awful head which felt as if the top was going to blow off. Cabinet lasted from 6 p.m. to 8.45 p.m. and I did not think I could last it out and felt sick with headache. Just off to bed hoping for a good night, but the buzz-bomb alarm is just starting."

" *July 25th.* A very long drawn out Chiefs of Staff meeting. First of all with the Joint Intelligence report, and secondly Duncan Sandys and the ' professor '," (Lord Cherwell) " to discuss flying-bombs and rockets. The large rocket is now taking very definite shape and may be expected any day. Meanwhile flying-bombs have greatly decreased during the last twenty-four hours mainly due to the bombing of Courtrai."

" Weather at last a little better, and two new offensives started in Normandy."

Chapter Seven

THE BREAK OUT

*My general objective is to pull the Germans on to Second
Army so that First Army can extend and expand.*

GENERAL MONTGOMERY TO C.I.G.S.
11 June, 1944

THE NEW offensives to which Brooke referred in his diary
on July 25th—a Canadian attack along the Caen-
Falaise road and an American one southwards towards
the western base of the Cotentin peninsula—marked the culmination of the battle of the bridgehead which Montgomery
had been directing for the past seven weeks. They were the
prelude to the break-out on the American front which had
been his unchanging objective since he first formulated his
plans on taking command of the invasion land-forces in
January. His strategy, as he had explained it to his subordinates and chief again and again, was " to draw the main
enemy forces to battle on our eastern front and to fight them
there so that our attack on the western flank may proceed the
easier."

But General Eisenhower, though he had made himself
responsible for his lieutenant's strategy, never seems wholly to
have understood it. In the closing stages of the battle for
Caen he had written him a letter, which Montgomery at once
forwarded to Brooke, urging him to try to break out, not on
the American front but the British. " I am familiar," he
explained, " with your plans for generally holding firm with
your left, attracting thereto all of the enemy armour while
your right pushes down the peninsula and threatens the rear

238

and flank of the forces facing the Second British Army." None-the-less, the advance on the right had been slow and laborious and it seemed to him therefore that a determined effort was now necessary to prevent a stalemate and the necessity of fighting a major defensive battle in an insufficiently deep bridgehead. As the Allies had not yet attempted a major full-dress attack on the left flank, he suggested that this should now be made, supported by everything that could be brought to bear. " I will back you," he ended, " up to the limit in any effort you may decide upon to prevent a deadlock. . . . If you could use in your attack on your left flank an American armoured division I would be glad to make it available. . . . Please be assured that I will produce everything that is humanly possible to assist you in any plan that promises to get us the elbow room we need."[1]

To this Montgomery had replied on July 8th—the day before Caen fell—" I do not need an American armoured division for use on my eastern flank; we really have all the armour we need. The great thing now is to get First and Third U.S. Armies up to a good strength and to get them cracking on the southward front on the western flank and then to turn Patton westwards into the Brittany peninsula." Ten days earlier he had told Brooke of the difficulties he was having in getting the Americans to the positions from which their offensive was to be launched:

> " I tried very hard to get First U.S. Army to develop its thrust southward towards Coutances at the same time as it was completing the capture of Cherbourg. . . . But Bradley didn't want to take the risk; there was no risk really: quick and skilful regrouping was all that was wanted. . . . I have to take the Americans along quietly and give them time to get ready; once they are really formed up, then they go like

[1] Gen. Eisenhower to Gen. Montgomery, 7 July, 1944. *Pogue* 184-5; Lord Alanbrooke, *Personal Files*. " Ike has been smouldering and to-day burst out with a letter to Monty which, in effect, urges him to avoid having our forces sealed in the bridgehead, take the offensive, and Ike would support him in every way." Butcher, *Diary*, 520 (7 July, 1944).

hell. I have got to like them very much indeed, and once you get their confidence they will do anything for you."[1]

For though the thickly wooded, marshy bocage through which they were fighting towards the more open country to the south was harder even than that through which the British and Canadians were struggling south-west of Caen, Montgomery had no doubt of the Americans' ability to break the German lines when they were in position.[2] And having tied down Rommel's armour on his left, he knew that, once they were through, the enemy would be unable to hold them. " Of one thing you can be quite sure," he ended his letter to Eisenhower, " there will be no stalemate."

After the capture of Caen on July 9th, the British and Canadians had continued to pin down the German armour by attacks west of that city and along the Odon, while Bradley's army fought its way south towards the Périers-St. Lô road where its tanks could deploy for the break-through. " Once it can get a footing on the road," Montgomery wrote to Brooke on the 14th, " it will be able to launch a real ' blitz ' attack. . . . The time has arrived to deliver terrific blows designed to write off and eliminate the bulk of the enemy's holding troops. I doubt if he can collect more troops to rope us off again *in the west*, and it is in the west that I want territory."[3] " We require the Brittany ports," he wrote a week later, " so that we can develop the full resources of the Allies in Western Europe and we must get them soon."

But after July 18th, when the British and Canadians, after clearing the last suburbs of Caen, started a new offensive to the south-east and the Americans captured St. Lo, the operations of both armies were brought to a standstill by a week's continuous rain which turned the bocage into a quagmire and deprived them of the air support which was their trump card.

[1] Gen. Montgomery to C.I.G.S., 27 June, 1944. Lord Alanbrooke, *Personal Files*.
[2] On July 9th Rommel, asked how long the German front in the West could be held, replied, " At the most fourteen days to three weeks. Then the break-through may be expected. We have nothing more to throw in." *Speidel*, 123.
[3] Gen. Montgomery to C.I.G.S., 14 July, 1944. Lord Alanbrooke, *Personal Files*.

It was not till July 25th that Montgomery was able to launch the decisive blow on his right—Operation *Cobra* which was to lead to the capture of the Brittany ports and the sweep round the German left flank and rear towards Le Mans and the Seine. Preceded by a terrific air-bombardment, it was delivered that day and the next by the Americans in overwhelming strength on two sectors of a twenty-mile front. By the evening of the 26th, the way for Patton's armour was open. " The main blow of the whole Allied plan has now been struck on the western flank," Montgomery wrote; " that blow is the foundation of all our operations and it has been well and truly struck."

Yet this was the moment chosen by the Supreme Commander, still in England, to complain of his Commander-in-Chief to the Prime Minister. A week earlier Eisenhower had been reported by his naval aide-de-camp as being " blue as indigo over Monty's slowdown "; Montgomery, he declared, always stopped " to draw up his administrative tail ". During a flying visit to Normandy on July 25th and 26th, he was up and down the line, according to his Chief of Staff, " like a football-coach exhorting everyone to aggressive action "; what he wanted, Bedell Smith wrote, was " an all-out co-ordinated attack by the entire Allied Line which would at last put our forces in decisive motion ". " From one or two things Ike said yesterday when he was here," Montgomery reported to Brooke, " public opinion in America is asking why the American casualties are higher than the British and why they have captured so many more prisoners."[1]

Thus it came about that, while the German line was on the point of breaking and the American armour massed for the kill, Eisenhower appealed to the Prime Minister " to persuade Monty to get on his bicycle and start moving ".[2] Fortunately Churchill's earlier resentment against the British Commander-in-Chief had been dissipated by the C.I.G.S.'s prompt action

[1] Gen. Montgomery to C.I.G.S., 26th July, 1944. Lord Alanbrooke, *Personal Files*.
[2] *White House Papers*, II, 803.

on the 19th and by his own subsequent visit to Montgomery's headquarters. Brooke's diary records the sequel:

" *July 26th.* At 4 p.m. I was sent for by Winston and kept for an hour. Eisenhower had been lunching with him and had again run down Montgomery and described his stickiness and the reaction in the American papers. The old story again:—' H.Q. was sparing British Forces at the expense of the Americans, who were having all the casualties.' "

" However, Winston was in a good mood and receptive to argument. He even said that on all military matters I was his *alter ego*! In the end I was asked to dine to-morrow night to meet Eisenhower and Bedell Smith."

" Then at 6 p.m. a long Cabinet on man-power which lasted till 8.45 p.m., and at which nothing was settled . . ."

" *July 27th.* I have earned my pay to-day! Started with a very rushed hour examining telegrams and being briefed for C.O.S. meeting. At 10.30 attended C.O.S. meeting with Planners at which we discussed many papers of importance. Back to War Office to have an hour with Secretary of State discussing post-war policy in Europe. Should Germany be dismembered or gradually converted to an ally to meet the Russian threat of twenty years hence? I suggested the latter and feel certain that we must from now onwards regard Germany in a very different light. Germany is no longer the dominating power in Europe—Russia is. Unfortunately Russia is not entirely European. She has, however, vast resources and cannot fail to become the main threat in fifteen years from now. Therefore, foster Germany, gradually build her up and bring her into a Federation of Western Europe. Unfortunately this must all be done under the cloak of a holy alliance between England, Russia and America. Not an easy policy, and one requiring a super Foreign Secretary."

" After lunch long man-power meeting with Weeks and

Kennedy trying to organize post-war German forces. At 6 p.m. Cabinet meeting on German rockets and flying-bombs, which lasted till 8 p.m. Then dinner with P.M., Ike and Bedell Smith, intended to bring me closer to Ike and to assist in easy running between Ike and Monty. It did a lot of good. I have offered to go over with Ike if necessary to assist him in handling Monty.

" The strategy of the Normandy landing is quite straightforward. The British (on left) must hold and draw Germans on to themselves off the western flank whilst Americans swing up to open Brest peninsula. But now comes the trouble; the Press chip in and we hear that the British are doing nothing and suffering no casualties whilst the Americans are bearing all the brunt of the war."

" There is no doubt that Ike is all out to do all he can to maintain the best relations between British and Americans. But it is equally clear that Ike knows nothing about strategy. Bedell Smith, on the other hand, has brains, but no military education in its true sense. He is certainly one of the best American officers, but still falls far short when it comes to strategic outlook. With that Supreme Command set-up it is no wonder that Monty's real high ability is not always realised. Especially so when ' national ' spectacles pervert the perspective of the strategic landscape."

Next morning Brooke wrote to Montgomery about his talk with the Supreme Commander.

" The trouble between you and the P.M. has been satis-factorily settled for the present, but this other trouble I spoke to you about is looming larger still and wants watching very carefully.

" Ike lunched with P.M. again this week and as a result I was sent for by P.M. and told that Ike was worried at the outlook taken by the American Press that the British were not taking their share of the fighting and of the casualties.

There seemed to be more in it than that, and Ike himself seemed to consider that the British Army could and should be more offensive. The P.M. asked me to meet Ike at dinner with him, which I did last night; Bedell was there also."

" It is quite clear that Ike considers that Dempsey should be doing more than he does; it is equally clear that Ike has the very vaguest conception of war! I drew his attention to what your basic strategy had been, i.e. to hold with your left and draw Germans on to the flank whilst you pushed with your right. I explained how in my mind this conception was being carried out, that the bulk of the armour had continuously been kept against the British. He could not refute these arguments, and then asked whether I did not consider that we were in a position to launch major offensives on each front simultaneously. I told him that in view of the fact that the German density in Normandy was $2\frac{1}{2}$ times that on the Russian front whilst our superiority in strength was only in the nature of some 25% as compared to 300% Russian superiority on Eastern front, I did not consider that we were in a position to launch an all-out offensive along the whole front. Such a procedure would definitely not fit in with our strategy of mopping up Brest by swinging forward western flank."

" Evidently he has some conception of attacking on the whole front, which must be an American doctrine judging by Mark Clark with Fifth Army in Italy! However, unfortunately this same policy of attacking (or ' engaging the enemy ') along the whole front is one that appeals to the P.M. Ike may, therefore, obtain some support in this direction."

" I told Ike that, if he had any feelings that you were not running operations as he wished, he should most certainly tell you and express his views. That it was far better for him to put all his cards on the table and that he should tell you exactly what he thought. He is evidently a little shy of doing so. I suggested that if I could help him in any way by telling you for him I should be delighted. He said that he might perhaps ask me to accompany him on a visit to you! So if you see me turn up with him you will know what it is all about."

" Now, as a result of all this talking and the actual situation on your front, I feel personally quite certain that Dempsey must attack *at the earliest possible* moment on a large scale. We must not allow German forces to move from his front to Bradley's front or we shall give more cause than ever for criticism. I shall watch this end and keep you informed, but do not neglect this point; it is an important one at present. . . ."[1]

To this Montgomery replied that night:

" Your letter received 1830 hrs. . . . Everything will be thrown in. Gave orders to Dempsey this morning that attack is to be pressed with utmost vigour and all caution thrown to the winds and any casualties accepted and that he must step on gas for Vire. Americans are going great guns, and with Second Army drive south from Caumont I think results may be good."

Brooke's diary for the 28th continued:

" *July 28th.* A Chiefs of Staff meeting as usual with its variety of problems. Then an interview with Secretary of State. At 3 p.m. another Cabinet meeting which lasted two hours, and at which we spent all our time discussing rockets and flying-bombs. All this should have been finished yesterday. Winston relating all his old reminiscences connected with the various Cabinet appointments he has held, none of which have any bearing on the points under discussion. I remain very fond of him, but, by Heaven, he does try one's patience! "

During the week-end, while the C.I.G.S. spent a quiet Sunday at home, the Americans were racing south, exceeding the wildest expectations of their commander, Bradley. The leading armoured division of Patton's newly formed Third

[1] C.I.G.S. to Montgomery, 28 July, 1944. Lord Alanbrooke, *Personal Files.*

Army reached Avranches—the key road junction at the south-western base of the Cotentin peninsula, thirty miles from the starting point of the offensive—on the evening of the 30th. Next day it entered Brittany, and von Kluge, the German Commander in the West, who had succeeded Rundstedt four weeks before, telegraphed to Hitler's headquarters, " The whole Western Front has been ripped open. . . . The left flank has collapsed." At the same time the Russians, who had advanced two-hundred-and-fifty miles since the start of their summer offensive, reached the Niemen at Kovno and the Vistula near Warsaw. On August 1st the people of the Polish capital, believing their deliverance to be at hand, rose against the oppressors.

" *August 1st.* August—the month when wars usually start. I wonder whether this one may look like finishing it instead? "

" Our C.O.S. meeting laboriously ploughed through the weekly report by the Joint Intelligence Committee, followed by the Flying-Bomb Committee, Cherwell, Duncan Sandys, Bottomley,[1] etc. A great deal of talking and, from my point of view as Chairman, a great difficulty to keep discussion to the point. Cherwell must show his mathematical genius and Duncan Sandys insists in letting one see that he has a great political future."

" *August 2nd.* Brocas Burrows attended our C.O.S. meeting and we discussed the organization of some Staff centre at Moscow, although I feel that it is highly unlikely that Stalin will ever agree to any such organization being established."

" News to-night excellent. St. Malo, Rennes, Vitré, have been captured, the latter being the last but one of the headquarters that I occupied in France."

" *August 3rd.* The war news goes on improving daily. If things go on as they are doing now, we should be able to clear the Brest peninsula fairly quickly. Beyond that

---

[1] Air Chief Marshal Sir Norman Bottomley, Deputy Chief of Air Staff.

it is rather hard to see what the Boche can do except to retire to the line of the Seine, and it is doubtful if he can succeed in doing this in view of our great preponderance in the air."

" Buzz-bombs very noisy last night; hope they behave better to-night."

Yet though next day Montgomery ordered Patton's triumphant armour to wheel east on Le Mans, and a smiling Eisenhower greeted his A.D.C. with " We are to hell and gone in Brittany and slicing 'em up in Normandy ", the C.I.G.S., as always by the time his strategy was being tested on the battlefield, was busy on new projects with his colleagues and political chief.

" *August 4th.* Mountbatten is due to arrive to-night: on Monday (Bank Holiday) we are to discuss his plans with him. Then Tuesday and Wednesday we are to discuss them with the P.M. with the object (we hope!) of getting a decision on the Pacific strategy by Wednesday so that Winston can start for Italy that night. Portal and I have said we could not go with him that night as we shall have to put this decision into effect. We intend to follow in about a week and just spend a week only in Italy."

" To-day Eisenhower has asked for the famous South of France landing to be cancelled and that same force to be transferred to Brittany instead. That is actually what we had suggested to the Americans and they had turned it down. It is far the best solution."

" *Later.* Winston did not keep us long. Told us that Ike had lunched with him and read a paper with the suggestion that the South of France landing should be transferred to Brittany, which Winston thoroughly agreed with. He gave us the impression that Ike had already sent a telegram about it to America. Winston had drafted a telegram to the President supporting this proposition strongly. I told him that, although I entirely agreed with the proposal, I was convinced that he was wrong in wiring to the President. This could only have the effect of swinging the Americans against us. He did not agree, decided to send his telegram and asked us to send one to the American Chiefs supporting him."

" *August 5th*. Dickie Mountbatten turned up from India, and we had a preliminary meeting with him to discuss his plans. Then slipped home."

" *Sunday, August 6th*. Was called up on the telephone (scrambler) to be told that Eisenhower had never sent any telegram to America and that he was strongly opposed to any change in the South of France attack plan. Who has been " double-crossing " whom? In any case, we have certainly not improved our relations with the Americans."[1]

" *August 7th*. Bank Holiday, but a busy one. Back early. Dickie Mountbatten and Wedemeyer came to our C.O.S. meeting and explained their Burma strategy. It is clear that now that Stilwell has led us down to Myitkyina we shall have to go on operating in Burma. It is equally clear that the best way of doing so is to take the whole of Burma by an airborne attack on Rangoon. Furthermore it is clear that such an enterprise must reduce our effort in the Pacific. Finally, as a background to it all, when will Germany be finished off and allow us to transfer our strength to the Far East? "

" All these points we discussed repeatedly in a series of conferences throughout the day. Now it remains to make up our minds—not the easiest part of the task! "

" *August 8th*. Started with C.O.S. meeting at 10.30 and at 11 a.m. met the P.M. till 1.30 p.m.; meeting attended by Eden, Lyttelton, Attlee, Mountbatten, Wedemeyer and Chiefs of Staff."

---

[1] This episode is dealt with in Vol. VI 50-62, of Sir Winston Churchill's *Second World War*, in Ehrman's *Grand Strategy* V, 361-4, Eisenhower's *Crusade in Europe* and Hopkins's *White House Papers*, though in none of them completely. On the 5th, according to Butcher, the Prime Minister lunched at Eisenhower's Headquarters near Portsmouth and spent the afternoon trying to convert the Supreme Commander to his view. " Ike said No, continued saying No all afternoon, and ended saying No in every form of the English language at his command." *Butcher*, 545.

" Meeting resumed again from 6 p.m. to 8.30 p.m. and is due to meet once more from 10.30 p.m. to ——? Up to the present we have settled absolutely nothing and, as far as I can see, we are unlikely to settle anything to-night. We have been discussing the Pacific strategy, recommending the capture of Burma by a landing at Rangoon, combined with a Pacific strategy of Naval, Air and Dominion forces operating from Australia. Winston still hovers back to his tip of Sumatra and refuses to look at anything else."

" *Later at 1 a.m.*. Just back from our evening conference with the P.M. We have conferred for seven hours with him to-day to settle absolutely nothing. . . ."

" *August 9th*. Met C.O.S. at 10.30 when we discussed previous evening's work and as a result of it drafted our conclusions on the South-East Asia strategy. At 12.30 we met the P.M. with Anthony, Oliver and Attlee. The P.M. produced a document of his own which he read out. It was not far off ours. I said so and suggested that ' Pug ' should draft a document combining our two papers. I told him privately that he was to draft it on our paper but with P.M.'s phraseology."

" After lunch meeting with Sosnkowski who is very upset that we are not providing more assistance to the underground Army fighting Germans in Warsaw. I had some difficulty in calming him."[1]

" Then Cabinet at 5.30, first of all to discuss dispatch of forces to Greece in event of German evacuation. I had discovered that Paget was intending to use 5th Division for this purpose, whilst this division is intended for Italy. Cabinet lasted till 8.50 p.m."

[1] ' Sosnkowski's visit that day was a tragic one. Throughout the war they had fostered this underground Army in Warsaw and had trained and equipped it with great difficulty. It was destined to bide its time till the Russian liberation forces were on the verge of attacking the Germans in Warsaw. The appropriate moment arrived, the Poles checked up with the Russians to make certain they were ready and then they rose. But the Russians never moved and allowed the Germans to eliminate the bulk of the Poles. The Poles in London were of course infuriated and Sosnkowski was endeavouring to get me to send one of our Airborne brigades into Warsaw to help their underground Army.' *Notes on My Life*, XIV, 18.

" After dinner another meeting with the P.M. at 10.30 which lasted till 1.30 a.m. at which we finally arrived at a policy for South-East Asia. It is not what we started out for and not ideal, but it saves as much as it can out of the wreck, whilst also meeting the more rapid American advance and the necessity for liquidating our Burma commitment by undertaking the capture of Rangoon. On the other hand, it still gives scope for the use of our naval forces in the Pacific and for the formation of a British Task Force there."

" *August 10th.* This morning we drafted carefully our wire to America to put into effect last night's decision. A difficult wire to word, as it had to remain acceptable to the Americans whilst remaining within the requirements of the P.M. Two opposites very hard to reconcile . . ."

" Winston started to-night by air for Italy. But not until he had re-drafted our wire to the American Chiefs of Staff and put it into a form and words in which it is unmistakable and bound to be recognized as emanating from him and consequently crash any hope of getting it through! "

" *August 11th.* We had to reconsider the P.M.'s amendments and refuse to accept them with consequent delay. I then had a busy day with interviews, culminating with letters from Dickie Mountbatten to Marshall which he sent me to look at. I had to tell him that he could not send any of them and should attend C.O.S. meeting on Monday with Wedemeyer, and we should then tell the latter what he should say to Marshall."

• • • • • • • •

By this time the climax was at hand of the great drama set in train by the strategy agreed at Casablanca, Quebec and Teheran. On August 8th, ignoring Hitler's attempts to cut his lengthening communications, Patton's armour entered Le Mans; on the previous day the British and Canadians, having captured the dominating height of Mont Pinçon, opened an all-out offensive towards Falaise. By the 14th they were only four miles from the town, while the Americans, having wheeled northwards to capture Alençon on the 12th, were on the outskirts of Argentan, ten miles south-east of Falaise. Between and to the west of these two places fifteen German divisions and the bulk of their armour in the West lay trapped in a narrowing sack. In Italy, having reached the banks of the Arno at the beginning of August, the Allies entered Florence on the 13th, and prepared to assault the Gothic Line before debouching on to the Lombardy plain. By the following night the landing-craft carrying the American-French army which was to liberate Marseilles and Toulon were closing on the Riviera coast. If von Kluge's army in Normandy and Kesselring's in Italy were to collapse, with the Russians nearing the East Prussian frontier and pouring into Rumania, anything might happen.[1]

" *Monday, August 14th.* Back to War Office by 9.30 a.m. News very good and every chance of rounding off some Boche on Monty's front."

" At C.O.S. meeting Dickie and Wedemeyer attended, the latter most helpful, and I hope he assists in putting the case to the Americans. Adam to lunch and long talks with him prior to my visit to Italy. Cabinet at 5.30 p.m. run by Attlee and finished in half the time."

" To-night landings in Southern France near Toulon and St. Raphael are to take place."

' It was a relief to feel that at last these landings were taking place and could no longer produce heated arguments. The Americans' original idea was to launch them in May before *Overlord* and seriously at the expense of operations in Italy. Coming as they did now, they could no longer do all the harm they would have done at an early date. But I still wonder whether we derived much benefit from them.'

[1] Field-Marshal Smuts wrote on August 12th to the Prime Minister, " A decisive stage has now been reached in the war, and an all-out offensive on all three main fronts against Germany must lead to the grand finale this summer." *Churchill* VI, 94.

" *August 15th.* Life has a quiet and peaceful atmosphere about it now that Winston is gone.[1] Everything gets done twice as quickly."

" A full morning at the C.O.S. meeting studying with the Joint Intelligence Committee the German reactions to the Allied successes on all fronts. It is a wonderfully thrilling period. Apparently the Germans are contemplating holding the line of the Seine and Marne."

" After lunch visit to Amery who is very perturbed about Indian grain situation. He is calling for our assistance and is very nervous lest Archie Wavell should resign the Viceroyship owing to the lack of support he is obtaining from the Government."

" At 5 p.m. Cabinet, run by Attlee, on the rocket bomb and the desirability of giving Germans false reports through agents so as to move mean point of burst farther south."

" Monty's great encircling move in France is making good progress and still holds out great hopes."

" *August 16th.* Most of the C.O.S. meeting was taken up with problems as to how to support the Polish underground rising in Warsaw. The Russians seem to be purposely giving no assistance and the Poles here are naturally frantic."

" The landing near Toulon seems to be going well, whilst the operations in Normandy are working up towards a climax. There are great hopes of delivering a smashing blow which might go a long way towards clearing the road for the rest of France."

" *August 17th.* The Joint Planners came to attend our C.O.S. meeting and we discussed all difficulties facing us if we are to stage a Rangoon attack by next March. The War Office has been raising just one series of difficulties and delays. Their examination proved that it was impos-

[1] He was at that moment watching the almost unopposed American landing on the Riviera of which he disapproved so strongly. " As far as I could see or hear," he wrote, " not a shot was fired either at the approaching flotillas or on the beaches. . . . There seemed to be nobody there." *Churchill* VI, 85.

sible to do it by that date. I, therefore, had a two hours'
meeting this afternoon to prove to them that it is possible
and must be done."

"It is extraordinary how exhausting it is having to
drive a plan through against opposition. First on the part
of P.M., and now on the part of those responsible for it
in the War Office. There are moments when I would
give anything just to get into a car and drive home,
saying I was fed up with the whole show and they could
look for someone else to fill my job. The making of plans
is child's play as compared with putting them into
execution. I feel worn out and very glad at the thought
of going to Italy for a change and rest."

"*August 18th.* We had a final interview with Dickie
Mountbatten to discuss our plan for the capture of
Rangoon which is based on our being able to start with-
drawing the 6th Division from the European Theatre on
Oct. 1st. It is a gamble, but I believe one worth taking."

"During afternoon a Cabinet at 5 p.m. to discuss the
underground rising in Warsaw and lack of support on
the part of the Russians. Then various interviews all in
preparation for my departure to-night with Portal for
Italy. We leave Northolt at midnight hoping to make
Rabat about 7 a.m. and Naples about 4 p.m. to-morrow."

. . . .

The C.I.G.S.'s flight on August 19th to join the Prime
Minister and consult with Wilson and Alexander in Italy
coincided with the closing of the Falaise pocket. By that day
50,000 Germans had made good their escape towards the
lower Seine crossings, but 30,000 remained in the Allies' cages,
including three divisional commanders and one corps commander, and another 15,000 lay dead on the battlefield. A day
earlier von Kluge—the second Supreme Commander in the
West to be dismissed by Hitler in seven weeks—committed
suicide, after sending the latter a letter urging him to end the
war. Orléans, Chartres and Dreux had already fallen to the

Americans; on the night of August 19th the French Resistance rose against the garrison of Paris.

The situation awaiting the C.I.G.S. in Italy was dominated by three factors. The first was the withdrawal from General Alexander's command, at the instance of the American Chiefs of Staff, of seven American and French divisions at the very moment when victory had seemed within his grasp and their descent, on August 15th, on the South of France, where during the next few critical and decisive weeks they could play little or no part in either the Italian or the *Overlord* campaign. The immediate effect of their appearance on the Riviera had been, as Brooke had foreseen, the dispatch by Hitler—sure now that no further landing on either the Italian or Dalmatian coast was to be feared—of three crack divisions from Italy to Northern France. The second factor was the belief of the Prime Minister and General Alexander that, despite the removal of a quarter of the attacking army, a victory over Kesselring's forces could still be won which would make an invasion of Austria through Venetia and the Ljubljana Gap possible before the winter for a link-up in the Danube valley with the Russian forces advancing into Rumania and the Balkans. The third was the fact that Kesselring, an officer of great ability, now disposed of as many divisions as Alexander, and, with his flanks and rear no longer threatened from the sea, held a strongly fortified mountain line whose defences he had been preparing throughout the summer while his men withdrew up the mountain spine of Italy.

Despite Anglo-American command of the air, the prospects of Alexander's offensive—now timed to begin on the night of August 25th—did not, therefore, in the cold light of military logic seem as hopeful as either he or the Prime Minister supposed. Having tried first to stop, and then to divert, the Riviera landing by every argument at his disposal, even to warning Eisenhower that he would have to go " to the Monarch and lay down the mantle of his high office ", Churchill arrived in Italy on August 17th, his vigour, as he wrote, " greatly restored by the change and movement and the warm weather " and his hopes set on seeing the victor of Tunis smash his way through the Gothic Line to Lombardy.[1]

In his letters to Brooke, Alexander had nursed similar hopes; " I shall be eternally grateful to you," he wrote three weeks after Washington's refusal to cancel the Riviera landings, "if you can do everything to ensure that this theatre of operations does not sink in the minds of the people at home into a secondary affair. . . . I believe, and I am sure you do too, that this may become a decisive front. I have only to get through the Ljubljana Gap and it will be."[2] Having been forced to accept the American strategy, the C.I.G.S. was less sanguine and on July 20th had sent Alexander one of his characteristically laconic communications, bidding him to do the best he could with what he had.

" 1.   Many thanks for your letter of 12 July.

2.   I hope forthcoming visit will be a great success . . .

3.   I thought I had made it quite clear that neither 6 Ind. Div. nor 31 Ind. Arm. Div. could be spared. We have done all we can to find troops for you but cannot denude the Middle East entirely.

4.   Smythe is being sent by air.

5.   R.E. units in Madagascar. There are only 40 British personnel.

6.   Many congratulations on Arezzo, Ancona and Leghorn.

7.   Hope you will not let your fox go to ground and have to dig him out."[3]

This, in fact, was what had happened. Brooke's view of the Italian campaign remained what it had always been: that it was not an end in itself but a means to an end—the weakening

---

[1] Prime Minister to the King, 17 August, 1944. *Churchill* VI, 86.

[2] Gen. Alexander to C.I.G.S. 18 July, 1944. Lord Alanbrooke, *Personal Files.* " I am most grateful for all the help and assistance for my Italian campaign which I feel convinced will pay a big dividend. Everything is ' *en train* '—and we must all act with speed and decision so that we are not beaten by Father Time. . . . I am looking forward to the P.M. coming out here and I hope you will come too— and then you must manipulate things so that you can stay on here after he has left." *Idem*, 12 July, 1944.

[3] C.I.G.S. to Gen. Alexander, 20 July, 1944. Lord Alanbrooke, *Personal Files.*

of Germany's capacity to strike back on the decisive fronts in Northern France and Russia—and that, the U.S. Chiefs of Staff having thrown away its tactical possibilities, first by with-holding in favour of their Pacific offensive the means of using sea-power against the peninsula's exposed coastline and then by checking Alexander's victorious advance in mid-course, it was useless now to expect too much from it. His attitude was expressed in a letter he had written the Supreme Commander, Mediterranean, at the beginning of August.

" It was a great pity that we were defeated over *Anvil* in the end: Alex's talk about his advance on Vienna killed all our arguments dead. It is a pity because I do not see Alex advancing on Vienna this year unless he does it in the face of a crumbling Germany, and in that case he has ample forces for the task and greater than he will be able to administer over snow-covered mountain passes. However, I do not feel that *Anvil* can do much harm at this stage of the war, and it may well prove of some use in introducing French forces to reinforce the *Maquis*.

" I am rather disappointed that Alex did not make a more definite attempt to smash Kesselring's forces up whilst they are south of the Apennines. He has planned a battle on the Apennine position and seems to be deliberately driving the Germans back on to that position instead of breaking them up in the more favourable country. I cannot feel that this policy of small pushes all along the line and driving the Boche like partridges can be right. I should have liked to see one concentrated attack, with sufficient depth to it, put in at a suitable spot with a view to breaking through and smashing up German divisions by swinging with right and left. However, it is a bit late for that now. . . ."[1]

Brooke reached Caserta in Southern Italy on the afternoon of August 19th, having flown three thousand miles since leaving Northolt at midnight. " It is a wonderful feeling," he wrote

[1] C.I.G.S. to Supreme Commander, Mediterranean, 2 August, 1944. Lord Alanbrooke, *Personal Files*.

as his aircraft headed across the Sicilian Narrows, " comparing this flight with my first journey down the Mediterranean before Alex and Monty were installed in Egypt. I then slunk along in a twin-engine Dakota under cover of darkness and very glad to get through safely." " Punctually on the stroke of 4 p.m.," he added that night,

" we landed just north-east of Naples, having been fourteen hours in the air out of the last twenty-four hours. We were met on the aerodrome by Slessor and Gammell.[1] We went up to Wilson's H.Q. and there discussed plans and prepared a programme for the next few days. I then had a long talk with 'Jumbo' Wilson and finally came up to the hunting lodge above Caserta which he is living in."

" *August 20th. Caserta.* Spent the whole morning in conference. We examined recent success near Toulouse, discussed future of the Southern France invasion, planned Mediterranean strategy, re-occupation of Greece when Germans collapse, etc."

" After lunch more conferences to dinner. Paget turned up in the evening from Middle East and I spent some time talking over some of his problems with him."

" *August 21st. Alex's Hqrs. south of Florence and near Siena.* Left Naples aerodrome at 8.30 a.m. and flew past Mount Camino, Mount Cassino and Monastery Hill where we did two rings round and I had a most excellent view of the whole position. We then flew up the Liri valley looking at all the ground I had looked at on my map and model time and time again. From there over Anzio bridgehead which we examined carefully. Finally landed outside Rome."

" We did a three-hours' tour of Rome. At 1 p.m. we went to the British Embassy to lunch with Charles, the

[1] Air Marshal (now Marshal of the Royal Air Force) Sir John Slessor, Commander-in-Chief, R.A.F., Mediterranean, and Lt.-Gen. Sir James Gammell, Chief of Staff to Supreme Allied Commander, Mediterranean.

Ambassador. For lunch P.M. who had just arrived, Macmillan, ' Jumbo ' Wilson, Portal."

" After lunch conference with P.M. on the question of Greece, got him to agree that the Greek Government should be moved over to Italy. After meeting he kept me on to tell me that ' Jumbo ' Wilson was interfering too much with Alexander. This is not right, and I cannot believe that Alex would have been guilty of suggesting such a thing . . ."

" Embarked in plane at 6 p.m. and flew on up to Alex's H.Q. He met me on the aerodrome and we had a lovely drive up to his small camp. Here I am very comfortable in one of his caravans."

" *August 22nd. Near Siena.* Attended 9 a.m. Intelligence conference of Alex's to hear latest news on all fronts. We then started off on a long tour of the front. First we visited Murray who had just taken over command of 6th Armoured Division on right of XIII Corps. We had collected Kirkman, commander of XIII Corps, on the way. From there we visited Russell, commander 8th Indian Division, and then went on to an Artillery H.Q. from which we had a very good view of Florence. We also had a shot at the Boche from there."

" Came back about 7 p.m. and had a long discussion with Alex on questions of organization of the Mediterranean command. Found Alex very upset; evidently . . . relations between Alex and Wilson are not of the best. This is troublesome and will require a good deal of working at."

" *August 23rd. Near Siena.* Attended Alex's conference at 9 a.m. and then started in a jeep for the landing-strip near the camp. There we took off in "whizzers" for the Siena aerodrome where we changed into Alex's Dakota. We flew across Italy to a landing ground just west of Ancona. There I met Anders of the Polish Corps and found him in great spirits in spite of the Warsaw troubles with the Russians. His attitude being: ' We Poles have two deadly enemies, the Germans and the Russians. We are now engaged with the Germans—well, let us make a job of this enemy first.' "

" We then drove up to Oliver Leese's H.Q. where we discussed his forthcoming offensive. On way back I had an interview with Burns commanding the Canadian Corps. Flew back to near Siena. Finished up the day by dining with the P.M. in his villa where he had come back to for a few days to be near on-coming battle! "

" *August 24th. Gibraltar.* After listening to the morning's Intelligence report I left for the aerodrome and by 10.45 a.m. we were off for Naples. We made good time and arrived at 12.15 p.m. There I found Gammell who had various points he wanted to discuss. Portal was there also, and by 12.45 p.m. we had started for Gibraltar."

" After a very good run arrived at Gibraltar at 7 p.m. We were met by ' Rusty ' Eastwood and went up to Government House for dinner. Had hoped to start again by 11 p.m. but owing to foggy weather at home our departure was put off till 4 a.m. We went down to the plane shortly after midnight and put in some sleep before taking off."

" *August 25th.* We crossed the coastline somewhere about 10 a.m. and by 11 a.m. were landing at Northolt, having flown under 7000 miles in the six days we had been away."

" Spent most of the day getting into the picture and telling P.J." ' (Grigg) ' " about my trip and the conditions in Italy. The news of German decay on all fronts continues to be almost unbelievable."

For while Brooke had been absent the pace of events across the Channel had quickened further. On the day before his return the last Germans crossed the Seine, having lost in their disastrously prolonged defence of Normandy more than two thousand armoured vehicles and half a million men, nearly a quarter of them prisoners. On the same night French and

American troops entered Paris. Meanwhile, robbed by Britain's Mediterranean strategy and Hitler's refusal to yield ground of the central strategic reserve which, with her swift east-to-west communications, could have kept Germany's assailants at bay, the *Wehrmacht's* defence of South-Eastern Europe had suddenly collapsed. With fifty-five divisions still tied up in the Mediterranean littoral[1] and another fifty isolated in the Baltic States by Zhukov's drive to the Prussian frontier, on a three-hundred-mile front between the Carpathians and Black Sea the Germans had only two armoured divisions and no reserves at all. Here, striking on August 20th, two Russian Army Groups swept across the Pruth into Central Rumania. On August 23rd the pro-Axis dictatorship in that country was overthrown by a palace revolution; on the 25th the new Government declared war on Germany. Next day the Bulgarians sued for peace, and four days later the Russians reached the Ploesti oil-wells. Greece, Yugoslavia, Hungary and the Danube valley lay wide open to the advance of the Red Armies.

Brooke at this time was expecting the Germans to collapse. " It becomes more evident every day," he had written to General Maitland Wilson three weeks earlier, " that the Boche is beat on all fronts. It is only a matter now of how many more months he can last. I certainly don't see him lasting another winter."[2] But on August 22nd, with the Axis tottering to its fall and victory within the Allies' grasp, General Eisenhower, backed by the American Chiefs of Staff and the whole weight of American public opinion, announced his intention of taking operational command of the Liberation Armies. By this time the United States had twenty-two divisions in France, including the three now advancing up the Rhone valley from the Riviera, while Britain and Canada had only seventeen. " The Americans now feel," Brooke had written in his letter to Wilson, " that they possess the major

[1] Field-Marshal Alexander's *Dispatches*, Numb. 38937. London Gazette, 12 June, 1950.
[2] C.I.G.S. to Supreme Commander, Mediterranean, 2 August, 1944. Lord Alanbrooke, *Personal Files*.

forces at sea, on land and in the air, in addition to all the vast financial and industrial advantages they have had from the start. They look upon themselves no longer as apprentices in war but as full-blown professionals. As a result they are determined to have an ever-increasing share in the running of the war in all its aspects."

It had always been understood that, as soon as the U.S. had two armies in action, a separate American Army Group, independent of the original 21 Army Group, should be formed under Omar Bradley, leaving Montgomery in command of a purely British and Canadian Army Group. This had been effected at the time of the American break-out at the beginning of August, but throughout that month of victory the direction of the Allied ground forces continued in Montgomery's hands. But, for all his military genius, that officer was little loved by his immediate American subordinates, and the apparent ease of their break-out and the rapidity of their advance compared with the slow, slogging pace of the British and Canadians in the bocage had filled them with self-confidence. It seemed essential to them now, not only that there should be an American Supreme Commander, but that he should act and be recognized as Commander-in-Chief as well.[1] And several senior British Army and Air Force staff officers at S.H.A.E.F., who, like everyone else who worked closely under Eisenhower, loved and admired him, agreed with them.

Having used the Americans to break out on his right flank and sweep to Paris, Montgomery at that moment was preparing to launch the British on his left in a similar all-out drive across the Lower Seine and the Picardy and Flemish plain towards Brussels and Antwerp. It was his belief that, by doing

[1] As early as February 6th, Eisenhower's A.D.C. voiced this growing American feeling. " Generally speaking the British columnists write that General Ike's contribution to the Mediterranean were administrative accomplishments and friendliness in welding an Allied team. They apparently dislike to believe that General Ike had anything to do with the military decisions in those campaigns. They don't use the words ' initiative ' and ' boldness ' in talking of Ike, but often do in speaking of Alex and Monty. Yet Ike had to make numerous important military decisions and take the final responsibility for all of them. I should think he would get sour on being written about as ' Chairman of the Board.' " *Butcher*, 417.

so and directing his own and Bradley's army group as a solid compact mass of forty divisions towards the Lower Rhine and Ruhr, he could strike Germany a blow from which in its present shaken state there could be no recovery. But Eisenhower, who was essentially a staff officer with little knowledge of the realities of the battlefield, did not share this belief. He was obsessed with the logistical problems—which were immense —of supplying his forces, now advancing far from their inadequate Channel bases, and of maintaining them throughout the winter as they moved into Germany, and felt that he could only do so if they went forward on a wide front, using as many roads as possible. And like nearly all senior American military commanders at the time, except the genius MacArthur, he was a believer in the classic Civil War doctrine of frontal assault, of " Everybody attacks all the time." He disapproved of Montgomery's plan for allocating all the available maintenance to the north to enable the Allied left to drive through the Low Countries into the heart of the Ruhr. He wished instead to divide his resources between Montgomery's British and Canadians in the north, Bradley's Americans in the centre— now spreading out and advancing on Nancy and Metz—and Devers's Americans and French moving up from the Rhone towards Alsace, and then, having got them neatly into position on a six-hundred-mile front, to assail Germany simultaneously with them all.

Brooke's diary for Monday, August 28th, reflects this difference in strategic view and the problems raised by Eisenhower's decision.

" Difficult C.O.S. meeting where we considered Eisenhower's new plan to take command himself in Northern France on Sept. 1st. This plan is likely to add another three to six months on to the war. He straight away wants to split his force, sending an American contingent towards Nancy whilst the British Army Group moves along the coast. If the Germans were not as beat as they are this would be a fatal move; as it is, it may not do too much harm. In any case I am off to France to-morrow to see Monty and to discuss the situation with him."

" Meanwhile Paris is liberated, Rumania out of the war, and Bulgaria tumbling out next. The Germans cannot last very much longer."

" Attended Thanksgiving Service in the Crypt of St. Paul's Cathedral for Liberation of Paris at 12 noon. Hearing the ' Marseillaise ' boom out gave me a deep thrill. France seemed to wake again after being knocked out for five years."

" *August 29th*. Left here at 9 a.m. for Hendon where I took off in pouring rain with an escort of three fighters for Normandy. Arrived there 11 a.m. and met by de Guingand who said that weather was too bad for flying on to Monty's H.Q. I therefore had a two-and-three-quarter hours' drive in pouring rain along a muddy road crammed with lorries and at times heavily scented with dead horses. We went through Caen, Falaise and Chambois. The latter was a regular shambles of broken tanks, lorries, carts and dead horses."

" Arrived Monty's H.Q. by 2 p.m. Had long talk with him about recent crisis with Eisenhower. Apparently he has succeeded in arriving at a suitable compromise by which First U.S. Army is to move on the right of 21 Army Group and head for area Charleroi, Namur, Liége, just north of the Ardennes. Only unsatisfactory part is that this Army is not under Monty's orders and he can only co-ordinate its actions in relation to 21 Army Group. This may work; it remains to be seen what political pressure is put on Eisenhower to move Americans on separate axis from the British."

" Left at 3.30 p.m., had another two-and-three-quarter hours back to aerodrome and a murky fly home through clouds, reaching Hendon at 7.45 p.m., having lost my escort of three fighters in the clouds. I hope they returned safely."

" Winston returned from Italy this evening with a temperature of 104°."

" *August 30th.* Apparently Winston has again got a minor attack of pneumonia; not much, and they think they can get him right to start by sea in the *Queen Mary* for Quebec next week. I was sent for by him at 7 p.m. Found him looking ill. I explained to him the difficulties that had been arising with Eisenhower taking control from Monty and wanting to direct the American forces on Nancy and Frankfurt, leaving the British forces to deal with the German forces in Northern France."

" He informed me that he wanted to make Monty a Field-Marshal, the appointment to coincide (Sept. 1st) with the date of Eisenhower assuming command of Land Forces. He felt that such a move would mark the approval of the British people for Montgomery's leadership."

Chapter Eight

LOST OPPORTUNITY

Optimism was in the air, the whips were got out, and the Supreme Commander urged everyone on all along the front. Everyone was to be fighting all the time. . . . All my military training told me he could not get away with it and that we would be faced with a long winter campaign with all that that entailed for the British people.

FIELD-MARSHAL MONTGOMERY

THE TIME had now come for finally resolving what part Britain was to play in the assault on Japan. For nine months the Prime Minister had sought by every means to avoid implementing the Cairo agreement of the Combined Chiefs of Staff that the Navy should operate after the defeat of Germany with the American Fleet in the Pacific. Now, with a collapse of Germany imminent, a decision could no longer be avoided. And decision could only be reached in consultation with the American President and Chiefs of Staff, whose forces by their capture that summer of Guam and Saipan in the Marianas were now only 1300 miles from Tokyo.

On Roosevelt's return in mid-August from the Pacific, where he had been planning an invasion of the Philippines with his admirals, MacArthur and Churchill had proposed a conference at Quebec in September. Owing to Stalin having rejected an earlier suggestion of a three-Power meeting in Scotland, the conference, like its predecessor of a year earlier, had to be confined to the Western Powers. The issues were the orders to be given the Supreme Commanders in North-Western Europe and the Mediterranean for administering the *coup de grâce* to Germany and the strategy for the coming campaign against Japan.

During their visit to London in June the American Chiefs of Staff had, with reservations, tentatively approved a proposal— put forward in the spring by their British colleagues as a con- cession to Churchill and agreed with the Australian and New Zealand Prime Ministers—of a British sea and land offensive based on Australia and directed towards Amboina and Borneo.[1] But just before the Normandy break-out, encouraged by the growing reluctance of the American admirals to let the Royal Navy share their triumphs, the Prime Minister had suddenly repudiated this " middle strategy ", as it was called, and reverted to his old idea of a purely British naval campaign in the Indian Ocean whose objective was to be the occupation of Northern Sumatra as a jumping-off ground for Burma and Malaya. Since the repulse at midsummer of their invasion of Assam, the Japanese facing the British Army on the Burmese- Indian frontier had lost their old ascendancy and were now in retreat. But their expulsion from that land of monsoons and primitive communications was certain to monopolize all Britain's available military and air resources, whether it was to be effected solely by an advance from the jungle hills into the Mandalay plain as the Commander-in-Chief of Fourteenth Army, General Slim, now believed to be possible, or simul- taneously, with the aid of additional divisions from Europe, by an air and seaborne attack on Rangoon as proposed by Mount- batten and approved that August by Brooke and his colleagues as an acceptable plan—since it would re-open land communica- tions with China—for submission to the Americans at Quebec. This was to be coupled, as before, with an offer of the British Fleet for operations against the Japanese homeland or, failing that, in the South-West Pacific under MacArthur. But for this the Prime Minister continued to show no enthusiasm, his mind being set on two amphibious projects of his own—one to

---

[1] See p. 217. But see also *Ehrman* V, 483-4, where the American objections to this strategy are stated.

Sumatra as a stepping-stone to Singapore,[1] the other to invade Istria across the head of the Adriatic in order to outflank the German armies in Italy and capture Vienna, " a stab for Germany," as he called it, " in the Adriatic armpit ".

The C.I.G.S., therefore, awaited the journey to Quebec with considerable misgiving.

" *September 1st.* Winston is improving rapidly and it looks as if we should all be starting for Quebec on Monday evening. . . . During morning and afternoon repeated telephone calls from Winston to find out whether Alex could re-assume his senior position to Monty when he is made a Field-Marshal at a later date."

" *September 4th.* A lot of messages in, and many preparations all day for our departure. Cabinet at 5.30 attended by P.M. who was not looking at all well. I very much wonder whether he will be up to the strain of this trip."

" This evening our troops are reported in Brussels and advancing on Antwerp. It is very hard to believe it all."

" *September 5th. Queen Mary.* Left the flat this morning shortly after 9 a.m. for Addison Road. There I joined the P.M.'s special train. Shortly after we had left the P.M. sent for us, and we had a conference on Greece with him. He seems to be still very much of the opinion that we might be justified in dropping a parachute brigade (about 2000 to 3000 strong) near Athens with some 150,000 Germans still in Greece. I had to convince him that such a plan was out of the question and that the dropping of this party was dependent on the Germans evacuating Greece or being prepared to surrender. He was looking much better and in very good form."

" By about 7 p.m. we arrived on the Clyde and came

[1] " Here is the supreme British objective in the whole of the Indian and Far Eastern theatres. It is the only prize that will restore British prestige in this region." Prime Minister to General Ismay for C.O.S. Committee, 12 Sept., 1944. *Churchill* VI, 146.

straight on board the *Queen Mary*. After dinner went up on to the bridge with Cunningham and Portal and watched the start of our journey."

" Winston has agreed to our airborne campaign on Burma but limits his sanction to the capture of Rangoon alone without the clearing of the rest of Burma. This makes the expedition practically useless and, what is worse, converts it into one which cannot appeal to the Americans since it fails to affect Upper Burma where their air route is situated. . . . ."

" *September 6th. Queen Mary.* Woke up to find the *Queen Mary* gliding down the Irish Channel, with the Irish coast in view. At 10.30 we held a C.O.S. meeting to discuss our line of action with the Americans. We discussed the possibility of beginning the withdrawal of forces from Europe for the war against Japan and came to the conclusion that, as far as could be judged at the present moment, we were justified but should await events of the next few days before taking any final decision."

" We then discussed future of Italian campaign and came to the conclusion that it must become of secondary importance as soon as the Pisa-Rimini line had been broken and Kesselring's forces defeated and driven back. Unfortunately it will not be easy to get Winston to see eye to eye with us . . ."

" *September 7th. Queen Mary.* Started the day again with a C.O.S. meeting which we got Leathers to attend in order to discuss the shipping situation which will arise when Germany is eliminated. The call on personnel shipping will be enormous, what with the move of forces to the Japanese war, repatriation of our prisoners, return of Americans to U.S.A. and on to Japanese war, Canadians to Canada, New Zealanders to their homes and South Africans to South Africa, and on top of it all civilian requirements. It is going to be a difficult problem to lay down priorities."

" Cunningham, Portal, Laycock and I went to lunch with Winston and Clemmie. He was not looking at all well and was most desperately flat. A good deal of it may be due to the M & B which he has been taking. . . ."

" Last night we passed close over a German submarine and intercepted his signal reporting having seen us. We are now level with Cape Finisterre and have just turned due west, making straight for Halifax. Destroyers have now left us and we have only one cruiser as escort. We are doing about 28 knots and the cruiser is having some difficulty keeping up with us."

" *September 8th. Queen Mary*. We have been travelling in the Gulf Stream all day and consequently living in a Turkish bath of hot clamminess. We began with a short C.O.S. meeting and at 12 noon had a meeting lasting till 1.30 p.m. with the P.M. He looked old, unwell and depressed. Evidently found it hard to concentrate and kept holding his head between his hands. He began by accusing us of framing up against him and of opposing him in his wishes. According to him we were coming to Quebec solely to obtain landing-ships out of the Americans to carry out an operation against Istria to seize Trieste, and there we were suggesting that, with the rate at which events were moving, Istria might be of no value! We also suggested moving troops from Europe for Burma and had never told him that the removal of these forces was dependent on the defeat of Hitler—a completely false accusation! He further said that we had told him only one division was required for Burma, and now we spoke of five—here again a complete misstatement of facts.[1] It was hard to keep one's temper with him, but I could not help feeling frightfully sorry for him. . . ."

" We made no progress and decided to go on to-morrow. He finished up by saying:—' Here we are within 72 hours

[1] " The Chiefs of Staff stated on 9th September that ' the fundamental problem, stated in its simplest terms, is the movement of 370,000 men and 24,000 vehicles from the European theatre to India in the shortest time.' " *Ehrman*, V, 509.

of meeting the Americans and there is not a single point that we are in agreement over.' "

" I spent the afternoon working up notes for to-morrow's meeting with him."

" *September 9th. Queen Mary.* We received two Minutes from the P.M. to-day. His arguments are again centred on one point—Istria; we have come for one purpose only, to secure landing-craft for an operation against Istria; all else of importance fades into the shade of secondary considerations. But what is more serious, he now repudiates what we secured from him weeks ago and which we sub-mitted to the Americans with his approval; namely the possible formation of a British Task Force under Mac-Arthur. A subject discussed with Curtin and Fraser during the Imperial Conference and repeatedly thrashed out in the War Cabinet is now disapproved as a matter of dis-cussion with the Americans. . . . We were to have met him this evening but he had started another temperature and had to remain in bed, cancelling an invitation for us to dine with him. I am afraid that he is definitely ill."[1]

' He had got into his head that we were going to " frame-up " (he used those actual words to me) with the American Chiefs against him. As he knew that the American Chiefs could handle the President fairly easily, he feared he would be faced with a military bloc of Chiefs of Staff plus the President. As matters stood we were very far from " framing-up " with our American colleagues even if we had wished to.'

" *September 10th. Queen Mary.* We had another meeting with Winston at 12 noon. He produced arguments to prove that operations could be speeded up so as to leave us an option till December before having to withdraw any

[1] In a letter to Harry Hopkins written a few days earlier, the American Ambassador Winant wrote of Churchill, " His message to the President will have told you of his illness . . . which is only known to a dozen people here. To-night his temperature is back to normal and he seems on the way to a quick recovery. But each journey has taken its toll, and the interval between illnesses has been constantly shortened." J. G. Winant to H. Hopkins, 1 Sept., 1944. *White House Papers*, II, 806.

forces from Europe. He knows no details, has only got half the picture in his mind. . . ."

" Immediately after lunch we went ashore. By about 3 p.m. our special train had left for Quebec."

" *September 11th. Quebec.* We arrived here at 10 a.m. to find that the President's train had arrived before us. Conference after lunch and then several hours of reading messages. Finally dinner at the Citadel by the Athlones for Winston and Roosevelt. All the rank, fashion and clergy of Quebec, plus all American Chiefs of Staff. . . ."

．　．　．　．　．　．　．　．

The Conference, however, proved easier than Brooke had expected. When the British and American Chiefs of Staff met on September 12th their arms had been crowned with continuous success for many weeks on every front. On the first of the month the Eighth Army had penetrated the Gothic Line and the Americans had entered Pisa. Next day Finland asked for an armistice and the British liberated Lille. On Sunday the 3rd the latter freed Brussels and, on the 4th, Antwerp. By the end of that week Ostend had fallen to the Canadians, the Americans and French, advancing up the Rhone valley, had reached Burgundy, and the Russians had invaded a dissolving Bulgaria. On the day before the Conference began, the first American patrol crossed the German frontier and the port of Havre surrendered next day.

In the first flush of victory allies find it easy to be cordial. In August the American Chiefs of Staff had delayed for three weeks before replying to their British colleagues' latest proposals for the Far East, and had then—when the latter were already on their way to Quebec—ignored their offer of their Fleet for the Central Pacific. But when on the opening day of the Conference, loyally advancing the thesis he had so long opposed, the Prime Minister stressed his country's wish to see its Navy co-operating with America's against Japan, the President replied that the offer was no sooner made than accepted. He would like, he said, to see the British Fleet used

wherever and whenever possible.[1]   And when the C.I.G.S.
outlined Britain's military proposals for the Italian campaign
and, in view of the possibilities that might arise if operations
against the Gothic Line were successful, asked that the
American forces and landing-craft should remain in the theatre
for the present instead of being transferred to France or the
Pacific, the Joint Chiefs of Staff unexpectedly and cordially
agreed, with a proviso that the matter should be reconsidered
on October 15th when the result of the Allied offensive in
North Italy was known.

" *September 12th.   Quebec.*   To-day we started work and,
after a Chiefs of Staff meeting at 10 a.m., we had our first
Combined C.O.S. meeting from 12 noon till lunch and
again from 2.30 to 4.30 p.m.   It went off most satis-
factorily and we found ourselves in complete agreement
with American Chiefs of Staff.   They were prepared to
leave American divisions in Italy till Alex had finished
his offensive.   They were also prepared to leave tank
landing-ships for Istrian venture if required."

" At 4.30 p.m. we had an ordinary Chiefs of Staff
meeting to discuss latest minute by P.M. on Pacific
strategy.   He is gradually coming round to sane strategy,
but by Heaven what labour we have had for it!   He now
accepts the naval contingent for the Pacific, a Dominion
Task Force with MacArthur, etc.   At 6.30 p.m. we had
to go up to the Citadel for a meeting with him.   He was
all smiles and friendliness for a change.   How quickly he

---

[1] On Sept. 1st Winant had written to Harry Hopkins: " The really gallant
people of Great Britain are as anxious to join us in the fight against Japan as we
are ourselves to defeat Japan, and yet for all that there has seeped into this country
through military channels a belief that the British Navy is not wanted in the Pacific.
I know . . . that many of our Navy men feel that the British Navy was built for
short hauls . . . and that conversion would mean clogging our Navy Yards and
strengthening the British Navy in the post-war years. . . . Yet if we allow the British
to limit their active participation to recapture areas that are to their selfish interests
alone and not participate in smashing the war machine of Japan . . . and if we
shuck the British Air Force in order to prove our own dominance in the air, we will
create in the United States a hatred for Britain that will make schisms in the post-
war years that will defeat everything that men have died for in this war." *White
House Papers*, II, 807-8.

changes! An April day's moods would be put to shame by him."

" Lunched with Marshall, Leahy and Dill, the former as charming as usual. . . ."

" Dined at Citadel with Athlones; Roosevelt, Churchill, American Chiefs of Staff and British Chiefs of Staff. I sat on President's right and found him very pleasant and easy to talk to."

" *September 13th. Quebec.* Started with a C.O.S. meeting at 9 a.m., as we were to meet the Americans at 10 a.m. However, the P.M. sent for us and informed us it was essential for him to see us at 10 a.m. As a result we had to put off our meeting with the Americans. However, when we met him we found he had nothing special to see us about."

" At 11.30 we had a long Plenary meeting, which consisted of a long statement by the P.M. giving his views as to how the war should be run. According to him we had two main objectives, first an advance on Vienna, secondly the capture of Singapore![1] However, he did support the employment of naval forces in the Pacific."

" After lunch another meeting with American Chiefs followed by another C.O.S. meeting at 4 p.m. which lasted till nearly 6 p.m."

" *September 14th. Quebec.* At 7.30 a.m. told that the P.M. wanted to see me at 9 a.m. and that ' Pug ' Ismay would like to see me before that. I hurried with breakfast and some office work and then saw Ismay. Found him very upset. P.M. had on his own wired to Dickie Mountbatten to find out how it was he was now wanting six divisions to capture Burma, having originally said he only wanted two from outside. Dickie had wired back giving full details of the series of changes in plans that had occurred. As a result Winston had accused us all to

[1] ' Neither of them in our plans. We had no plans for Vienna, nor did I ever look at this operation as becoming possible. Nor had we any plans for the capture of Singapore. By mentioning these objectives he was not assisting in our discussions with the American Chiefs.' *Notes on My Life,* XIV, 45.

Ismay of purposely concealing changes of plans from him to keep him in the dark, that we were all against him. Ismay had written out a letter to him handing in his resignation and asked for my advice as to whether he should send it in. I told him that this decision must rest with him."[1]

" I then started off to see Winston at 9 a.m., wondering what awful row I should find myself mixed up in. To my surprise I found him in his bed and in a very good mood. Another wire from Dickie had arrived with new suggestions. He had now got over all his bad humour; he was prepared to move 2nd Indian Division from Alexander, which he would not look at before. He was in such a good humour that I tackled him about the transfer of Oliver Leese from Alexander to Dickie, and got him to agree."

" I then dashed back for a C.O.S. meeting at 9.30 a.m. which was followed by a Combined meeting at 10 a.m. lasting till 12 noon. A very successful meeting at which we got Americans to accept the British Fleet in Central Pacific, and also the Burma operation. We had great trouble with King who lost his temper entirely and was opposed by the whole of his own Committee. He was determined, if he could, not to admit British naval forces into Nimitz's Command in the Central Pacific."

" At 12.15 we had another short C.O.S. meeting to decide as to how to deal with King's evident animosity towards the conclusions we had arrived at. We decided to get the P.M. at the final Plenary meeting to cross the t's and dot the i's in this respect."

" My mind is now much more at rest. We have nearly finished this meeting. Things have gone well on the whole in spite of Winston's moods."

.   .   .   .

[1] ' That dear old patient ' Pug ' had at last reached the end of his tether is some indication of what we had been through. I believe he did hand in his resignation and that Winston refused to take any notice of it. But for all that it relieved the tension.' *Notes on My Life*, XIV, 47.

The decisions reached by the Conference for once satisfied both sides. Though, at Brooke's instance, they stressed " the advantages of a northern line of approach into Germany as opposed to the southern ", the Combined Chiefs of Staff accepted Eisenhower's proposals for a broad advance instead of the single concentrated thrust on the Ruhr urged by Montgomery. The decision to leave overall operational control to the Supreme Commander had been agreed from the start, and it was impossible for the British Chiefs of Staff, at such a time of victory, to question the competence of the officer to whom both Allied Governments had entrusted their forces. Over both the Italian and Burma campaigns the allies found agreement easy. General Wilson was to be informed that no major units would be withdrawn from Italy until the outcome of Alexander's offensive was known, and was to submit plans to the Combined Chiefs of Staff before October 10th if he wished to make further use of the existing amphibious lift in the Mediterranean. The Supreme Commander, South-East Asia, was to launch two new major operations to clear Burma before the summer monsoon of 1945, preparatory to invading Malaya in the last quarter of the year. While the small-scale offensives on the two flanks were to be maintained—by the British in Arakan and by Stilwell's Chinese in the northern mountains— the British Fourteenth Army was to make a concerted drive across the Chindwin towards the Irrawaddy and Mandalay, while a force of six British and Indian divisions, to be withdrawn from the Mediterranean and North-West Europe, was to make a sea and air descent on Rangoon in the spring.

Despite the unanimity of the opening day, agreement on the Pacific campaign had proved much harder. Determined to deny the Royal Navy any share in the coming victory which his own Service had made such sacrifices to achieve, Admiral King put up a strong delaying action. On the first evening of the Conference the British Chiefs of Staff received from their American colleagues a Memorandum, drawn up before the morning's Plenary session, welcoming British naval participation but adding that it should be confined to the South-West

Pacific, that is, to a subsidiary theatre. The British had therefore resumed the attack on the 14th, Brooke opening proceedings by saying that, while he realised the American Memorandum had been written before the previous day's agreement, he and his colleagues were gravely disturbed by the reference to the South-West Pacific. For political reasons, he urged, it was essential that Britain should take part in the main operations against Japan. This had led to a denial by King that any mention of the Central Pacific had been made at the Plenary session and an angry refusal to commit himself as to where the British Fleet should be employed. But the British Chiefs of Staff, having won their long struggle with the Prime Minister, were adamant, and King's colleagues, in view of their President's promise, felt unable to support him. In the Combined Chief's Final Report it was agreed that the British naval contingent should be a balanced and self-supporting force[1] operating with the main American Fleet, while the details of its employment were to be decided from time to time according to circumstances. The earlier proposal of a British Empire Task Force under MacArthur in the South-West Pacific was, therefore, withdrawn, and the Chief of Air Staff was asked to prepare a paper outlining the contribution the Royal Air Force could make to the attack on the Japanese homeland. The controversy of the past nine months on Far Eastern strategy was thus resolved on the lines the British Chiefs of Staff had urged from the start.

" *September 15th. Quebec.* Started with a C.O.S. meeting at 9 a.m. followed by a Combined meeting at 10 a.m. There we succeeded in winding up the work of this meeting and produced our final Report to President and Prime Minister. On the whole we have been very successful in getting the agreement which we have achieved, and the Americans have shown a wonderful spirit of co-operation . . ."

[1] It was to consist of four of the most modern battleships, five or six fleet-carriers and twenty light-fleet and convoy-escort carriers, with an appropriate number of cruisers and destroyers. *Ehrman* V, 519-24.

'In my diary I have made very little reference to Dill. This is not due to the fact that he was playing any lesser part than usual; on the contrary, he continued to act as the most invaluable link between Marshall and me. I did however notice at this Conference that he was very far from being his old self. He seemed to be wasting away and both mentally and physically he was showing signs of slowing up. When walking down the passages of the hotel with him one had continually to check one's pace. When speaking to him one had frequently to repeat sentences as if his brain only slowly absorbed statements. I was very distressed to see him in this state but had no idea that this was the last occasion on which we should meet. Thank Heaven I did not know; the parting would have been too hard.'[1]

" In the evening we met the P.M. at 6 p.m. He did his best to pull the whole of our final report to pieces, found a lot of petty criticisms and wanted to alter many points which we had secured agreement on with some difficulty. Anthony Eden was there and did his best to help us, but unfortunately Winston was in one of his worst tempers. Now Heaven only knows what will happen to-morrow at our final Plenary meeting. He may between now and to-morrow alter his outlook, but I doubt it. The tragedy is that the Americans, whilst admiring him as a man, have little opinion of him as a strategist. They are intensely suspicious of him. All his alterations or amendments are likely to make them more suspicious than ever."

" *September 16th.* The last day of the Conference. We started with a C.O.S. meeting at 9.30 a.m., expecting to receive amendments by the P.M. to our Final Report.

[1] *Notes on My Life*, XIV, 50-1. Dill had had to go to hospital in July and had written to Brooke on August 1st: " I had better wait till these doctors have finished with me. I am really all right except for a low blood-count which is getting gradually better. Marshall keeps me well in touch with what is going on." ' It was a real tragedy,' Brooke wrote, ' that Dill was so seedy. I missed his contacts and influence with Marshall tremendously. It made me realise more than ever what an immense debt we owed him.' *Notes on My Life*, XIII, 89.

We did not quite know how we should deal with them as the Final Report was one which we had agreed with the American Chiefs; it was therefore not possible for us now to bring in any alterations. However, he must have thought better of it, as those remarks never turned up and instead we were told that he wanted to see us ten minutes before the Plenary meeting."

" At 11 a.m. we had our final Combined meeting and then went up to the Citadel where we met Winston. The first thing he informed us was that he wanted us all for a meeting at 5 p.m.; we had previously make it quite clear that we proposed starting on our fishing trip at 2.30 p.m.! We told him that planes were ordered and all plans made. He said we should not be seeing each other for ten days and that he must have a meeting."

" The (final Plenary) meeting went off well, and we returned to the hotel to counter-order our plans. However, while we were at lunch we received a message from P.M. saying that, after all, he would not have a meeting and would not want us. We had a desperate rush and by 3 p.m. left the hotel for the aerodrome. Our party consisted of Cunningham, Portal, Leckie (Canadian Chief of Air Staff) and self. We took off in two amphibian planes and had an hour's very interesting flight north-west from Quebec towards Hudson's Bay. Country mainly virgin forest and masses of lakes. After about 150 miles we reached the Oriskany Lake where the fishing camp is situated . . ."

" We landed on the lake, taxied up to the landing stage, had tea, put up rods, and started off in canoes to fish. Each one of us had a canoe and guide; we moved from lake to lake by ' portage ', the guide carrying the canoe on his head. . . . As it was getting dark I caught a nice two-pounder. Returned to camp by torch-light. I had caught fourteen trout but only one good one."

" *September 17th. Oriskany Camp.* We got up at 6 a.m.

and after a cup of coffee started off with canoes and guides. We again went through Deep Lake to Silver Lake and from there on to Yate Lake and Spurey Lake and back to Silver Lake, having completed a circuit which brought us to a small log-hut where breakfast had been sent out. After breakfast we set out again through Lakes Bladelrun, Zion, Sundause to Blue Lake. . . . In the evening we worked our way home by a series of ' portages ' the way we came. How my little guide, who must have been nearly as old as I am, carried that 80-lb. canoe all that distance is a marvel."

" We reached home after dark tired and hungry after a delightful day."

" *September 18th. Lac Des Neiges.* Up at 6 a.m. and out to troll for grey trout in the main Oriskany Lake. We had breakfast at 9 a.m. and then sallied out by car to fish another lake. I caught another ten trout bringing my total up to thirty-four, averaging about $\frac{3}{4}$ lb. weight."

" After lunch Cunningham took off for Quebec and New York, whilst Portal and I took off for Quebec, hoping to be able to fly on to the Lac des Neiges. Unfortunately the latter is some 3000 feet up and was in the clouds, so we had to go by road. Our host, Colonel Clark, met us on the aerodrome and motored up with us. We stopped for tea at La Cabane, his river camp where Winston stayed last year. We hurried on to try and put some fishing in before dark, but only had half-an-hour before it became too dark."

" *September 20th. Quebec.* Up again at 6 a.m. and fished hard till 2.30 p.m. when we had to leave. I finished the day with forty-four trout which brought up my total for the two days to a hundred-and-six, averaging a good $1\frac{1}{2}$ lbs. and out of which twelve were grey trout. It is certainly the most wonderful lake for fish that I have ever seen."

" On the way down we stopped again at La Cabane.

As we had a few minutes to spare while tea was being prepared,[1] we filled in the time fishing in the river opposite the log-hut. During those few minutes Portal caught a trout of $5\frac{1}{2}$ lbs.—the biggest ever caught in that pool."

" As we reached La Cabane we were handed an official looking telegram which had been sent up for us. It was from Winston and ran as follows:—

' GUNFIRE (305).

Following for C.I.G.S. and C.A.S. from Prime Minister. Please let me know how many captives were taken by land and air forces respectively in battle of Snow Lake.'

Portal worded the following reply:—

Following for Prime Minister from C.I.G.S. and C.A.S. Your gunfire 305 only just received. Battle of Snow Lake began at dawn 19th and finished 2.30 p.m. on 20th. Enemy forces were aggressive throughout and put up fierce resistance at all familiar strong points, particularly Churchill Bay and Brooke Bay. Casualties inflicted by our land and air forces were approximately equal and totalled about 250 dead, including the enemy general who surrendered to the land forces on Tuesday afternoon. In a short rear-guard action at Cabane de Montmorency our air forces accounted for the largest submarine yet seen in these waters.

We trust that you have had a comfortable journey.' "

" *September 21st. In the Clipper.* Got up at 5 a.m., left hotel at 5.30 and embarked on the clipper in the St. Lawrence at 6 a.m. By 7 a.m. we had taken off and were flying past the Frontenac Hotel looking into my bedroom window. We had a comfortable journey over the clouds reaching Botwood about 12 noon, when we had lunch. At 2 p.m. we took off again for England. I went up to the pilot's seat to see the last of Newfoundland before

---

[1] 'Clark had prepared a mass of food of all descriptions for us to take away with us. I have seldom met anybody kinder or more hospitable.'

we set out across the Atlantic. By 8.30 a.m. we were over Plymouth Bay, nosing our way about in a very misty sky. However, we made a beautiful landing."

" *September 22nd. London.* We started the day by going to the R.A.F. Mess for breakfast. While we were there we were informed that the mist had now cleared from Poole harbour where our special train was waiting for us. So we re-embarked and flew on to Poole, caught our train and were in London by 2.30 p.m."

" I went to the office and worked till 7.30 p.m., including an interview with P. J. Grigg. Then motored home where I arrived shortly after 9 p.m."

* * * * * * * *

During the week following the conclusion of the Quebec Conference and while the British Chiefs of Staff were recrossing the Atlantic, the consequences first became felt of Eisenhower's assumption of the command of the ground forces in North-Western Europe. At the beginning of September, when Montgomery had once more urged his chief to halt his armies on every front save one and allocate the whole of his available petrol, transport and ammunition to a single ' powerful and full-blooded thrust ' of forty divisions, either in the north under himself or in the centre under Bradley, the Germans had only twenty-five disorganized and under-strength divisions left in the West. According to their Commander-in-Chief they had fewer guns and tanks to hold the two-hundred crucial miles between the Scheldt estuary and Luxembourg than had been available to defend Britain after Dunkirk.[1] Nor had they any hope of reinforcement from the East where a hundred-and-twenty overstrained German divisions—little more than half the number at the beginning of the year—were struggling against three times as many Russian divisions, or from the

---

[1] At the beginning of September SHAEF Intelligence described the German Army in the West as " no longer a cohesive force, but a number of fugitive battle groups. . . . Organized resistance under the control of the German High Command is unlikely to continue beyond 1 December 1944, and . . . it may end even sooner." *Pogue* 244-5.

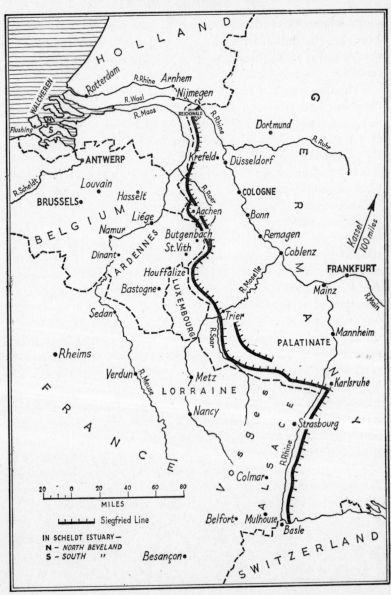

THE FRANCO-GERMAN BORDER

south where Alexander's men were battering on the Gothic Line in the hills north of Florence and where, beyond the Adriatic, a Communist-led Yugoslavia was ablaze with rebellion.

Yet, as a result of the Supreme Commander's attempt to maintain from overstrained supply-lines the momentum of his advance along the entire Western Approaches to the Reich, Hitler and the German High Command were given the time they needed to halt the northern drive towards the Ruhr—a target far more vulnerable and accessible than any comparable prize elsewhere and whose capture at that moment might have ended the war. On September 5th—the day the British Chiefs of Staff sailed for Quebec—in conformity with a S.H.A.E.F. plan for an advance on both sides of the Ardennes made before the sudden enemy collapse in Normandy, Eisenhower sent a signal to Montgomery and Bradley that, as the bulk of the German Army had been destroyed, he proposed to exploit his success by simultaneously breaking the Siegfried Line, crossing the Rhine on a wide front and seizing both the Saar and the Ruhr.[1] At the time of dispatching this telegram—part of which took four days to reach Montgomery owing to the lack of facilities for exercising operational command from Eisenhower's personal headquarters—the Supreme Commander was isolated, with a sprained knee, in a remote Normandy villa nearly four hundred miles from the battle-line with which he was out of both radio and telephonic touch. Eager as " the policeman of Allied unity " to reconcile the competing demands of his high-powered American and British subordinates, obsessed like the sound staff officer he was by the logistical nightmare of supplying, from distant and inadequate ports, their diverging

---

[1] " This I intend to do with all possible speed." Montgomery, *Memoirs*, 273. " Ike," Captain Butcher wrote in his diary after a conversation with him as late as September 11th, ". . . expects to go through the Aachen gap in the north and the Metz gap in the south and to bring the Southern Group of Armies to the Rhine south of Coblenz. Then he thinks he should use his airborne forces to seize the crossings over the Rhine to be in a position to thrust deep into the Ruhr and to threaten Berlin itself." *Butcher*, 567. There is little contemporary evidence to suggest that, in rejecting Montgomery's plea for concentration, Eisenhower was influenced by the danger of counter-attack by a powerful German reserve on which he subsequently laid such stress in his post-war memoirs.

and runaway columns, yet unrealistically sanguine about their progress, this impartial and conciliatory commander failed to give the consistent and categorical orders which, by halting the rest of his army, might have enabled part of it to break through the enemy's momentarily disorganized defences. While Montgomery and Bradley both pleaded for priority of supply—the one to strike through Holland across the Lower Rhine at the Ruhr and the Hanover plain, the other to drive through the hillier Saar and Palatinate towards Frankfurt and Central Germany—Eisenhower, inclining first one way, then another, remained what Brooke had seen him to be, an arbiter balancing the requirements of competing allies and subordinates rather than a master of the field making the decisive choice which alone could turn the " option of difficulties " that is war into victory.[1]

The opportunity for delivering the *coup de grâce* by rushing the Ruhr, if it ever existed, lasted only for those few days of early September. By the 10th, when in response to Montgomery's repeated entreaties Eisenhower flew from his sick-bed to Brussels[2] to give his approval to a plan for using the Allies' airborne forces to seize, ahead of the halted British Second Army, the canal and river crossings of the Maas, Waal and Rhine, the chance to drive through Holland to the Ruhr was already passing. Not till the 12th, in response to the Combined Chiefs of Staff's Quebec Directive urging precedence for the northern thrust, did the Supreme Commander agree to allocate sufficient additional transport and petrol to 21 Army Group to make even this belated project

---

[1] " I believe that in August 1944 a Supreme Allied Commander . . . . could have ended the war by Christmas by decisively backing either Montgomery or Bradley. But there was . . . no strong hand at the helm, no man in command. There was only a conference, presided over by a Chairman—a shrewd, intelligent, tactful, careful Chairman. . . . The man on whose shoulders the title of Supreme Allied Commander rested had been especially selected for his ability to conciliate, to see both points of view, to be above national interests—and to be neither bold nor decisive, neither a leader nor a general. . . . It was the sudden necessity of choosing between Montgomery's and Bradley's battle plans that was his trouble—and that necessity was thrust upon him unexpectedly by History." R. Ingersoll, *Top Secret*, 168-9.
[2] The interview took place in Eisenhower's aircraft as he was too lame to get out. Montgomery, *Memoirs*, 275.

possible. And he still continued in private to stigmatize Montgomery's demand for complete priority of supply as " crazy "[1] and failed to halt Patton in Lorraine.

It was a case of too little too late. During the five days that followed Eisenhower's decision and while the proposed aerial offensive—Operation *Market Garden*—was being mounted, the German strength in Montgomery's path doubled. On September 17th, with only part of the Second Army supplied and in a position to fight its way across the sixty-four miles of enemy-held territory that separated it from the northernmost landing-zone at Arnhem, one British and two American airborne divisions were dropped beside the Rhine, Waal and Maas crossings. Simultaneously Patton, using supplies which might have made all the difference to his northern colleagues, launched a major attack on Metz. During the next five days, fighting desperately, Montgomery's troops advanced more than fifty miles to join hands with the American paratroopers who, with their aid, captured the bridges across all but the farthest of the five waterways. But the British First Airborne Division, dropped by ill-luck in the middle of a German parachute corps and isolated on the northern bank of the Rhine, was faced by a task beyond its powers. Deprived by bad weather of air support and reinforcements, for a week the men held out in their encircled positions. Then, on September 24th—two days after Brooke's return to England—Montgomery ordered the withdrawal of the survivors to the south bank of the river.

Not till September 22nd, after calling a conference of his senior commanders at Brussels, did the Supreme Commander agree to the general northward shift of the main American effort that he had refused for four crucial weeks. By then the battle for the Rhine at Arnhem had been lost, and fourteen German divisions were opposing the British Second Army. The opportunity for decisive victory at the decisive point before winter had passed. With the last Channel ports still uncaptured and Antwerp, though in Allied hands, blockaded

---

[1] " Monty's suggestion is simply—'Give him everything'. This is crazy." *Eisenhower's war diary entry for September 12th, 1944*, quoted in Kay Summersby's *Eisenhower Was My Boss*, 155.

by the Germans at the mouth of the Scheldt, the logistical problems which had militated against decisive action when it seemed still practicable had assumed dimensions that could only now be solved by shortening the Liberation Army's supply-lines.

For though at the beginning of September, after their crushing defeats in Normandy and the Balkans, the Germans were off balance and stripped of reserves, their recovery was swift. The bewildered generals and officers captured during the Allied race through Northern France and Belgium had declared, with truth, that there was nothing between their captors and Berlin, that the Western Wall was unmanned, and that there were no reserves in Germany nor plans for resistance. But awakened to the urgency of their peril, Hitler and his satraps soon made both. By calling up boys of sixteen and combing the Navy, *Luftwaffe* and reserved occupations, the Führer during the autumn of 1944 created forty new divisions to form the central reserve which he had lacked since the Italian collapse a year before. With this, as soon as it could be trained and equipped, he planned to strike back at the commander who had failed to overwhelm him when he was at his mercy. And while thousands of civilians and slave-workers toiled to strengthen the Siegfried Line, Germany's toughest generals—the Models and Students to whom, under Von Rundstedt, the defence of the West had been entrusted—gathered fighting men from every fortress, depot and training establishment and flung them, with veteran paratroopers and the remnants of the defeated and retreating divisions, in the path of the allies.

To Brooke, returning from the Quebec Conference, all this was tragic. When he had left England the invasion of northern Germany by Montgomery's victorious armour had seemed imminent.[1] Now the gates of the Ruhr had been closed and

[1] While he was in Quebec he sent a personal Order through the V.C.I.G.S. to Montgomery who had just circulated his subordinate commanders about their security arrangements and personal safety when they entered Germany. It read:
" You yourself have conspicuous appearance and dress and are therefore obvious target for the enemy.
" Little doubt that definite and concerted efforts will be made by desperate men to kill you.

barred and the empty ramparts were manned. In Italy, too, where at the end of August Churchill, Alexander and Wilson had all confidently hoped for an autumn invasion of Istria and Austria, the failure to strike at Germany's heart was exerting its melancholy influence. Instead of abandoning the Apennines and Lombardy plain as the Reich behind them went down in flames, Kesselring's men, conscious that the homeland was being saved, put up as staunch a fight as any in German history. And, having at the beginning of September driven a twenty-miles-wide wedge into the Gothic Line and captured Rimini, Alexander, his troops confronted by one grimly contested mountain ridge after another, was forced on the 26th to write to the C.I.G.S.:

"The trouble is my forces are too weak relative to the enemy to force a break-through. . . . We shall have to continue the battle of Italy with about twenty divisions, almost all of which have had long periods of heavy fighting this year, and some for several years, against the twenty German divisions committed to the battle-front. . . . We are inflicting very heavy losses on the enemy and are making slow but steady progress, but our losses are also heavy and we are fighting in a country where, it is generally agreed, a superiority of at least three to one is required for successful offensive operations. It will be small wonder, therefore, if we fail to score a really decisive success when the opposing forces are so equally matched."[1]

To which Brooke could only reply: "It is not possible to send reinforcements to the Mediterranean and you will have to continue to live on your own resources." For the chief sufferers from the failure to follow up Montgomery's victory

---

"It is therefore your duty to put aside your feelings and take most stringent and thorough steps for your personal safety. You can no longer afford to be casual in these matters.

"Please regard this message not as a suggestion but as a definite order from C.I.G.S."   Montgomery, *Memoirs*, 294.

[1] Gen. Alexander to C.I.G.S., 26 Sept., 1944. cit. *Ehrman* V, 530.

were the British who, having thrown their last military reserves into an all-out effort to end the struggle in Europe in 1944, now faced its almost certain continuance into another year and as a result, a growing gap between their man-power needs and resources.[1] And though the obstinacy with which the Germans clung to the last Apennine passes continued to serve the C.I.G.S.'s plan of drawing Germany's reserves and supplies away from the one front where the decisive blow at her heart could be struck, it availed little when the commander who alone could deliver it failed to strike home.

Nor were the repercussions of Eisenhower's indecision confined to Europe. They affected South-East Asia too. At Quebec the Combined Chiefs of Staff and the Prime Minister and President had approved a plan for reinforcing Mountbatten's forces in India with six British and British-Indian divisions from Europe, including one armoured and one airborne division—with their administrative and supporting troops some 352,000 men and 24,000 vehicles[2]—for an air and seaborne expedition to capture Rangoon before the 1945 monsoon. But by the beginning of October, for all the Prime Minister's pleas to Roosevelt for American reinforcements to release British divisions from Italy, it was clear that no troops could be spared from Europe during the coming winter at all. A month earlier, with the equivalent of twelve armoured divisions against Model's remaining two-hundred tanks, Eisenhower could, in General Blumentritt's words, " have torn the weak German front to pieces and ended the war "; [3] by now his fifty-six divisions—eight of them still in Normandy for lack of transport—were so extended against the growing forces in their path that, like Gamelin in 1940, he was without any strategic reserve at all. A reluctant decision had, therefore, to

[1] " Taking all possible sources of supply, the Minister of Labour calculated that only 140,000 men and women could be made available for the Services during the year. Against this the Services were demanding a further 225,300. . . . The Man-power Committee had therefore to try, in uncertain and largely unknown circumstances, to close a gap of some 85,000." *Ehrman* VI, 23-4.

[2] *Ehrman* V, 509. By the end of September the Vice-Chiefs of Staff, by drawing on more troops from India and other devices, had been able to reduce the number of troops to be transported to the East to a quarter of a million. *Idem*, 532.

[3] *Wilmot*, 539.

be made by the British Chiefs of Staff and Prime Minister to postpone Operation *Dracula*, as the Rangoon landing was called, until after the end of the war in Europe, leaving General Slim to reconquer Burma, if he could, by driving with such troops as he already possessed out of the mountains and jungles across which he had retreated in 1942.

. . . .

When Brooke resumed his Whitehall routine on September 25th—the day the Arnhem battle ended—the necessity for this had not yet become a certainty, and the Chiefs of Staff were still considering the Vice-Chiefs of Staff's proposals for reducing the number of troops to be transported to India.

" *September 25th*. Back to work with C.O.S. at 11 a.m. when we worked out plans for recapture of Rangoon next month. . . ."

" *September 26th*. Went to Euston Station at 10 a.m. to meet P.M. on his return from America. Large crowd as usual. He arrived looking very fit and cheerful."

" From there to Chiefs of Staff when we went further into the questions of next March operations for recapture of Burma."

" *September 27th*. Cabinet at 6 p.m. at which Winston wanted to discuss the desirability or otherwise of responding to German requests to send food in for the British population of the Channel Islands. Decided not to send any in and to reply to Germans that it was their duty to keep population reasonably fed or to surrender if they were unable to do so."

" *September 28th*. A short C.O.S. meeting attended by Planners when we discussed the man-power problem in relation to our future effort in the war against Japan."

" *October 2nd*. A longish Chiefs of Staff meeting when we discussed the Foreign Office attitude to our paper on dismemberment of Germany. We had considered the possible future and more distant threat to our security in the shape of an aggressive Russia. Apparently the Foreign Office could not admit that Russia might some day become unfriendly."

" Cabinet at 5.30 p.m., and at 10 p.m. meeting with P.M. to discuss Burma operation. Just before dinner I had received a message from Montgomery saying that he could not spare either 52nd Division or 3rd Division, 6th Airborne Division or 6th Guards Armoured Brigade or a Corps H.Q., and drawing our attention to the fact that there is still heavy fighting in front of us before defeating Germany. Operations in Italy are also lagging behind and do not admit of the withdrawal of forces. I, therefore, advised against trying to stage Rangoon operation before next monsoon, and P.M. agreed. It is very disappointing, but I think the correct decision. We were lucky to find the P.M. in a very reasonable and quiet mood. We might otherwise have failed to obtain any decision from him."

" P.M. suddenly informed us that he and Anthony Eden were off to Moscow on Saturday next, and that he wanted me to come with him! This is a bit of a surprise and clashes with my plans to go to France on Wednesday till Sunday. I shall have to shorten the French trip."

" *October 3rd.* Plans for Moscow are taking shape, and we start on Saturday evening as far as I can see. A large explosion has just gone off in the vicinity. Presumably, a rocket."[1]

" The C.O.S. was attended by representatives of the Foreign Office whilst we discussed organisation of Control Committees for Germany after defeat. In the afternoon, first of all a Selection Board meeting and then interviews with Urquhart, the commander of the 1st Airborne Division just back from Arnhem. Then Oliver Leese,

---

[1] The first German rocket-bomb fell on London on the evening of September 8th. During the autumn and winter about five hundred of these missiles fell in the London area, killing nearly three thousand and wounding more than six thousand persons.

back from Italy prior to going out to Burma to relieve Giffard."

" *October 4th. Versailles.* After lunch started off for Heston aerodrome to visit Eisenhower at Versailles. He had sent over his special Mitchell machine that cruises at 260 miles per hour. We had a somewhat bumpy journey through storms. It gave me a great thrill going through Versailles again. The last time had been in 1939 when driving up from Laval to Lille."

" We drove round to Ike's office in an annexe of the Hôtel Trianon. I had a good talk with him and met Bedell Smith and de Guingand. We then drove up to Ike's small château in Saint Germain, the one Rundstedt had occupied before he left Paris. Bertie Ramsay, Humfrey Gale, Leigh-Mallory and Whiteley came to dine."

" During the night I heard one of the rockets landing in Paris."

" *October 5th.* A conference by Ike at 11.30 of his Army Group commanders. Ike ran the conference very well. It consisted first of all of statements by Army Group commanders, followed by the Air and Navy. Ike then explained his future strategy which consisted of the capture of Antwerp, an advance to the Rhine in the north and south, forcing the Rhine north and south of the Ruhr, capture of Ruhr, followed by an advance on Berlin either from Ruhr or from Frankfurt, depending on which proved most promising. Meanwhile Devers in the south to threaten Munich as a cover plan. During the whole discussion one fact stood out clearly, that (access to) Antwerp must be captured with the least possible delay."

" I feel that Monty's strategy for once is at fault. Instead of carrying out the advance on Arnhem he ought to have made certain of Antwerp in the first place. Ramsay brought this out well in the discussion and criticized Monty freely. Ike nobly took all blame on himself as he had approved Monty's suggestion to operate on Arnhem.[1] The atmosphere was good and friendly in spite of some candid criticisms of the administrative situation."

" After lunch I flew back, doing the journey Paris-London in one hour and ten minutes. Found Gammell in the office and had a long interview with him to discuss plans for Istrian operations."

" After dinner called up by P.M. to go round to him. All he wanted was to discuss with me my visit to Eisenhower and to hear the gossip. I found Portal there fixing up final details for the trip to Moscow which are now settled."

" *October 6th.* A busy day, first of all catching up ground lost during visit to France, and secondly polishing off last bits before starting for Moscow."

" Finally left London at 7 p.m. for home so as to have clear day at home before starting for Russia."

" *October 7th.* A quiet day at home with early dinner so as to be ready for Boyle at 8.30 p.m. when he is to pick me up for Lyneham airfield where I am to meet Anthony Eden and depart at midnight."

" *Later.* Boyle turned up and we had a good run through Basingstoke, Newbury, Hungerford, Marlborough. We arrived a little before Anthony, who turned up after having dined with Queen Mary."

" At 12.10 a.m. sharp we took off into the darkness."[2]

---

[1] Despite the stress put at this Conference on the importance of opening the Scheldt estuary, in a message to Montgomery and Bradley two days later Eisenhower defined the first objective of both Army Groups as " the gaining of the line of the Rhine north of Bonn as quickly as humanly possible." According to Montgomery, it was only on October 9th, after the latter had reported this to be now impossible without the prior opening of Antwerp, that Eisenhower wrote, " Unless we have Antwerp producing by the middle of November, entire operations will come to a standstill. I must emphasize that, of all our operations on our entire front from Switzerland to the Channel, I consider Antwerp of first importance." Montgomery, *Memoirs*, 283.

[2] Churchill states that he left London with Eden, Brooke and Ismay on the night of October 5th. This must be a mistake. *Churchill* VI, 192.

Chapter Nine

MOSCOW

THE CHIEF reason for the Prime Minister's and Brooke's visit to Moscow was Churchill's determination to solve the Polish problem. That autumn Russia's attitude towards Poland had broken across the accord established between the Eastern and Western allies at Teheran and consolidated by the success of the " Second Front ". During the Warsaw rising in August, the Kremlin had behaved with gross inhumanity, not only making no attempt to use its armies—then only a few miles away—to aid the Polish insurgents but flatly refusing to allow the British and American air forces landing-fields from which to drop supplies on the city. As a result the rising had been crushed with the slaughter of 200,000 Poles, including the flower of those who might have re-created an independent Poland after the war, while a number of British and American airmen had needlessly lost their lives. Stalin's contemptuous excuse—so far as he deigned to give any—was that the Polish Home Army was worthless and led by irresponsible " criminals " and " adventurers ".

A few days before the Warsaw rising the Red Army had captured the Polish city of Lublin and had at once set up there, in opposition to the exiled Polish Government in London, a " National Committee of Liberation " of Moscow-trained Communists. Behind this façade the Kremlin now proposed to re-draw Poland's frontiers so as to incorporate nearly half its pre-war territory in Russia while it denounced the Polish Ministers in London as fascists and traitors. As Great Britain had gone to war to preserve the independence of Poland and had given shelter to its Government and Army in exile, Churchill was faced by a grave moral challenge.

He met it with his habitual courage, proposing an immediate visit to Moscow and using his powers of persuasion to induce the Polish Prime Minister, Mikolajczyk, a man of moderation and goodwill, to meet the Russians half-way and collaborate with the hated Lublin Committee. In this he received small encouragement from Roosevelt, who was determined to do nothing that might injure the prospects of an American-Russian working understanding which was his recipe for the future governance of mankind. With this in mind, the President warned Churchill and Stalin that, while his Ambassador in Moscow, Averell Harriman, would attend their talks as an observer, they should be regarded only as exploratory preliminaries to a three-Power meeting which he would convene after the forthcoming Presidential election.[1]

There were other questions for discussion with Russia—the demarcation between Soviet and British areas of operations and influence in the Balkans where the Red Army was now in complete control of Rumania and Bulgaria and where the Germans, threatened with encirclement from the north, were on the point of evacuating Greece; the proposals which had been under discussion at Dumbarton Oaks for a world organisation to maintain peace after the war; and, most pressing of all, the provision of some kind of co-ordination between the Red Armies in Poland and the Balkans and the Anglo-American armies in North-West Europe and Italy. The British landing in Istria, if it was to take place as Churchill still hoped, needed in particular to be synchronised with the Russian advance towards the Danube; on the way to Moscow the Prime Minister and the C.I.G.S. were to break their journey at Naples to discuss the possibilities of this operation with Generals Wilson and Alexander. In view of the heavy drain on the latter's troops of the autumn offensive against the Gothic Line and the impossibility of reinforcing them, there seemed little chance now of staging this till February, and before the

[1] *Feis*, 442-3.

Prime Minister left London the Director of Military Operations had furnished him with an appreciation of the situation to prepare his mind for what he was to be told by General Wilson.[1]

" *October 8th. Cairo.* We had a good trip and arrived in Naples at 7.10 a.m. after exactly seven hours flying. We landed just in time; as a very heavy rain thunderstorm broke and obscured everything, we should have had a job getting down in it. We landed just behind Winston's plane and were met by ' Jumbo ' Wilson, Alexander, Macmillan, John Cunningham, etc. We drove to a villa in Naples where we had a bath, shave and breakfast. We then had a conference with P.M., Wilson, Alex, Eden, ' Pug ' and Jacob to discuss best plan to adopt to retain the American divisions and landing-craft in Italy and to prevent them being withdrawn. Plans are difficult to make; Alex is getting stuck in the Apennines with tired forces and cannot spare any for amphibious operations. At the same time Hungary is suing for peace, Russians are advancing into Yugoslavia and Tito's partisans making ground. It is, therefore, hard to estimate what the situation will be when Alex can find forces, namely in February."

" At 11.30 a.m. we took off again, Eden having changed over into Winston's plane, who had asked me to come also; but I thought I had better remain in my plane and get on (with) drafting a wire to London with Ismay and Jacob on results of our conference in Naples. I am now in the air again, writing this as we fly down the leg of Italy on our way to Cairo."

" *Later.* We finished a very good flight to Cairo and arrived at 6.30 p.m. (8.30 local time) and did an excellent landing in the dark. Unfortunately the P.M.'s machine did a bad landing and damaged the under-carriage and

[1] D.M.O. to C.I.G.S. 7 Oct., 1944. Lord Alanbrooke, *Personal Files*. See *Ehrman* VI, 47-8.

was unable to fly on. Paget met me and drove to ' Casey Villa ' where Moyne now lives."[1]

" After dinner we drove out at midnight for our departure for Moscow. We had to do a reshuffle, as the P.M.'s machine could not fly on owing to the damage to its under-carriage. He therefore changed over into my plane."

" *October 9th. In the air over Kharkov.* We took off at 1 a.m. and flew out over the Aegean, round by the Dardanelles into the Black Sea so as to avoid having to climb over the mountains of Turkey, as flying high is bad for P.M. We struck Russia over the Crimea but it was still dark. I got up at 8 a.m. and just as I had finished dressing and shaving we passed over Dnepropetrovsk and had a very good view of the famous dam over the River Dnieper. Beautiful clear day, and most interesting looking down on this country that has been so much fought over."

" P.M. seemed very tired last night. He is still asleep now which should do him good."

" *Later.* Spent rest of journey looking at the country and picking up all the old signs of the war, such as derelict trenches, gun-emplacements, demolished houses, anti-tank ditches, etc. From what I saw there is no doubt that the war has not left such deep scars on Russia as it has on the heavily fought-over sectors of France and Italy. I was struck by the density of the population of the country we flew over, very much heavier than what I had met when flying up from Baku through Kuibyshev to Moscow."

" When we approached Moscow it became evident that the pilot was not quite clear as to where he was, and he started hawking around and finally found an aerodrome on which he came down and was told that the right aerodrome was some thirty kilometres farther on. We took

---

[1] Lord Moyne, Minister for State, Middle East, who a few weeks later was assassinated by Jewish terrorists.

off again and were very soon over Moscow. However, our next difficulty was that the under-carriage would not come down properly, and the emergency compressed-air had to be used to get it fixed. Finally we landed just before 12 noon (Moscow time), having done the trip from London in exactly thirty-four hours. We were met by Molotov, Maisky, a bevy of Russian generals, Clark Kerr, Harriman, Brocas Burrows etc. A guard of honour to be inspected and marched past, the whole of 'God Save the King' and the Russian National Anthem. Finally a broadcast speech by Winston."

"I then drove off to the National Hotel; 'Pug', Jacob, etc., are all here with me. Winston is in a small house by himself, and Eden is at the Embassy. I lunched with Brocas in his flat and discussed with him the Russian dislike for him which has resulted in our having to withdraw him. Then on to Embassy to see office arrangements that have been made for me. From there on to the British Mission buildings which I visited with Brocas and had talks with a good few of the Mission personnel."

"*October 10th. Moscow.* I had a wonderful sleep and then went round to the office they have established for me in the Embassy. Beyond a few telegrams there was little work for me there, but I discovered we were all invited by Stalin to a large lunch for 2.30 p.m. The party consisted of Winston, Stalin, Eden, Molotov, Gusev,[1] Maisky, Harriman, Ismay, Burrows, Deane, Jacob, representatives from the Dominions, Russian generals and Foreign Office staff. Great smartness all round, and all Foreign Office staff, including the interpreters, have now blossomed out into uniforms of a grey colour."

"Stalin greeted me with congratulations on my promotion and was in a most affable mood. The lunch was a complete banquet, starting with masses of hors-d'œuvres which included caviar. We passed on to sucking-pig, then small scallops of mushrooms, followed by fish, then

[1] Russian Ambassador in London.

chicken and partridges, finishing up with ices. We had, as usual, a series of speeches proposing everybody's health. Molotov started with the health of the P.M., then Eden, then myself, then Ismay, then Harriman etc., etc., and we all had to reply in turn."

" Finally Stalin himself got up and began a long speech. He referred to Winston's and Harriman's speeches in which they had mentioned the unreadiness for war of Britain and America. Stalin said this was the same in the case of the Russian forces. Why was this? The reason was easy to find, we were all three peace-loving nations with no aggressive thoughts. Germany and Japan, both aggressors, were ready for war because they wanted war. How was this to be prevented in future? Only by the co-operation of the three peace-loving nations, provided they maintained the power to enforce peace when necessary, etc. Finally Molotov said he was in an aggressive mood and that he insisted we all fill our glasses with champagne to drink an important toast he had to propose and one for which there must be no heel-taps, and he himself would see that the glasses were emptied. He then proposed the health of the three leaders, and we had to drain our glasses. Luckily up to then I had got off lightly and had only had one vodka and one glass of white wine."

" It was 5.30 p.m. when we rose from the table. We had sat for three solid hours, listening to politicians and diplomats informing each other of their devotion and affection and expressing sentiments very far detached from veracity. We had not yet finished, but went into the next room for coffee, brandy, smokes and fruit. Finally at 6.15 p.m. we broke up and returned to the Embassy to read the latest telegrams."

" *October 11th.* Started with a visit to my office at the Embassy. At 11 a.m. Brocas Burrows came to collect me to do some shopping. However, the shopping though interesting was most unsuccessful; there is practically nothing worth buying, although a lot of junk is changing hands at very high prices. I then lunched at the American Embassy to discuss the lines on which we should work with the Americans when we come to discuss military questions."

" In the afternoon drove out to a small height outside Moscow from which Napoleon watched the burning of the town. Drove back through the ' Park of Culture ' where they have got an exhibition of captured German weapons of all types from veterinary equipment to aeroplanes. A very well-run show. At 6.30 p.m. proceeded to a cocktail party given by Molotov. Found Maisky and Mme. Maisky there, also Litvinov and Madame and all the rest of the people we have been meeting. Back to the office and the hotel for a bath and then to the Embassy at 9 p.m. for dinner attended by Stalin and Winston. The speeches this time were kept till the end, but even then we only rose at midnight."

" During dinner a salute was fired for the capture of Cluj, a wonderful display of fireworks which were reflected in the Kremlin windows. After dinner a large reception of those who could not be fitted into the dinner. Finally the diplomatic heads with Stalin and Winston got into a huddle in a small room and remained on indefinitely. I escaped at 2 a.m. and went off to bed, delighted at last to get some sleep."

" *October 12th.* There is some fable about some hunters going out to shoot a bear who on the eve of the shoot became so busy arguing about the sale of the skin and the sharing of the proceeds that they forgot to shoot the bear! I feel this is what we are doing here. Ever since we have arrived we have been busy discussing post-war settlements and as a result have completely neglected up to date the problem of how we are going to finish the war."

" During the morning I went over to see Winston in bed and settled various points about appointments with him and the question of the withdrawal of Brocas Burrows. I also succeeded in riding him off any idea of trying to withdraw divisions from Italy to try still to carry out the Rangoon attack before the monsoon. He was mainly influenced by his desire to do something for Mountbatten. I also arranged with him some of the details of the military talks we are to have with the Russians either Saturday or Sunday. He aims at leaving here on Monday and returning to London by Friday; I hope he keeps to this plan."

" In the afternoon I drove off with Moran to see the monastery of the First Virgin's Cemetery.[1] It is just on the edge of Moscow. We visited the Greek church, walls covered with 16th century mural paintings in excellent condition, also lovely old ikons and clergy clothes. Outside was a large cemetery and in it is buried Stalin's first wife; the tombstone is a stone pillar broken at top and with a head carved out of the break. Well-kept garden round it."

" In the evening I went to the opera to see *Prince Igor*. A vast theatre with the stage larger than the auditorium. Very fine music, singing, scenery and dresses; in fact far better staged than anything that could be done in London. It was a wonderful and most impressive performance. The theatre was packed, all stalls being reserved for Commissars and officers. No sergeants allowed in them, and this is a country of supposed equality. We had tried to take stalls for some of our sergeant clerks, but were informed that they could not be admitted! "

" Opera lasted from 7.30 to midnight."

" Poles have now been fetched over from London, and to-day is to be devoted to discussions concerning the future of Poland."

" Weather turned much colder."

' That morning whilst I was with Winston he suddenly looked up at me and asked, " Why did not the King give Monty his baton when he visited him in France." I replied

[1] " I visited a monastery near Moscow where 7000 virgins were collected annually as a tax to the Tartars to keep them quiet! " Gen. Brooke to Lady Brookeborough, 6 Nov., 1944.

that I did not know, but that, as batons were not Woolworth stores, they had to be made and that probably one was not ready. " No! " replied Winston, " that is not it. Monty wants to fill the Mall when he gets his baton! And he will not fill the Mall! " I assured him that there was no reason for Monty to fill the Mall on that occasion. But he continued, " Yes, he will fill the Mall because he is Monty, and I will not have him filling the Mall! " '

' Apparently he went on turning this matter over in his mind, for on the journey home he suddenly turned to me and said:—" Monty will not fill the Mall when he gets his baton! " '

' I took the first opportunity I had to warn Monty to keep his visit to Buckingham Palace as quiet as possible.'

" *October 13th.* Spent the morning preparing my notes for to-morrow's military meeting when I am to describe the situation on the French front, Italian front and Burmese front. It will not be an easy matter as I shall have to work through an interpreter."

" After lunch went out with Brocas to visit the site of an old wooden castle owned by the Tsars and a special favourite of Ivan the Terrible. It used to overlook the Moscowa River and vast forests, all cut down, on the far side. Nothing is left of the 16th century wooden castle as it decayed away, but in one of the subsequently built stone houses they have got a wonderful scale model of the castle, which gives one an excellent idea of the astounding work they carried out in wood. A woman guide took us round; she looked like an illiterate peasant woman but was very far from it. She had made a special study of Russian history and it was quite impossible to stump her."

" Came back for a time to the office to read the latest telegrams, and then back to the hotel for tea and two boiled eggs before going to the Opera again. This simple meal was just Heaven after all the orgies of food that we have been struggling through."

" The opera was *Eugen Onegin* and, I think, on the whole was better than last night. The scenery was again uncannily good; the duel scene was by half light in the snow amongst snow-covered birch trees, with a cold mist rising up from the valley and a changing sky of pearl grey with a few occasional breaks of light. The singing was also quite beautiful. I could not help wondering what the effect of these wonderfully reproduced episodes of aristocratic life must have on the Communist audience. The State Ball scenery and dresses were magnificent, and I was interested to see that the audience was so impressed that it clapped spontaneously as the curtain was raised."

" The tendency towards better turn-out both in men and in women is most noticeable since I was here last. The officers are competing against each other to turn out better and better. The women have not much chance of doing anything very great with the limited resources at their disposal, but they are certainly making the best of them and are showing a tidiness which was totally absent last time I was here."[1]

" It is very distressing to hear from the Mission here how impossible it is to build up any sort of social relations with the local inhabitants. They will never come for meals and never ask any of our representatives to come out. A vast gap exists which apparently cannot be bridged."

Up till now Brooke had had little of importance to do in Moscow and had spent the time mainly in sight-seeing, in which, according to General Ismay's secretary who organized the social activities of the British delegation, he took an almost boyish delight.[2] The primary purpose of the visit being

[1] In August 1942, when Stalingrad was at its last gasp and Russia was half-starving. See *The Turn of the Tide*, pp. 459-71.

[2] Communicated by Mrs. Philip Astley (formerly Miss Joan Bright). " One of my major problems was finding a party for Brooke to go to. We all used to have breakfast together—he, ' Pug ', some brigadiers and various other officers and me—and would meet in various degrees of hangovers. Brooke always had some joking remark to make about the appearance of the brigadiers and he always turned and asked me what he could do that day and whether that night there

political, the brunt was borne by the Prime Minister who on the night of his arrival, after thirty-six hours almost continuous travelling, embarked on a highly successful conference with Stalin as to the demarcation of British and Russian spheres of military control in the Balkans.[1] On the 13th, ignoring a temperature, the indomitable old man had two long trying sessions with his host, first with the Polish Prime Minister whom he had summoned from London in the hope of a settlement that would establish some kind of independence for Poland, and then with the Lublin Committee, trying with infinite patience to persuade the one to accept a realistic eastern frontier which would satisfy Russia, and the other to take the hand of their non-Marxist countrymen instead of abusing them and repeating the parrot demands and denunciations of Moscow.

The time had now come for the C.I.G.S. to play his part: to explain the British and American strategy and intentions to the Russian General Staff and Generalissimo, and, by gaining their confidence, to obtain what the Western Allies so much needed to know, the Red Army's dispositions and plans for the coming winter in Europe and—a matter of even greater moment to Washington—their proposals for their promised campaign in Manchuria against Japan. So far, neither at Moscow in 1942 nor at Teheran in 1943, had the Russian military leaders shown the slightest disposition to reveal anything to their allies at all. But Brooke now had the prestige of the summer's victories in France and Italy behind him, and he was not handicapped, as at Teheran, by any need, in his exposition of Western strategy, to carry his American colleagues with him or slur over differences between them. He did not even have to seek the prior agreement of his friends, the British Chief of Air Staff and First Sea Lord. Though he

wasn't perhaps some party or other he could attend. He loved music and knew something about it, and was interested in any and everything he was shown. I was very impressed that a man of such importance should consider so little of himself that he was able to feel really happy that he *wasn't* needed at the big council table and that he was able to throw his professional cares away and set out to enjoy himself."

[1] *Churchill* VI, 197-200. *Ehrman* VI, 104-5. *Feis*, 447-8.

spoke for them all, the manner in which he did so was for once entirely his own.

Brooke's exposition was a triumph, and the Russians, who liked his tough, direct approach and uncompromising expression of his views much better than did the Americans, became far more frank about their own military plans than they had ever been before. They even, through Stalin, proposed a British invasion of Istria and a joint attack on Vienna, presumably because the German resistance in the Danube valley was proving tougher than they had anticipated and they needed their allies' help to break the deadlock[1]—a possibility which, however, for the present was outside the West's capacity owing to Eisenhower's committal of his reserves and Washington's refusal to send American troops to Italy that could not yet be maintained in France. Even though, despite all his persistence, Churchill failed in his objective of saving Poland's independence,[2] the Moscow Conference proved the heyday of Anglo-Russian friendship.

" *October 14th*. I spent the morning reading up notes in anticipation of our evening meeting with Stalin in the Kremlin. Then back to Embassy to read latest telegrams.

" At 5 p.m. I had a meeting with General Antonov, who represents Voroshilov who is up at the front; Burrows came with me and we were there for an hour. I found him most friendly and communicative. He explained how the Russian forces had been attacking on both flanks, i.e. Baltic and Balkans, where the going was softer, and how the surrender of Hungary might open up possibilities for attacks on Germany from the south. He said, however, that the Hungarian Army was not conforming to the conditions of the surrender, that it contained many German officers and might yet give serious trouble. I then gave him a brief account of French and Italian fronts."

[1] *Feis*, 444-7.
[2] When he left Moscow the Prime Minister half thought he had succeeded, writing to Roosevelt on October 22nd that he was hopeful that in the next fortnight a settlement might be reached. *Churchill* VI, 209-11.

" Rushed off at 6 p.m. for Gala Ballet performance in main theatre. There we sat in old Tsarist Royal Box and our party consisted of Stalin, Winston, Eden, Molotov, Harriman, Maisky, Litvinov, Ismay, Clark Kerr, Burrows and self. The Ballet performance was perfect and was followed by a supper in an adjoining room. Many toasts and speeches as usual."

' Amongst the toasts Stalin made one which was not translated but which raised peals of laughter from all the Russians. The toast had been for Maisky, and, as he sat next to me and had not taken any part in all the laughter, I asked him what all the laughter was about. With a glum look on his face he replied, " The Marshal has referred to me as the poet-diplomat because I have written a few verses at times, but our last poet-diplomat was liquidated—that is the joke! " '

' Molotov said he had ordered tumblers to be served all round. He could not complete his toast till he was satisfied that all tumblers were full, and he would also satisfy himself that all tumblers were empty when the toast had been drunk. He then proposed the toast of the Red Army. I drained my tumbler and wondered what its effect would be on my strategic survey which was to follow!'

" Then back to the box for a fine performance of Red Army band, singers and dancers, including excellent Cossack dances. Performance finished at 9.30, and we then rushed to the Kremlin for a military discussion in Molotov's study."

" I had brought maps of France, Italy and Burma and described military situation, through an interpreter, of all these fronts to Stalin. He asked several questions and expressed various views and opinions. Deane[1] then described the Pacific war."

" Antonov then took up the running by describing the Russian front, and we asked him many questions. Stalin joined in the answers and we had a real satisfactory dis-

[1] Maj.-Gen. J. R. Deane, Head of U.S. Military Mission in Moscow.

cussion on the whole of the German Eastern front, including Russian immediate intentions and probable future moves. The whole was on a most open and free basis of discussion. We broke up at 1.30 a.m., well satisfied with our meeting. We have come a long way for it, and have had a long wait for it, but it has made up for these inconveniences."

" To-morrow we continue the discussion at 6 p.m. at the Kremlin and shall then be dealing with Japan."

" *October 15th.* Brocas Burrows picked me up at 10 a.m. and we started off for Zagorsk monastery. The monastery is situated about forty miles north of Moscow and represents the Canterbury of Russia. We had a lovely drive in beautiful sunshine and spent the morning going round some of the churches and the Abbot's house which has been retained with all its old furniture and was most interesting. We then started on the road back and stopped on the edge of a wood where we had a picnic lunch, sitting on rugs in the sun without our great-coats on. We were back here about 3 p.m. and I then went through the telegrams."

" At 6 p.m. we again met Stalin in the Kremlin but this time a smaller party, as Winston has got another go of fever. We discussed the war against Japan, and Antonov explained the situation as they saw it. They are allowing for a very large concentration of Japanese into Manchuria both from China and Japan—far more than the Japs will dare to withdraw. However, they are certainly taking steps to concentrate adequate forces and consider they may require some sixty divisions to deal with the forty-five Jap divisions that they expect."

" I asked them whether they considered that they could maintain sixty divisions and their strategic air forces over their trans-Siberian railway. Antonov replied in the affirmative but was corrected by Stalin who thought this was doubtful. The railway had a capacity of thirty-six pairs of trains per day, but of these only twenty-six could be counted on for military traffic, and the capacity of each train was from 600 to 700 tons. He (Stalin) considered that assistance from America across Pacific would be required."

" The meeting was most successful. There was never any doubt that the Russians were coming in as soon as they could and that they were prepared to discuss plans now. Stalin, however, drew attention to the fact that there was a political aspect to this problem which must also be tackled. What was Russia to get for her help? "

" The meeting finished at 8 p.m. and I dashed off to the Ballet to see *Swan Lake* which was quite excellent. Afterwards we went round to the American Embassy for supper and the chief Ballerina was also invited to come; she was very nice and simple."

" Bed at 1.30 a.m., well satisfied with our military discussions. We have achieved far more than I had expected."

' At our meeting with Stalin that day, when I asked Antonov whether he could maintain sixty divisions and the strategic air offensive over the trans-Siberian railway, I felt fairly certain that he knew the answer but was not certain what Stalin might want him to say. He looked round at him for some guidance but got no help; Stalin stood back with a complete poker-face.'

' Antonov, at a loss, said that they could, and was at once brushed aside by Stalin who then proceeded to explain technical matters such as the fact that the capacity of the trans-Siberian railway was limited to thirty-six pairs of trains per day. That five pairs were required for maintenance of railway and five for the population in the Maritime province. He did not think that a balance of twenty-six trains for military purposes with a lift of 600 to 700 tons per train would be adequate to maintain sixty divisions and the air offensive. He said that we had the example of Kuropatkin in the last Russo-Japanese war, who was brought to a standstill through lack of supplies, etc. He displayed an astounding knowledge of technical railway details, had read past history of fighting in that theatre and from this knowledge drew very sound deductions. I was more than ever impressed by his military ability.'

" *October 16th.* Luckily the reports of the P.M.'s health are much better; his temperature has gone down and he is normal again. It was a gloomy prospect last night— the thought that he might be seriously laid up here."

" This morning we were allowed a visit to the Kremlin. We started with the old part of the palace which used to be inhabited by Ivan the Terrible. All the original furniture is still there, and even his four-poster bed. In the room next to his bedroom he murdered his boy of sixteen. We then saw his special church, and from there passed through various more modern parts of the castle till we got to the 18th century front with some marvellous reception rooms. Especially the hall of the Order of St. George where all the names of the recipients of this Order are carved into the walls. One vast room has been converted into a Chamber of Assembly for the two Soviet representative bodies. Every deputy has his own seat, desk and a small loud-speaker on his desk."

" Finished the castle and went out to look at the church from the outside, and also to see the largest bell in the world which crashed when they tried to hang it up in the 17th century. It was left where it fell, half buried in the ground for over a hundred years, and then dug out and erected as a monument. We also saw a vast cannon and, what interested me even more, three great tits in the garden of the Kremlin, the first small birds I had seen up to date."

" Worked in the Embassy till 6.30 p.m. and then came home for a bath and a quiet evening, a relief after all the gaieties of the last few days."

" Our return journey has been put off for another twenty-four hours as Polish political discussions are hanging fire. It is a bore, as now that our military work is over I am longing to get off. It gets very trying being followed everywhere and completely shadowed by three detectives and a major in the Red Army! They are quite nice and supposed to be there to watch over me. Their authority over the crowd is absolute. Whilst shopping the other day a crowd had collected round me. One of the detectives walked round saying quite quietly, ' It would be better for you not to be here ', and they all dispersed and vanished at once."

" Weather continues glorious. I only hope we are not missing our chance of good flying weather."

" *October 17th.* Our departure has again been put off for twenty-four hours: this time to give the Russians an opportunity of staging a Kremlin banquet. If we leave without such a banquet the impression will be created throughout Russia and reflected in Germany that the conferences have been a failure and that we are parting as a result of disagreement."

" To-day, as there was no work to be done, I went off at 11 a.m. to visit the offices of the newspaper called the *British Ally*. It publishes a paper weekly with articles showing British activities, photographs of interest and extracts out of the British Press. In addition, it runs a library of books to lend out to Russians, the whole institution being most popular."

" From there I went to the Moscow equivalent of Selfridges and walked round two floors. The building was crammed and every counter buried with purchasers in spite of the frightful prices, i.e. an eiderdown for £10 and a rug for £8 etc. And yet there were many articles which you could not find in an English shop. Children's toys for the small were far better than in London."

" For lunch we were taken out by Brocas Burrows to the house he has rented in the forest outside Moscow. We drove out about thirty miles and then took to four-wheel-drive vehicles to follow the track across the woods.

Finally we arrived at a delightful wooden two-storied house. We had a walk through the woods; I hoped to see a black woodpecker which had been seen before, unfortunately he did not show up. After lunch we drove back to the Embassy. I had a meeting with the Ambassador at 6.30 p.m. to discuss the future of the Mission and whether we should replace Brocas, which we decided not to do for the present. We then went to an evening show of Russian folk songs and dances which was very good."

" As all military and political discussions have been brought to an end, I hope that we start early, as settled, the day after to-morrow."

" *October 18th.* This has been a day of filling in time. In the morning I visited the Red Army Club and Red Army Theatre. The former is a centre where the Red Army can meet. It contains a museum, small theatre or cinema, libraries, playing rooms, and runs all outdoor-sports grounds. There are similar centres in other towns, and the Moscow one acts as the parent organization. The museum was very interesting, containing masses of maps, diagrams, etc., from the various fronts, but it would require hours to get full value out of it."

" The Army theatre is a vast one, quite as large as the largest London theatre; it seats 1600 people and could hold close on 2000 on the stage. It is run entirely by the Army and gives daily performances. After lunch I visited site of the castle started by Empress Katherine, but abandoned by her as she did not like it when half finished."

" Now I have the awful ordeal of the Kremlin dinner in front of me, and to-morrow we are by way of starting at 10.30 a.m."

" *Later.* The evening turned out to be quite a mild one. We met at 8 p.m. in the room of the Order of St. Katherine. It was a very representative party from the Russian point of view. Stalin, Molotov, Maisky, Litvinov, Gusev, Voroshilov, Antonov, the heads of Artillery, Tanks,

Aviation, Engineers, Railway, Supply, State Production, Navy, etc., etc. On our side P.M., Eden, Ismay, Jacob, and self. Diplomatic—Clark Kerr, Balfour, three Dominion representatives, Americans, Harriman and Deane."

" The dinner was good and less oriental than last time: caviar, hors d'œuvres, soup, fish, chicken or beef, partridge and ice-cream. The usual toasts and speeches went on continuously. To start with they were proposed by Molotov and later by Stalin himself. Molotov proposed my health with some very nice words, and I had to reply."

" We rose at about 11.30 p.m. and went into the next room for coffee and fruit and remained there till about midnight. We were then taken off to see two films which lasted till 2.15 a.m. but were very good. After that we broke up and went home."

" *October 19th. In plane on my way to Cairo.* Left the hotel at 9.45 a.m. for the aerodrome where I found that Eden and Clark Kerr had already arrived. It was drizzling very unpleasantly and cold. We then had to wait in the rain for the arrival of the P.M. However, the next arrival of importance was that of Stalin himself! A great honour that he should have come himself. We went on standing in the rain, wondering how late Winston would be and whether he was still possibly drying himself after his morning bath. Luckily he was not very late. We then had National Anthems, followed by inspection of the guard of honour and march-past. Small speeches in the microphone by Winston. Much hand-shaking, and at last the P.M.'s plane slipped off to the runway, followed closely by ours and by the Liberator behind. By 11 a.m. we were sailing over the top of Moscow and seeing the Kremlin recede into the distance."

" We are now in the air heading for the Crimea in lovely sunshine, our work in Moscow finished and far more satisfactorily than I could ever have hoped for."

" *Later*. We had a cloudy flight down, and did not see much of the ground till we crossed the sea leading into the Crimea. We landed at 3.30 p.m. and were met by the Commissar for the Crimea and the Admiral commanding the local ground and air forces. We were given cars and driven off to Simferopol, about an hour's drive. There a house had been prepared for us to rest and feed in. P.M. remained there for a sleep, whilst Eden, Ismay and I and rest of party drove off into the mountains towards Yalta to see the country."

" Unfortunately there was not sufficient time to reach Sevastopol, but we were able to form a good general idea of the country. The main impression I gained is that the Crimea is far more prosperous than the rest of Russia that we saw: houses better, clothes better, and general impression of more amenities of life. The Commissar told us that the population had been a million but was reduced to 500,000 by the Boche, and they were forced at present to introduce additional population from Russia."

" We returned to our house at Simferopol by about 7 p.m. for a vast dinner, accompanied by a series of toasts as usual. Finally we returned to the aerodrome and took off at 1 a.m. for Cairo."

" *October 20th. Cairo*. We had a good journey, but I found it hard to sleep with a heavy cold and sore-throat. At 8 a.m. we landed outside Cairo and drove to breakfast with Moyne. Dickie Mountbatten also there.

" *Later*. At 10.30 a.m. I ran a conference till 1 p.m. with Dickie Mountbatten, Wedemeyer, Ismay and Jacob on the question of offensives from India. I discussed Dickie's new plan with him and all his various difficulties."

" Lunched at the hotel and then round to Moyne's villa to attend conferences with P.M. on the question of Dickie's future plans. The conference went well, and we got the P.M. to agree to plans connected with freeing Arakan of Japs. The plans require examining in much more detail . . ."

" Conference lasted till 5.30, and at 6.30 we had another, with Paget attending, to discuss the undesirability of letting French troops be sent to Syria and Lebanon. This conference lasted till 7.30 p.m., when I dashed back to Mena Hotel for a bath and change before dining with Moyne, P.M., Eden etc. Towards end of dinner P.M. was in great form and produced several gems. He also informed me suddenly that we were to start at 11 a.m. to-morrow instead of at midnight. Delighted; this should get us back twelve hours sooner."

" I had a very useful talk with both Paget and Dickie after dinner settling various difficulties of theirs."

" *October 21st. In the air over the Mediterranean between Benghazi and Messina.* Throat much better. Left Mena Hotel at 9.45 a.m. and drove to aerodrome with Paget. The P.M. had asked me to come with him in his plane. By 11 a.m. we were off and have so far had an excellent flight. We went from Cairo to Benghazi, and from there swung round to head for Naples. We could not go straight as it would have meant flying over Crete which is still held by Germans."

" I have spent the whole morning reading all the P.M.'s secret documents on the world situation. P.M. very particular about the temperature of the aircraft and walks about with a small thermometer. He is complaining of a cold. I pray to Heaven that it does not develop into anything before we get home."

" *Later.* At 4 p.m. local time we landed outside Naples, having taken exactly seven hours. We were met by ' Jumbo ' Wilson, Gammell, Macmillan and John Cunningham. Drove straight up to Wilson's Guest House in Naples, had tea and sat down to a conference which lasted from 5.30 to 8.15 p.m. P.M. was there for the beginning part and we discussed the possibilities of carrying out the Istria operation by landing on the Dalmatian coast. P.M. then left, and I went on discussing a series of points connected with reinforcements, equipment, Polish forces and their expansion, raising of Italian forces, etc. I find it very weary work running conferences after a long flight, even though it is carried out in the greatest of comfort."

" For dinner P.M., Alex, Wilson, Cunningham, Macmillan, etc. P.M. in the very best form but unfortunately kept us up till 1 a.m. local time but 3 a.m. Cairo time, which was the time we had got up by."

" *October 22nd. In the air over Southern France.* We were told last night that the weather report was very bad, that it was highly unlikely that we should be able to fly by day but that we might fly to Malta in the afternoon so as to make use of their night-flying facilities and take off in the dark for home. I was to be told at 7 a.m. As I had been told nothing I was comfortably in bed at 8.30 a.m. when I was suddenly informed that the weather had improved, and that we were due to leave the house at 9 a.m. I had to rush my shave, dressing and breakfast and succeeded in being ready before the P.M."

" At 10.10 a.m. we took off and flew along Italian coast across to north point of Corsica where we flew over Bastia and had a grand view of North Corsica silhouetted against a stormy sky. From there on to cross the French coast at Narbonne."

" *Later.* The weather turned nasty over France and we had to go up higher to get above the clouds and from then on saw nothing of France till we were over the Cherbourg peninsula. We passed west of the Isle of Wight, over Andover and swung in to Northolt which we reached at 5 p.m., having done our journey in six-and-three-quarter hours. We found Clemmie on the aerodrome to welcome Winston, and Archie Nye and ' Barney ' had come for me. We were not long in getting off, and here I am back in the flat which I left only just over a fortnight, and I have covered 10,500 miles. It has been a remarkably successful trip with a great deal accomplished. I have now got a lot to do to put the results of our conferences and talks into effect."

" Winston seemed none the worse for the journey and arrived back in great form. I am glad we have got him back safely and that he did not fall sick in Moscow. With this flight I have now passed the 100,000 miles in the air since doing this job."

" *October 23rd.* Started in again with the usual routine of C.O.S. meetings and Cabinet meetings. I am glad to have had a bit of a change from this form of life, and it is rather hard to step into it again. However, by this evening I felt as if I had never left London, and Moscow seemed as far away in the past as it is in miles from here."

" I am very glad to have been back to Russia again; it is a country with much food for thought. One more of these vast experiments which humanity periodically carries out: experiments which lead to much bloodshed, upheaval, suffering and finally, when all is examined, some progress. In my mind all have their purpose; they turn the wheel of destiny one or two cogs forward towards the path of general progress. Humanity surges forward like the tide flowing. Successive waves of one or other ' ism ' romp up the beach, only to be sucked back almost to where they started from. But in that ' almost ' lies the progress forward."

. . . .

Three days after his return from Moscow Brooke received a telegram from his old colleague and adversary, General Marshall. It read:

" Dear Brooke: From what I hear from Harriman who is here, Deane in Moscow and Wedemeyer who was in Cairo, you did a beautiful job with Stalin.

Congratulations and sincere thanks.

G. C. Marshall."[1]

[1] Gen. Marshall to C.I.G.S., 25 Oct., 1944. Lord Alanbrooke, *Personal Files.*

Chapter Ten

HITLER'S LAST THROW

The Americans were strung out all along the front; everyone was attacking everywhere and every day; there were few reserves available.

FIELD-MARSHAL MONTGOMERY

WHILE THE C.I.G.S. had been in Moscow the fears he had expressed in his diary when Eisenhower assumed operational command in North-West Europe had been realised. It was now certain the war would continue for another winter. The failure to strike at the Ruhr in early September had been accompanied by a simultaneous failure to free the mouth of the Scheldt and make use of Antwerp.

The Supreme Commander who, on taking over control of ground operations, had shrunk from the one for fear of further extending his communications, had omitted to ensure the other which would have shortened them. As a result, though the last of the Channel ports fell at the beginning of October, throughout that month and November the docks of the great Belgian port which Montgomery had captured unscathed at the beginning of September remained as useless as though the Germans were still in occupation. To open it the Canadian left wing of 21 Army Group struggled, with the aid of the Navy, through mud and flood to expel the blockading garrisons from Breskens and the islands of South Beveland and Walcheren—now strongly fortified and defended. Even after November 4th, when the Canadians and British had forced the enemy to relinquish his stranglehold on the estuary,

316

at least three weeks were needed to clear the river of mines and enable ships to come in.

Rain and winter set in early that autumn, partially grounding the Allies' tactical air forces and depriving them of what till now had been their greatest asset. Not only was the weather unfavourable to the offensive—the November rains proved the worst for years—but, owing to their overstrained supply lines, the Allies were short both of men and ammunition. New divisions were piling up in the United States but they could only be put into the battle line as and when they could be transported and supplied through the inadequate and damaged Channel and Riviera ports. Ammunition was so short that it had to be rationed and, owing to shipping shortages and miscalculations in Washington, even minimum requirements were not being met.[1]

Yet, following a conference on October 18th with his senior commanders at Brussels, Eisenhower persisted in what his naval A.D.C. called his " strategy of stretch-out ". On the 28th, rejecting Montgomery's renewed plea for concentration against the Ruhr, he issued orders for a general offensive, as soon as the approaches to Antwerp could be cleared, along a two-hundred-mile front from Arnhem to Metz. The main effort was to be made by the American First and Ninth Armies through the Aachen gap towards Krefeld, Cologne and Bonn, but the American Third Army in Lorraine was also subsequently —" when logistics permit "—to renew its attempt on the Saar. Bradley, however, who was in charge of the offensive and believed that " if all the armies . . . attacked simultaneously, it might well end the war ", overlooked even this reservation and allowed Patton to launch his attack at the beginning of November, so robbing his main thrust north of the Ardennes of any possibility of success. Confident from his Sicilian

---

[1] " From Ike's conferences up front, he found that the one thing worrying everybody is the shortage of artillery ammunition. The shortage was not caused merely by port capacity and distribution, but by too few shipments from the U.S. or by limitation of production at home. He cabled General Marshall of his concern." Butcher, *Diary* 585 (20 Oct., 1944). In the middle of November Eisenhower was forced to broadcast an appeal to the American people for more ammunition. *Ehrman* VI, 25-7.

triumphs and his almost unopposed advance across the Orléans plain, Patton assured him he could reach the Saar in three days and " easily breach the West Wall ".[1] Despite his superiority in men and armour, owing to weather and the enemy's skilful defence he made little progress. Meanwhile, by spoiling counter-attacks and the use of strong defensive positions, the Germans in the north were able to ward off every attempt towards the Lower Rhine. The Ruhr beyond it—" the only real worth-while objective on the western front ", as Montgomery called it—remained as far away as ever.

The stalemate in France and the Low Countries was paralleled in Italy. Helped as before by the Allies' failure to use their maritime resources to exploit their Mediterranean strategy, the Germans were contesting every rocky coign and watercourse in order to tie down the attackers and prevent any move across the Adriatic to cut off the Hungarian bauxite on which their aircraft industry depended. Because of Eisenhower's difficulties no reinforcements could be sent to Alexander; " all of us ", Roosevelt wrote to Churchill on October 16th, " are now faced with an unanticipated shortage of man-power, and overshadowing all other military problems is the need for quick provision of fresh troops to reinforce Eisenhower in his battle to break into Germany and end the European war."[2] On October 25th, after fighting its way half-way from Rimini to Bologna, the Eighth Army was halted by torrential rains. The attempts of the Fifth Army on its left to break out of the Apennines were equally unsuccessful. Here, as elsewhere, having failed to concentrate and strike with all they had at the decisive point and moment, the Allies were just not strong enough to force a decision. And, as the last hope faded of breaking into the Lombardy plain before winter, one of the attacker's divisions had to be sent in haste to Greece where, as Brooke had feared, the British force landed when the Germans withdrew in October was proving far too small to preserve order in that passionately partisan country.

Nor was the prospect less disappointing in Yugoslavia where, after the high hopes of the autumn, not only had the Germans stabilized the situation but, as a result, it was suspected, of Russian intrigues, the guerrilla leader, Tito, had turned against the West. Only in the Danube valley, where the Red Army was knocking at the gates of Budapest, and in the Pacific, where months ahead of programme the Americans had invaded the Philippines, was the initiative retained. Here at Leyte Gulf, during the last week of October, the greatest naval victory of the war was won, the Japanese, in an attempt to oppose MacArthur's landing, losing three battleships, a fleet-carrier, nine destroyers and thirteen cruisers. It marked the end of their naval power. A fortnight later the *Tirpitz*, Germany's last remaining battleship—immobilized by earlier underwater and air attacks—was sunk in a Norwegian fiord by the Royal Air Force.

. . . .

These events and the problems they raised were mirrored in Brooke's diary after his return from Moscow and the resumption of his normal routine, as a weary Britain entered upon her sixth winter of war.

" *October 26th.* We had the Planners in this morning and discussed with them the wonderful telegram from Marshall in which he seems to consider that if we really set our hearts on it and bank on its happening, irrespective of what happens in the future should we fail to do so, we ought to be able to finish the war before the end of the year! . . ."

" *October 30th.* Long C.O.S. meeting with many Minutes from the P.M. Cabinet at 6 p.m. and finished up with a 10 p.m. meeting with the P.M. He was in a good mood, and we got through surveys of the French front, Italian front and Burma front by midnight."

" *October 31st.* We were concerned with the intended bombing of defences near Flushing, P.M. objecting from humanitarian reasons and Ike pressing for it to save casualties in the infantry attack—P.M. agreed."

" *November 2nd.* Lunch with P.M. at 10 Downing Street to meet Bedell Smith. Found out that Ike's plan as usual entails attacking all along the front instead of selecting main strategic point. I fear that the November attack will consequently get no farther than the Rhine at the most."

" P.M. not in his usual form and on the flat side. However, his fighting spirit the same as usual and he said that if he was a German he would get his small daughter to put a bomb under some British bed; he would instruct his wife to wait till some American was bending over his basin washing to strike him on the neck with a chopper, whilst he himself sniped at Americans and British indiscriminately! "

" *November 3rd.* Sent for by the P.M. at 10.45 a.m. He told me that he had been thinking over the desirability of replacing Dill now that he would be unable to carry on. It was only yesterday at lunch that he had stated that it was unnecessary to replace him, and we had all remonstrated with him. His suggestion now is to send ' Jumbo ' Wilson there and to relieve him with Alexander, whilst Clark should relieve Alexander. It is probably the best solution but will all depend on how ' Jumbo ' hits it off with Marshall. Last year in Cairo Marshall had a good opinion of him."

" I then tackled the P.M. on the question of making ' Jumbo ' a Field Marshal. He refused at first and said it was quite unnecessary; however, by working away at him I got him to agree and only hope he does not go back again."

" In the evening again sent for by the P.M., this time to discuss his proposed visit to France. He is to start on the 10th, attend Armistice ceremony in Paris, then fly to Besançon to visit French forces under De Lattre de Tassigny. From there to visit Ike and Monty. He wants me to come with him which will be great fun and very interesting. We are to send detachments of British Forces to take part in the November 11th ceremony. The only bad part is the security side; the French have already announced his visit, and there might well be remnants of Germans or Vichy representatives who would be only too ready to take advantage of a chance to have a shot at Winston."

" *November 5th.* On the wireless at 9 a.m. the death of Jack Dill was announced. . . . His loss is quite irreparable. Without him at Washington I do not know how we should have got through the last three years."

' To my mind we owe more to Dill than to any other general for our final victory. I had unbounded admiration for him combined with the deepest of devotion, whilst Marshall had grown to admire, respect and like him. Any success that I may have had in getting Marshall finally to accept our Mediterranean and Italian strategy was. entirely due to Dill's help. The American opinion of him cannot be better exemplified than in his place of burial.[1] Twice P. J. Grigg and I did our best to secure him a peerage; this was never turned down by the P.M., but nothing ever came of it.'

" *November 6th.* Usual early start from home, and a difficult C.O.S. meeting at which we discussed the problem of the partition of Palestine for the Jews. We are unanimously against any announcement before the end of the war, but our hand may well be forced."

" At 5.30 p.m. our usual Cabinet. P.M. announced that Lord Moyne had been shot in the neck by terrorists . . ."

" *November 7th.* Started our C.O.S. meeting with a wire Winston wished to send to the President in which he proposed that Wilson should take Dill's place in Washington and that Alexander should take over from Wilson. Unfortunately he went on to suggest Alexander should combine the duties of Supreme Commander and

---

[1] A grave for him in the Arlington National Cemetery was offered by General Marshall to Lady Dill—a unique honour for a British soldier.

his own present ones at the same time. He went further
to suggest that Greece should return to Middle East
where we have just taken it from, and in every possible
way proposed upsetting the organization of Command in
the Mediterranean. He had tried to bounce in with the
telegram yesterday, and now again it must go off by
3 p.m. to-day!"

"However, we had to pull it to pieces badly and sent
it back mutilated with our reasons. He has been unable
to send it off, but has decided to have a 10.30 p.m.
meeting with us."

"Monty came to lunch with me, in very good form
but full of criticism of Ike and of his methods of running
a war."

"After lunch a Selection Board, and at 5.30 p.m.
another Cabinet to finish off what we had left over
yesterday. We spent hours discussing desirability of
sending some food to Holland, Norway and Channel
Islands and never arrived at any very decisive results."

"*Later*. Just back (1 a.m.) from our meeting with the
P.M., Anthony Eden attending. As I had suspected,
he was responsible for the change in the P.M.'s plans.
He had just come back from Italy where he had been
seeing Alexander. As a result he had recommended
combining the Supreme Commander and Army Group
Commander into one, and wanted, in fact, to commit the
error which Eisenhower has just made in France. We had
a long discussion, luckily quite a pleasant one and not too
heated. After much arguing I made my point, namely
Wilson to replace Dill, Alex to replace Wilson, and Clark
to replace Alex. It is not ideal, but it is the best that can
be made of a very complicated problem with many personal factors. Anthony Eden behaved well and did not
press his point."

"*November 8th*. We discussed at the C.O.S. meeting
the telegram drafted by the secretariat as a result of our
meeting last night and sent it on for the P.M. to dispatch

to the President. We also had our weekly meeting with Cherwell and Sandys on the flying-bomb and the rocket. I am afraid that both of these are likely to interfere with the working of Antwerp harbour, a matter of the greatest importance in the future."

" I then had an interview with Joubert de la Ferté and he gave me some interesting side-lights on Mountbatten's H.Q. He said that the Anglo-American relations continued to be bad; the Americans full of criticisms of our management of India and expressing openly the opinion that if they had their way there would be no British Empire after the war. He was followed by Robertson from Italy to discuss the administrative situation in Italy which is bad. Also had long discussion with ' Boy ' Browning and Crawford on the provision of glider pilots from the Air Force, and the necessity for training these pilots in ground fighting as well as in their gliding training."

" Meanwhile the plans for our trip to Paris are materializing fast, and we are due to leave on Friday 10th."

" This evening Cyril Falls, Military Correspondent of *The Times*, came to see me. He said that he was disturbed at the system of Command in France with Eisenhower commanding on two planes, namely commanding the Army, Navy and Air forces in his capacity of Supreme Commander and at the same time pretending to command the land forces (divided into three Groups of Armies) directly. He has hit the nail on the head and found the weakness of this set-up which the Americans have forced on to Eisenhower. Unfortunately it becomes a political matter, and the Americans, with preponderating strength of land and air forces, very naturally claim the privilege of deciding how the forces are to be organized and commanded."

" Falls had been seeing Monty, and there is no doubt that Monty had been rubbing it in hard! It is, however, a very serious defect in our organization, and one that may have evil repercussions on the strategy of the war. I do not like the lay-out of the coming offensive and doubt whether we even reach the Rhine. It is highly improbable that we should cross over before the end of the year."

" *November 9th.* We had the Planners in for our usual weekly talk and to discuss further Mountbatten's plans for the spring. Then attended Mansion House lunch to install the new Mayor. Winston made his usual speech; I think it must be the fourth that I have listened to there, but it was not quite as good as some of the previous ones. As there was no Archbishop of Canterbury, Lord Simon took that job on."

" During the afternoon I had a talk with Monty before he returns to France. He still goes on harping over the system of command in France and the fact that the war is being prolonged. I agree that the set-up is bad, but it is not one which can be easily altered, as the Americans naturally consider they should have a major say. Perhaps, after they see the results of dispersing their strength all along their front it may become easier to convince them that some drastic change is desirable, leading to a concentration of force at the vital point . . ."

" I finally had a long meeting with Weeks to discuss whether we should cannibalize one or two divisions in the Mediterranean. He is inclined only to do one; personally I feel certain we shall have to do both ultimately and would sooner make one bite of the cherry. I expect P.J. will prefer to do one at a time, in the hope that he could get one division through easier than two with the P.M. But the alternative will necessitate returning twice to the P.M., which in my opinion will be worse."

" All the preparations for Paris are made; if fine we fly, if not we go by destroyer, and I pray to Heaven we may not have to go in the destroyer! The Channel is very rough at present."

" *November 10th. Paris*! After spending a usual morning and attending the C.O.S. meeting I had an early lunch and left for Northolt aerodrome where our party assembled ready to embark in two Dakotas for Paris. The party consisted of P.M., Anthony Eden, Mrs. Churchill and Mary, ' Pug ' Ismay, Cadogan etc. We had an excellent flight and arrived at 4.30 p.m. just south of Paris. Met on aerodrome by guard of honour of National Guard, De Gaulle, Juin, many members of Cabinet and officials."

" With a long procession of cars we drove through Paris with streets lined on either side. We went to the Quai d'Orsay where Winston is stopping. There we deposited him and drove on to the Continental Hotel, Juin's H.Q., where I am putting up. The hotel as such is closed. In my room I found a set of the most priceless bird books which had been drawn out of the Natural History Museum Library for me to look at! Juin had asked Archdale of the Mission here if there was anything I might care for in my room to entertain me, and he had suggested bird books, knowing me well. They are quite lovely and most of them original drawings."

" In the evening I went to dine with the P.M. at the Quai d'Orsay. Party consisted of P.M., Mrs. Churchill, Mary, Anthony and Beatrice Eden, the two Duff Coopers, Cadogan. P.M. in excellent form. Said last time he had been in the Quai d'Orsay building was 1940 when the French were busy burning the archives, preparing to depart. I was not able to escape before midnight."

" *November 11th. Paris*. At 10 a.m. General Juin's A.D.C. came to collect me, and we started off for the great function of the day. We drove to the Arc de Triomphe where we waited for the P.M. and de Gaulle. When they arrived they went up together to lay a wreath on the unknown soldier's grave and for de Gaulle to relight the perpetual flame."

" De Gaulle then presented medals to a group of

officers. After that we marched on foot down the Champs Élysées to a stand which had been put up. As no places had been marked, and half of them were already occupied, there was some scramble to get accommodated. I stood next to a French general who said:—' *La foule, comme d'habitude, déborde la police!* ' This was very much the case; there were the usual very futile *agents* quite incapable of handling the crowd, especially Press photographers. The security side was appalling and I had some uneasy feelings for Winston at times."

" He had a wonderful reception, and the Paris crowd went quite mad over him, with continuous cries of ' Churcheel! Churcheel! ' After we had taken our places on the stand there was a parade of troops lasting an hour, starting with the *Garde nationale* and its band and mounted troops (which have remained intact throughout the war), and passing on to bands and detachments of British, Canadian and American troops. We had an excellent band, a naval detachment, a grand Guards' composite Company, and an R.A.F. detachment. French forces followed, some Moroccan and Algerian detachments, some French Forces of the Interior units transformed into *Chasseurs Alpins*, part of the new division being raised in Paris, and a fine detachment of the Airborne troops who worked with us in Normandy."

" After the review we drove off to Clemenceau's statue where we deposited wreaths; from there to Foch's grave. Finally we went to the Hôtel de la Presidence (where de Gaulle is installed) for an official lunch. It was a very large lunch with sixty-eight guests, including the whole of the Cabinet. De Gaulle made a short speech followed by Winston, after which we rose for coffee and cigarettes. I had a long conversation with old Giraud and discussed his recent wound when a sentry shot him through the neck, the bullet coming out half-way between the nose and the corner of his mouth without breaking his jaw. He told me that his wife, two daughters and seven grandchildren were still all held as hostages in Germany and he could not even obtain a word from them."

" This morning's parade stirred me up deeply. It was a wonderful feeling to be standing in Paris watching a review of French troops after the last four years of planning and struggling to get back to France and to drive the Germans out of it. I even wondered at times whether I might be dreaming and that I should suddenly wake to find ourselves back where we were a year ago."

" In the evening we dined with Gen. Juin."

" *November 12th. Paris.* At 11.30 went to Gen. Juin's office for a talk. He told me of his designs to raise eight French divisions as soon as possible. Equipment is, as usual, the crux; what could we do to assist? He was very reasonable in all his requests and an easy individual to get on with. Later lunched with Juin *en famille*."

" 'Barney'[1] and I then went for a short walk before having to go for a meeting with de Gaulle. He received us in the same room that Clemenceau used to work in during the last war. He discussed the raising and arming of forces, very much on the same lines that Juin had in the morning. He was in one of his more pleasant moods and quite affable. We were with him for about an hour."

" Finished the day by dining with Koenig, who had two generals dining who had taken a great part in the Resistance movement. They were most interesting about their experiences and lives led under a dozen names and carried on from dozens of residences. Four months was the most that the majority survived before getting caught by the Gestapo."

" Finally I drove to the Gare de Lyon where we embarked in the Presidential train for Besançon. A very comfortable train in which I have an excellent cabin, but the line is very rough, hence my bad writing."

' I was interested to meet the Resistance generals and to hear their views on de Gaulle. They did not think much of

[1] Capt. A. K. (" Barney ") Charlesworth, Brooke's A.D.C.

the part he had played. One of them said to me:—" De Gaulle! What did he do? Evacuated his family to London from the start, where he followed them. There he lived comfortably throughout the war, whilst we were risking our lives daily in contact with the Germans, living in the cellars with them overhead and expecting daily to be apprehended by the Gestapo. Meanwhile from his safe position he had the impertinence to say: ' *Je suis la France!* ' " They were very bitter and had little use for him.'

" *November 13th. Besançon.* Woke to find the whole country we were travelling through covered with snow. And a grey morning with snow falling fast."

" We arrived in Besançon well up to schedule by 10 a.m. There we were met by General de Lattre, the *Préfet*, the Mayor and a mass of other officials. Outside the station a band, a guard of honour and a large crowd. We solemnly stood in the snow whilst most of ' God Save the King ' the ' Stars and Stripes ' (sic) and ' La Marseillaise ' were played through."

' As we arrived in the station which was filled with generals, bands, guards of honour and dignitaries of every description, Winston was expected to alight from the train gracefully. However, at this moment Winston was still only half dressed, and as he completed his toilet, a process that lasted a full quarter of an hour, General Lattre and all his comrades were rapidly being converted into Father Xmases! Finally Winston emerged in the dining-carriage dressed as an airman. There Sawyers, his valet, proceeded to adjust his coat whilst he admired the general effect in the glass. At the correct moment Sawyers handed him from behind the two ends of the belt. This produced a thunder-storm of abuse: " Sawyers, you damned fool, why have you not removed that bastard! You know I never want that bastard round me again! Cut off the damned thing!" Mary was standing beside me at the door that led into the corridor, and, not knowing what further language the paternal anger might produce, withdrew gracefully down the corridor with a smile.'

' Finally and at last Winston was ready and out he stepped into the snow with a smile on his face, large cigar, and his coat no longer adorned by that " bastard thing ".'

" We then started off in cars, leading car P.M., de Gaulle, de Lattre and Mary; next came General Juin, ' Barney ' and self. We had a long drive of some sixty miles in the snow to a place called Maiche, where de Lattre had his Advanced H.Q. He had hoped to take us forward to an observation-post from which we could have seen the beginning of the battle which was to start today. But it was snowing far too heavily to see anything. There was already quite a foot of snow and the attack had had to be put off."

" The P.M.'s car punctured twice and we got temporarily stuck in the rut at the side of the road. However we finally arrived at Maiche. The P.M. was very cold and miserable looking and I hope will not be any the worse for it."

" On arrival we were given by de Lattre a description of the front held by the First French Army and the plans for the attack. Considering that the divisions for the attack are on a thirty-kilometre front each, have been fighting without rest for two and a half months and also have just been reorganized by absorbing white personnel in lieu of the Senegalese who have to go back to Africa, the whole plan of attack struck me as being fantastic. It is another case of Eisenhower's complete inability to run the land battle as well as acting as Supreme Commander. Furthermore it is another example of the American doctrine of attacking all along the line. The American Army just north of de Lattre is attacking in an impossible country in the Vosges; all he will do there is lose men. He ought to establish a defensive front there and concentrate his forces on the Belfort gap. Any successful offensive there would turn the line of the Vosges and render this expensive attack unnecessary. The French realise these errors only too well and are fretting at being subjected to their results."[1]

" We were given lunch which finished off with a speech by Winston in French, followed by de Gaulle and de Lattre, and I was then ordered by the P.M. to make one in French also. There was nothing for it but to make the best of the situation."

" After lunch we started driving back in the snow with darkness coming on. But on the way home we had to visit a training camp where new *Maquis* recruits are being turned into reserves. We also saw a battalion of the ' Legion ' which marched past. A most impressive sight. Then some tanks loomed past in the semi-darkness, and, to finish, one of the new battalions did some community singing. Winston looked frozen, and I pray Heaven that he will not be any the worse for it."

" At 7 p.m. in darkness and snow we rejoined the train, having been nine hours on the go in cold and snow, and very glad to get back to the warmth of the train."

" Throughout the day de Gaulle was most affable and pleasant, but I very much doubt whether he has the personality to unite France for concerted action at this critical time. General Juin is a very pleasant type, easy to get on with, a proved good general in the field . . . De Lattre seems a fighting commander, with plenty of character and determination, but how good he really is would be hard to judge without seeing more of him."

" Finished off the day by dining with de Gaulle in his dining-car on the train. I sat on de Gaulle's left, Mary on his right. Winston was in excellent form, and even de Gaulle unbent a little! "

[1] The French did, in fact, six days later do precisely what Brooke advocated and broke through the Belfort gap, so reaching the Upper Rhine and freeing Mulhouse and later Strasbourg. But the victory was never followed up and the operations south of the Ardennes failed to relieve the impasse in the north, where alone decisive results could be achieved. See *Ehrman* VI, 34; *Wilmot*, 569-70.

" Now midnight and I am very sleepy. Train far too bumpy to write more."

' Of all the sights that day the one that remained most rooted in my mind was the march past of that Foreign Legion battalion. We had just been inspecting units formed out of *Maquis* personnel, good, tough-looking boys that promised well, when de Lattre said he would like to march past a battalion of the Foreign Legion which he had in reserve.'

' They had their own band and out of the darkness came the wildest strains of a march, played on some weird sort of pipes, which transported one to North Africa. Then out of the fast-failing light and through the falling snow-flakes came a sight I shall never forget. The grandest assembly of real fighting men that I have ever seen, marching with their heads up as if they owned the world, lean, hard-looking men, carrying their arms admirably and marching with perfect precision. They disappeared into the darkness leaving me with a thrill and a desire for a division of such men.'

' One other incident that day that left a mark in my mind was Winston at lunch. He arrived completely frozen and almost rolled up on himself like a hedgehog. He was placed in a chair with a hot-water-bottle at his feet and one in the back of his chair; at the same time good brandy was poured down his throat to warm him internally. The results were wonderful, he thawed out rapidly and when the time came produced one of those indescribably funny French speeches which brought the house down.'

" *November 14th. Rheims.* The train left Besançon shortly after we got into it and travelled throughout the night to Paris where it arrived about 6 a.m. Then the coaches with de Gaulle, Juin and the Ministers were cut off and we went on to Rheims. We arrived at 11 a.m. and were met by Ike who drove us out to his camp situated on the golf links built by the big champagne merchants.[1] He went

[1] Like Montgomery, Eisenhower preferred to live in a small " Forward Headquarters " away from his vast SHAEF Headquarters at Versailles. At Rheims he slept in a caravan, while his personal staff of devoted American and British aides,

over the dispositions on the front and seemed fairly vague as to what was really going on."

" We had lunch with him and then drove to the aerodrome where we took off at 3 p.m. for Northolt which we reached at 4.45 p.m. after a very comfortable flight."

" It was a relief to get the P.M. safely back from his trip, and I have now got a much clearer idea of the situation as regards developing French forces. We should most certainly get busy with giving them equipment as soon as port facilities admit."[1]

. . . . . .

" *November 15th.* Started the old C.O.S. life again, and worried about P.M.'s ideas as to what Command implies. This was all connected with the move of Wilson to replace Dill, and Alexander to replace Wilson, whilst Clark is to take over from Alexander. Winston had wired to Alexander through secret channels without telling me."

' Winston had a habit of occasionally sending private telegrams to commanders without telling me that he was doing so. These telegrams were usually connected with some subject I had fully discussed with him and had disagreed with him over. He then tried to get commanders to agree with him and consequently to disagree with me. Fortunately all the Commanders-in-Chief throughout the war served me with exceptional loyalty. I had a rule with them that, if ever they sent a telegram to the P.M., they always sent me a copy. In this case, and in a few similar ones, my staff on applying to the Cabinet Office were unable to trace

---

secretaries, clerks and batmen occupied the local clubhouse. Two of them—his U.S. Naval A.D.C., Captain Butcher, and his British lady driver and later personal secretary, Mrs. Kay Summersby—published books after the war describing this informal and very democratic menage. Accustomed to the more rigid hierarchy of the British Army, Brooke during his visit was surprised to find Mrs. Summersby presiding over the head of the luncheon table, with the Prime Minister on her right. *Notes on My Life* XV, 29. See K. Summersby, *Eisenhower Was My Boss* and Butcher, *Diary*, passim.

[1] As with all his journeys abroad, when there was any chance of his falling into enemy hands, the C.I.G.S. had opened a new volume of his diary for his trip to France, closing it on his return.

the P.M.'s original wire to which the telegram in question was the answer. After considerable difficulties they found the original had gone through without the P.M.'s secretaries even knowing about it! '

' Once I had obtained the original I took it, together with the copy of Alex's reply, to the P.M. and said that I was surprised that he considered it necessary to send this wire as we had previously fully discussed the matter and he knew my views. He showed some surprise that I had secured the original but never any shame over what he had done! '

" *November 16th.* Started our C.O.S. meeting with John Anderson on the question of atomic bomb. He was very interesting and gave us an excellent account of what he knew about the research work going on in Germany and the likelihood of arriving at some conclusion in the near future, which does not seem to constitute a danger for the present."[1]

" *November 17th.* We found at the morning Chiefs of Staff meeting that Winston was still confused about the system of Command in Italy and the Mediterranean. Having tried hard to warp the whole organization while Wilson was Supreme Commander and Alex commanding the Group of Armies so as to try and put Wilson in the shade for the benefit of Alexander, now that he places Alexander as Supreme Commander he is frightened lest his powers should be restricted in the manner he has endeavoured to reduce those of Wilson! We had to meet at 4 p.m. and, after laborious explanations, I at last got him to accept matters as they are."

" *November 20th.* Early start from home. Fairly long C.O.S. meeting with several post-war problems. Also a discussion as to the unsatisfactory state of affairs in

[1] Sir John Anderson, then Chancellor of the Exchequer. An American Scientific Mission—ALSOS—was at this time searching in France for clues of German progress in atomic research. A week later, when the French captured Strasbourg, one of Germany's leading nuclear physicists fell into Allied hands together with his laboratory, whose records revealed that enemy was still a long way from being able to make an atomic bomb.

France, where Eisenhower completely fails as Commander. Bedell Smith lives back in Paris quite out of touch; as a result the war is drifting in a rudderless condition. Had a long and despondent letter about it from Montgomery over the week-end. Am preparing a case, as we shall have to take it up with the Americans before long . . ."

In the letter Brooke had received from Montgomery, written on November 17th, the latter reported that he had neither seen nor spoken to his chief on the telephone since October 18th, and had only met him four times since the end of the Normandy campaign. " He is at a Forward Headquarters at Rheims ", he wrote; " the Directives he issues from there have no relation to the practical necessities of the battle. It is quite impossible for me to carry out my present orders . . . Eisenhower should himself take a proper control of operations or he should appoint someone else to do this. If we go drifting along as at present we are merely playing into the enemy's hands and the war will go on indefinitely . . . He has never commanded anything before in his whole career; now, for the first time, he has elected to take direct command of very large-scale operations and he does not know how to do it."

" The Germans ", he continued, " are bound to bring divisions to the Western Front—from Norway, from the Russian front and from elsewhere . . . Bradley tells me the American ammunition situation is going to be worse and his allotment is already being scaled down; the reason is that the Pacific theatre is now coming to the fore and ammunition has to be diverted there; the Americans have not enough ammunition to give adequate amounts to two theatres—both going at full blast. So the urgency to finish the German war quickly is very great ". The only way, Montgomery thought, to achieve this was " to concentrate great strength at some selected place and hit the Germans a colossal crack, and have ready the fresh divisions to exploit the success gained ". The question was what was he himself to do? " I would be grateful for your advice as to whether you think I ought to take the initiative again in the matter. I put the whole matter to Eisenhower early in October; he did not agree and I told him that so far as I was concerned the matter had ended—and he would hear no more from me on the subject. A month has passed since then and I am getting rather alarmed; I think we are drifting into dangerous waters . . . I have always valued your advice and I would be grateful for it now." [1]

To this the C.I.G.S. replied on the 20th, in a confidential letter sent by the Chief of Air Staff who was visiting the Front: [2]

" . . . Without any hesitation I would advise you:—
   (a) not to approach Eisenhower for the present;
   (b) to remain silent now, unless Eisenhower opens the subject.

I thoroughly appreciate how unsatisfactory the situation is and how essential it is to try and rectify matters, but, after having told Eisenhower ' he would hear no more from you on the subject ', you would be in the wrong if you re-opened the matter.

I do not believe that up to now anything could possibly have been done; the Command organization and strategy had to prove themselves defective by operational results before they could be satisfactorily attacked.

I feel pretty certain that the results of the current offensive will provide us with sufficient justification for requesting the American Chiefs of Staff to reconsider the present Command organization and the present strategy on the Western Front.

We shall within the next week or fortnight have ample proof of the inefficiency of the present set-up and this will justify our making the strongest representations to Washington.

I feel certain that in view of the American preponderance in strength they will insist on any Land Commander

---

[1] Field-Marshal Montgomery to C.I.G.S., 17 Nov., 1944, Lord Alanbrooke, *Personal Files.*
[2] " This is the letter I mentioned. It is one of a very secret nature. I shall be most grateful if you will deliver it to Monty." C.I.G.S. to C.A.S. 20 Nov., 1944. Lord Alanbrooke, *Personal Files.*

appointed being an American. I do not think that either politically or militarily we can resist this claim. This being so, do you consider that Bradley is fit for the job? Will he be able to control Patton and Devers? Would he discuss plans with you sufficiently?

Give me replies to the above. Meanwhile don't open the matter with Ike again. I am working out the best line of attack from here, but I won't conceal from you that I anticipate the greatest difficulties in getting the American Chiefs of Staff to agree to any change in the set-up . . ."

" American attacks round the Vosges ", the C.I.G.S. wrote in his diary next night, " have been doing better to-day, but I still feel certain that final results will fall far short of our hopes ". Meanwhile Montgomery, after discussing the matter with Portal, had sent home by him a further letter.

" The whole problem here . . . can really be solved very simply by having a proper organization for Command. Within the American armies they seem to have a curious idea that every Army Commander must have an equal and fair share of the battle . . . I do not believe we shall ever get a Land Commander. I have offered in writing to serve under Bradley, but it is no use; Ike is determined to do it himself! . . .

I suggest the answer is this.

1. Ike seems determined to show that he is a great general in the field. Let him do so and let us all lend a hand to pull him through.

2. The theatre divides itself naturally into two fronts— one north of the Ardennes and one south.

3. I should command north of the Ardennes and Bradley south of the Ardennes.

4. Ike should command the two fronts, from a suitable Tactical Headquarters, having the air C.-in-C. with him—who must be Tedder . . ."[1]

[1] Field Marshal Montgomery to C.I.G.S., 22 Nov., 1944. Lord Alanbrooke, *Personal Files*.

Brooke did not agree and replied on the 24th.

". . . As regards your letter, frankly I don't think much of your plan! You have always told me, and I have agreed with you, that Ike was no commander, that he had no strategic vision, was incapable of making a plan or of running operations when started."

"Now you state that, 'This solution is so very simple and would solve all problems. Ike would allot forces to each front as demanded by his plan.' How is he to do this if he can't make a plan? Further, 'He must decide on his strategic plan *now*, lay down objectives, allot resources, and so on.' Is that not exactly what he has up to date proved himself incapable of doing? And again:—'Bradley and myself then carry on, and Ike co-ordinates as necessary.' Can you see Ike judging between the requirements of the two fronts, overriding American clamour for their Commander being in charge of the main thrusts, etc., etc.? I can't!"

"All you are suggesting is that Ike, instead of trying to command the Land Forces organized on a three-group basis should do so on a two-group basis. You may overcome a proportion of the defects but you won't get at the root of the matter, and the same evils will persist."

"Furthermore, you are asking for the Command of the Northern Group. You must remember that you have repeatedly affirmed that the Northern line of advance is the one and only one that has any chance of success. Namely the one on which the major effort must be directed and at the expense of the Southern front."

"You are therefore proposing yourself for the one and only front that can play any major part in the Western offensive on Germany. Have you considered whether you are likely to be very acceptable in American eyes for this Command? I have grave doubts in view of their present claims to being definitely the predominating partner in the Western offensive."

" Personally I consider Bradley much better suited to carry out the tasks of Land Force Commander than Ike; he might make plans, decide on objectives, allot forces, co-ordinate etc. I agree that the front could be divided into two groups, and consider a suitable set-up to be Bradley Land Forces Commander, yourself Northern Group, and Patton Southern Group. With that set-up there might be some chance of your being accepted for the Northern Group."

" Now Weeks informs me of a new plot by which you are contemplating re-opening the matter with Ike by asking him whether he has any objections to your doing so! As I told you in my letter, personally I think you are wrong in doing so."

" I should now like a reply from you by return telling me exactly what you are doing and how you reconcile your new plan with everything you have said up to date."[1]

To make doubly sure that his brilliant subordinate took no precipitate action, Brooke also sent him a telegram telling him he was sending a letter by special messenger and urging him to do nothing until he received it.

That night—the 24th—the C.I.G.S. wrote in his diary:

" At the end of this morning's C.O.S. meeting I showed the secretaries out and retained only ' Pug '. I then put before the Committee my views on the very unsatisfactory state of affairs in France, with no one running the land battle. Eisenhower, though supposed to be doing so, is on the golf links at Rheims—entirely detached and taking practically no part in the running of the war. Matters got so bad lately that a deputation of Whiteley, Bedell Smith and a few others went up to tell him that he must get down to it and RUN the war, which he said he would."

" We discussed the advisability of getting Marshall to come out to discuss the matter, but we are doubtful if he would appreciate the situation. Finally decided that I am to see the P.M. to discuss the situation with him. It

[1] C.I.G.S. to Field-Marshal Montgomery, 24 Nov., 1944. *Idem.*

is one of the most difficult problems I have had to tackle. I know the only solution, but doubt whether we can bring it off. Bradley should be made Commander of the Land Forces with Tedder as the Air Commander working closely with him. The front should then be divided into two Groups of Armies, one north of the Ardennes under Monty and one south under Patton, whilst Ike returns to the true duties of Supreme Commander . . ."

Next day Montgomery wired the C.I.G.S. to assure him that, though he had arranged a visit from Eisenhower on the 28th, he would do nothing further without his instructions and suggesting that he should fly back to England next day for consultation. Brooke's diary for Sunday, November 26th describes this visit.

". . . Monty flew over from Belgium and landed at Hartfordbridge Flats at 11.30 a.m. I sent a car for him to drive him to Ferney Close, where we had an hour together prior to his flying back. We decided that there were three fundamentals to be put right:—

(a) to counter the pernicious American strategy of attacking all along the line.

(b) to obviate splitting an Army Group with the Ardennes in the middle of it, by forming two Groups (a Northern and a Southern) instead of three as at present.

(c) to appoint a Commander for the Land Forces. The problem is how to get this carried out! What we want is Bradley as a Commander of Land Forces, Montgomery Northern Group of Armies, with Patton's Army in his Group—by substituting Third Army for Ninth Army—and Devers commanding Southern Group."

" Monty is to see Eisenhower on Monday[1] and, if he opens the subject, Monty is to begin putting forward the above proposals. Meanwhile I am to have a talk with

[1] Actually on Tuesday the 28th.

the P.M. suggesting that Marshall should be asked to come over to discuss the matter. Without some such change we shall just drift on and God knows when the war will end!"

" *November 27th.* Returned early. Had a long C.O.S. meeting . . . Cabinet at 6.30 to 8.30 p.m.—P.M. evidently beginning to realise that all is not well in France. He is now pressing for the clearing of Holland during the next few months, which he thinks could be done ' in no time with two or three divisions '."

" *November 28th.* ' Jumbo ' Wilson came to attend our C.O.S. meeting and gave us his views on future operations in Italy and across the Dalmatian coast. These are pretty well in accordance with the Directive we had prepared for him."

" At 12.30 I went to see the P.M., having asked for an interview with him. I told him I was very worried with the course operations were taking on the Western Front. I said that when we looked facts in the face this last offensive could only be classified as the first strategic reverse that we had suffered since landing in France. I said that in my mind two main factors were at fault, i.e.,

(a) American strategy;
(b) American organization."

" As regards the strategy, the American conception of always attacking all along the front, irrespective of strength available, was sheer madness. In the present offensive we had attacked on six Army fronts without any reserves anywhere."

" As regards organization, I said that I did not consider that Eisenhower could command both as Supreme Commander and as Commander of the Land Forces at the same time. I said that I considered Bradley should be made the Commander of the Land Forces, and the front divided into two Groups of Armies instead of the three, with the Ardennes between them; Montgomery to command the Northern and Devers the Southern."

" Winston said that he also was worried about the Western Front. He agreed with most of what I had said, but was doubtful as to the necessity for a Land Forces Commander. I think I succeeded in pointing out that we must take the control out of Eisenhower's hands, and the best plan was to repeat what we did in Tunisia when we brought in Alex as a Deputy to Eisenhower to command the Land Forces for him."

" I told Winston that the only way of putting things right was to get Marshall to come over. He agreed; we decided to wait for a few more days before doing so."

" At 2 p.m. conference with P.J. and Weeks on the ammunition situation. At 5 p.m. conference with ' Jumbo ' Wilson, Weeks and Nye on the organization of Command in Italy. Finally conference from 6 to 8 p.m. with Winston on the ammunition situation and methods of boosting up production to meet war dragging on into 1945."

.   .   .   .

The offensive which Eisenhower had ordered in October, which Patton had anticipated by his attacks south of the Ardennes and which Bradley, after waiting a fortnight for the weather to clear, had launched on a far too wide front in mid-November was now petering out. Except for the capture of the Metz forts, it had achieved nothing; neither the drive on the Saar nor the drive on Cologne got the Americans anywhere or even engaged the German reserves. The weather was appalling, ammunition ran short, and, after a fortnight's struggle in drenched fields and quagmires in which an advance of only eight miles was achieved at the point of greatest penetration, the Siegfried Line remained unbreached. As Montgomery had warned Eisenhower when he refused to concentrate, the Western Allies were now in a " strategic strait-jacket ". They were bogged down and reduced to the trench warfare it had always been their object to avoid. Until spring dried the ground, and reinforcements from America could again tip the scales in their favour, they were back where their predecessors had been in the days of Gamelin and the Maginot Line.

All this Montgomery proceeded to rub in when Eisenhower visited him on November 28th. That night he reported to the C.I.G.S.

" Ike visited me to-day and we have had a very long talk. I put following points to him.

1st. That the plan contained in his last Directive had failed and we had, in fact, suffered a strategic reverse. He agreed. 2nd. That we must now prepare a new plan and in that plan we must get away from the doctrine of attacking all along front and must concentrate our resources on selected vital thrust. He agreed. 3rd. That it seemed a pity he did not have Bradley as Land Force Commander to take off him the work of running the operations on land. He did not, repeat not, agree. 4th. That the theatre was divided naturally by Ardennes into two definite fronts. There should be one commander north of the Ardennes and one south. To this he agreed in principle. 5th. That I should command north of the Ardennes and Bradley south. He considered there would be difficulties about this, as main objective lay in Northern zone. But he said he would be quite prepared to put a strong Army Group under Bradley north of the Ardennes and to put Bradley under my operational command, thus putting me in operational charge north of the Ardennes."

" We talked for three hours in a most friendly way and I proved to him that we had definitely failed and must make new plan and next time we must quite definitely not (repeat not) fail. He admitted a grave mistake has been made and in my opinion is prepared to go almost any length to succeed next time. Hence his own suggestion I should be in full operational command north of the Ardennes with Bradley under me and 6 Army Group in a holding role in South . . ."

In a further telegram next morning Montgomery added,

" Had a further talk with Ike this morning before he left and there is no doubt our discussion last night has left him worried and ill at ease. He thought he and Bradley between them could do the business, and he now understands clearly that they made a very grave error and the net result is complete failure to do what was intended. When I suggested last night that Bradley would be suitable as Land Force Commander under him he definitely shied right off it, and it is my impression this morning that he thinks Bradley has failed him as an architect of land operations. There is no doubt he is now very anxious to go back to the old set-up we had in Normandy and up to 1st September and to put Bradley under my operational command with both our Army Groups north of the Ardennes. In fact, he now definitely wants me to handle main business but wants Bradley to be in on it and, therefore, he will put him under me. In my opinion Ike will never agree to appointment of a Land Force Commander for whole front as he wants to do this himself. If he reverts to the system we had in Normandy it means that I shall in reality be in operational charge and be able to influence whole land battle by direct approach to Ike myself . . ."[1]

Brooke's reaction to these communications is shown by his diary for November 29th.

" Received telegram from Monty. He had had a talk with Eisenhower. The latter had agreed that strategy was wrong, that results of offensive were strategic reverse, that front wanted reorganizating. Would not agree that command of land forces was necessary, but prepared to put Bradley with a large Group north of the Ardennes under Monty's orders, leaving Devers south of the Ardennes. This may be all right, but I still have grave doubts, as Ike is incapable of running a land battle and it is all dependent on how well Monty can handle him . . ."

[1] Lord Alanbrooke, *Personal Files.*

343

Next morning, November 30th, before embarking on a day of discussions with the Secretary of State and General Wilson on the forthcoming changes in the Mediterranean, Brooke sent a signal to Montgomery:

" Have been very interested in both your telegrams but am not quite clear on several points. Am sending over D.M.O.[1] as you suggest to obtain details from you and to let you know my views. On the whole, I feel that your conversation may lead to considerable improvements, provided that as a result of further discussions minds are not altered and decisions changed."

Either because of this communication or because of doubts of his own, Montgomery on the 30th sent Eisenhower a letter which crossed the t's and dotted the i's of what he supposed to be their agreement.

" My dear Ike,
In order to clear my own mind I would like to confirm the main points that were agreed on during the conversations we had during your stay with me on Tuesday night.
We have definitely failed to implement the plan contained in the SHAEF directive of 28 October, . . . and we have no hope of doing so. We have therefore failed; and we have suffered a strategic reverse.
We require a new plan. And this time *we must not fail.*
The need to get the German war finished early is vital, in view of other factors. The new plan *MUST NOT FAIL.*
In the new plan we must get away from the doctrine of attacking in so many places that nowhere are we strong enough to get decisive results. We must concentrate such strength on the main selected thrust that success will be certain . . .
The theatre divides itself naturally into two fronts: one north of the Ardennes and one south of the Ardennes. We want one commander in full operational control north of the Ardennes and one south.

[1] Major-Gen. J. W. Simpson, Director of Military Operations.

I did suggest that you might consider having a Land Force Commander to work under you and run the land battle for you. But you discarded this idea as being not suitable, and we did not discuss it any more. You suggested that a better solution would be to put 12 Army Group and 21 Army Group both north of the Ardennes, and to put Bradley under my operational command.

I said that Bradley and I together are a good team. We worked together in Normandy under you, and we won a great victory. Things have not been so good since you separated us. I believe to be certain of success you want to bring us together again; and one of us should have the full operational control north of the Ardennes; and if you decide that I should do that work—that is O.K. by me . . .

I am keeping

$\left.\begin{matrix} \text{Wed. 6 Dec.} \\ \text{Thurs. 7 Dec.} \end{matrix}\right\}$ next week

free for a meeting at Maastricht with you and Bradley.

Will you let me know which day you select. I suggest that we want no one else at the meeting except Chiefs of Staff, who must not speak.

Yours ever,
B. L. Montgomery."

Brooke's diary continued:

" *December 1st.* Went to see Winston at 10 a.m. to tell him about Monty's wires. Found him in bed finishing his breakfast, surrounded by birthday presents. ' This is delicious butter sent to me by my doctor, his wife makes it with her cow, she milks it and beats it up! etc.' He was in good mood and approved the steps that Monty had taken, including the latter's letter to Ike laying down in black and white the results of their talk together."

" If only all Monty thinks he has settled materializes we shall be all right, but I have fears of Ike going back when he has discussed with Bedell Smith, Tedder, etc."

" *December 2nd.* . . . In the evening I was called up by the P.M. who had drafted a wire to Eisenhower which he wanted to send, referring to the conversations which Monty has been having with Ike, and which the latter does not even know that Monty has told me about. I tried to stop him, explaining to him the harm it would do, but he would not agree, stating that the interview had been much publicized by the Press; it was a matter for Government decision, and not a matter to be settled by military men on their own. I told him that if he treated private wires that way it would make me very reluctant to show them to him again. However, I finally got him to hold his hand till Monday."

" *December 3rd.* A quiet Sunday spoilt by a mass of correspondence sent down by dispatch-rider, and several telephone calls. Trouble brewing up in Greece and all my worst forebodings coming true. Also telephone call from Simpson just back from visiting Monty, and with Monty's latest news. Monty has now received Ike's reply, and it does not look too good; he seems to be changing round since seeing Bradley! "

" *December 4th.* . . . At 3.15 p.m. I went off to complete my argument with Winston. I found him in a good humour and succeeded in getting him to withdraw a Minute he had written to me after our talk on Saturday. He also agreed not to send that wire to Eisenhower and not to do anything till Monty and Ike had had their talk next Thursday."

" During our discussion, he said he did not want anybody between Ike and the Army Groups, as Ike was a good fellow who was amenable and whom he could influence. Bradley, on the other hand, might not listen to what he said! I replied that I could see little use in having an ' amenable ' Commander if he was unfit to win the war for him."

" Cabinet at 6 p.m."

" *December 5th.* The Greek situation is getting more and

more confused. Winston spent most of the early hours from 3 a.m. onwards sending telegrams to 'Jumbo' Wilson, Scobie and Leeper.[1] Meanwhile Wilson was sending me wires which did not fit in with the instructions Winston was sending him. Leeper, having originally asked for 5000 men as being ample to set the Greek Government firmly on its feet, has now got over 40,000 and considers that 'the military have badly under-estimated the strength required' and should send more troops at once. This is *exactly* what I have predicted from the very start. Winston had been trying to induce Wilson to leave the Parachute brigade in Greece whereas it is urgently required for operations in Italy. Added to which these operations are Anglo-American, and the approved Directive to Wilson from the Combined Chiefs of Staff stated that the operations in Greece must on no account be allowed to interfere with those in Italy."

" I asked for an interview with Winston; was told 12.15 p.m. He kept me waiting till 12.45 p.m., as he was in the House and having a bad time about the Greek situation. When he returned I put the whole case in front of him. I found him rather rattled about the situation; however, he agreed that the withdrawal of the Parachute brigade should be proceeded with as settled."

" I do not see much daylight yet in that Greek situation. And I feel certain we shall have to send far more troops there . . ."

" *December 6th.* A very long C.O.S. meeting which Alexander attended for a bit. I am afraid that it was an eye-opener to him to find some of the problems and difficulties he is to be up against as Supreme Commander in Mediterranean. God help him, and may God help us! "

" *December 7th.* Another long C.O.S. meeting during which we examined the American plans for the Pacific.

[1] Lt.-Gen. (now Sir) Ronald Scobie, G.O.C. Greece, and Sir Reginald Leeper, British Ambassador at Athens.

They are based on the war in Europe ending before the end of this year and do not bear any very direct relation to facts. They will have to slow up the estimates of their rate of advance."

" *December 8th.* . . . After dinner called up by Winston to find that he wanted to send a wire to Wilson to reinforce Greece by two brigades. He is doing it without being able to estimate what the situation is. However, one thing is certain, we must now get out of the mess that this Greek venture has let us in for. Consequently I agreed to additional force being sent, since the greater the force, the quicker the job will be done. I warned him, however, that we shall be falling foul of the Americans and that we shall have to have the Supreme Commander Mediterranean's Directive adjusted."

. . . .

Meanwhile the conference with the Supreme Commander that Montgomery had proposed in his letter of November 30th had taken place at Maastricht on December 7th. It had been proceeded by a further exchange of correspondence. The British commander's letter had not only made the position crystal clear; it had made Eisenhower very angry. For all his good nature, the Supreme Commander was a tough " West Pointer " and could never have reached his position otherwise. However acquiescent he may have seemed when he was Montgomery's guest, when confronted with his letter—which, according to Captain Butcher, made him " hot under the collar "—he indignantly rejected the description of the autumn campaign as a " strategic reverse ". " You have stated ", he replied, " your conception of the points that were agreed upon during our conversation, whereas there are certain things in your letter in which I do not concur . . . I do not agree that things have gone badly since Normandy, merely because we have not gained all we hoped to gain . . . I have no intention of stopping Devers's and Patton's operations as long as they are cleaning up our right flank and giving us *capability of concentration* . . . I beg of you not to continue to look upon the past performances of this great fighting force as a failure because we have not achieved all that we could have hoped."[1]

Genuinely fond of Eisenhower like everyone who served under him, Montgomery had been quick to assure him that he had never said or intended any such thing but had been referring only to the failure of the November offensive. Whereupon, with characteristic generosity, the Supreme Commander had replied:

" You have my prompt and abject apologies for misreading your letter . . . I do not want to put words or meaning into your mouth, or ever do anything that upsets our close relationship."

Yet, despite their personal cordiality, Montgomery's meeting with Eisenhower and his other principal subordinates, Bradley and Tedder, proved a failure. Three days before it took place, after receiving the Supreme Commander's apology, he had optimistically telegraphed Brooke asking him to leave matters to him and not to take up the reorganization of the Command at a higher level, as the C.I.G.S. was proposing.[2] But after the conference he wrote to him in despair.

" Eisenhower has obviously been ' got at ' by the American generals; he reversed his opinion on all major points on which he had agreed when he visited me on the 28th Nov. . . . I personally regard the whole thing as quite dreadful. I can see no good coming out of this business. Eisenhower and Bradley have their eyes firmly fixed on Frankfurt, and the route thence to Kassel. We shall split our resources and our strength, and we shall fail."

As always, Montgomery had pleaded for concentration and the building up of powerful striking reserves at a single point

[1] Supreme Commander to Montgomery 1 Dec., 1944. *Pogue*, 313-14; Lord Alanbrooke, *Personal Files*.

[2] " I recommend very strongly that for the moment you leave the matter to be handled between myself and Ike. There is a sporting chance that we may pull it off. But any outside interference might be fatal at this juncture." Montgomery to C.I.G.S., 4 Dec., 1944. Lord Alanbrooke, *Personal Files*.

for an early spring offensive, in the north against the Ruhr and the open Hanover plains beyond; " once the war becomes mobile, that is the end of the Germans." But, though they had parted on the friendliest note,[1] Eisenhower and his companions had remained unmoved by the British Commander-in-Chief's pleas. Their contention was that the broad-front winter offensive on both sides of the Ardennes was paying dividends, that, though costly and immediately unspectacular in results, it was wearing the enemy down and that, as the Allies' only objective was to kill Germans, it did not matter where they did it. Like the " Westerners " of First World War legend, they put their faith in attrition. " I played a lone hand against the three of them ", Montgomery concluded; " they all arrived to-day and went away together. It is therefore fairly clear that any points I made which caused Eisenhower to wobble will have been put right by Bradley and Tedder on the three-hour drive back to Luxembourg . . . I can do no more myself . . . If we want the war to end within any reasonable period you have to get Eisenhower's hand taken off the land battle. I regret to say that in my opinion he just doesn't know what he is doing. And you will have to see that Bradley's influence is curbed."

The onus of action was now on the C.I.G.S. Though Montgomery, confident that he could handle the situation himself, had hitherto been averse to his doing so, Brooke had already taken preparatory steps. On December 4th the Prime Minister had written to the President asking, in view of the stalemate in France and Italy, for a meeting of the Combined Chiefs of Staff. Roosevelt's reply, prompted by Marshall, was

[1] " I may say that we all had a very cheery lunch and parted afterwards with much laughter." Montgomery to C.I.G.S., 7 Dec., 1944. Lord Alanbrooke, *Personal Files*. The letter, one of the longest Montgomery ever wrote, runs to over forty numbered paragraphs and ends, " Before he left I made it clear to Eisenhower that it was for him to command and for me to obey; but I was the Commander of the armed forces of one of the principal allies, and as such he must know what I thought about things. I said that in this case we differed widely and on fundamental issues. He said he quite understood and we parted great friends." Tedder, who supported Eisenhower's and Bradley's views, also sent a report of the meeting to Portal who passed it on to Brooke on Sunday, December 10th, with a note, " Tedder has a very clear head for this sort of thing; I expect it can be taken as being accurate."

not encouraging. The agreed broad strategy, he declared, was developing according to plan, General Eisenhower estimated that he was inflicting losses in excess of the German capacity to form new units, the Western Allies' ground and air forces were " day by day chewing up the enemy's dwindling man-power and resources " and a decisive break in their favour was bound to come soon. As Washington's only recipe, as before, was to leave everything to Eisenhower, an immediate invitation to meet the Prime Minister and British Chiefs of Staff in London was sent to the Supreme Commander and his Deputy.

The meeting took place, as Brooke's diary records, on the evening of December 12th in the Prime Minister's map room.

" *December 12th*. I have just finished one of those days which should have been one of the keystones of the final days of the war. I feel I have utterly failed to do what is required, and yet God knows how I could have done anything else."

" I started by going to the P.M. at 10 a.m. to discuss with him Monty's letter. Found him in bed eating his breakfast and absorbed by the last telegram from Alex on the situation in Greece. He was quite incapable of concentrating on anything but the Greek situation. I remained till 10.30 a.m., found he had not even read Monty's letter and knew nothing about it. I tried to explain but he kept returning to Greece."

" Went to the C.O.S. meeting, which lasted till near 1 p.m. Was informed during lunch that War Cabinet was to meet at 3 p.m. on Greece. We wasted one-and-a-half hours deciding whether Archbishop should be appointed a Regent. Finally Cabinet decided that this should be done and drafted a Minute to that effect to the King of Greece."

" At 6 p.m. met Ike and Tedder with P.M. in the latter's Map Room, with the whole Chiefs of Staff. Ike explained his plan which contemplates a double advance into

Germany, north of Rhine and by Frankfurt. I disagreed flatly with it, accused Ike of violating principles of concentration of force, which had resulted in his present failures. I criticized his future plans and pointed out impossibility of double invasion with the limited forces he has got. I stressed the importance of concentrating on one thrust. I drew attention to the fact that with his limited forces any thought of attack on both fronts could only lead to dispersal of effort."

" Quite impossible to get the P.M. to understand the importance of the principles involved. Half the time his attention was concentrated on the possibility of floating mines down the Rhine![1] He must get down to detail. . . . "

" Finally dined at 10 Downing Street with P.M., Ike, Tedder, Cunningham, Portal and Ismay. Conversation again to the same topic of the strategy, but I got no further in getting either Winston or Ike to see that their strategy is fundamentally wrong. Amongst other things discovered that Ike now does not hope to cross the Rhine before May! "

" *December 13th.* I was very depressed last night and seriously thought of resigning, as Winston did not seem to attach any importance to my views. I found, however, to-day that the situation was far better than I thought. After the C.O.S. meeting I went to see Winston at 1 p.m. He told me that he had had to support Ike last night as he was one American against five of us with only Tedder to support him. And also he was his guest. I think he felt that I had been rather rough on Ike, but on the other hand I found that I had convinced him of the seriousness of the situation. What I had said last night had had far more effect on him than I had thought. He decided that the War Cabinet must assemble at 5.30 p.m. this evening

[1] The *Royal Marine* operation with air-dropped mines and aerial torpedoes with which Churchill had hoped to immobilize the German offensive in the spring of 1940.

and that I must put before them the whole strategic situation. In addition he wanted me to put in a paper on the whole matter."

" At 5.30 p.m. we met at 10 Downing Street and I ran through the situation after the P.M. had given a general introduction. The date of May for the crossing of the Rhine had a profound effect on the Cabinet. However, it has cleared the air well, and the Cabinet now know what to expect, which is a good thing to counter the over-optimistic attitude of the newspapers."

For the rest of that week Brooke's staff was busy under his direction preparing the paper for which the Prime Minister had asked and which the Chiefs of Staff were to present on Monday the 18th. It began by recalling the Directive which in September the Combined Chiefs of Staff had given Eisenhower and, in which, at the C.I.G.S.'s instance, they had stressed the importance of the northern line of approach into Germany as opposed to the southern. Despite, however, the Supreme Commander's lip service to these instructions in his orders for the November offensive, the concentration in the north had never taken place and there had been dispersion of effort along the whole line, the main attacks on the Ruhr and Saar fronts having been launched with forces of approximately equal strength. Both had failed. The Supreme Commander's latest proposals had the same defect. Though by the spring he would probably have from eighty to eighty-five divisions, at least twenty would be needed to hold the rest of the front between the North Sea and Switzerland, and, so long as Germany had the reserves in hand she was now known to have built up, the sixty or so remaining divisions available for the offensive would be insufficient for the double enveloping movement Eisenhower envisaged. " We consider ", the Report continued, " that it is important to decide on one major thrust. Sufficient forces could then be allotted to this thrust to ensure that it is made in overwhelming strength with fresh formations always available to keep up the momentum of advance . . . We still think that the opinion of the Combined Chiefs of Staff last September was the correct one and that this main thrust should be made in the north."

The paper ended with a recommendation that the Combined Chiefs of Staff should request General Eisenhower to submit, as a matter of urgency, an account of his recent operations and his plans for the rest of the winter and spring. It was a subject on which the British felt strongly, for, by needlessly prolonging the war in the West as they thought, the American Supreme Commander was presenting them with a man-power problem likely to prove unsoluble. Within the past fortnight the Government had announced a new military call-up. It meant a corresponding loss in war production, and there would be no further possibility of making up battle wastage. After six years of war, with a higher proportion of her population mobilized than any other belligerent, Britain had reached the bottom of the barrel.

. . . .

Yet though the Western Allies had temporarily lost the initiative which British strategy had won for them two years before, though their reserves had been committed and their hand— formerly so skilfully concealed—been disclosed, the stalemate was about to be broken by a greater optimist than Eisenhower. By his fanatic refusal to yield ground Hitler had already allowed the Western Allies to destroy two great German armies—one in Tunisia in 1943 and the other in Normandy in 1944—as he had enabled the Russians to destroy another at Stalingrad and blockade another in the Baltic provinces. Ever since his reprieve in September, he had been husbanding the new army of young fanatics he had raised by his drastic autumn call-up,[1] not to create the central defensive reserve which, with her foes closing in from east and west, was Germany's supreme need, but to form the wherewithal for a second *blitzkrieg* which should do against the Americans and British what its predecessor had done against the French and British

[1] He had, *inter alia*, reduced the call-up age from $17\frac{1}{2}$ to 16.

354

in 1940. Rather than rely on the interior lines that were his country's chief military asset and play the patient defensive game which had enabled his hero, Frederick the Great, to snatch victory from defeat, the Führer had decided to stake everything on a single throw, " to win or lose it all ". And because he despised the Americans and believed them to be more likely to break under such a blow than the Russians, he had resolved to leave the Eastern front to look after itself and make his desperate bid for victory in the West.

Though his generals regarded Hitler's project as dangerously unsound and even impracticable with the limited resources at his disposal, it offered a possible chance of a victory which no defence, however skilful and prolonged, could have offered Germany at the end of 1944. Its object was to drive a wedge between the two main halves of the Anglo-American forces which Eisenhower had aligned on either side of the Ardennes and, by striking from there at the point of maximum potential confusion where the Americans and British forces joined, to reach Brussels and Antwerp in the latter's rear, encircle and, this time, destroy them. After that, Hitler felt he could deal with the remaining Americans to the south as he had dealt with the French after Dunkirk. Once the Western Allies had been driven from the Continent, his new submarines, jet-fighters and rockets would force their discredited statesmen to sue for peace. With Russia left to face the uninterrupted might of a revived Reich, the end of the Coalition would follow.

In view of Germany's unbroken defeats of the past two years and the enormous Allied preponderance in the air and in war material, it all seemed the wildest fantasy. Yet with less than seventy American and British divisions as yet on the Continent and with their forces—exhausted by their non-stop offensives and deployed for yet another double thrust—so strung out as to be without reserves at all, a repetition of 1940 was just conceivable. And by staging his gamble in the dead of winter and at a time when the Allies' air forces might be unable to intervene, Hitler, who since the autumn had carefully husbanded and concentrated his own small air force, hoped to be able to keep the American and British bombers at bay until he had secured the Meuse crossings and broken the Allies' lines wide open.

The point chosen for the assault was the same hilly and wooded Ardennes across which the first *blitzkrieg* had been launched. Here, owing to Eisenhower's dividing his main forces between the Ruhr and Saar, four American divisions were guarding nearly a hundred miles of front. Against them, in the utmost secrecy, Hitler had concentrated twenty-eight divisions or nearly 400,000 men, including ten armoured divisions, with another six divisions ready to attack farther south—a larger striking force than he had been able to assemble on any front since the Allies had struck in the Mediterranean two years before.

On December 12th, the day on which Churchill and the British Chiefs of Staff tried to persuade Eisenhower to regroup his forces, the Führer had harangued his generals at a secret meeting place. Stripped of their weapons and brief-cases and with armed S.S. guards standing behind them, they listened for two hours to his final orders and an impassioned justification of his policy. Four days later, at dawn on Saturday the 16th, the Germans struck. By nightfall, before Bradley and Eisenhower at their distant headquarters had realised what was happening, they had broken through on a wide front. By the morning of the 17th the Panzers were pouring through a fifty-mile gap, with broken American units flying in confusion before them. That evening the enemy's spearheads were twenty miles inside Belgium.

On Monday December 18th, when the Chiefs of Staff were to have delivered their report on the Supreme Commander's strategy to the Prime Minister, Brooke wrote in his diary:

" *December 18th.* Germans are delivering strong counter offensive against Americans, who have no immediate reserves to stem the attack with. They ought ultimately to hold it all right and to have an opportunity of delivering a serious counter-blow which might well finish off

Germans. But I am not certain whether they have the skill required."

" It is a worrying situation. If I felt that the American Commanders and staff were more efficient than they are, there is no doubt that this might turn out to be a Heaven-sent opportunity. However, if mishandled, it may well put the defeat of Germany back for another six months."

" I feel that Rundstedt, in launching this counter-offensive, feels that as ' a good officer ' he is doing the right thing to put off defeat by means of a counter-offensive destined to upset the Allied plans. However, he must realise the great risks he is taking of achieving exactly the reverse result if the Americans can take advantage of the risks he takes. Perhaps as ' a good German ' he considers that these may be definite advantages in bringing this war to an early conclusion and consequently accepts all risks, great as they are."

" *December 19th.* Very little more news of the war in France. Eisenhower seems quite confident, and so do his Staff, that they can deal with this situation. I only hope that this confidence is not based on ignorance."

" *December 20th.* Received telegram from Monty which showed clearly that the situation in France was serious. American front penetrated, Germans advancing on Namur with little in front of them, north flank of First American Army in state of flux and disorganization, etc. Also suggesting that he should be given command of all forces north of the penetration."

" I sent a copy to P.M. who sent for me at 3.30 p.m. in the Map Room . . . I got him to telephone to Ike to put the proposal to him that Monty should take over the whole of the northern wing whilst Bradley ran the south. Ike agreed and had apparently already issued orders to that effect."

" We were then summoned to the 6 p.m. Cabinet to discuss the French situation. Cabinet took it well on the whole. I rather doubt whether they realised all the possible implications."

Montgomery's telegram which Brooke received that morning had begun—from one who was the reverse of an alarmist—with the ominous words, " The situation in American area is not—not—good." After naming the points to which the enemy had penetrated, it went on: " In that part of the First Army north of line Udenbreth to Durbuy there is great confusion and all signs of a full-scale withdrawal. There is a definite lack of grip and control and no one has a clear picture as to situation . . . There is an atmosphere of great pessimism in First and Ninth Armies due, I think, to the fact that everyone knows something has gone wrong and no one knows what or why. Bradley is still at Luxembourg but I understand he is moving, as his Headquarters are in danger. I have no information as to where he is moving. I presume Ike is at Rheims but I have heard nothing from him or Bradley . . . I have myself had no orders or requests of any sort. My own opinion is that . . . the American forces have been cut clean in half and the Germans can reach the Meuse at Namur without any opposition. The Command set-up has always been very faulty and now is quite futile, with Bradley at Luxembourg and the front cut in two. I have told Whiteley[1] that Ike ought to place me in operational command of all troops on the northern half of the front. I consider he should be given a direct order by someone to do so. This situation needs to be handled very firmly and with a tight grip."[2]

To the C.I.G.S. it was not unreminiscent of the days of Gamelin and the 1940 Battle of the Bulge, when he and Montgomery had been left without information of the state of the French and Belgian armies on their flanks and their troops had had to fight their way out of chaos without orders. He at once wired back to the British Commander-in-Chief:

---

[1] Maj.-Gen. (now Lt.-Gen.) Sir John Whiteley, a senior British officer of the SHAEF Staff.

[2] Montgomery to C.I.G.S., 20 Dec., 1944. Lord Alanbrooke, *Personal Files.*

" 1. Many thanks for your very informative telegram which with your previous ones has thrown on this confused situation a light which we have been unable to obtain from other sources.

2. We are not clear here about number of American formations available elsewhere in France and time it will take to move these to the battle area, but we hope to obtain this information shortly from SHAEF. At least one U.S. Airborne division seems to be moving up between enemy northern penetration and Namur area.

3. I consider action proposed in your para 6 is right and proper. It will ensure safety of your southern flank and enable you to help American counter-stroke later if required.

4. Eisenhower has just reported to Combined Chiefs of Staff that his general plan is to plug the holes in the North and launch co-ordinated attack from the South. He has ordered whole front south of Moselle to go on defensive with Devers taking over most of present Third Army front. Patton is moving north with six divisions to organize major counter-blow with target date of 23 or 24 December. Eisenhower appreciates his weakest spot is in direction of Namur. No doubt you have already had all this direct from SHAEF, but otherwise you should keep this information to yourself.

5. As regards your para 7 I fully sympathize with what you are feeling and agree that it would be a great advantage to have one commander (preferably yourself) for all troops on northern half of front. But only Authority which can order Eisenhower to do so is Combined Chiefs of Staff, and I see no chance of our being able to convince U.S. Chiefs of Staff at present that necessity exists for Combined Chiefs of Staff to take the drastic step of instructing Eisenhower on his conduct of the battle.

6. I think you should be careful about what you say to Eisenhower himself on subject of Command set-up as it may do much more harm than good, especially as he is

now probably very worried over whole situation. It is a different thing, however, to make suggestions to Whiteley as you have done and these may well bear fruit.

7. I have sent the Prime Minister a copy of your telegram."[1]

By this time, however, on the advice of Bedell Smith and despite Bradley's protests, Eisenhower had already acted as Montgomery wished. Following a brief message on the previous day to the Combined Chiefs of Staff, whose purport the C.I.G.S. had communicated in his telegram, he contacted the British commander on the morning of the 20th by telephone. " He was very excited ", Montgomery reported, " and it was difficult to understand what he was talking about; he roared into the telephone, speaking very fast. The only point I really grasped was that ' it seems to me we have now two fronts ' and that I was to assume command of the Northern front. This was all I wanted to know. He then went on talking wildly about other things; I could not hear and said so; at last the line cut out before he finished."[2] Later in the day Eisenhower also gave the news by telephone to the Prime Minister at Downing Street. Brooke was in the room at the time but took no part in the conversation, as he did not wish to appear to be short-circuiting his American colleagues of the Combined Chiefs of Staff. The Prime Minister said that he supposed the Supreme Commander was " working on a pincer-nip from the north and the south upon the German offensive bulge " and suggested that this could be best effected by putting Montgomery in command of everything north of the German break-through and Bradley of everything south of it. Eisenhower explained that this was exactly what he had done.

Montgomery, who had already taken steps of his own to guard the British Army's exposed flank and rear, wasted no time in assuming control of the cut-off American forces. In a telegram to Brooke that night he described how, within two hours of his talk with Eisenhower, he visited the commanders of the First and Ninth Armies; a British officer who was

[1] C.I.G.S. to Montgomery, 20 Dec., 1944. Lord Alanbrooke, *Personal Files.*
[2] Lord Alanbrooke, *Personal Files.*

present said that he strode into Hodges's H.Q. "like Christ come to cleanse the temple". "Neither Army Commander", he reported to Brooke, "had seen Bradley or any of his staff since the battle began . . . There were no reserves anywhere behind front. Morale was very low. They seemed delighted to have someone to give them firm orders." These took the form of an immediate reorganization of the front in order to form a reserve of three divisions. "All bridges over the Meuse", Montgomery added, "from south-east of Liége to north-east of Givet are now held by British garrisons . . . I have every hope the situation can be put right now that we have a properly organized set-up for Command and proper super-vision and control can be kept over the battle. It will take a day or two to get American front reorganized and in better shape and we may have a few more shocks before that is com-pleted . . . But it is necessary to realise that there was literally no control or grip of any sort of the situation and we shall never do any good so long as that goes on."

Montgomery's assumption of the northern command only took place just in time. At dawn on the 21st twelve fresh German divisions, seven of them armoured, were flung against the American First Army, whose tired, battered units had been fighting back, with supreme gallantry but little co-ordination or direction from above, in an attempt to stem the tide where they stood. "The American armies in the north," Mont-gomery wrote subsequently, "were in a complete muddle; Bradley had not visited either Army since the attack began; there had been no grip or tight control of the battle; the Army Commanders did what they thought best."[1] Behind their strained lines lay the Meuse crossings, guarded by the British detachments which Montgomery had sent there to protect his rear when news of the offensive first reached him. At one point the enemy's advance guards came within four miles of Dinant. And beyond the Meuse lay the open Belgian plain, with Antwerp little more than sixty miles away.

For though the full force of the assault had fallen, as Hitler

[1] Montgomery to C.I.G.S., 25 Dec., 1944. Lord Alanbrooke, *Personal Files.*

had intended, on the Americans, its real objective was the encirclement of the British and northern forces whose life-line ran through the Belgian port. ' Had Rundstedt achieved a little more success ', Brooke wrote after the war, ' Antwerp might have been very seriously threatened. That he did not achieve this success is, in my opinion, mainly due to Monty's prompt action. Rundstedt had proved how faulty Ike's dispositions and organizations were. Spread out on a long front, with no adequate reserves and no Land Force Commander to take charge immediately, Eisenhower was temporarily thrown off his balance.'[1]

Yet though the American High Command had been found wanting, the American soldier was not. Wherever he was given the chance he and his junior commanders, many of whom displayed qualities of the highest leadership, proved worthy of the men of Antietam and Gettysburg. At St. Vith and Butgenbach to the north of the breach and at Bastogne to the south, the fighting men of America stood like rock amid the advancing grey tide. The beleaguered commander's reply —" Nuts "—to von Lüttwitz's demand for the surrender of Bastogne epitomized the battle. Though without Montgomery's handling of the situation in the north the American refusal to yield ground and impatience to counter-attack might have played into the enemy's hands, the bastions on either flank of the German break-through held.

Nor in the hour of crisis was the Supreme Commander unworthy of the men he led. Calamity acted on Eisenhower like a restorative and brought out all the greatness in his character. It was he who, as soon as the news of defeat reached him, overruled Bradley, halted the offensive south of the Moselle and ordered Patton to march north against the Germans' flank; who threw in the two airborne divisions— his sole reserve—to hold Bastogne and the Meuse crossings; who opened a conference of his senior commanders with the words, " I want only cheerful faces ", and declared that the

---

[1] *Notes on My Life* X, 52. For a confirmation of Alanbrooke's view of Montgomery's influence on the battle, see *The Battle of the Ardennes* by the official U.S. military historian, Robert Merriam.

situation should be regarded as one not of disaster, but opportunity. His Order of the Day—comparable to Haig's " Backs to the Wall " Order of 1918—contained the prophecy, " By rushing out from his fixed defences the enemy has given us the chance to turn his great gamble into his worst defeat."[1]

It was the knowledge that Montgomery was now in control of the real danger point in the north that caused Brooke to write in his diary for December 21st:

> " News of the war in France much better. Provided the two gate-posts hold on either flank, there may be a chance of annihilating a great many of the troops that have broken through. If only the Americans are up to it."
>
> " *December 22nd*. German offensive appears to be held in the north, but I am a little more doubtful about the south. Patton is reported to have put in a counter-attack; this could only have been a half-baked affair, and I doubt its doing much good."[2]

For a week after the break-through the thick wintry weather upon which Hitler depended for victory continued, grounding the Allied air forces. The German armour and grey infantry masses went forward in fog and snow without interruption from above, penetrating the thin Allied line in places to a depth of sixty miles. The sole unengaged troops Eisenhower could throw into the battle were a raw division fresh from the United States which was disembarking at Havre and the two airborne divisions. He was only able to release Patton's Seventh Army for operations in the North at the expense of giving Devers permission to abandon Strasbourg and the ground recently won by the French in Alsace—an order which precipitated a major crisis with de Gaulle's Government. And

---

[1] *Butcher*, 620-2. He himself was threatened with assassination by paratroopers reported to have been dropped for this purpose in American uniforms and had, to his disgust, to be guarded night and day.

[2] Brooke was right. Though Patton was able to relieve Bastogne on the 26th, it was not till well on in January that he made any real impression on the southern flank of the German salient. " In the south," Montgomery wrote on Christmas Day, " Bradley is trying hard to get to Bastogne to relieve 101 Airborne Division. He may possibly get that place, but he admits himself that he is not strong enough to get any farther."

Patton's belief that he had only to hurl his armoured divisions against the German salient to break it proved, as Brooke had foreseen, illusory. For all the speed and fury with which he acted, he could make little headway over snow-blocked roads and fields against the strongly held German defence-points. As Montgomery with his clear grasp of military reality saw, the enemy's drive could only be broken, not by throwing troops piecemeal into the battle but by yielding inessential to secure essential ground and by winning time to form reserves with which to counter-attack when the impetus of the offensive was expended.

On December 23rd, two days before Christmas, the blanket of cloud and fog over the confused battlefield lifted and the Allied air forces went into the attack. While Montgomery, restraining the impatience of his American subordinates, waited until he had built up an adequate striking force and steadily edged the German columns away from the Meuse crossings south-westwards where they could do no harm,[1] thousands of bombers and fighters harried Rundstedt's armour and communications and made his supply position, always precarious, impossible. Thanks to the American fighting-man's tenacity and the British Commander-in-Chief's prescience the Panzers never reached the Allied petrol dumps where they were to have refuelled for the final drive across the Belgian plain and, for lack of oil, ground slowly to a standstill in the snow-clad foothills to the south and east of the Meuse. By the 26th, though in sight of the river, their advance was at an end; by the 30th, though Montgomery was still not yet ready to counter-attack, they had begun to yield ground. Hitler's eleventh-hour throw for victory had failed.

During the last few days of 1944 Brooke was on leave, taking a brief much-needed rest after a year which had seen the capture of Rome, the invasion and liberation of France, the defeat of Hitler's Western Army, the Allied Conferences in London, Quebec and Moscow, and the long drawn-out dis-

---

[1] " It was not," wrote the indignant Bradley, " until January 3rd, twelve days later, that Montgomery completed his primping and attacked." *Bradley*, 479.

putes with the Americans over ' *Anvil* ' and the Italian campaign and with the Prime Minister over Far Eastern strategy. " Situation in France gradually improving ", he wrote on the closing day of the year, " and Rundstedt's offensive appears to be held. Importance now rests in counter-strokes to be delivered."

Chapter Eleven

A NEW DIRECTIVE

No more let us falter!
From Malta to Yalta!
Let nobody alter!

PRIME MINISTER TO PRESIDENT

THERE WAS no doubt that the Americans had had a severe shock. Their commanders had chosen to ignore the two most elementary rules of war—concentration and the possession of a reserve to counter the enemy's moves and keep the initiative. As a result, though Germany was all but broken, she had been able, like a wounded tiger, to inflict on them grave injuries. Their casualties had amounted to over 75,000 men, nearly 30,000 killed or missing.

But the British, who had so repeatedly warned them, had had a worse shock. And they took longer to recover from it. With their man-power and resources all but exhausted after five years of war and with no possibility of making good further losses, they had staked everything on an early victory in the West and had seen it, as they felt, thrown away by the inexperience of the American High Command. The war, instead of ending in 1944, had been prolonged into another year and, unless a very different method of conducting it was now to be adopted, seemed likely to continue until, not only their own position, but that of Europe was desperate. Eisenhower's statement at his meeting with the British Chiefs of Staff on December 12th that he did not expect to cross the Rhine before May had been almost as grave a blow to Churchill and Brooke as the German offensive that had followed.

There seemed only one remedy: to induce the American

High Command, while shaken by its reverse, to concentrate at last on a single decisive blow and to prevent Eisenhower and Bradley from again indulging their preference for attacking everywhere at once. And this, as Brooke was aware, could only be achieved by persuasion; with more than fifty American divisions already in France to the Commonwealth's fifteen, it was not in Britain's power to dictate. Her ally had had a lesson, and it was possible, as he had predicted in his letter to Montgomery of November 20th,[1] that, having seen the consequences of their strategy, the American leaders might now take advice. Yet unless it was tactfully tendered, such advice was more likely to offend than persuade.

Feeling thus, Brooke had written to Montgomery on the day after the latter had been entrusted with the American First and Ninth Armies:

" I would like to give you a word of warning. Events and enemy action have forced on Eisenhower the setting up of a more satisfactory system of command. I feel it is most important that you should not even in the slightest degree appear to rub this undoubted fact in to anyone at SHAEF or elsewhere. Any remarks you may make are bound to come to Eisenhower's ears sooner or later and that may make it more difficult to ensure that this new set-up for Command remains even after the present emergency has passed. I myself have all along felt you were right, and now events have proved it. The fact will sink in of its own weight more effectively than if any of us try to drive it in. We must watch, however, that things do not go wrong again, and, I hope, therefore, you will continue to keep in close touch with me on these matters."[2]

Unfortunately this was not advice Montgomery found it easy to follow. On Christmas Day, when Bradley visited him, he did not disguise his view that the American Command had deserved what had happened. " I was absolutely frank with him," he wrote that evening, " I said the Germans had given

[1] See p. 335.
[2] C.I.G.S. to Montgomery, 21 Dec. 1944. Lord Alanbrooke, *Personal Files.*

us a real ' bloody nose'; it was useless to pretend that we were going to turn this quickly into a great victory; it was a proper defeat, and we had much better admit it. . . . I then said it was entirely our own fault; we had gone much too far with our right; we had tried to develop two thrusts at the same time, and neither had been strong enough to gain decisive results. The enemy saw his chance and took it. Now we were in a proper muddle."

Bradley, Montgomery reported, " looked thin, and worn and ill at ease. . . . He agreed entirely with all I said. Poor chap; he is such a decent fellow and the whole thing is a bitter pill for him. But he is man enough to admit it and he did. . . . He stayed only half an hour and flew straight back." Bradley's own account of the interview suggests that the Field-Marshal misunderstood his feelings. They were not so much of repentance for past errors as of resentment at the way they had been pointed out.[1]

Three days after Christmas Eisenhower had himself visited Montgomery. The discussion between them had turned on whether, in a new offensive to cross the Rhine, Montgomery should be given general co-ordinating powers to synchronize the operations of the American northern armies with his own, as the Supreme Commander was ready to agree, or whether, as the Field-Marshal insisted, he should have full operational direction of the entire attack.[2] In his report of the interview to the C.I.G.S., Montgomery stated that he had carried his point, though he admitted that he had had difficulty in doing so. Brooke, in his diary, expressed his doubts.

> " Monty has had another interview with Ike. I do not like the account of it. It looks to me as if Monty has been rubbing into Ike the results of not having listened to advice ! "

[1] " So scrupulously did we conceal our irritation with Monty," Bradley wrote after the war, " that I doubt he was even aware of it. . . . I am quite certain he never knew just how exasperated we had become." *Bradley*, 299, 487.

[2] As before, Montgomery had offered to serve under Bradley if Eisenhower preferred to appoint an American to command the northern thrust, but Eisenhower had replied that he had no intention of giving Bradley such a Command.

" According to Monty, Ike agrees that the front should now be divided in two and that only one major offensive is possible. But I expect that whoever meets Ike next may swing him to any other point of view."

Brooke's fears were quickly realised. On the day after the Supreme Commander's visit the British Commander-in-Chief had followed his usual practice of underlining what he had said by a letter. After recalling that before the German break-through Bradley had opposed any idea of Montgomery's exercising operational control over his Army Group, he went on:

" I therefore consider that it will be necessary for you to be very firm on the subject, and any loosely worded state-ment will be quite useless. I consider that if you merely use the word ' co-ordination,' it will NOT work. The person designated by you must have powers of operational direction and control of the operations that will follow on your Directive. . . . One commander must have powers to direct and control the operations; you cannot possibly do it your-self and so you would have to nominate someone else. I suggest that your Directive should finish with this sentence:

' 12 and 21 Army Groups will develop operations in accordance with the above instructions. From now onwards full operational direction, control and co-ordination of these operations is vested in the C.-in-C. 21 Army Group, subject to such instructions as may be issued by the Supreme Commander from time to time.'

I put this matter up to you again only because I am so anxious not to have another failure.

I am absolutely convinced that the key to success lies in:

(*a*) *all* available offensive power being assigned to the Northern line of advance to the Ruhr.

(*b*) a sound set-up for Command, and this implies one man directing and controlling the whole tactical battle on the Northern thrust.

I am certain that if we do not comply with these two basic conditions, then we will fail again."[1]

The arrival of this uncompromising document at S.H.A.E.F. coincided with a major crisis in Anglo-American relations. During the Ardennes offensive articles had appeared in the British Press criticizing Eisenhower's handling of the campaign and suggesting that its operational command should revert to Montgomery. This had produced an outburst in the American Press, whose writers—doubly sensitive at their troops having been caught off their guard—retaliated by attacking Montgomery, whom they accused of intriguing for the Command. The American Chiefs of Staff had been equally irritated, and, on the day before the end of the year, Marshall had sent a telegram to Eisenhower telling him that it would be quite unacceptable to give a British general command of any substantial American forces and that, in his handling of the campaign, he had the fullest confidence of the President, himself and the whole of America.

On receipt of this telegram Eisenhower did as Brooke had predicted. He wrote to Montgomery on December 31st to tell him that he could not agree to one Army Group Commander giving orders to another Army Group Commander. He enclosed an outline plan which provided for a crossing of the Rhine as soon as the enemy forces to the west of it had been destroyed, the main preliminary effort to be in the North, as Montgomery had recommended, with the latter commanding and with the American Ninth Army still under his orders, while Bradley's 12 Army Group—to which Hodges's First Army was to return as soon as the Ardennes salient had been eliminated—was to drive north-eastwards towards the Rhine. He proposed, too, to build up a strategic reserve to reinforce success and to give Montgomery the power of emergency decision in any question affecting co-ordination along the boundaries of the two attacking Army Groups. Further than this, he wrote, he could not go, and, in view of Marshall's telegram and the fury of his principal American subordinates against the British

[1] Montgomery *Memoirs*, 317-19.

Commander-in-Chief,[1] it was further than might have been expected.

" You know," Eisenhower ended his letter,

" how greatly I've appreciated and depended upon your frank and friendly counsel, but in your latest letter you disturb me by predictions of ' failure ' unless your exact opinions in the matter of giving you command over Bradley are met in detail. . . . I know your loyalty as a soldier and your readiness to devote yourself to assigned tasks. For my part I would deplore the development of such an unbridge-able group of convictions between us that we would have to present our differences to the Combined Chiefs of Staff. The confusion and debate that would follow would certainly damage the good will and devotion to a common cause that have made this Allied Force unique in history.

As ever, your friend,

Ike."[2]

Montgomery, whose outspokenness was equalled by his loyalty, made no further attempt to alter the Supreme Commander's decision. He had been privately informed by his Chief of Staff of Marshall's telegram and, before receiving Eisenhower's letter, had on the evening of the 31st sent the latter a telegram saying that he understood his difficulties and would support him in whatever he decided. At the same time he reported what had happened to the C.I.G.S. " I am now going to withdraw from the contest," he told him. " It is clear to me that we have got all we can and that we shall get no more. I have told Ike that I have given him my views and he has given his decision and that I will now weigh in one hundred per cent to make his plan work. He is delighted and has sent me a very nice telegram in which he thanks me for my under-standing attitude. So everything is friendly."[3]

[1] According to his own account, Bradley informed Eisenhower that, sooner than serve under Montgomery, he would resign, and Patton promised to resign with him. *Bradley*, 487-8.

[2] Montgomery, *Memoirs* 320-1.

[3] Montgomery to C.I.G.S., 1st Jan., 1945, Lord Alanbrooke, *Personal Files.*

Such was the position when Brooke returned from leave and resumed his diary on January 1st.

" A new year started and let us hope the last one of the war with Germany! I have now done three years of this job and am very, very weary. I left home early this morning and, after a dark, cold and slippery drive through fog, landed at the War Office at 9.25 a.m. Not much trouble in getting into my stride as I had had brown bags sent down daily with all current news."

" P.M. has sent in a regular flow of Minutes throughout the afternoon. . . ."

' This,' Brooke added after the war, ' may have been the afternoon when I received fifteen such Minutes! ' At this time the Prime Minister was particularly active, even for him. On Christmas Eve, as a result of civil war in the Greek capital and a deadlock between the British Government's representatives and the King of Greece, he had suddenly decided to fly to Athens. This he had done on Christmas Day, disregarding his seventy years and E.L.A.S. bullets. " Winston," the C.I.G.S. wrote in his diary,

" has done a spectacular rush to Greece to try and disentangle the mess. The rest of the 46th Division is now off to Greece; this completes the 80,000 men I had originally predicted. And what are we to get out of it all? We shall eventually have to withdraw out of Greece and she will then become as Communist as her close neighbours consider desirable. Meanwhile the campaign in Italy stagnates."

' I was quite wrong,' Brooke admitted afterwards,

' Greece was saved from Communism. I do not think that I realized sufficiently the vital importance of preventing Greece from giving Communism a door into the Mediterranean.'

" Ike's . . . plan does all we want except in the realm of command. The weight is in North, and 9 U.S. Army is put into 21 Army Group. 12 Army Group with First and Third Armies is to drive north-east on general axis Prüm-Bonn."

The diary for 1945 continued:

" *January 2nd.* . . . Started Chiefs of Staff meeting at 10.30 with a meeting of Joint Intelligence Committee. This lasted till 12.15 p.m., when we adjourned to meet the P.M. in his Map Room. The first point was to discuss Alex's visit to Moscow. Winston had himself expressed the wish that Alex was to run the battle in Italy and I asked him how he expected him to do so if he was to go to Athens twice, to Moscow once, then Belgrade, followed probably by going to the Crimea to attend our Combined meeting there? This defeated Winston temporarily."

" He then propounded strategies based on ensuring that British troops were retained in the limelight, if necessary, at the expense of the Americans. We only escaped at 1.45 p.m. Finally a Cabinet which lasted from 5.30 p.m. to 8.30 p.m. and might easily have been finished in one hour."

" Little news from France to-day, but heard that Bertie Ramsay had been killed in a plane crash in Paris. His is a desperate loss."

' The news of Bertie Ramsay's death was a very sad blow. After working closely with him for one and a half years at the Imperial Defence College I had formed a deep affection for him and unbounded admiration for his ability. I attached the highest importance to his opinion on most matters and repeatedly benefited by his advice during the War. It was the saddest of tragedies that he should be killed just now, when his advice at Ike's H.Q. could be of such assistance. In his death the country lost one of its ablest admirals.'

" *January 3rd. Versailles.* Left Northolt by plane at 12.30 p.m. with the P.M. for Paris. Bumpy passage and dirty weather; took us an hour and three-quarters for the trip. Eisenhower met us on the aerodrome and drove us to his new house in Versailles. He has left Rundstedt's old house in St. Germain and is now in the President's house just on the approach to the Trianon."

" We found a very worried Ike, as de Gaulle had taken exception to his proposed dispositions in Alsace-Lorraine to withdraw front to the Vosges and leave only an outpost line. De Gaulle stated that such an abandonment of Strasbourg and of the Alsatians and Lorrainians would lead to an outcry throughout France, which could bring his Government crashing to the ground."

" It had been arranged for de Gaulle to come to Versailles to see Ike this afternoon. So after lunch we went round to Ike's office and held a memorable conference consisting of P.M., de Gaulle, Ike, Juin, Bedell Smith, an interpreter and myself. De Gaulle painted a gloomy picture of the massacres that would ensue if the Germans returned to portions of Alsace-Lorraine. However, Ike had already decided to alter his dispositions so as to leave the divisions practically where they were and not to withdraw the two divisions that were to have been moved up into Patton's reserve."

" The P.M. then withdrew for a political talk with de Gaulle, and I remained for a discussion with Eisenhower about his front. He seemed worried about the turn of affairs, but I avoided returning to any questions of command-organization or of strategy, as it is quite useless."

" To dinner Morgan, Whiteley, Eaker, Curtis, Strong and Gale. Long night, P.M. only being moved off after 1.30 a.m. He then dragged me into his bedroom for a further talk. He said that he was beginning to see that any operation from Italy towards Vienna had little prospects. This is the result of many patient hours' work swinging him away from this venture. He agreed that any divisions rendered spare by a withdrawal of Kesselring to the Adige could better be employed on the main Western Front. This is most satisfactory. He then went on about Alex, saying that he could not leave him in Italy once this front had become a subsidiary one with only small forces there. He suggested that, as Tedder was wanted back by the Air Ministry, we might replace him by Alex. This also seems a sound move and one which might assist in keeping Ike on the rails in future. He asked me to sound Ike about this suggestion and find out what his reactions would be."

' As we arrived at the aerodrome that day, we found the most depressed looking Ike. It was only on the previous day that Bertie Ramsay, one of his best friends, had been killed on this very aerodrome. Then he had the background of the serious reverse he had just suffered and which he did not even then seem quite to understand. And now on top of it all, de Gaulle was turning sour. He seemed genuinely pleased to see Winston and to feel that he would have his support in his interview with de Gaulle. And yet when pressure was put on him he very soon altered his dispositions again.'

" *January 4th. In Ike's train on way to Monty's H.Q.* Woke up to find it snowing hard. Impossible to fly up to Monty; shall have to go by train instead. After breakfast went with Ike to his H.Q. when we went through the situation with Whiteley, Strong and Robb.[1] On the whole the counter-attacks appear to be making some progress towards narrowing down the corridor at Bastogne; unfortunately the Air unable to function owing to this foul weather."

" *Later.* Duff Cooper turned up for lunch, and at 4.30 p.m. we left for Versailles station to get on board Ike's train which is to take us up to Monty's H.Q. through the night. After lunch Winston put the move of Alex to replace Tedder forward to Ike, who said he would welcome him."

" We had a very comfortable dinner on the train and a comfortable night, travelling up through Amiens, Arras, Lille, Brussels to Hasselt."

" *January 5th.* We arrived about 7.30 a.m. Monty turned up at 9 a.m., and I had about three-quarters of an hour's

[1] Air Chief Marshal Sir James Robb.

talk with him before the P.M. He seemed quite pleased with his attack which had started yesterday on Hodges's Army front and which was making good progress. I gathered from him that a large number of American divisions on his front were badly under strength and had lost their offensive value temporarily. He seemed fairly confident that between him and Bradley they could deal with the western end of the German salient but said that the base of the salient would present a more difficult problem. I told him about the possibilities of obtaining, later on, reinforcements from Italy and of the possible scheme of Alex replacing Tedder. He said that he was all for such a plan which might go some way towards putting matters straight."

" By 11.15 a.m. we left by car for Brussels aerodrome. We passed through Louvain, which woke many memories of 1939 and of my discussions with Monty about the defence of Louvain. How little did I expect that last day when I drove back from Monty's H.Q. along that road that over five years later I should be driving down that same road with Winston as Prime Minister! "

" About 12.30 p.m. we arrived at the aerodrome east of Brussels which the Boche used to bomb so heavily. We lunched on the plane and in an hour and three-quarters were at Northolt. Went straight to the War Office, where I had meetings with Secretary of State, Adjutant-General, Quartermaster-General, Vice-C.I.G.S., Director of Military Operations and Director of Intelligence."

" *January 8th.* Monty's offensive seems to be progressing very favourably, but I am not at all so certain that matters are all right in Alsace-Lorraine. Alexander is also worrying me by committing more and more troops in Greece without much hope of getting them out."

" *Later.* Had to go round to P.M. at 10.30 p.m. He wanted, first of all, to gloat over the reply from Stalin, promising an offensive in middle of January, which he had received in answer to the wire he had sent asking for information and promising he would only divulge reply to Eisenhower and to myself."[1]

" He was already in bed when I arrived, sipping coffee, drinking brandy and smoking a cigar. We discussed all the evils of Monty's Press Interview, which resulted in a call to Eisenhower and the sending for Brendan Bracken. Shortly afterwards Andrew Cunningham turned up, followed by ' Pug ' Ismay. Then a typist was sent for and a wire was dictated to Roosevelt. Then the red stylo-pen was lost and Sawyers was sent for, new pen was brought, followed by old one being found inside the bed! etc., etc. Finally at 1.30 a.m. we all withdrew."

' Eisenhower, when talking to P.M. on telephone, had mentioned that Bradley was very seriously upset by what Monty had said in his interview with the Press. I think that Ike had said that, in view of the excellent work he had done in meeting Rundstedt's thrust, Ike would present Bradley with some decoration. The Prime Minister said, Excellent, he would call him up next morning to congratulate him and that would all assist to calm him down. Next morning before going to Chiefs of Staff meeting I was called up by Winston to ask me whether I had noticed the American Press reaction to Monty's Interview. I said I had and that I had been surprised what a good Press it had received. Winston replied: " So was I. I do not think it is now necessary for me to call up Bradley.". . .'

Whatever the repercussions in America of this Press Conference of Montgomery's, its effect on the American generals was anything but happy. On January 6th, after assuring the War Office that his relations with Eisenhower were now

[1] In view of the German concentration in the West Eisenhower had sent his Deputy, Tedder, to Moscow to find out if and when the Russians intended to attack. On learning of this, Churchill had volunteered to write to Stalin and had done so on the 6th, with the welcome and unexpected result that Stalin had replied next day, promising an offensive not later than the middle of January. *Churchill* V, 243.

" extremely friendly ",[1] the Field-Marshal had sent a private telegram to the Prime Minister telling him that he was proposing next day to explain to British and American correspondents how, during the Battle of the Ardennes, the whole Allied team, throwing national considerations overboard, had rallied to the call and how Allied solidarity had saved the situation. " I shall stress," he wrote, " the great friendship between myself and Ike and tell them that I myself have an American identity card and am identified in the Army of the United States, my finger-prints being registered in the War Department at Washington." To which, with characteristic enthusiasm, Churchill replied that he thought that what the Field-Marshal proposed would be invaluable.

Yet when next day Montgomery, in his usual categorical manner, did as he proposed, the impression his words made on the by now hyper-sensitive American commanders was that he had single-handed rescued a shattered American Army from the consequences of their inexperience and folly.[2] His account —followed though it was by praise of the Supreme Commander and the American fighting man—of how he had tidied up the battlefield in " one of the most interesting and tricky " operations he had ever handled, infuriated Bradley and Eisenhower's staff. As Montgomery himself admitted afterwards, it was probably a mistake " to have held the Conference at all ".[3]

All this involved further troubles for the C.I.G.S. For Eisenhower's new plan had not solved the problem inherent in the U.S. top commanders' inexperience of handling large masses in battle. The American corps and divisional commanders—men like Collins and Ridgway—had proved themselves as good in action as, if not better than, the best British generals of equal rank. But their superiors had never had the

---

[1] As an illustration of it he mentioned that Eisenhower had offered to replace his private Dakota which had just been destroyed in an accident. " This offer," the Director of Military Operations reported to the C.I.G.S., " seems to have gone right to F. M. Montgomery's heart."

[2] *Bradley*, 484-5.

[3] Montgomery, *Memoirs* 314-15. " What I did *not* say was that in the Battle of the Ardennes the Allies had got a real ' bloody nose,' the Americans had nearly 80,000 casualties, and that it would never have happened if we had fought the campaign properly after the great victory of Normandy."

essential experience of field command. Before being appointed to command the American ground forces Bradley's only active service had been a few weeks as a corps commander in Tunisia and Sicily. Eisenhower himself had not even had that. In spite of the more realist proposals which the Supreme Commander had now put forward, Brooke doubted whether, in the absence of a more effective overall control of the ground forces, the offensive in the North would receive either the concentration or the sense of urgency needed for its success. He feared that, as before, pressure by individual American Army Commanders would deflect forces from the main into subsidiary efforts and that time would be lost in clearing up unimportant pockets of resistance in the south and centre before striking at Germany's heart in the Ruhr and Hanover plains, where the Allies' immense superiority in armour and in the air could be adequately used.

Because of these doubts and because Montgomery had been forced to accept a continued Command set-up which left the control of the campaign in Eisenhower's hands, Brooke now pinned his hopes on being able to persuade the American Chiefs of Staff to see the necessity for some reorganization of the higher direction at S.H.A.E.F. He was not sanguine. The growing preponderance of American forces in France, the sensitivity of injured American feelings and the distrust of Montgomery at Washington and Versailles, all militated against it.[1] But he hoped to some extent to be able to offset the first, as soon as Britain's military commitments to Greece could be reduced, by

[1] " The British Chiefs of Staff are proposing to the Combined Chiefs that General Ike be called upon for a Report as to his plan of campaign following the elimination of the Bulge. Representatives of the British Chiefs have discussed with General Marshall the advisability of a single commander for ground operations and the opinion has been expressed that General Ike has too many other pressing duties of supply, of political complexity, etc., and, that, therefore, more concentrated direction of ground operation is required. . . . The British Chiefs desire a Directive to be issued by the Combined Chiefs which would point out to General Ike that the best results would be achieved if one man were given operational control and co-ordination of all ground forces for the main thrust. General Marshall asked for the Supreme Commander's views and added his own opinion that the British proposal stems from the Prime Minister's recent visit to France and Field-Marshal Montgomery's evident pressure to get a larger Command." *Butcher*, 626-7. (9 Jan. 45.)

transferring to France British divisions from the Mediterranean and Italy, where the campaign to contain the German reserves had by now served its purpose. And owing to the prospect of an early meeting between the Heads of the three Allied Governments, there was now a chance, for the first time since the campaign went awry in the autumn, of discussing matters round a table with the American Chiefs of Staff. Ever since the failure of the Allies' hopes in November Churchill had been urging on Roosevelt the need for another Conference, and, though Stalin had refused to consider one anywhere except in Russia, the President had agreed to leave America immediately after the Inauguration ceremonies of his Fourth Term on January 20th to attend a Conference at Yalta in the Crimea. It was, therefore, proposed that the Western leaders' military advisers should meet on the way, at Malta, at the end of the month.[1]

Brooke refers to these anxieties and hopes in his diary.

" *January 9th.* C.O.S. meeting at which I pointed out the necessity to draft a new Directive to Alex telling him to finish off Greek enterprise at earliest possible moment, rest troops in Italy, prepare offensive, drive Kesselring back to Adige and provide troops for France."

" *January 11th.* C.O.S. trying to disentangle the plans for our next Combined meeting in the Crimea with a preliminary meeting in Malta. The latter is too small to accommodate everybody, and the former very uncertain as to what accommodation exists."

" We then discussed with the Planners the next Directive for Alexander based on early evacuation of Greece and transfer of forces from Italy to France. . . ."

" Bitterly cold day with periodic snow."

" *January 12th.* A very nice quiet day for a change,

[1] " Would it not be possible for you to spend two or three nights at Malta and let the Staffs have a talk together unostentatiously? " Prime Minister to President, 5 Jan., 1945. *Churchill* VI, 296. " I am still thinking it of high importance," Churchill telegraphed on the 8th, " that our military men should get together for a few days before we arrive at Yalta." *Idem*, 298. The President finally yielded to his importunity on the 10th.

which gave me an opportunity to write a long letter to Alexander. . . ."

"*January 15th*. Usual early start back for the War Office. Plans for our journey to Malta and the Crimea are gradually taking shape."

"*January 16th*. Good news coming in from Russia; it looks as if they had started their winter offensive in earnest. I hope so, as it should make all the difference towards speeding up the end of the war."

The Russians had proved as good as their word. On January 12th, without waiting longer for the weather, they had struck on the frozen plains of Southern Poland. Hitler's attempt to snatch victory in the West by concentrating almost his entire available armour against Eisenhower played into their hands. A few days earlier his new Chief of Staff, Guderian, had pleaded with him to reinforce the Eastern front, where seventy-five weak divisions[1]—starved of petrol and supplies—were holding six hundred miles from the Baltic to the Carpathians against Russian forces nearly three times as great. Striking with massive concentration, first at one point and then at another, the Red Army broke through the thin enemy defences and poured westwards towards the Silesian and Prussian frontiers. The flood that at the end of the summer seemed about to submerge the Reich from the West now burst on her from the East.

That week brought good news, too, from Burma. Here, after the abandonment in the autumn of Mountbatten's plans for an amphibious expedition across the Bay of Bengal, Slim's Fourteenth Army, heartened by its victory at Imphal, had struck through the hills and jungles on the Assam frontier and, advancing two hundred miles in six weeks, had reached the Irrawaddy, which it had begun to cross, fifty miles north of Mandalay, on January 14th. Contrary to all expectation, there now seemed a chance of liberating Burma from the north before the monsoon with the forces already in the theatre, and on the

[1] As compared with 110 now in the West, Italy and Yugoslavia and another 17 contained by British sea-power in Scandinavia. *Wilmot*, 621.

17th General Browning—Mountbatten's new Chief of Staff—arrived from Ceylon to ask for an airlift to make it possible.

"*January 17th.* A specially long C.O.S. meeting as we had 'Boy' Browning back from Kandy, having been sent by Dickie to plead his case for more transport aircraft for Burma operations. There is no doubt that the operations there have taken quite a different turn, and there is now just a possibility of actually taking Rangoon from the north. This is due to the Japanese forces beginning to crumple up."

"One of our difficulties arises from the fact that the transport aircraft belong to the Americans and that the reconquest of Lower Burma does not interest them at all.[1] All they want is North Burma and the air-route and pipeline and Ledo road into China. They have now practically got all these, and the rest of Burma is of small interest to them. . . ."

"*January 18th.* A long meeting with C.O.S. preparing our Directive for Alex in the Mediterranean and trying to damp down his ardour in Greece. How difficult war is to run owing to the personalities one has to handle and how terribly dull it would be if they were all soulless cog-wheels without any personal idiosyncrasies! But to handle them you must be young and full of vigour and enthusiasm. Whereas every day I feel older, more tired and less inclined to face difficulties."

"*January 19th.* The Canadian Mission attended our C.O.S. meeting and I had to give them a short review of the situation on all fronts. In the afternoon 'Boy' Browning came to say goodbye before returning to Ceylon. Tedder on his way back from Moscow to give results of his meeting with Stalin. He had not much to say

[1] General Slim in his war memoirs describes how on December 10th, 1944, he had been awakened by the sound of seventy-five American Dakotas, on which he was relying for his Army's maintenance, taking off for China where they had suddenly been ordered by the American High Command to counter a new Japanese advance. "It meant that the second foundation . . . on which all our plans had been based was swept away. The loss threatened to bring operations to a standstill." *Defeat into Victory,* 395-6.

beyond what had been developing in the wonderful Russian advance, which looks like speeding up the end of the war."

" As I returned home to flat I found a call from P.M. wanting to see me. So off I started again. I found it was in connection with Greece and the fears he had that we should ' frame up ' with the American Chiefs of Staff against him in an endeavour to extricate forces out of Greece prematurely.[1] I assured him that, although strongly opposed to our original venture in Greece, now that we were committed I fully realised the difficulty and impossibility of extracting forces out of Greece until such time as Greek forces had been organized and trained to take on the job. It was a commitment which we had incurred against my military advice, no doubt based on excellent political reasons. But now that we were committed, I fully realised all implications."

" *January 20th*. We had a fairly full Chiefs of Staff meeting which completed our record week for the maximum number of items handled in one week since the war started. It is a strange thing what a vast part the C.O.S. Committee takes in the running of the war and how little it is known or its functions appreciated. The average man in the street has never heard of it."

* * * * * * * *

On January 16th, exactly a month after the Ardennes breakthrough, Montgomery's and Bradley's forces, battling their way from north and south against stubborn German resistance, met at Houffalize and sealed off the breach in the Allied lines. Two days later Hodges's First Army reverted to Bradley's Army Group, leaving only the American Ninth Army under Montgomery's command. Meanwhile, so the latter felt though perhaps unjustly, under pressure from his American lieutenants —almost as eager now to beat the British Commander-in-Chief

---

[1] A truce had been signed on January 11th for an armistice, which came into effect on the 15th, under which the E.L.A.S. or Communist forces withdrew from Athens and Attica.

to the post as to avenge themselves on the Germans—Eisenhower had again begun to wobble.

Three days before the junction of his own and Bradley's Army Groups, Montgomery had sent Brooke the details of the plan for the forthcoming offensive in the north—Operation *Veritable*—which he had agreed, or thought he had agreed, with Eisenhower. As it was essential to wrest the initiative from the enemy as soon as possible, and as, after their heavy losses of the past month, the American First and Third Armies did not seem strong enough to break through the Siegfried Line, everything was now to be put into Montgomery's attempt, first to close on, and then to cross, the Rhine north of the Ruhr. With this object the American Ninth Army under his command was to be made up to four corps with thirteen divisions, while another U.S. corps of three divisions was to be transferred to the British Second Army, thus giving 21 Army Group control of sixteen American divisions. Eisenhower, Montgomery assured the C.I.G.S., was delighted with the plan and liked it very much; " the one snag " was " the old one of whether the main effort which contains a good many American divisions can be solely in the hands of a British commander."

To this and the detailed dispositions which the British Commander-in-Chief sent him, Brooke replied on the 15th in a letter written at his instructions by the Director of Military Operations. " C.I.G.S. agrees," the latter wrote,

" that the first essential is to get the firm base necessary for an offensive, and then to put in the greatest possible concentration of force at the point at which it is decided to make the vital thrust. Everyone is agreed, too, that this thrust must be made in the North. . . . Your proposed plan, if adopted, will ensure that the necessary concentration of force is made at the right point.

" C.I.G.S. feels that there may well be difficulties in deciding what forces are necessary to secure the long defensive portion of the front south . . . of the southern boundary of your offensive operations. . . . As you probably

well realise, General Eisenhower cannot help but be sensitive
—sometimes for political and sometimes for military reasons
—to enemy threats to certain portions of the southern parts
of his front. It is just possible that the proposed SHAEF
reserve at Namur may not remain inviolate as regards both
quantity and quality in the face of such threats. C.I.G.S.
thinks this point will have to be watched very carefully.

" C.I.G.S. does not think that Rundstedt is capable of
mounting another counter-offensive on the scale of his
December thrust. The chances of anything really worrying
even on a smaller scale have grown much less as the result
of the start of the Russian winter offensive. Once *Veritable*
starts, of course, these chances become much smaller still,
as the initiative which you will then have regained will
go a very long way to giving you the security you need.

" C.I.G.S. says that . . . he could not help feeling you
were being somewhat pessimistic over the future, especially
as it now does not seem in Rundstedt's power to stage any
substantial counter-offensive. On the other hand, when he
received your two telegrams of yesterday, he wondered
whether you were not being a little over-optimistic as regards
the U.S. forces which could be allotted under your command
for the thrust towards Düsseldorf. We have not sufficient
information here at present to know whether the required
number of divisions of good quality can, in fact, be available.
If they can, and Rundstedt decides, as seems likely, to fight
a decisive battle west of Düsseldorf, you then ought to have
just the opportunity you want.

" What C.I.G.S. is not quite clear about is how you view
the next phase. The successful completion of your plan
would put you on the west bank of the Rhine from Düsseldorf
to Arnhem. He wonders whether this will be a long enough
stretch to enable you to achieve the necessary tactical surprise
for the movement across the river to the north of the Ruhr.
He thought it would probably be desirable first to clear up a
further stretch of the west bank of the Rhine, say down to
Bonn, if the necessary forces can be made available.

" General Eisenhower has been asked to submit his plan to the Combined Chiefs of Staff by the end of this month. This will of course be in the form of a full Appreciation and plan for the whole operation for the final defeat of Germany in the West, and will, therefore, be much wider and go further than your plan. C.I.G.S. asked me to tell you that, if adequate U.S. forces can be made available for your plan and it is accepted by General Eisenhower, it will, as far as it goes, fit well, he thinks, into the bigger concept."[1]

Next day, January 16th, the plan Montgomery had so confidently outlined was discussed at S.H.A.E.F. Headquarters: a wholly American meeting, he reported, except for the presence of Major-General Whiteley. To meet national susceptibilities it was proposed that the American divisions under Montgomery's command should be cut from sixteen to twelve and that the deficiency should be met by Bradley's and Hodges's First Army taking over part of 21 Army Group's line and so having a small share in the operation. With these modifications, to which the British Commander-in-Chief agreed, Whiteley assured him there would be no further trouble about the Command and that the American Ninth Army and the whole conduct of operations would be entrusted to him. " I have told SHAEF," Montgomery informed the C.I.G.S., " that if plan is agreed and I can be given six American divisions by 1st Feb., it will be possible to launch operation *Veritable* by about Feb. 10th. Operations *Veritable* and *Grenade* "—a subsidiary drive by the Ninth Army towards Düsseldorf—" will altogether be a terrific party and there will be little rest for most of us once we begin."[2]

Yet though the plan, as modified, was approved by S.H.A.E.F., and the British Commander-in-Chief on January 18th had what he described as " a fine conference with Bradley " in which agreement was reached on all points, by the 20th all was in the melting-pot again. On that day an alarmed Montgomery reported to the C.I.G.S. that he had received a

[1] 15 Jan., 1945, Lord Alanbrooke, *Personal Files.*
[2] Montgomery to C.I.G.S., 16 Jan., 1945. Lord Alanbrooke, *Personal Files.*

Directive, dated the 18th, which, far from being in accordance with what he supposed had been agreed, showed that Bradley was once more " going off on his own line " and that, " instead of one firm, clear and decisive plan, there was great indecision and patchwork ". Instead of closing down the Ardennes counter-offensive so that his forces could be re-grouped in order to launch *Veritable* on February 10th, the Supreme Commander was now proposing to continue the Ardennes battle till the first week in February and to do " a great many other things ", which in Montgomery's view would result, as before, in his not being strong enough at the place that really mattered. " Both Ike and Bradley are emphatic that we should not—not—cross the Rhine in strength anywhere until we are lined up along its entire length from Nijmegen to Switzerland. If we work on this plan we shall take a long time to get anywhere."

This was precisely what Brooke had feared. And during the week-end worse followed. " Not only was the Ardennes battle," as Montgomery put it, " being continued for the sole reason of keeping Bradley employed offensively ", but new demands in the South and Centre threatened to draw away the divisions which were to have been allocated to Montgomery's offensive and to the general reserve at Namur. " My latest information," Montgomery wired the C.I.G.S. on the 22nd,

" is that SHAEF are very worried about situation in South about Colmar and Strasbourg. . . . Whiteley tells me that they may have to send considerable strength down there to get that area well in hand. If this is done it will mean that *Grenade* will be put right back indefinitely. That would put *Veritable* back, as the two operations are inter-dependent. The prospect of getting by degrees sufficient numbers of really good fresh divisions for *Grenade* is fading away. . . ."

" I fear," Montgomery ended, " that the old snags of indecision and vacillation and refusal to consider the military problem fairly and squarely are coming to the front again. . . . The real trouble is that there is no control and the three Army Groups are each intent on their own affairs. Patton to-day issued a stirring order to Third Army, saying the next step would be Cologne. . . . One has to preserve a sense of humour these days, otherwise one would go mad."[1]

On the same day, Monday January 22nd—a week before the proposed meeting of the Combined Chiefs of Staff at Malta—the C.I.G.S. received Eisenhower's Appreciation of his future plans.

> "*January 22nd.* Eisenhower's Appreciation was in. It leaves us again with a most confused picture; still hankering after the Frankfurt line of advance and in the end backing both and being insufficiently strong for either. . . ."

Nor was it only with Eisenhower and the American Chiefs of Staff that Brooke had to contend if German resistance in the West was to be broken by the summer. Before the meetings at Malta and Yalta he had also to obtain from the Prime Minister a firm decision as to the line to be pursued by the British with their allies. Having agreed to a transfer of divisions from the Italian to the Western front to strengthen Montgomery's hand, Churchill had now suddenly reverted to his old idea of an advance on Vienna. By doing so he reduced the C.I.G.S. almost to despair.

> "*January 23rd.* We met Winston this morning to try and get from him some decisions prior to our meeting the American Chiefs of Staff. We wanted to get approval for our proposed Directive to the Supreme Commanders. The first was one to Alexander, laying down that forces should be withdrawn from Greece as soon as political situation admitted and that some six divisions should be transferred from Italy to France. I had obtained full agreement from him before to these moves; now he began to haver and say we were crippling the Italian front, yet he agreed that there was nothing now to be done in Italy or in Yugoslavia. He did not know what he wanted, but would not agree to anything."
>
> "Then Eisenhower's Directive, urging that only one

[1] Montgomery to C.I.G.S., 22 Jan., 1945. Lord Alanbrooke, *Personal Files.*

388

offensive should be carried out and that in the North, a much more debatable point[1]. It was the only point he expressed any sort of agreement with. Next, probable date of end of war, sufficiently vague to require little decision, and yet he refused to approve circulation of the paper to the Cabinet; Chiefs of Staff to make a statement instead."

" Next, American suggestion of worn-out bombers being flown empty in to Germany. Again no definite decision although he had ridiculed the proposition in the Cabinet the previous day.[2] Finally the conversion of Long Range Penetration Groups to an Airborne division for operations in Burma; a flat refusal to give a decision after the whole case had been put before him and a statement that he would send a decision in writing! A matter of complete detail which he ought to have nothing to do with at all. . . ."

" *January 24th.* This afternoon Anders, back from Italy, came to see me about the future of the Polish Forces. Apparently they are anxious to start planning for the eventual assembly of Polish Forces in France and to form them into an Army with Anders at its head. They do not want to return from Italy to Poland via Vienna, as they consider this likely to lead to a clash with the Russians! They would sooner join up in France and swell their numbers with Poles from Germany, gradually returning through Germany and, if necessary, carrying out a period of occupation of Germany. I foresee that this may well lead to many complications politically and must discuss this matter with Anthony Eden."

" *January 25th.* A long meeting with the Planners to fix up final points for our meeting with the American

---

[1] " Before the Conference began the British Chiefs of Staff had prepared draft Directives . . . for submission to the Combined Chiefs of Staff." *Ehrman* VI, 87.

[2] This project—launching pilotless bombers laden with explosives against industrial targets in Germany—is referred to in President Truman's *Years of Decision*, 32-3. It was opposed by Churchill and the British Chiefs of Staff on the ground that the already massive bombing of Germany by the R.A.F. and American Air Force made it unnecessary and that its only consequence would be retaliation against London.

Chiefs of Staff. Most points are now squared up, except that we have been unable to get agreement with P.M. over moves of divisions from Italy to France. He is basing his objections on the delays of the move. As we have cut down the times required for the move to one-and-a-half instead of two-and-a-half months, he should not now object any more. Unfortunately the whole matter is mixed up with the reduction of Alexander's Command and the difficulty of finding another appointment for Alex. He has no alternative strategy for Italy and agrees that it must now become a secondary front."

" Monty was to fly over and come to lunch with me, as he is again very depressed with the American strategy and Eisenhower's inability to retain a definite policy. However, flying weather was too bad, and he is to come to-morrow instead."

" *January 26th.* . . . Monty came to lunch and I had a good talk with him. The old trouble keeps turning round and round in his head. Lack of organization of Command on the part of the Americans and their failure to concentrate their effort on the vital point."

" At 3 p.m. back to a Cabinet meeting to discuss the present overall shortage of shipping and to have approved the line of action to take with the Americans at the coming Conference. . . ."

" *January 27th and 28th.* Quiet Saturday at home and a call in the evening, stating that owing to bad weather departure had been put off. Sunday, motored up after dinner to complete final arrangements in anticipation of early departure to-morrow morning."

. . . .

" *January 29th. Malta.* We left Northolt at 9 a.m. A poisonously cold morning, driving through a snow-covered Hyde Park in half darkness. I loathed this idea of launching myself into cold space and longed to be able to remain at home! However, we had a wonderful trip mostly at

12,000 ft. over the clouds and in brilliant sunshine. The little bits of France that we saw were covered with snow till we got close to Toulouse when the snow disappeared. We passed over Le Mans, Tours, Narbonne, then over Sardinia, after which we descended into more bumpy going and by 2.45 p.m., after $5\frac{3}{4}$ hours, were over Malta. By 3 p.m. we had landed."

" Schreiber[1] met us at the plane and took me off to the Palace. There ' Jumbo ' Wilson and Bedell Smith are stopping. The rest are scattered throughout the island. All the American Chiefs of Staff are in the Artillery Mess, Andrew Cunningham with C.-in-C. Mediterranean, Portal with A.O.C.-in-C. There are rumours that P.M. is arriving to-night, but nothing certain about it."

" *January 30th.* C.O.S. meeting at 10 a.m. to decide on our line of action. At 12 noon we met the Americans to decide on the times of our meetings and the programme. I then lunched with ' Jumbo ' down at the Club, after which we again met the Americans at 2.30 p.m. We discussed the Western Front and Ike's Appreciation. Started with Bedell Smith and Bull[2] giving a description of Ike's plan. This description was very much in line with what we have always asked for, but not in line with what Ike had put down in his plan. This resulted in considerable discussion; Bedell Smith had to agree that Ike's paper did not entirely agree with what he (Bedell) had been propounding."

" As a result, I said that we would probably be prepared to approve Bedell's statement and take down in the Minutes of the meeting that we could not approve the Appreciation by Eisenhower. I do not know how this will be received."

" The P.M. arrived last night at 4 a.m. and at once developed a temperature. However, it dropped again later on and he moved out to his cruiser where he is now. I had

[1] Lt.-Gen. Sir Edmond Schreiber, Governor of Malta.
[2] Brig.-Gen. H. R. Bull, Eisenhower's Assistant Chief of Staff, Operations.

to go out and see him there at 6.30 p.m. Found Alex just coming away and Anthony Eden waiting to see him. Anthony and I went in and found him in bed. He asked me how we had got on to-day and I told him. I then asked him if he had talked matters over with Alex and whether he, P.M., was now in agreement with us about the withdrawal of divisions from Italy. He said that he was now entirely with us and that I could now go ahead and discuss it with the Americans. This is a godsend, as I was wondering how we should get through to-morrow's meeting with the Americans without this agreement."

" He told me that he had also suggested to Alex that he should replace Tedder as Deputy to Ike and that Alex was pleased with the idea. I shall have to see Alex to-morrow and find out what his real reactions are."

That day's discussions with the Americans had begun with the C.I.G.S., who was in the chair, explaining the British objections to the proposals for two main thrusts as set out in Eisenhower's Appreciation. He and his colleagues feared that, unless the latter was tied down more specifically than he had been by the Combined Chiefs of Staff's last Directive in September, he would again interpret it as he had then done and with the same stultifying results. They profoundly distrusted the phrase in his Report that his operations west of the Rhine should be so designed as to enable him to close the river throughout its length, feeling that this would again be used as an excuse for substituting a general attack all along the line for a concentrated and adequately supported break-through. The new draft Directive to the Supreme Commander which they had prepared for the consideration of their American colleagues, therefore read:

" (*a*) All the resources which can be made available for offensive operations should be concentrated on one main thrust. This thrust should be made in the maximum possible strength with sufficient fresh formations held available to keep up the momentum of advance.

Only such forces as cannot be employed to support this main thrust should be used for subsidiary operations. Only if the main thrust is held and the subsidiary operations prosper, should the latter be exploited.

" (b) If tactical considerations allow, this main thrust should be made in the North, in view of the overriding importance to the enemy of the Ruhr area.

" (c) The best results will be achieved if one Land Force Commander, directly responsible to you, is given power of operational control and co-ordination of all ground forces employed in the main thrust."[1]

To this the American Chiefs of Staff, who were attended by Eisenhower's Chief of Staff, Bedell Smith, replied that, while accepting the British contention that the main thrust should be in the North, they considered that both the Supreme Commander's past operations and his future plan were designed for this end. " The Southern advance," they argued, " was not intended to compete with the Northern advance but must be of sufficient strength to draw off German forces to protect the important Frankfurt area and to provide an alternate line of attack if the main effort failed." As communications limited the force that could be used in the North to thirty-six divisions with ten in reserve, twelve divisions could be safely allocated to the subsidiary advance which it was proposed that Patton should make towards the Middle Rhine. Brooke and his colleagues agreed that this placed quite a different interpretation on Eisenhower's Appreciation. They were also relieved to find that, despite the recent triumphs of their allies in the Pacific and the titanic scale of their offensive there, they still regarded the unconditional surrender of Germany as their first objective and at the earliest possible date. And Eisenhower now accepted the need for urgency and had sent a message to the Combined Chiefs of Staff that, in view of the Russian advance, " the factor of time " had become all-important.

It was, therefore, agreed that the British Chiefs of Staff and

[1] *Ehrman* VI, 87-8.

Bedell Smith should redraft the crucial paragraph in the Supreme Commander's Appreciation to make it conform more closely to the meaning which his Chief of Staff assured them that it had. As amended by them it read:

" My plan is
    (*a*) To carry out immediately a series of operations north of the Moselle with a view to destroying the enemy and closing the Rhine north of Düsseldorf.
    (*b*) To direct our efforts to eliminating other enemy forces west of the Rhine which still constitute an obstacle or potential threat to our subsequent Rhine crossing operations.
    (*c*) To seize bridgeheads over the Rhine in the North and the South.
    (*d*) To deploy east of the Rhine and north of the Ruhr the maximum number of divisions which can be maintained (estimated at some 35 divisions). The initial task of this force will be to deny to the enemy the industries of the Ruhr.
    (*e*) To deploy east of the Rhine, on the axis Frankfurt-Kassel, such forces, if adequate, as may be available after providing 35 divisions for the North and essential security elsewhere. The task of this force will be to draw enemy forces away from the North by capturing Frankfurt and advancing on Kassel."[1]

This revision was telegraphed to Eisenhower, who at once accepted it. In replying to Bedell Smith he wired:

" You may assure the Combined Chiefs of Staff that I will seize the Rhine crossings in the North immediately this is a feasible operation and without waiting to close the Rhine throughout its length."

To this, however, he added the rider:

" I will advance across the Rhine in the North with maximum strength and complete determination as soon as

[1] *Ehrman* VI, 91-2.

the situation in the South allows me to collect the necessary forces and do this without incurring unnecessary risks."

So suspicious had the British become as a result of past disappointments that they feared that even this sentence would be used as an excuse for further procrastination.

This now almost undisguised lack of faith in Eisenhower's judgment was intensely resented by the Americans and particularly by Marshall. According to one account, the latter assured Eisenhower before the Conference, that never, while he remained Chief of Staff, would he allow the British to saddle him with an overall Ground Commander.[1] Indeed, so sensitive were the Americans about this latter suggestion that it was never formally considered at the Conference at all, but only secretly discussed by the Combined Chiefs of Staff in closed session without recorded Minutes or anyone present but themselves.

Brooke's diary continued:

"*January 31st.* We started the day with our C.O.S. meeting when we had some difficult points to consider. There was the question of the Western Front strategy, of Eisenhower's Appreciation which points to no decisive action. Then there was Bedell Smith's interpretation which was very close to our own view and was recorded in the Minutes of the previous day. We decided to adopt Bedell's statement and to ignore Ike's Appreciation."

"However, when we met at 2.30 p.m. the situation was more confused than ever, as Bedell Smith had sent another wire to Ike which was also impossible and Ike had wired back. So we were again stuck! However, we made good progress with the Directive for Alexander withdrawing divisions from Italy for France, and also in getting the South-East Asia Directive approved, contemplating the clearing of Burma and then proceeding with Malaya."

[1] K. Summersby, *Eisenhower was My Boss*, 196. Harry Hopkins, on a visit to Versailles a few days earlier, told Captain Butcher that he thought "Ike had conducted the campaign beautifully and had the complete support of all people at home, official and unofficial." *Butcher*, 636. (27 Jan., 1945.)

" After the meeting I had a long and useful interview with Alex. Discussed the withdrawal of forces from Italy and also the possibility of his move to Deputy to Ike, which he is prepared to do. Finally told him that some of us had doubts as to whether Macmillan or Alexander was Supreme Commander of Mediterranean. This had, I think, the required effect. But, by Heaven, how I loathe being unpleasant in this way."

' I had the highest regard and affection for Alexander, both as soldier and man, but felt that, in his absorption in the Greek episode, he was being too much influenced by his very able political partner, the Resident Minister of State.'

" I then attended a large dinner party with John Cunningham in the house of the C.-in-C. Mediterranean, Nelson's old Headquarters. I felt swept off into the old ages, imagining him here with his romance and his wars."

" Returned here and was just off to bed when Bedell Smith came in and we had at least an hour's talk trying to find some settlement to the difference that lies between us. I think that the talk did both of us good and may help in easing the work to-morrow."

" It has been a long day with much work and I am feeling very tired and old."

' My talk with Bedell Smith,' Brooke recalled after the war, ' had at any rate shown me that he was quite able to appreciate the dangers of Ike's strategy, and I felt satisfied that he would use his influence to guide him.' The C.I.G.S.'s distrust of Eisenhower as a commander sprang from the readiness with which in the past he had been deflected from his objective by the views of others. The very sympathy with which he listened to all-comers—one of the qualities that made him such a unique co-ordinator of Allied differences—left him dangerously open to the latest comer's suggestion. It was the fear that he would again dissipate his resources that made Brooke depart from his normal rule of leaving a commander in the field a free hand.

But if Bedell Smith, a far abler soldier in the C.I.G.S.'s view than Eisenhower, now realised the need for concentration in the North, there was far less danger of Bradley and Patton being allowed to turn the secondary thrust towards Frankfurt into a major operation capable of stifling the main offensive. For, unlike Bradley, Bedell Smith was at Eisenhower's shoulder and was always entrusted by him with the drafting and execution of his plans. And, as the rest of the campaign in the West was to prove, Bedell Smith had learnt his lesson.

" *February 1st. Malta.* . . . Rather a rush with telegrams, etc., before our C.O.S. meeting at 10 a.m. This lasted till 1.15 p.m., and was long and difficult. We discussed shipping shortage, allocating shipping to liberated countries, stocks of oil in England, etc."

" I then rushed off to lunch with Anthony Eden on his cruiser where he had Stettinius, Harry Hopkins and Harriman. I sat next to Stettinius and found him pleasant and easy to talk to. Then rushed back to arrive in time for the Combined Chiefs of Staff meeting at 2.30 p.m. There we had more difficulties about the Western Front. Marshall wished to go into ' closed session '; he was opposed to cramping Eisenhower's style by issuing any Directive to him! He wanted us to approve his quite unacceptable Appreciation and plan. I refused to do this, but said I would be prepared to ' take note ' of it, which we finally settled to do. This allowed Marshall to express his full dislike and antipathy for Monty. Other points we settled were South-East Asia and Mediterranean strategy."

" P.M. sent for me at 6 p.m. on the cruiser *Orion*. I gave him an account of our proceedings."

Though to the C.I.G.S. the meeting with the all-powerful Americans had seemed unsatisfactory, two factors—over and above Bedell Smith's new awareness of the dangers of Eisenhower's strategy of dispersal—had transformed the military situation since the British Chiefs of Staff had drafted their proposed Directive for the Supreme Commander in the days of the Ardennes offensive. One was the sudden brilliant success of the Russians who, by threatening Berlin and overrunning the Silesian coalfields, had already drawn off two of Hitler's Panzer armies from the West and whose advance, coupled with the tremendous Anglo-American air attack on Germany's communications and oil production, made it impossible for the defenders of the Siegfried Line to repeat their former exploitation of American mistakes. ' The other,' Brooke wrote, ' was the condition of the German forces. It was clear that after the failure of Rundstedt's offensive German morale had deteriorated and that from now on we could take greater liberties. Under these new circumstances an advance on a wider front might present advantages. Ike's faulty strategy of dispersal had nearly led to a serious disaster on the occasion of the German thrust in the Ardennes. When this thrust failed, with the last German offensive repulsed, the Germans were as good as defeated. From then on defeat was certain; with the loss of hope the incentive for fighting had also gone. No serious opposition was likely to be encountered, the double attack might soon become a pursuit and as such fully justified.'[1]

For, though Brooke felt that the Americans had dominated the Conference and that he could no longer make his strategic conceptions prevail as in the past, the British had, in fact, achieved their essential aim. After four wasted months the Americans had accepted the need for concentration in the North, and it was no longer necessary to deny a supplementary and now justified offensive to Bradley in order to ensure success for Montgomery. With the edge of the German sword blunted in the Ardennes and the Russians on the Oder, the Western Allies were by now strong enough to undertake both. As Ismay reported to the Prime Minister after the British and American military advisers had agreed on their Directives, " General Eisenhower's intentions are more or less exactly what you and the Chiefs of Staff would have them be."[2]

Over Italy, too, the British had got their way. Not only

[1] *Notes on My Life* XV, 52, 83.
[2] *Ehrman* VI, 93.

had the Americans approved the transfer of five British and Canadian divisions to reinforce Montgomery—three of them immediately and the other two as soon as the political position in Greece admitted—but they had agreed to leave their own troops in Italy. With the forces remaining to him—roughly two-thirds of those with which he had captured Rome—Alexander was now directed, " by means of such limited offensive action as may be possible and by the skilful use of cover and deception plans ", to contain the Germans and take advantage of any weakening or withdrawal of their forces.

Chapter Twelve

YALTA

Of one thing I am certain, Stalin is not an imperialist.
PRESIDENT ROOSEVELT

FEBRUARY 2ND was the last day of the " Argonaut " conference. It began for Brooke with a great personal tragedy.

" *February 2nd—Malta.* This morning when I went to the office Brian Boyle met me with the ghastly news that the plane ' Barney ' was travelling in had crashed last night in the sea near Pantelleria. Of the twenty passengers[1] only seven had been saved. In spite of several telegrams to try and obtain names of the survivors it was not till just on 8 p.m. that I obtained the news that ' Barney ' was amongst the killed. It is a frightful blow as ' Barney ' had grown to be a most intimate companion. I always knew I could discuss anybody or anything with him without any fear of his ever repeating anything. He was always cheerful and in good humour no matter how unpleasant situations were. I shall miss him most awfully and feel so very, very sorry for Diana."

' The loss of ' Barney ' Charlesworth was one of the worst blows I had during the war. He had come to me as A.D.C. in France in 1940, we had been through Dunkirk together and since then had lived in the same flat and during most of my time as C.I.G.S. had had most of our meals, the two of us together. The circumstances of the crash were tragic.

---

[1] Including senior Foreign Office officials on their way to Yalta.

Owing to some fault in the navigation the plane arrived over Pantelleria in the dark thinking they were over Malta. They kept calling up for the aerodrome to be lit up. Finally after flying round for some time they sent a message that they were running out of fuel and would land on the sea. The pilot chose a small bay and, I believe, did an excellent landing. Unfortunately there was a submerged wreck which ripped off the bottom of the plane and killed the occupants. That, at any rate, was the account I was given.'

" The day has been a very busy one and I have found it extremely hard to concentrate my thoughts and not let them wander off to 'Barney'. We started a Chiefs of Staff meeting at 9.30 and had Leathers in for another discussion on shipping. At 12 noon we met the Americans and finished off most of the items we wanted to do before leaving for the Crimea. We also produced an interim report for the President and P.M. on our work up to date. After lunch we had arranged a short tour for the Americans to the Palace, the Library and the Cathedral of the Knights of St. John. This lasted till 4 p.m."

" At 5.30 p.m. we all went to the President's battleship for our interim Plenary meeting. The paper was passed and agreed in its present form."

" After the Plenary meeting Winston asked me to stop on to discuss with him and the President and Marshall the proposal for Alexander to replace Tedder. The President and Marshall considered that politically such a move might have repercussions in America if carried out just now. It might be considered that Alex was being put to support Ike after his Ardennes failure. They were, however, quite prepared to accept this change in about six weeks time after further offensive operations will have been started and the Ardennes operation more forgotten."

" After dinner, just on midnight, I drove to the aerodrome where we took off for the Crimea."

" *February 3rd. Crimea.* We had a good and smooth

journey. Got up about 6 a.m. to have a shave and breakfast. We were then flying over clouds over the Black Sea. At about 7.30 a.m. clouds cleared and we sighted Eupatoria on the west coast of the Crimea. Shortly afterwards we made a safe landing, having taken a little over 7½ hours for the journey. Molotov, Gusev, Vyshinski and many others were on the aerodrome. We were given a cup of tea and then started off by car for Yalta. We drove by Simferopol and Alushta to Yalta and then on to near Alurka. Here we are lodged in one of the large Crimean houses of Tsarist nobility days, built by a Scottish architect in semi-Moorish, semi-Scots style. The mixture is somewhat startling! We have got the P.M., Anthony Eden, three Chiefs of Staff, Clark Kerr, Leathers and a few others."

" The drive took us some four and a half hours over a fairly good road with a certain amount of snow. Here the snow is gone and the temperature much milder than I had expected. We are also much more comfortably established than I had ever hoped for."

" *February 4th. Yalta.* We had a short C.O.S. meeting at 10 a.m. to discuss our line of action. We finished by about 11 a.m. and had nothing to do for the rest of the morning. I only wish we had a real full day to keep my thoughts from wandering off to poor old ' Barney '."

" After lunch Stalin came at 3 p.m. to call on Winston and we all met him in the hall. He then spent an hour with Winston, and Eden told me afterwards that he had raised the suggestion that we should send a force from Italy through northern Yugoslavia to operate on their left flank. This is a bore, as we had been banking on transferring troops from Italy to France and have got all agreed with the Americans."

" At 5 p.m. we met at the American Headquarters. They are living in the old Yalta Tsar's palace. We had a round table conference consisting of Stalin with Maisky interpreting for him (a new departure), Molotov, Antonov, their Admiral and Air Marshal,[1] President, Leahy, Marshall, King, Stettinius, Harriman and Deane, P.M., three Chiefs of Staff, Eden, ' Pug', Alex and Clark Kerr."

" Meeting started with the usual compliments, followed by an opening statement by Stalin calling on Antonov to give an account of the war. He gave an excellent and very clear talk, but not much we did not know. Marshall then described the situation on the Western Front. To-morrow at 12 noon we are to discuss the co-ordination of our military actions and offensives, as Stalin considered the war might well go on till the summer and it was very desirable that our offensive actions should coincide."

" Weather again quite lovely and wonderfully mild."

The Allied leaders and their train of several hundred experts and clerks had arrived at Yalta at a moment when Russian military prestige stood at its highest. Eight months before, when the men of the West stormed the Normandy beaches, the main forces of the Red Army had been six hundred miles from the Brandenburg frontiers of Germany. Even at the beginning of September, 1944, after the great Soviet victories in the south had opened the gates of the Balkans, the Russian lines still lay to the east of Warsaw, while the Western Allies had not only overrun most of Italy and liberated France and Belgium but, after a triumph as complete as Hitler's in 1940, seemed on the point of breaking into the Ruhr and advancing across Northern Germany. But, having missed their opportunity, they were now no nearer Berlin than they had been then. And because Hitler, seeing this, had starved his immense Eastern front in order to stake all on an eleventh-hour victory in the West, the Russians had now seized the chance their allies had failed to grasp. Since smashing the thin German lines in Poland three weeks before, their armies had swept westwards for nearly three hundred miles and were now only forty miles from Berlin and in possession of almost the whole of East Prussia and Silesia, as

[1] Admiral of the Fleet Kuznetsov and Marshal of Aviation Khudyakov, Chief of Soviet Air Staff.

well as of Hungary and Slovakia, while a third of Hitler's Eastern forces had been encircled and cut off in Courland.

The Russians were, therefore, in a mood of elation. They were ready to welcome their allies with their usual profuse oriental hospitality, but they meant to use the opportunity given them by the West's procrastination to drive the hardest possible bargain. They were no longer mainly concerned with defeating Germany but with dominating as much of Europe as possible. They meant to keep the eastern half of Poland and the Baltic republics that their bargain with Hitler in 1939 had given them, to ignore Britain's and America's pledges to Poland and subordinate the rest of that Christian land to a Communist servitude under the guise of a " People's Republic ". They meant, too, to make similar satellite States of Rumania, Bulgaria, Hungary, Albania, Yugoslavia and, if they could overrun them before their allies, of Austria, Czechoslovakia, Denmark, Norway and the eastern half, or even whole, of Germany. By doing so they would both enlarge the bounds of Communism and safeguard Russia's future.

Yet though this tempting prospect was offered them by their victories, as well as by the faith of the now fast-failing American President who had come to Yalta determined to establish a world republic of independent liberal nations and who believed that, unlike Churchill and the British " colonialists ", Stalin was ready to underwrite such a world, the Russians knew that the dying German beast could still bite. In their three weeks' advance they had far outrun their supplies, and the order to halt on the Oder and consolidate the conquered rear-areas had already gone out. They were haunted, as always, by memories of Tannenberg and the threat of Germany's interior lines, and they wished to make sure that their allies contained Hitler's Armies in the West and South by continuous offensives until, with the re-establishment of its communications and the hardening of the ground in May, the Red Army was ready to resume its advance on Berlin, Vienna and Prague. The Western Powers, too, wished for assurances that the Soviet High Command would maintain pressure on Germany during the

March and April thaw while they were engaged in the hazards of forcing the Rhine.

It was this that Brooke and Marshall and their naval and air colleagues had come to Yalta to discuss with their Russian counterparts while Roosevelt, Churchill and Stalin wrestled with one another in the Livadia Palace over the political future of Germany, Poland and the world. Their tasks were to co-ordinate the converging offensives from West and East so as to prevent the Germans from transferring troops and aircraft from one front to another, to settle their respective military responsibilities in the occupied areas, and to make arrangements for the entry of Russia into the Japanese War as soon as possible after the defeat of Germany.

" *February 5th.* We started our day with a C.O.S. meeting at 10 a.m. to decide the line on which we should run our meeting with the Americans and Russians. At 11.30 we drove to Antonov's H.Q., half-way to Yalta. After many examinations by sentries we were admitted. Meanwhile the Americans had lost themselves and came down to this house. As a result they were half an hour late, which was all to our advantage, as I got into a huddle with Antonov whilst Portal and Cunningham got hold of their opposite numbers and proceeded to break the ice and make friends."

" When Marshall, Leahy and King finally turned up we proceeded to our conference room and started work. The first point to settle was who should take the chair for the meeting—a duty I finally found myself stuck with. I, therefore, opened up on the question of co-ordination of theatres, pointing out that immediate co-ordination was covered by the Western Front February offensive. I then stated that, as this offensive would continue during March and April at least, we hoped that the Russians would find it possible, in spite of the thaw and their long line of communications, to continue their offensive through March and, if possible, April."

" Marshall then expanded this statement, and finally Antonov replied that it was their intention to continue as long as circumstances admitted. He then referred to the Italian front and to the possibility of operating through the Ljubjana Gap towards Vienna. I replied, pointing out difficulties of such action and our decision to reinforce the Western Front with divisions from Italy."

" From there we passed on to air action on both fronts and its co-ordination. This led to Leahy putting up proposals for Eisenhower having a mission in Moscow (a step we have always been against). Before Antonov had time to reply I stepped in, saying that, whilst we were in complete agreement with the Americans as to desirability of liaison, we considered this should be based on a sound organization: namely, a Commission in Moscow whose duty it would be to settle all questions of co-ordination of higher strategy with the American and British Chiefs of Staff, whilst on a lower level we established liaison with Theatre Commanders and Russian Army Group Commanders concerned. Antonov agreed to the former, but not to the latter without reference to Stalin. From the discussion it appeared that Marshall was also in agreement with us, but not Leahy who seemed to understand very little about the problem."

" We finished up our meeting with a discussion on the co-ordination of strategic air bombing, a difficult matter.[1] Antonov produced an arbitrary line running through Berlin, Leipzig, Vienna and Zagreb, which did not suit us and which we reserved for our next discussion, which was settled for the following day at the same time. Finally after three hours we broke up at 3 p.m. and drove home for lunch."

" I then had a look at the birds on the sea-front of our house. There I picked up a Great Northern Diver,

[1] Owing to the danger of the converging allies in Austria and Germany bombing each others' forces and the determination of the Russians to extend and preserve their special spheres of military and political influence. See *Ehrman* VI, 96-8.

cormorants, many gulls and other diving ducks. Also dolphins feeding on shoals of fish. At 6.30 p.m. we had a short Chiefs of Staff's meeting to decide what action to take at to-morrow's meeting with Americans at 10.30 prior to meeting Russians."

" At dinner Winston came up to me and asked me to come round to his dinner table in his room as soon as I had finished to give him results of our meetings. I gave him a full account and asked him how he had been getting on. The highlight of his remarks was that the President had said that the Americans would only remain in Germany for two years after the end of the war. France could assist in the Army of Occupation but was not to be represented on the Inter-Allied Commission in Berlin. Last night Stalin showed great reluctance to propose the King's health, stating that he was a republican; Americans failed to take our part. Stalin made excellent speech proposing Winston's health, stating that he alone had stood up against the might of Germany at the critical moment and supported Russia when she was attacked, a thing he would never forget! "

" *February 6th*. At 10 a.m. the American Chiefs of Staff came here for a conference. We cleared up several minor points which had remained unsettled when we were in Malta, and we also settled our future line of action with the Russians. At 12 noon we went to Antonov's H.Q. and had a three hours' conference."

" I was again appointed chairman and we had a very friendly meeting. Our discussion centred round the use of a bomber line of demarcation for strategic purposes. We solved this by appointing a technical committee consisting of the Chiefs of Staff of the Air to settle the final details."

" From that we passed on to many questions as to co-ordination of the Western offensive with the Russian operations. On the one side, the crossing of the Rhine governs dates, on the other, questions of thaw conditions. But on the whole the co-ordination is fairly good. We then finished up with a run-over of operations in the Pacific. Admiral King gave the Pacific fighting, and I referred to the situation in Burma."[1]

" While we were at work the Foreign Secretaries met at 12 noon, and the high ones again at 4 p.m. I have not seen the P.M. this evening so do not know how they got on."

" Weather colder and inclined to rain."

" *February 7th*. A most interesting day. We left at 9 a.m. for Sevastopol and to see the British Crimea battlefields on the way. We had finished our military discussions, the political ones were still in full swing, so this was a good chance to have a day off. We warned Winston and he agreed provided I trained some officer who could show him the Balaclava battlefield. So I took Peake[2] along with me to show him what I had gathered from books lately and to relate it to the ground we should see. We had good cars with excellent drivers, which was good as our lives were in their hands at several points of the winding mountain road."

" We drove by what is known as Vorontzov's Road, the road constructed by the former owner of the house we are in when he was Viceroy of the Crimea. This is a most lovely road winding high up on the mountainside above the sea, with the most wonderful views. We drove within sight of the sea till we arrived at Baidai Gate, a stone gate on the top of Phoros Pass, after which we dropped down to the old Tartar village of Baidai. There we saw fat, healthy children, full of fun and waving cheerfully to us, a good sign and evidence they are beginning to put the famine behind them."

" From there we drove on through a long pass on the banks of the Black River tributary. This led us straight on to the battlefield of Balaclava. There was the port on our extreme left, on our immediate left the site of the charge of the Heavy Brigade, and on our right the site of

[1] Where General Slim was developing his offensive to liberate Mandalay and where on January 27th the overland route to China had been reopened.
[2] Brigadier R. Peake.

408

that memorable charge of the Light Brigade. And, on top of it all, the confusion of recent tank battles connected with the two last sieges of Sevastopol. I had brought with me diagrammatic sketches of the battles, and also a copy of George Blackenbury's ' Campaign in the Crimea ' with its excellent sketches by William Simpson."

" We could see Balaclava port quite clearly and could imagine its working organization as a base, the mud, the storms, the frightful difficulties, the awful sufferings, etc. And then, on top of it all, as if this small corner of the world had not witnessed sufficient human suffering, there were ample signs of the last recent conflicts for the capture of Sevastopol and then for its liberation. A grave beside a wrecked aeroplane here, a broken-down tank there, rows upon rows of shell and bomb craters, twisted iron chevaux-de-frise, tangled barbed-wire, odd graves, and the usual rubbish of battlefield."

" From the Balaclava battlefields we drove over the approach gaps to Sevastopol, with Inkerman on our right, and shortly the ghost of Sevastopol loomed up in front of us. Such a ghost! Hardly a house standing, and those that stood had no roofs, but over the whole port rested that inexplicable atmosphere of pride such as one only feels on rare occasions. Verdun always gave me that feeling. I had it strongly to-day. If the Russians succeeded in holding out for eleven months against double their numbers of Germans favoured by overwhelming superiority in the air and in armour, whilst suffering great privations on the supply side, then there is no doubt in my mind that the Russian is a very, very great fighter."

" We dropped into Sevastopol, drove between shattered houses to the Russian Admiral's H.Q. There we were given a wonderful reception. First of all, a three quarter's of an hour lecture on the defence of Sevastopol, then a lunch, with several toasts. After lunch we drove up to the old ' Flagstaff Hill ' of the Crimean War, and from there studied the attacks of the British in 1855, the Germans in

1941/42 and the Russians in 1944, against Sevastopol. From there we drove to the site of the famous Malakov Redoubt and had another wonderful view out towards the Inkerman heights. We then dropped back into the port, said goodbye to our Russian Admiral and went out to see the *Franconia*, the large trans-Atlantic transport that had been got ready for us in case we required a Headquarters. They had certainly made a first-class job of her."

" Finally we started the journey home, but on the way out visited the old Crimean British cemetery; it is in a bad way. Evidently it has acted as a strong point in the recent fighting and it has been heavily shelled. Nearly all the Memorial Chapels and graves have been badly smashed. A pathetic sight."

" We had a lovely journey back with lights caused by the setting sun, and reached home close on 7 p.m. in the dark."

" *February 8th*. We started with a Chiefs of Staff meeting at 10 a.m. to examine the results of the Committee that had been sitting on oil and shipping during yesterday. These two troublesome matters had at last reached a stage of agreement. At 12 noon we drove over to meet the Americans for our final meeting with them to pass the shipping, oil and equipment for Greek Forces. This all went through quite early and now we are at liberty to draw up our final Report which we are to consider tomorrow. We have, however, been invited to a banquet by Stalin to-night at 9 p.m. This will mean one of those late nights with many toasts and much vodka."

" *Later*. Our dinner was, as I expected, a lengthy affair. We left here at 8.45 p.m. and returned shortly after 1 a.m. The dinner, as usual, consisted of a series of toasts[1] which went on continuously with the result that most courses were cold before they reached one or before one could settle down to try and eat them. Stalin was in the very

---

[1] Including one by Molotov to Brooke and his colleagues, " the three representatives of the Army, Air Force and Navy of the country which went to war before we did." *Churchill* VI, 317.

best of form, and was full of fun and good humour, apparently thoroughly enjoying himself."

" The standard of the speeches was remarkably low and mostly consisted of insincere, slimy sort of slush! I became more and more bored, and more and more sleepy, and on and on it dragged. On my right I had General Antonov who speaks just a little French, but not enough to be able to keep up a flowing conversation with him. Finally at about 12.45 a.m. the party broke up and we rose from the table, shook hands with Stalin and departed for home and a welcome bed."

" *February 9th.* A short C.O.S. meeting at 10 a.m. to run through the final version of our Final Report. At 11 a.m. we met the Americans for our conference with them to pass the Final Report. At 12 noon we had our Plenary meeting with the P.M. and President and had our Final Report approved, and received our usual reward of compliments on our good work! Drove back our half-hour journey to our home for lunch. Barely was this finished when we had to start off again on our half-hour drive to the American H.Q. for the photographs. This was a most disorganized procedure with no one getting the people in their places for the various military and political groups."

" I then had a quiet afternoon writing letters and finally had to dine at 9 p.m. with Winston who had invited Marshall and Alexander. We never got up from the table till 12.30 a.m. and then only to go into the map room for half an hour. Finally Marshall left, Winston disappeared and I was left alone with Alex. I hope our talk may be of use. It was not till close on 2 a.m. that I rolled into bed."

" A satisfactory feeling that the Conference is finished, and has on the whole been as satisfactory as could be hoped for, and certainly a most friendly one."

. . . .

With the military work of the Conference over, and with Montgomery's great offensive to close on the Rhine launched two days earlier, Brooke and his colleagues were anxious to return at once to England. They set out next morning, leaving Churchill to continue for two more days his losing battle for Europe's future against the cynical chauvinism of his Russian partner and the credulity and growing weariness of his American one.

> " *February 10th. In the air between Greece and Italy.* We made an early start with breakfast at 7 a.m., and by 8 a.m. we were off after all the necessary goodbyes. We had a lovely drive of some four and a half hours to the aerodrome we landed at near Eupatoria. Then we had more goodbyes together with vodka and an egg! The Chief of the Air Staff had been sent down by Stalin to see us off."
>
> " At 1 p.m. sharp we took off and made straight for the Turkish coast above Istanbul. We must have crossed at about Midye but could not see anything as we were above the clouds. Shortly afterwards we saw the ground again and found ourselves at the point of the Gallipoli peninsula flying over Gulf of Saros with Suvla Bay on our left. The beaches of the landings of the last war were quite clear. We then had an excellent view of Imbros and Lemnos with Samothrace to the north of us. Shortly afterwards clouds obliterated the ground and we saw nothing more till we found most beautiful snow-covered mountains projecting above the clouds. We were flying north of and parallel to the Corinth Gulf; gradually the clouds broke and we had a glorious view of a series of snow-covered peaks. We touched the sea again at the mouth of the Gulf and from there flew on over the island of Cephalonia. Now we are over the sea south of the foot of Italy. We hope to arrive in Malta about dark."
>
> " *Later. Malta.* At 7 p.m. (Russian time, 5 p.m. Malta time) we landed in Malta, having had an excellent trip.

I went straight to the cemetery where ' Barney ' has been buried and laid a wreath on his grave."

" *February 11th. Flying over France.* At 1.15 a.m. Portal was woken up by the pilot saying that last reports of weather over England were bad, that unless we started at once we might not get away for two days. We decided to start at once. We had a very good night's journey and were called at 7 a.m. and told that in an hour we should be in Northolt and the weather good enough to get down. So I got up, shaved and dressed and had a cup of tea."

" Close on 8 a.m. we began occasionally to see the ground through the clouds. I saw a river which I tried to fit in with the Thames. There was a large town, but it certainly was not Reading. Suddenly Portal came and said, ' Do you know where we are?—over Paris! ' (He had seen the Eiffel Tower.) We were then again lost in heavy mist; the atmospherics were so bad that the wireless could not be used and we wandered about Northern France lost in the clouds. Luckily after some flying the pilot recognised Fécamp in a gap in the clouds. We then pushed on over the Channel which was barely visible for fog, rain and mist. On crossing the English coast we found the weather slightly better and finally landed at Northolt at 9.30 a.m., being one and a half hours overdue."

" I went straight to the flat and was glad to be able to escape at once from the flood of ' Barney ' memories by driving home."

Chapter Thirteen

RHINE CROSSING
AND VICTORY

As soldiers we looked naïvely on the British inclination to complete the war with political foresight and non-military objectives.

GENERAL BRADLEY

ON FEBRUARY 8th—two days before Brooke left Yalta—Montgomery's offensive to clear the Lower Rhineland opened with the biggest barrage of the war. Two great armies were engaged in it—the Canadian First, strongly reinforced from the British Second Army, and the American Ninth reinforced at the last moment from 12 U.S. Army Group. But before the American Ninth Army on the right could open its attack, planned by Montgomery for February 10th, the Germans smashed the discharge-valves of the last uncaptured Roer dam on Bradley's front to the south and flooded the valley in the Americans' path, holding them up for a fortnight. Until then the British and Canadians had to advance unsupported along a narrow corridor between two rivers which Hitler had ordered to be defended to the death. Fighting their way eastwards through the Reichswald and across the Siegfried Line, over mined and sodden fields and woods and the rubble of bomb-shattered towns, they engaged eleven German divisions—half of them armoured or composed of fanatic young Parachute troops resolved at all costs to keep the invaders from reaching the Rhine and stopping the movement of the Ruhr coal and steel on which, now that the Silesian industrial basin had been lost to the Russians, the Reich's fast-disintegrating war industry depended.

414

During the first two weeks after the C.I.G.S.'s return from Yalta, while Montgomery, repeating a familiar pattern, drew the German reserves into the mêlée on his left so as to weaken resistance to the impending American attack on his right, Brooke's diary recorded little of importance. It did not even mention the situation reports—concise and lucid—which every night Montgomery dictated for him after receiving the latest battle news from his liaison officers. Brooke felt acutely the absence of ' Barney ' Charlesworth in the empty flat in Westminster Gardens; " I never realised," he wrote, " how much I should miss him and what an awful void he would leave in my life." On the Friday after his return he entertained his widow and tried to comfort her.

> " It was very heart-breaking for both of us. She is wonderfully plucky outwardly, but it was only too clear that inwardly she was torn in two with grief. I wish I could have done more to help her."

" Back to flat for a lonely dinner," he wrote that night. " The absence of dear old ' Barney ' just haunts me the whole time."

One night, in that first " grizzly and gloomy week", Brooke dined at the Palace with his colleague, the Chief of Air Staff.

> " It was a very small party, just the King, Queen, Portal and myself. The King and Queen were as usual quite extraordinary hosts and made us forget at once the regal atmosphere of the meeting. The King thrilled about the new medal ribbons he was devising and had an envelope full of them in his pocket; the Queen charming and captivating, interested in everything, full of talk and quite devoid of any stiffness. There is no doubt that they are a wonderful pair."

On another evening the Deputy Prime Minister, Attlee, sent for Brooke to hear his account of the Malta and Yalta Conferences. Churchill, who had broken his return journey at Athens and Cairo, did not reach England till the 19th when, the C.I.G.S. wrote, the usual Monday evening Cabinet meeting was

" interrupted by Winston's return from the Mediterranean in tremendous form ".

By February 20th Brooke's life had resumed its normal course.

> " *February 20th.* We had our usual weekly run round the world with the Joint Intelligence Committee. There are certainly a few small cracks beginning to appear in the German fighting machine but no indications of a general cracking up. It is quite impossible to estimate how long it may last."

> " I had to go to Winston at 2.45 to discuss Eisenhower's last letter in which he proposes to employ Alex in the back areas if he comes to him as a Deputy! Winston had drafted a good letter which we ran through and made a few alterations in. In it he suggested coming out next Thursday with me on a visit."

For though the C.I.G.S. had supposed that he failed to make much impression on the Americans at Malta, he had achieved more than he knew. His talk with Bedell Smith had convinced that officer and, through him, the Supreme Commander, that concentration was essential if the German resistance in the West was to be broken by the spring. The latest attempts of the American Army Commanders to whittle down Montgomery's build-up in the North in favour of operations elsewhere had failed; Eisenhower at last was standing pat behind the new plan that he and Bedell Smith had drafted. And Montgomery was delighted. " Ike agreed with everything I was doing," he wrote after a meeting with him on February 14th,

> " he is giving me two more American infantry divisions for Ninth Army. . . . He reaffirmed his intention to concentrate all resources, Ground and Air, on doing one thing at a time. The first thing to be done was for 21 Army Group to line up on the Rhine from Düsseldorf northwards and to get bridgeheads firmly established across the river; all resources would be concentrated on doing this. He stated his intention to

leave the Ninth U.S. Army of twelve divisions in 21 Army Group for the rest of the war. All this is very good and I do believe that we are at last all well set with a fair wind to help us into harbour. We have had a few storms, but the sky is now clear."[1]

In Montgomery's view this rendered unnecessary the change in the Command set-up and the appointment of an overall Ground Commander for which he had pleaded so urgently before Christmas. The expedient of calling in Alexander as Deputy Supreme Commander in Tedder's place, which Churchill and Brooke had discussed with Roosevelt and Marshall at Malta, no longer appealed to him. For the rumour of it had distressed his friend, Eisenhower, and made the latter suspect he was intriguing against him. " I am sorry this was said at Malta," Montgomery wrote in his diary that night, " it got back to Ike very quickly and was, no doubt, attributed to me; he is such an awfully decent chap that I hate to see him upset." He had therefore assured him that he regarded the present Command set-up as wholly satisfactory and did not want it changed. Whereupon, delighted at having his formidable lieutenant's backing, Eisenhower had written to the Prime Minister that, if Alexander was appointed in Tedder's place, he could only allow him to handle such routine matters as administration in the rear areas.[2]

It was to this letter that the C.I.G.S. had referred in his diary on February 20th.

" *February 21st.* Twice during the day I have received amendments of Winston's reply to Eisenhower. However, they were not important alterations and all fitted in equally well. Monty replied to my telegram that next week's visit was all right and welcome."

" Morgan[3] came in the afternoon prior to going out to

---

[1] Montgomery to C.I.G.S., 14 Feb., 1945. Lord Alanbrooke, *Personal Files.*
[2] Montgomery, *Memoirs* 325.
[3] Gen. Sir William Morgan, who had been Alexander's G.S.D.I. in the retreat to Dunkirk, and, having been Chief of Staff to Home Forces and more recently G.O.C. Southern Command, had now been appointed Chief of Staff in the Mediterranean.

Alexander (as Chief of Staff *vice* Harding). I had a long talk with him putting him into the picture and explaining to him what I required of him."

" *February 22nd*. This afternoon the Dutch Ambassador came to see me about two additional ships for relief of Dutch in occupied Holland. Heaven knows they deserve it, but the difficulty is to find spare ships."

" Then Hawkesworth back from Greece and very interesting on conditions in Greece."

" Finally a very trying hour with General Anders, who is back from Italy. He had been to see the P.M. yesterday, but was still terribly distressed. According to him the root of the trouble lay in the fact that he could never trust the Russians after his experiences with them, whilst Winston and Roosevelt were prepared to trust them. After having been a prisoner, and seeing how Russians could treat Poles, he considered he was in a better position to judge what Russians were like than the President or the P.M. He said that he had never been more distressed since the war started. When in a Russian prison he was in the depth of gloom, but he did then always have hope. Now he could see no hope anywhere. His wife and children were in Poland and he could never see them again; that was bad enough. But what was infinitely worse was the fact that all the men under his orders relied on him to find a solution to this insoluble problem. They all said,—' Oh! Anders will go to London and will put matters right for us,' and he, Anders, saw no solution and this kept him awake at night. I felt most awfully sorry for him; he is a grand fellow and takes the whole matter terribly hard. He is to see Winston again next Wednesday and me afterwards. I shudder at the thought of this next interview."

" *February 23rd*. We had one of our usual monthly examinations of the rocket-bomb threat with Cherwell attending the C.O.S. meeting. It is pretty clear that no air action has much effect on this form of enemy attack. There is only one way of dealing with them, that is by clearing the area from which they come by ground action, and that for the present is not possible."

" Adam came to lunch and we discussed our possible successors. Possibly Monty as C.I.G.S.; Nye or Swayne as Adjutant-General; Robertson if he will take on Q.M.G.; Alex either Army Control in Germany or C.-in-C. in India; Dempsey C.-in-C. British Troops of Occupation in Germany; MacCreery C.-in-C. British Troops in Austria; V.C.I.G.S. Swayne or Browning. All C.'s-in-C. at Home Commands will also want changing with younger men. There will be one mass of post-war problems which will require young and energetic men to solve them."

. . . .

That morning of February 23rd, before dawn, Simpson's Ninth Army on Montgomery's southern flank was able to launch its long-delayed attack. Moving across the subsiding floods of the Roer, it had surprised the Germans whose reserves had all been drawn into the fight against the British and Canadians to the north. During the week-end, advancing with great dash and negligible casualties, it broke clean through the Siegfried Line. " I ordered that advance be pressed relentlessly," Montgomery informed Brooke, " and that every legitimate risk be taken to get forward. The weather is fine and the ground is drying up and the enemy had few reserves immediately to hand with which to stop an advance, and it is important to take full advantage of this situation."[1] The next few days were almost as dramatic as those that followed the American break-through in Normandy. " I visited the Ninth Army," Montgomery wrote on the 28th, " and saw the Corps Commanders and many of the divisional generals. They were all in very great spirits and report that the troops are in tremendous form. The Army has gained a great victory with very few casualties and this has raised morale to a high level." By March 2nd the triumphant Americans had reached the

[1] Montgomery to C.I.G.S., 24 Feb., 1945. Lord Alanbrooke, *Personal Files.*

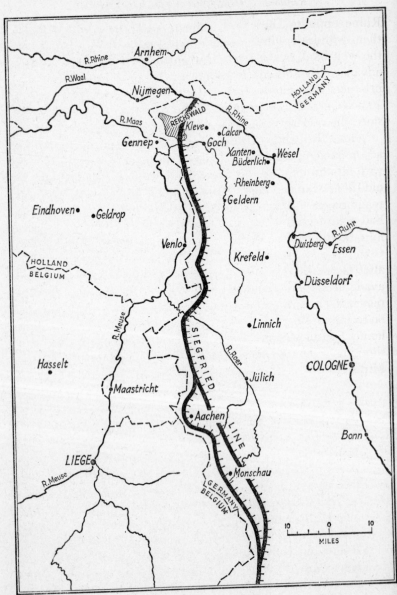

THE LOWER RHINE

Rhine opposite Düsseldorf. Owing to Hitler's refusal to let them withdraw, fifteen German divisions were now caught on the west bank of the river between the jaws of Montgomery's advance. By the end of the first week of the month 50,000 prisoners had passed through the Allied cages and another 40,000 Germans were estimated to have been killed or wounded since the offensive began on February 8th.[1]

While the victory was still being exploited the C.I.G.S. accompanied the Prime Minister on a visit to the front. He took with him his new A.D.C., Brigadier " Rollie " Charrington, an old friend who had been invalided out of the Service after commanding the 1st Armoured Brigade in Greece in 1941 and who had volunteered to fill Charlesworth's place. On the day before their departure Brooke had a long morning at the C.O.S. Committee wrestling with the allocation of Personnel Shipping after Germany's defeat—" an almost insoluble problem as the available shipping cannot begin to cater for the multitude of moves, such as Americans and Canadians back to America and on to Japan, British home and on to Far East, New Zealanders home, South Africans home, prisoners to be repatriated, civil shipping." Afterwards he and his wife lunched with the Prime Minister:

" Winston in good form; said that if he were Hitler he would have himself flown over to this country, hand himself to the Government stating that he alone was responsible for all the evils of Germany and was prepared to stand the racket. According to Winston this would face us with a difficult problem."

" All preparations are now ready for our visit to Monty and Ike to-morrow."

" *March 2nd. Geldrop near Eindhoven.* We left War Office, Rollie and I, at 9.45 a.m. for Northolt where we were to leave with the P.M. for France at 10.30 a.m. He was as usual late, and it was just after 11 a.m. when we left.

---

[1] *Normandy to the Baltic*, 245. The British and Canadian losses were 15,634 and the American losses 7478.

We travelled by his new C.54 machine. A beautiful and most comfortable machine, far quieter than the York. We were met on the aerodrome by ' Maori ' Coningham[1] and Mary Churchill. Coningham took us off to his H.Q. in Brussels."

" After lunch we flew on to Eindhoven aerodrome in two Dakotas. There Monty met us and drove us to his H.Q. After that we went to the station and found Eisenhower's train which he had sent for us to live in. We changed and then went round to dine with Monty. After dinner we attended the interview which he holds every evening with his liaison officers. It was most interesting and most impressive. After completing this interview he dictated his daily wire to me based on his conception of the situation arrived at from the liaison officers' reports."

" The battle is going wonderfully well, and there are signs from all sides of decay setting in in the German Army."

" *March 3rd. Train in siding at Geldrop.* At 9.15, P.M. and I started off with Monty in his two Rolls cars. We motored straight to Maastricht. There we went to the Ninth Army H.Q. and met Simpson, the U.S. commander. He introduced us to his staff, and Winston and I had to make small speeches to them. We then drove on, Simpson with P.M. and Monty with me. We drove on towards Aachen, but stopped on the Siegfried Line on the way to examine the dragon's teeth defence against tanks and to look at some of the pill-boxes which had been blown up by the Americans."

' As we were leaving Simpson's H.Q. Simpson asked Winston whether he wished to make use of the lavatory before starting. Without a moment's hesitation he asked, " How far is the Siegfried Line? " On being told about half-an-hour's run, he replied that he would not visit the

[1] Air Marshal Sir Arthur Coningham.

lavatory but that we should halt on reaching the Siegfried Line! On arrival there the column of some twenty to thirty cars halted, we processed solemnly out and lined up along the Line. As the photographers had all rushed up to secure good vantage points, he turned to them and said, " This is one of the operations connected with this great war which must not be reproduced graphically." To give them credit they obeyed their orders and, in doing so, missed a chance of publishing the greatest photographic catch of the war! I shall never forget the childish grin of intense satisfaction that spread all over his face as he looked down at the critical moment.'

" Aachen was very badly damaged, and it was a relief to see at last German houses demolished instead of French, Italian, Belgian and British. There were a few Germans in the town but not many. We drove on through to Jülich on the River Roer where we met the American Corps commander who carried out the crossing of the river. It must have been a very formidable obstacle, especially when the river was in flood."

" We crossed by the Bailey bridge and went to examine the Citadel, a Vauban brick fort with a large moat which had been held by a company. The Americans took it by bringing a gun to blow open the door and stormed the entrance whilst covering their attack with flame-throwers directed on the battlements. A very successful operation proving the value of flame-throwers."

" In the evening dined with Monty who had ' Bimbo ' Dempsey, Neil Ritchie and ' Bubbles ' Barker for dinner. It was a great joy seeing them again. After dinner we again went with Monty to listen to the reports from his liaison officers. The day's fighting had been most successful and we ought to be able to close up to the Rhine on its full length to Cologne within the next few days."

" *March 4th. Train siding at Geldrop.* We left again at 10.15 a.m. and drove through Eindhoven straight up the

Nijmegen road till we were short of that place. Then we stopped at Canadian Army H.Q. and met Crerar. We went into his map room and were given a very good short explanation of the fighting since the start of the operation to the present date. We then drove off through the Reichswald to a point on the far side where we ought to have been able to see the vast Rhine floods. Unfortunately it was raining and drizzling and we could see nothing."

" So we went to the Canadian Corps H.Q. where we found Simonds, the Corps commander. We then drove to Goch, which we went through to reach an 8″ gun which the P.M. was to fire. Surrounded by Press photographers, he pulled the lanyard and let her off."

" We then proceeded to Gennep to see the Bailey bridges which had been put up on the Meuse; they were even longer than the one I saw over the Sangro River last year. We finished up with a visit to the 51st Division who are out of the line and produced their Pipes and Drums. It was interesting to at last see this Division on German soil. I first came in contact with them when I took over the remnants after St. Valery when I returned to France subsequent to Dunkirk. They were next under my orders when I commanded Home Forces, and I visited them twice in Scotland. I saw them immediately after their arrival in Egypt and ready to move to the defence of Cairo against Rommel; in Tripoli after Rommel's defeat marching past the P.M.; at Bougie in Algeria prior to invasion of Sicily; and now at last in Germany."

" To-night we dined in the train and Monty and de Guingand came to dinner. Winston fretting because he was not allowed nearer the front, and trying to make plans to come back for the operations connected with the crossing of the Rhine! "

' De Guingand, not knowing the P.M., unfortunately adopted quite the wrong attitude with him and I at one time was afraid that we might have trouble. Winston was in deadly earnest in his desire to come out for the crossing of the Rhine and to be well forward in this operation. I knew we should have difficulties in providing for his security, but I was even more certain that de Guingand's rather grand-motherly arguments against Winston's wishes would ultimately lead to an explosion.'

" *March 5th. Rheims.* Shortly after midnight our train started off and at 10 a.m. we arrived at Rheims. Ike's A.D.C. came to collect us and drove ' Pug ', Rollie and me up to Ike's H.Q., a big Agricultural College near the station. There I found Ike with Bradley and had a long talk with him about the war in general. He took me into his map room and gave me the latest news about the situation on the front."

" We then went up to his Mess. Bradley remained for lunch, and P.M. turned up shortly before lunch. Whilst in the office I got Ike alone for a bit and told him that, if he had strong feelings about Alex not coming as his deputy, he should let the P.M. know. Apparently he is afraid that the introduction of Alexander would upset the outfit. Monty had also expressed the same opinion."

" After lunch I left Ike alone with the P.M. to give him a chance of expressing his views."

" For dinner Bedell Smith, Spaatz and Tedder came. I had a long discussion on fishing with Bedell Smith."

" *March 6th. Back to London.* Breakfast with Ike and another long talk with him. There is no doubt that he is a most attractive personality and, at the same time, a very, very limited brain from a strategic point of view. This comes out the whole time in all conversations with him. His relations with Monty are quite insoluble; he only sees the worst side of Monty and cannot appreciate the better side. Things are running smoothly for the present, but this cannot last, and I foresee trouble ahead before long. For all that, to insert Alex now is only likely to lead to immediate trouble for all, I gather. The war may not last long now, and possibly matters may run smoothly till the end. Therefore, I feel that it is best to leave Alex where he is. I think that Winston is now of the same opinion."

" We left Ike's mess at 10.30 a.m. and motored to the aerodrome outside, where we took off shortly before 11 a.m. We had a good journey over, arriving back shortly after 12 noon."

Brooke's advice to drop the project for changing the Deputy Supreme Commander was taken. In the light of Eisenhower's and Montgomery's views it seemed the only course. Three days after his return to England Churchill wrote to Alexander to tell him that, as Montgomery had now declared himself in perfect accord with S.H.A.E.F., it seemed better to leave him in the Mediterranean where the Greek situation, the delicate relations with Tito and the Yugoslav partisans and the possibility of a new offensive in Italy all made his presence as Supreme Commander essential. " I know," he wrote, " that you will . . . adhere to your becoming attitude of serving wherever you are ordered and discharging whatever duties are assigned to you." To which Alexander replied, " You already know that my only wish is to serve where I am most useful and, feeling that way, I am well content."

Brooke's familiar London routine now began again. It was just three years since he had taken over the chairmanship of the Chiefs of Staff Committee in the dark days of Singapore.

" *March 7th.* Herbert Morrison[1] attended the C.O.S. meeting to discuss what could be done to save London from rockets and buzz-bombs. He painted a lurid picture of the awful five years London had suffered and how wrong it was to expect her to go on suffering. He seemed to forget that theatres, cinemas, restaurants, night-clubs, concerts, etc., have been in full swing for the last few years. We listened as sympathetically as we could and then explained to him our difficulties in trying to deal with this

[1] Responsible, as Home Secretary and Minister of Home Security, for Civil Defence and the safety of the civilian population.

threat either by air or land action. (While I write I hear the rumble of one landing in the distance!) "

" Lunched with Franklyn[1] at Home Forces and gave them a talk on the world situation. Back to the office for a flood of files."

" *March 8th.* We were back on our shipping troubles again this morning, and the worst of it is that I cannot quite get to the bottom of them. We were by way of having settled it at Yalta, and now P.M. wishes to establish further cuts."[2]

" *March 9th.* This morning our main problem at the C.O.S. meeting was the Dutch P.M.'s lament to Winston concerning the starvation of the Dutch population and arguing for a reconsideration of our strategy so as to admit of an early liberation of Holland—one more of the continual repercussions of political considerations on strategical requirements. It is, however, pretty clear that our present plans for Monty's crossing of the Rhine cannot be changed. After crossing the Rhine, from a military point of view there is no doubt that we should work for the destruction of Germany and not let any clearing up of Holland delay our dispositions."

" *March 10th.* Just as I was rushing to make an early start home, a telegram turned up from Alex with certain underground peace proposals. These suggested the surrendering of the whole of Kesselring's army in Italy. However, as Wolff[3] was the main instigator and he is a

[1] General Sir Harold Franklyn, Commander-in-Chief Home Forces, who had commanded the 5th Division under Brooke in the retreat to Dunkirk.

[2] Faced at the Malta Conference with an apparently insoluble shipping shortage, the Combined Chiefs of Staff had agreed that, if deficiencies could not be made good, first priority should be given to " the basic undertakings in support of the overall strategic concepts ". But on March 2nd the Prime Minister directed that to meet the British deficit the main cuts would have to fall on military shipments to the Middle East and Indian Ocean. In the event the deficiencies proved to be a myth caused by American Service miscalculations, and the shipping subsequently released under pressure from the President resulted in an unexpected " flush of tonnage ". *Behrens* 416-36. *Churchill* VI, 626.

[3] General Karl Wolff, the S.S. Commander in Italy and as such responsible for liaison with the puppet Italian Government. " He was told that only

427

rabid S.S. follower of Himmler, it does not seem very plausible. We are following it up for the present and sending representatives to Switzerland to the selected spot."

" *March 12th.* 12.3.45! It is sad that this date will not return for another hundred years. It looks so nice! "

" A rushed morning with C.O.S. meeting and Cabinet, the latter luckily run by Attlee which shortened matters considerably. Long letter from Monty with all his plans for the attack across the Rhine on the 24th of this month. Also an invitation to the P.M. to come for it and stop with him. This is a result of the letter I had written to him."

" *March 14th.* We again discussed the underground movements towards capitulation of German forces in Italy. Somehow the whole business looks pretty fishy and not very promising."[1]

". . . In the evening I had to go to see the King to explain to him the situation on the Western Front and the coming offensive. He was very interested in them. After dinner had to go round to No. 11 Downing Street for a meeting on Distribution of Personnel Shipping after the defeat of Germany."

" *March 15th.* Our C.O.S. meeting was again concerned with trying to extricate divisions out of Greece."

" *March 19th.* This evening Crerar came to dine and I had a long and satisfactory talk with him after dinner. Thank heaven I have at last got the whole of the Canadian Army now assembled in France! "

' It had been a difficult task to get the Canadians finally

---

unconditional surrender would suffice and that the signature of the Commander-in-Chief was essential." When the C.I.G.S. replied to Alexander on March 10th, he emphasized that it was ' of first importance ' that the surrender should be agreed between the Combined Chiefs of Staff and that the Russians should be ' constantly and fully informed.' *Ehrman* VI, 122-3.

[1] The Russians protested vehemently at not being a direct party to these negotiations, though they never invited their allies to join with them in receiving military surrenders on their own front.

assembled as an Army in France. In the early stages McNaughton's opposition to the splitting of the Canadian forces had to be overcome. Then a portion had to be sent out to Italy, when I had difficulty with their lack of trained commanders. Finally they had to be withdrawn again from Italy and assembled as a whole Army for the final stages of the operations against Germany.'

.   .   .   .

Only four days now remained before the action that was to break open the line of the Rhine from the north, encircle the Ruhr and loose the British and American armour on the plains of North Germany. When Churchill and Brooke returned to England after their visit to the front on March 6th, the entire left bank of the Rhine from Nijmegen to Cologne had already fallen to the Allies. Next day an armoured patrol of Hodges's First Army, descending on the Rhine at Remagen twenty miles south of Bonn, captured a railway bridge over the river before it could be destroyed—a sign of the growing demoralization of Hitler's forces. Though it formed no part of his overall plan, Eisenhower ordered the immediate exploitation of this unlooked-for windfall and the formation of a bridgehead with as many divisions as could be spared without reducing the scope of Montgomery's impending blow in the North—a decision for which the tactful Supreme Commander was careful to seek that officer's approval.[1] A week later, while the British Commander-in-Chief was preparing for his crossing on March 24th, Patton had opened a new offensive. Having marched north at Christmas to contain the German break-through in the Ardennes and having gloriously avenged that battle in the early days of March by driving through the Eiffel to Coblentz, capturing with the First Army fifty thousand Germans in the process, the Third Army commander now struck south-east

---

[1] " I was consulted by Eisenhower by telephone this morning as to my opinion on this matter and said I considered it to be an excellent move, as it would be an unpleasant threat to the enemy and would undoubtedly draw enemy strength on to it and away from the business in North." Montgomery to C.I.G.S., 8 March, 1944. Lord Alanbrooke, *Personal Files.*

across the Moselle in two armoured drives, one along the left bank of the Rhine to cut the communications of the remaining Germans west of it, the other starting from Trier in the rear of the Siegfried Line, which Devers's Seventh U.S. Army from Marseilles and the French First Army were still vainly trying to force. Within a week, encircling the Siegfried Line defenders, he had rounded up many thousands more dispirited and demoralized Germans and cleared the whole remaining west bank of the Rhine. Then, once again—and this time rightly—jumping the gun to forestall Montgomery, the great cavalry leader obeyed Bradley's injunction to " take the Rhine on the run " and, on the night before the British were to make their crossing in the North, slipped a division across the now almost undefended river a few miles south of Mainz and established a second American bridgehead.[1]

Yet tremendous though the significance of these successes—for they showed that the Germans were at last losing grip along the entire front—both crossings were relatively small affairs compared with the majestic operation which Montgomery was now about to launch in the north. The Rhine at Wesel—" the greatest water obstacle in Western Europe "—was five hundred yards wide, and a million men had been assembled to cross it. Facing them was the flower of what remained of Hitler's Western Army after its tremendous losses in trying to hold the Rhineland and the transfer of most of its armour to the Eastern Front. That he should be present was the Prime Minister's intense desire and, after his disappointment over D-Day, he did not mean to be thwarted. Brooke, who in military matters was nearer him than any other man, was well aware of this. Immediately after their return from Germany he had written to Montgomery,

" As regards the P.M.'s proposals for his next visit, do not take this matter too light-heartedly; there are the seeds of serious trouble ahead. In his mind you stopped him before

[1] " Brad," he shouted on the telephone, " for God's sake tell the world we're across. . . . I want the world to know Third Army made it before Monty starts across." *Bradley*, 522.

the start of *Overlord* visiting troops, you tried to stop him in Normandy, and now you are attempting to do so again! Note that I said ' in his mind '; but that is the important point, as when he gets such ideas nothing on earth gets them out.

" De Guingand was working on the wrong lines after you left the night you dined; he was treating the whole visit as an impossibility. I can tell you he is determined to come out for the crossing of the Rhine and is now talking of going up in a tank! I feel the safest way would be to find some reasonably secure view-point (not too far back or there will be hell to pay) to which he can be taken and from which he can see and have explained what is happening.

" Discuss this with Simpson and let me know what you think."[1]

To this Montgomery replied,

" As regards the P.M. if he is determined to come out for the Battle of the Rhine, I think there is only one course of action: and that is to ask him to stay with me in my camp. I shall then be able to keep an eye on him and see that he goes only where he will bother no one. I have written him a letter; Simpson will show it to you; it should please the old boy! "[2]

Churchill himself had subsequently sent Montgomery a charming reply, assuring him that he would be no hindrance and would not come at all if he thought there was the slightest chance of his getting in the way or making inroads on his time and thought. He would come, he wrote, on D-minus-one, with only the C.I.G.S., Tommy—his A.D.C.—and his valet, four in all. And he mentioned the matter of the tank which, according to him, Eisenhower had suggested was the best way of seeing things.

Brooke, none the less, had doubts. " Tomorrow," he wrote in his diary,

[1] C.I.G.S. to Montgomery, 7 March, 1945, Lord Alanbrooke, *Personal Files.*
[2] Montgomery to C.I.G.S., 10 March, 1945, *Idem.*

" I start off with P.M. on this visit to see the Rhine crossing. I am not happy about this trip; he will be difficult to manage and has no business to be going. All he will do is to endanger his life unnecessarily. However, nothing on earth will stop him! "[1]

" *March 23rd. Monty's H.Q. Venlo, Germany.* We had our usual C.O.S. meeting after which I finished off some papers in the War Office. I then lunched with Winston at the Annexe, a small lunch, only Clemmie, Brendan Bracken and Winston. Clemmie very full of all the preparations for her journey to Moscow next week."

" After lunch I drove with Winston to Northolt. The road was up on the way and the driver was going to take the diversion, but this did not suit Winston and we had to go straight through. This meant lifting some of the barriers, driving on the footpath, etc., and on the whole probably took longer than going round. However, Winston was delighted that he was exercising his authority and informed me that the King would not take such action; he was far more law-abiding! "

" We left Northolt in a Dakota about 3 p.m. We had a very good two hours' flight over Calais, Lille and Brussels. On arrival here we reduced the party to four (P.M., Tommy, Sawyers and self) and drove on to Monty's H.Q. which is close to the aerodrome."

" We found Monty there, very proud to be able to pitch his camp in Germany at last. We had tea, after which Monty described plan of attack for the crossing of the Rhine which starts to-night on a two Army front, with Ninth American Army on right and Second British Army on left. Crossings take place throughout the night, and the guns have already started and can be heard indistinctly in the distance."

" After dinner Monty went off to bed early and Winston took me off. First of all, we walked up and down in the moonlight; it was a glorious night, and we discussed the

[1] *Diary*, 22 March, 1945.

situation we were in at the momentous moment of crossing the Rhine. We went back over some of our early struggles, back to Cairo when we started Alex and Monty off. How he had had to trust my selection at that time, the part that the hand of God had taken at the critical moment, etc. He was in one of his very nicest moods and showed appreciation for what I had done for him in a way in which he had never done before."

" We then went into the caravan and examined his Box which had just arrived. It contained a telegram from Molotov which worried him a great deal, connected with the Russian attitude to the peace negotiations which Wolff is trying to open in Berne and their fear lest we should make a separate peace on the Western Front without them being in. He dictated a reply, let his secretary out of the caravan, called him back, considered it, started writing another and finally very wisely left it till to-morrow to think over carefully."

" I am now off to bed. It is hard to realise that within fifteen miles hundreds of men are engaged in death-struggles along the banks of the Rhine, whilst hundreds more are keying themselves up to stand up to one of the greatest trials of their lives. With that thought in one's mind it is not easy to lie down and sleep peacefully."

" *March 24th. Venlo.* At breakfast Monty told me that from all reports he had received the forcing of the Rhine was going well. At 8.45 the P.M. and I started off together with Monty's A.D.C. We had a three-quarters of an hour's drive to a viewpoint about 2000 yards south of Xanten from which an excellent view can be obtained when the weather is clear. Unfortunately it was rather hazy, but we could just make out the line of the Rhine from Xanten to Wesel and could just see some of the boats ferrying across the Rhine where landings had taken place."

" We were in the middle of the battery positions supporting that portion of the front, and there was a continual roar of guns as they were busy engaging German

A.A. guns in anticipation of the arrival of the Airborne divisions. The 6th British and 17th American Divisions were due to start, arriving at 10 a.m., to land in the area about two to three miles beyond the Rhine, the far side of the Dienfordter Wald. The 6th Airborne Division was starting from East Anglia and the 17th Airborne Division from the Paris area. They arrived punctually to time, and it was a wonderful sight. The whole sky was filled with large flights of transport aircraft. They flew straight over us and over the Rhine. Unfortunately they disappeared into the haze before dropping their loads of parachutists. The flak could be seen bursting amongst them before they disappeared. Shortly afterwards they began to stream back with doors open and parachute strings hanging under them. A few of them burst into flames on their way back and shed their pilots who floated down in their parachutes."

" After about an hour's continuous stream the gliders began to arrive and sailed past, flight after flight."

" We remained at this viewpoint for about two hours and then embarked in two armoured cars, one each. We went down into Xanten where we turned north and through Marlenbaum at the north-east corner of the Hochwald and on to a bit of high ground just south of Calcar. There we had a good view looking out on to the crossing-place of the 51st Division, whose divisional commander was unfortunately killed this morning.[1] We lunched there and then dropped down to 3rd Division H.Q. in an old castle."

" Winston then became a little troublesome and wanted to go messing about on the Rhine crossings and we had some difficulty in keeping him back. However, in the end he behaved well and we came back in our armoured cars to where we had left our own car, and from there on back to the H.Q. P.M. went off for a sleep which he wanted badly; he had been sleeping in the car nearly all the way home, gradually sliding on to my knee."

[1] Maj.-Gen. T. G. Rennie.

" I washed dust away from my eyes and face, had tea, and then started off in Monty's plane for a fly-round to look at the front. We flew very low over the Meuse from Venlo to Gennep, looking at the wonderful defences the Germans had built for this line. At Gennep we swung north-east right through the Reichswald to Cleve, where we turned south-east and flew along main road Calcar-Xanten-Rheinberg. Finally we swung south-west through Geldern and back to Venlo. Total trip about a hundred miles and all of it most interesting. I was able to see most of the line of the Rhine beautifully."

" *Later.* I have now had dinner and attended Monty's conference with his liaison officers. From their reports there is no doubt that the operations have been an outstanding success. On the south each division has captured some thousand odd prisoners with only one or two hundred casualties. On the north the 51st Division has had a tougher time. It has been up against those hard-fighting parachute divisions, and for some six hundred prisoners has suffered over six hundred casualties, including the divisional commander. One of the outstanding successes of the day has been the employment of the Airborne divisions in close proximity and closely connected to the attack."

" Looking on the day as a whole and the successes of the American forces in recent weeks south of the Moselle, I am quite certain that the end of the Germans is very near indeed, and I would not be surprised to see them pack up at any moment. In a few days I feel that co-ordinated defence north of the Rhine will cease and that we shall be in a position to let Monty's eight armoured divisions operate boldly through North Germany, maintained by air-supply."

" On top of it all, we have those proposed negotiations of Wolff's suggesting Kesselring's surrender whilst still commanding forces in North Italy. Is it not likely that, with the hopeless situation confronting him on the front he has just taken over, Kesselring may well be induced to surrender the whole of the Western Front? If so, what about the Russian Front? It seems unlikely that the German soldier in the East will be induced to go on fighting when he hears the German soldier in the West has packed up."

" *March 25th. Palm Sunday. Venlo.* Started by going to church with Monty at his small Headquarters service. Winston came along too. The hymns were good, and the parson, a Presbyterian, preached a good sermon. After church we motored off to Rheinberg, where Anderson, commanding the 16th American Corps, had his H.Q. We were met there by Eisenhower, Bradley and Simpson."

" I had a talk with Ike on the question of the surrender of Kesselring and all the other purely military surrenders. He also wanted to know whether I agreed with his present plans of pushing in the south for Frankfurt and Kassel. I told him that, with the Germans crumbling as they are, the whole situation is now altered. Evidently the Boche is cracking and what we want now is to push him relentlessly, wherever we can, until he crumbles. In his present condition we certainly have the necessary strength for a double envelopment strategy, which I did not consider applicable when he was still in a position to resist seriously."

' On page 372 of Eisenhower's " Crusade in Europe " he refers to a conversation which took place between us on the day this diary-entry was written. I feel certain that he did not write down at once the statement which he attributes to me, and I can only assume that, when he came to write it, he did not remember clearly what I had said. According to him, when we stood together on the bank of the Rhine on March 25th, I said to him:—" Thank God, Ike, you stuck by your plan. You were completely right, and I am sorry if my fear of dispersed effort added to your burdens. The German is now licked. It is merely a question of when he chooses to quit.

Thank God, you stuck by your guns." When this statement is considered in connection with what I wrote in my diary that evening, it will be clear that I was misquoted. To the best of my memory I congratulated him heartily on his success and said that, as matters had turned out, his policy was now the correct one; that, with the German in his defeated condition, no dangers now existed in a dispersal of effort. I am quite certain that I never said to him, " You were completely right," as I am still convinced that he was " completely wrong." [1]

" Anderson then explained his situation and the rapid progress they had made since they had crossed the Rhine. We then had a light lunch in the garden of the house which had been the colliery manager's. After lunch we went down the Wesel road to Buderlich where a house stands on the bank of the Rhine with a wonderful view across, up to Wesel on one side and down to the bridge of boats farther south which the Americans have established."

" We then got into a tank landing-craft which was plying across the Rhine and crossed over. It was a great thrill setting foot on the far bank. We spent a little time examining the German river-defences and then recrossed the river. In doing so we attempted to work downstream towards the destroyed Wesel bridge, but could not owing to a string of buoys across the river."

" We got back into the car and motored to the main road bridge over the Rhine at Wesel. The bridge had been broken in several places but partly boarded over so that one could scramble about on it. Winston at once started scrambling along it for about forty yards. We found Wesel was still occupied and that considerable sniping was going on inside the town. About two hundred yards lower down, the bridging parties were getting ready to start a new bridge. They had apparently been seen by the Germans as shells began to fall some three hundred yards down

[1] *Notes on My Life*, XVI, 46.

stream. Reports then came in that the Germans were shelling the road behind us; at the same time shells began to fall about a hundred yards upstream of us. We decided it was time to remove the P.M., who was thrilled with the situation and very reluctant to leave! However, he came away more obediently than I had expected."

' I must interrupt the diary here, as I failed to record a picture which is as vivid in my mind as it was on that day. It is that of the U.S. General Simpson, on whose front we were, coming up to Winston and saying, " Prime Minister, there are snipers in front of you; they are shelling both sides of the bridge and now they have started shelling the road behind you. I cannot accept the responsibility for your being here and must ask you to come away." The look on Winston's face was just like that of a small boy being called away from his sand-castles on the beach by his nurse! He put both his arms round one of the twisted girders of the bridge and looked over his shoulder at Simpson with pouting mouth and angry eyes. Thank heaven he came away quietly. It was a sad wrench for him; he was enjoying himself immensely.'

" We then returned home, and after tea I started off for another fly-round in the small plane. This time I flew from Venlo up the Meuse to the junction of the Roer river. Then up the Roer river to just short of Jülich; there I turned north and went over Erkelenz, Gladbach and Krefeld. I wanted to go on via Mors, Rheinberg, Xanten and back, but we ran into dense smoke from the smoke-screens that are being built up over the river and were lost in a few minutes. We turned north-west and after some flying found ourselves over Geldern and then came home."

" This evening after dinner again attended Monty's evening séance with his liaison officers reporting results of their visits round the front. It is a most impressive scene: the modern form of the general and his gallopers and works admirably, but he has a very carefully selected team. Some commanders have objected to this system of his of collecting

information as short-circuiting them. Monty has, however, over-ruled such objections."

" The news of Patton's advance in the south is a clear
indication that the Germans are cracking fast."

" *March 26th. Return to London.* After packing up kit,
left camp at 10.15 a.m. for Neil Ritchie's (12 Corps) H.Q.
On the way up we picked up ' Bimbo ' Dempsey. On
meeting Neil we changed into jeeps and I got in with him.
We drove straight down to Xanten and on to the river on
the Bislich road. Here we found the new Class 40 bridge
which had just been completed and we drove over it and
up into Bislich; there we turned north and drove along
the bank of the Rhine to one of the tank landing-vehicles[1]
(known as ' Buffaloes ') crossing places. On the way we
passed a gang of newly captured prisoners, a weedy-
looking lot. We then got into the ' Buffaloes ' which had
been used in the assault crossing and recrossed the Rhine.
They are wonderful vehicles with tracks on both sides,
swim like a boat and crawl up the far bank with their
tracks."

" It was a strange feeling motoring along the east bank
of the Rhine with old Ritchie and looking back to our
retreat to Dunkirk together. I reminded him of it. I find
it almost impossible to believe, after these six years of
endless heartbreaking struggles, that we are now at last
on the threshold of the end."

" After recrossing the Rhine we motored farther north
to the site of the next bridge, a Class 9, which was also busy
pouring vehicles over on to the far bank. We then had
lunch on the bank of the Rhine just where our front line
had been up to now."

" After lunch we parted with Ritchie and drove back
to Monty's H.Q., then to the aerodrome at Venlo, and by
3 p.m. were airborne and sailing off homewards. At 7 p.m.
landed at Northolt, drove back to flat and revelled in the
first hot bath I had had since leaving. It has been a
wonderful trip and one which gave me a feeling of

realisation that all the last few years' toil and agony were at last producing results beyond my wildest hopes. Winston, I think, enjoyed his trip thoroughly and received a wonderful reception wherever he went."

' It was a relief to get Winston home safely; I knew that he longed to get into all the most exposed positions possible. I honestly believe that he would really have liked to be killed on the front at this moment of success. He had often told me that the way to die is to pass out fighting when your blood is up and you feel nothing.'[1]

.   .   .   .

" *March 27th*. Started C.O.S. work again and had one of our periodic meetings with Sandys and Cherwell to discuss rockets and flying bombs."

" In the afternoon had an interview with Alex's General Gruenther,[2] who had been sent over to prove how impossible it was for him to launch his offensive on April 10th if we took a division away from him. However, situation is now such that one additional division on the Western Front won't make much difference; the Germans are breaking fast and we have sufficient force there now to deal with them without importing any further divisions."

" Lovely spring weather, and wonderful news of success pouring in continuously."

" *March 28th*. This afternoon Archie Wavell came round to my office and remained there about an hour and a half. He was in very good form and looking very well, but worried at the prospects of his meetings with Winston.

---

[1] " He was determined to take every risk he could possibly take and, if possible, endanger his life to the maximum! I rather feel that he considers that a sudden and soldierly death at the front would be a suitable ending to his famous life and would free him from the never-ending worries which loom ahead with our Russian friends and others. Setting aside my natural reluctance to share such a fate, I foresaw endless squabbles in endeavouring to save his life for a few months at least. On the whole, he was fairly amenable and overjoyed when on the Wesel bridge we had some shells falling round and could hear sniping going on within a short distance." To Lady Brookeborough, 28 March, 1945.

[2] Gen. Alfred M. Gruenther, Alexander's chief U.S. staff officer.

From what he told me he is quite prepared to resign if he does not get what he wants, and I should not be surprised if he was eventually driven to take that course."[1]

" I received a copy of Monty's latest order; he is planning a bold drive to the Elbe with most of his armour, and, judging by the general situation, he has every chance of bringing it off."

" *March 29th.* A very long C.O.S. meeting with a series of annoying telegrams. The worst of all was one from Eisenhower direct to Stalin trying to co-ordinate his offensive with the Russians. To start with, he has no business to address Stalin direct, his communications should be through the Combined Chiefs of Staff; secondly, he produced a telegram which was unintelligible; and finally, what was implied in it appeared to be entirely adrift and a change from all that had been previously agreed on."

" At 5.15 p.m. we were sent for by the P.M. to discuss Ike's telegram to Stalin, and our proposed action. . . ."

" *March 30th.* Good Friday. Had a long C.O.S. meeting in order to finish off all the work for the week-end. Matters, however, looked rather ominous owing to Eisenhower's wire to Stalin."

" In the evening slipped off home full of hope of a long week-end at home and away from worries."

For the British, Eisenhower's telegram was one more disappointment and source of disillusion. Having gone to war in defence of Poland and the liberties of Europe at a time when Russia was in league with the aggressor and America concerned only with her own neutrality, they were now, with six years of struggle crowned by victory, forced to witness at the dictate of one of their principal allies the needless subjection of the whole of Eastern Europe to the totalitarian tyranny of the other. On March 28th, four days after Montgomery had crossed the Rhine

[1] The Viceroy had protested at the recent cut on civil supplies for India imposed by the shipping situation but had been overruled by the Cabinet which felt that his fears of famine were exaggerated.

and while strong German forces still barred the Russians' road to Berlin and Vienna, the Western Allies were confronted only by spasmodic resistance from a disintegrating, defeated Army whose mobility had been broken by their overwhelming air power and whose morale by the battle of the Rhineland and Westphalia in which it had lost, since the beginning of the month, 300,000 prisoners. On that day Montgomery's bridgehead was 35 miles wide and 25 miles deep, with twenty divisions and 1500 tanks already across the river, while the Americans had taken Frankfurt and Mannheim and Hodges's and Patton's armour was sweeping north-eastwards to encircle the Ruhr and join Simpson's Ninth Army in the rear of Model's routed forces. The green lights, it seemed, were clear for the long-awaited drive across the Hanover plains to the Elbe and Berlin—the goal of every Allied soldier since the start of the Western counter-attack at Alamein two and a half years before. " My intention," Montgomery had telegraphed the C.I.G.S., " is to drive hard for the line of the Elbe. . . . I have ordered Ninth and Second Armies to move armoured and mobile forces at once and to get through to the Elbe with utmost speed and drive. The situation looks good and events should begin to move rapidly in a few days. . . . My tactical H.Q. moves will be Wesel-Munster-Herford-Hanover—thence via the *autobahn* to Berlin, I hope."[1]

Yet on that very day, without reference to the Combined Chiefs of Staff or a word to the Commander-in-Chief of the British forces which still constituted nearly a third of his army, Eisenhower despatched a telegram to Stalin informing him that he proposed, after encircling the Ruhr, to concentrate in Central Germany for an advance, on an Erfurt-Leipzig axis, towards the Upper Elbe, there to await the arrival of the Russians. His object, he explained, was to cut Germany in half, separate its northern defenders from its southern and thereafter concentrate his main forces against the supposed " National Redoubt " in the Austrian Alps, in which, it was rumoured, Hitler and the Nazi fanatics intended to hold out until new

[1] Montgomery to C.I.G.S., 27 March, 1945. Lord Alanbrooke, *Personal Files.*

secret weapons or a split in the Grand Alliance came to their aid.

This unexpected message, of which copies were sent to London and Washington, received a cordial reception from the lord of the Kremlin, who had been perturbed by his Allies' sudden triumph and feared that the collapse of the Germans in the West would enable the British and Americans to reach Berlin while his own forces were still held up on the Oder.[1] He at once cabled back his approval of the Supreme Commander's intention to ignore Berlin, which he declared, had " lost its former strategic importance " and towards which, he assured him, the Soviet High Command now planned to allocate only secondary forces and then not till the middle of May. At the time of Eisenhower's intervention in the international scene, the relations between Moscow and London had been strained almost to breaking point by the Kremlin's bad faith over the Polish elections and by the arrogance with which it was imposing its rule on the nations of Eastern Europe, while even Washington's faith in Russian liberalism had been shaken by the treachery with which the Polish patriot leaders had just been tricked and kidnapped and the accusations of bad faith which Stalin was levelling against his erstwhile companions of Yalta over the German peace overtures in Italy.

Of all this, however, the Supreme Commander was unaware. To him, as he put it in his Memoirs, " in his generous instincts, in his love of laughter, in his devotion to a comrade and in his healthy, direct outlook on the affairs of workaday life," the Russian " seemed to bear a marked similarity to . . . the average American," and he apparently assumed that the rulers of Russia were equally guileless. But the British war leaders— the Chiefs of Staff for military reasons and the Prime Minister for political ones—viewed his abandonment of the direct drive on Berlin as yet another sacrifice, on the altar of American

[1] Churchill saw this clearly. " There is very little doubt in my mind," he wrote to Roosevelt on April 5th, " that the Soviet leaders . . . are surprised and disconcerted at the rapid advance of the Allied armies in the West and the almost total defeat of the enemy on our front, especially as they say they are themselves in no position to deliver a decisive attack before the middle of May." *Churchill* VI, 446.

military prestige of sound strategy, of Britain's war aims. These included the early liberation of Holland, the occupation of the North German naval ports and the freeing of Denmark.

For Brooke and his colleagues did not believe the Germans could maintain any serious resistance in the Austrian Alps and saw in Eisenhower's plan to exchange a concentrated British-American thrust across the Hanover plains to Berlin for an all-American advance in Central and Southern Germany the same danger of logistical dispersal which had dissipated the Allies' resources after their break-through in August and thrown away the opportunities presented by Montgomery's earlier victory. Apart from this they regarded Eisenhower's direct approach to Stalin as a usurpation of their authority. The Prime Minister, who attached much less importance to the strategic defects of the Supreme Commander's plan than his military advisers, was much more concerned at Eisenhower's readiness to minimize the importance of the German capital and to leave its capture to the Russians, who would then, as the captors of both Berlin and Vienna, appear as the real victors in the war and the sole " liberators " of Central Europe. " I deem it," he wrote to Eisenhower, " highly important that we should shake hands with the Russians as far east as possible."[1]

. . . .

It was this problem that faced Britain's war leaders when on the evening of Good Friday, with the war against Germany virtually won, Brooke set off for Hampshire for what he had hoped would be " a long week-end at home and away from worries ". He and his colleague, the First Sea Lord, had arranged to spend the Saturday salmon fishing on the Avon at the Mountbattens' home, Broadlands. But when he got back from what he described as " a windy day and unfortunately no fish up but for all that a very pleasant day in the country ", it was, " to find a message that the P.M. wanted a Chiefs of Staff meeting at Chequers next morning, Easter Sunday, at 11.30 a.m."

[1] Prime Minister to Gen. Eisenhower, 2 April, 1945.

" *April 1st.* Left home at 10.15 a.m. for Chequers. We sat in conference with P.M. from 11.30 to 1.30 p.m. checking a wire he had drafted to the President. We also discussed his wire to Ike, Ike's reply to him, and Ike's official reply to the Combined Chiefs of Staff. Now that Ike has explained his plans it is quite clear that there is no very great change, except for the fact that he directs his main axis of advance on Leipzig instead of Berlin. He also transfers the Ninth U.S. Army back to Bradley as soon as the Ruhr is surrounded and delays further advance whilst sweeping up this place. Most of the changes are due to national aspirations and to ensure that the U.S. effort will not be lost under British command. It is all a pity and straightforward strategy is being affected by the nationalistic outlook of allies. This is one of the handicaps of operating with allies. But, as Winston says, ' there is only one thing worse than fighting with allies, and that is fighting without them! ' "

" We then had lunch at Chequers, party consisting of P.M., Winant, Cherwell, Sandys and wife, Brendan Bracken, Sarah and three Chiefs of Staff. After lunch we had to go on till 5 p.m. drafting a reply to the American Chiefs' rather rude message. Finally returned home at 6.30 p.m."

In his reply to the Prime Minister the Supreme Commander had pointed out that, in making his main thrust towards Leipzig with an all-American Army under Bradley, he had no intention of neglecting the capture of Kiel and the North German ports which would be left to Montgomery whom, after he reached the Elbe, he would, if necessary, reinforce for that purpose. For the moment, he had explained, he was withdrawing the American Ninth Army from the latter's command to protect the northern flank of Bradley's advance towards Erfurt and Leipzig, but the British Commander-in-Chief would still be free to drive with the Second Army towards the Lower Elbe while the Canadians cleared up Holland and the Dutch coastline. With this the Prime Minister and British Chiefs of Staff had had to be content, for Marshall and his colleagues were adamant in their refusal to interfere with Eisenhower's discretion to dispose of his victorious forces as he chose and the President, now failing fast, was far too ill to respond to his old friend's repeated admonitions of the folly of allowing the Russians to overrun more of Europe than necessary.

There was a sequel, however, two days later when, after a quiet Easter Monday " putting in bookplates and pruning roses ", the C.I.G.S. returned to London.

> " *April 3rd.* Tedder attended our C.O.S. meeting and tried to explain that Ike was forced to take immediate action with Stalin, as Monty had issued a Directive that Ike did not agree with! I said that I was astonished Ike found it necessary to call on Stalin in order to control Monty. Furthermore, I could not accept this excuse, as the boundaries of 21 Army Group and Ninth U.S. Army still remained the same in Ike's Order as in Monty's, the only difference being the transfer of the Ninth Army from Monty to Bradley. Surely Stalin's help need not be called in for such a transfer! "

None the less, when a few days later the Prime Minister visited his wrath at Eisenhower's approach to Stalin on his unfortunate British Deputy, Brooke defended Tedder.

> " *April 12th.* We had to consider this morning at the C.O.S. meeting one of Winston's Minutes based on a complete misappreciation of the existing organization. It went back to Ike's direct approach to Stalin; he abused Tedder for having allowed him to do so without referring to us, forgetting that he himself had entirely undermined Tedder's position by continually communicating direct with Ike and cutting Tedder out. . . ."

Meanwhile a stream of telegrams had arrived from Montgomery who, at the very moment that he was setting his victorious columns towards the Elbe crossings and Berlin, found that his chief at S.H.A.E.F. was about to take the American part of his force from him and direct the Allied advance, not on the German capital but in the direction of Leipzig, a hundred miles to the south. " I consider we are about to make a terrible mistake," he wired the C.I.G.S. " The great point now is speed of action, so that we can finish off German war in shortest possible time. . . . S.H.A.E.F. never seems to understand that, if you suddenly make big changes in Army Groups, you create confusion in signal arrangements and administration generally. My communications have been built up on assumption that Ninth Army would remain in 21 Army Group until we had cleared Northern Germany and this was declared intention of Eisenhower. I have my main H.Q. moving this week to a site which will be well inside 12 Army Group. It seems doctrine that public opinion wins wars is coming to the fore again."

To this the C.I.G.S. had replied, in a telegram, on April 3rd.

" Eisenhower's plan covering phase of operations to which you refer is now subject of discussion between British and U.S. Chiefs of Staff. It seems likely that Eisenhower will have to be given a fairly free hand provided he keeps to the broad strategy hitherto agreed by the Combined Chiefs of Staff.

". . . Your point about command of Ninth U.S. Army had already been taken by British Chiefs of Staff who informed U.S. Chiefs of Staff that they were not happy about the proposed change which had become apparent from Eisenhower's own telegrams to London. We have done our best, but I doubt whether Combined Chiefs of Staff will feel able to forbid Eisenhower to make the change if he is set on it.

" I fully sympathize with your feelings and appreciate the difficulties in which such a change would place you. Nevertheless, . . . I feel that, as your views are already known to Eisenhower, you should take no further action."

For whatever the immediate tactical results and the ultimate political consequences of Eisenhower's change of command and axis of advance, to Brooke, the global strategist, the war in Europe was over. So far as the defeat of Germany was concerned, it mattered comparatively little what S.H.A.E.F. and its Supreme Commander now did, for, for all practical purposes Germany was defeated. Montgomery's forces were already on the Wesel even before Ninth Army reverted to Bradley's Command on April 4th, while the Ruhr, with the German Commander-in-Chief in the West and more than a quarter of a million troops, was by now surrounded; and, with a two-hundred-mile gap in the enemy's defences, no confusion of plans and purposes could prevent Eisenhower's highly mechanized armies from reaching the Elbe in a few days. If the American Chiefs of Staff and Supreme Commander chose to halt there along the demarcation lines of the future inter-Allied Zones of Occupation agreed at Quebec and leave it to the Russians to take Berlin and finish the war in Eastern Germany, nothing that Montgomery, the Prime Minister or the British Chiefs of Staff might say could prevent them.

It is this that gives to Brooke's diary for the rest of April a certain air of detachment and even unreality as of a man continuing to row after he was aware that the race had been won. The tragedy of the fighting in Germany—of ambushed and desperate stands, of pockets of fanatic resistance in wood and ruined town—continued; in the middle of the month, less than three weeks from the end of the war, a telegram from Alexander brought Brooke the sad news that his grand-nephew, the son of the head of his family, had fallen in action in Italy. But for the C.I.G.S. the urgency had gone out of the Western war; there was so little he could any longer do about it. When on April 5th he called at Edwards's bookshop in Marylebone High Street to look at a copy of Phillips's monograph on Ducks and on arrival was greeted by a telephone call to say that the Prime Minister had suddenly summoned the Chiefs of Staff to meet him at 3 o'clock, he remained looking at the book till 3.10 p.m., then drove to the Annexe and reached it at 3.15 p.m. with five minutes to spare before the Prime Minister arrived. " I felt," he wrote, " like Drake going on with his game of bowls when the Armada had been sighted! "[1]

On the evening of April 10th Brooke ended his diary entry,

> " The war has started another of its rather more sticky periods. We are not making very rapid progress just at present. The war looks like dragging on unless Stalin kicks off again, which I have every reason to believe he will before long! "

Next day the armoured vanguard of the American Ninth Army reached the Elbe at Magdeburg and secured a bridgehead over the river. But though his troops were now only fifty miles from Berlin and the Russians were still stationary nearly a hundred miles away on the Oder and Neisse, Eisenhower would permit no further advance. When told that his troops were restless and wanted to keep going till they entered the German capital, he replied that " it was much more important militarily to divide the Germans and to prevent them continuing to fight in Denmark and Norway or in the Southern Redoubt " and that " the taking of Berlin would be a mere show ".[2] " The essence of my plan," he informed the Combined Chiefs of Staff, " is to stop on the Elbe and clean up my flanks. . . . While it is true that we have seized a small bridgehead over the Elbe, it must be remembered that only our spearheads are up to the river and our centre of gravity is well back of there."

---

[1] *Diary*, 5 April, 1944. " He wanted us to discuss his reply to Stalin's last wire in which he accuses us of faking up a surrender of Kesselring's forces on the Western Front without telling him about it! He has accused the Americans of this also. To have their glorious victories belittled in this way suits them ill, but to be accused of cheating hits them on the raw. In his letter he " (Stalin) " certainly draws the allies together, if he does nothing else. We were kept for one-and-a-half hours and nearly dragged on to the subsequent Cabinet."

[2] *Butcher*, 669.

On the day that the Americans reached the river Roosevelt died at Warm Springs. His last message to Churchill, sent that morning, contained the words—the very epitome of the hopes he had nursed for a united world—" I would minimize the general Soviet problem as much as possible." Two days later, on April 16th, seizing for the second time the opportunity Eisenhower had failed to take, the Russians resumed their attack on the eastern defences of Germany. By the 21st—three days after Field-Marshal Model surrendered the Ruhr—the Red Army reached the outskirts of Berlin. By the 25th the city was surrounded, with Hitler inside it. On the same day Russian advance-guards, fifty miles to the south, met the waiting Americans at Torgau.

. . . .

During the second half of April, while Montgomery's 21 Army Group cleared Northern Germany and Holland and in the closing days of the month struck across the Elbe to capture Hamburg and Lübeck and save Denmark in the nick of time from absorption in the Communist empire, and while Patton's tanks were halted by the Supreme Commander's orders on the Czechoslovak border, the Chiefs of Staff were engaged mainly in preparations for the coming reinforcement of the war in the Far East and with plans for the military occupation and administration of Germany. On the 17th—when they broke their morning meeting to attend the Roosevelt Memorial Service in St. Paul's—and on the 18th, there were consultations with Eisenhower, who had come to London to " discuss action to be taken when we join forces with the Russians prior to our withdrawing into our respective Occupation Areas ". On the 20th Brooke noted:

> " The Russians are now moving properly and it should not be long before we join up with them on the Berlin-Dresden front. I feel that we still have several more weeks in front of us before we finish off the war. Several centres of resistance in Austria, Czechoslovakia, Denmark, Holland

and Norway will have to be worked off and may give considerable trouble. On the other hand, Hitler's suicide might well bring the end on rapidly."

" Anyway," he added, " I am off on leave to-morrow early for a week on the Dee and I pray and hope that I may not be recalled."

For, after close on four years of supreme responsibility and constant attendance, day and night, on his political master, the C.I.G.S. was at the end of his tether. " I find," he had written shortly before to his niece, Lady Brookeborough, " that I am beginning to break up with old age and work and find it hard to keep going. . . . The longing for the end of the war becomes almost unbearable at times." On the evening of the day that Roosevelt died, he broke his usual rule and allowed his wife, who had come up for the evening to help entertain the Secretary for War, to spend the night with him at Westminster Gardens. " P.J.," he wrote,

" asked me to stop on as C.I.G.S. with him if the Conservative Government was returned, as Winston has asked him to come back as Secretary of State. I told him I was quite ready to do so if he wanted me, but that I did not feel that I should remain on after the end of the year which would complete four years, which I considered already too long for a C.I.G.S. tenure of office. He was very kind in things he said as regards my influence with Winston and as to my being one of the few he had seen whom Winston would listen to.

" *April 13th.* You remained over for the day and we motored home together in the evening. A lovely evening, with all the lovely spring blossoms all at their best."

Brooke's week on Deeside brought him few fish but much happiness. " I just long," he had written a year earlier, " for a long, long spell by an excellent river, with no messages, no telephones and no possible contact with the P.M.! "[1]

[1] To Major Nigel Aitken, 18 Jan., 1944.

" *April 21st to 30th.* Flew up to Inverness on the 21st and inspected a brigade of Garrison gunners turned into infantry, finishing up at Cairnton. There I stopped with Blanche Cobbold and the two boys. A whole week's fishing, unfortunately under poor conditions. Caught two fish on my first morning, and no more after that. The only other fish I hooked the line broke! On 29th I flew down from Dyce to Odiham and arrived home for lunch. Two dispatch riders with brown bags filled up the evening with work."

" *April 30th.* The usual early start and back to work again, refreshed by a week away, but with a great disinclination to start work again! A long C.O.S. meeting, and a Cabinet. Alex has made the greatest advance he has yet brought off."[1]

" Dined with Archie Wavell at the Athenaeum. He was in very good form but worried with the reception his proposals were receiving from the P.M."

" *May 1st.* A very long C.O.S. meeting with three difficult subjects:—

   (*a*) Portal's desire to establish Long-Range bombers on island near Formosa.
   (*b*) Man-power paper on the re-deployment for war against Japan.
   (*c*) The transfer of South-West Pacific Area from American control to us.

In the afternoon a Selection Board and a long talk with Secretary of State."

" The crumbling of Germany is going fast. Forces in Italy may surrender to Alex tomorrow. At same time

---

[1] In Italy, despite the fact that the defenders slightly outnumbered the attackers on the ground, the Allies, relying on their immense superiority in the air, had opened their spring offensive on April 9th. In ten days they had broken through the last Apennine defences and reached Bologna on the 21st, and the Po two days later. Here a million Germans were now about to surrender to one of the divisional commanders—now Field-Marshal Alexander—who had served under Brooke at Dunkirk, while in Germany two million more were about to surrender to another—Field-Marshal Montgomery. The British Army had had its revenge.

Bernadotte is carrying on negotiations with Himmler. The end must come soon."

" *May 2nd.* Last night on the midnight news Hitler was reported as dead. After longing for this news for the last six years and wondering whether I should ever be privileged to hear it, when I finally listened to it I remained completely unmoved. Why? I do not know. I fully realised that it was the real full-stop to the many and long chapters of the war, but I think that I have become so war-weary with continual strain that my brain is numbed and incapable of feeling."

" The surrender of the German Army in Italy to Alex, expected at 2 p.m., did not take place, owing to Kesselring stepping in and sacking local commanders. However, Kesselring is prepared to carry on but asks for forty-eight hours more."

" Meanwhile Monty reaches the Baltic, and it is possible that Boche will surrender Northern Forces to him. I doubt whether Germany will last over the week-end."

" Meanwhile in Burma the landings south of Rangoon are going well."

" This afternoon Anders again came to see me, having returned from visiting his Corps of Poles in Italy. He says there are at least one million Poles in Western Europe whom he can (and wishes to) get hold of to swell his forces. He wishes to take part in the occupation of Germany and then has wild hopes of fighting his way home to Poland through the Russians! A pretty desperate problem the Polish Army is going to present us with."

" *May 3rd.* In the middle of the crumbling of Germany suddenly wild rumours appear that Guatemala is going to attack our colony of Honduras! Much discussion at C.O.S. meeting and much time wasted; only force available is Canadian battalion in Jamaica. Colonial Office must be approached and Foreign Office informed, owing to repercussions in America, etc. In the end it turns out to be a bad forest fire in Guatemala which had necessitated employing most of the Army to put out. This had put Honduras's nerves on edge. They saw ghosts everywhere and wasted our time unnecessarily."

" Meanwhile Germany crumbles. The Italian front has surrendered—Monty takes 100,000 prisoners—Hamburg gives in—and the negotiations with Monty look like the rest of North Germany and Denmark giving in! "

" During afternoon Gammell came to see me prior to his going to Moscow. Then Victor Fortune (commanding 51st Div. at St. Valery) back from his time as a prisoner. I had not seen him since 1939."

" *May 4th.* A memorable day in so far as it will probably be one of the last of the second war with Germany. Monty met Keitel this morning who surrendered unconditionally Holland, all North Germany, Schleswig-Holstein, Denmark, Friesian Islands and Heligoland. Keitel then went on to Ike's H.Q. to discuss the surrender of Norway. I had just got back to the flat when we were sent for for a C.O.S. meeting with the P.M. in the Cabinet Room, 10 Downing Street. We found him on the telephone busy telling the King about his conversation with Ike and Monty. He then told us all about it, and he was evidently seriously affected by the fact that the war was to all intents and purposes over as far as Germany was concerned. He thanked us all very nicely and with tears in his eyes for all we had done in the war and all the endless work we had put in ' from El Alamein to where we are now.' He then shook hands with all of us."

" On the 9 p.m. news the announcement was made. To-morrow we should hear the rest. The only part I am not clear about yet is whether Keitel has sufficient authority to stop the forces (some fifty divisions) in Czechoslovakia. If they stop to-morrow then the war is over, as they now form the only large force left."

" *May 5th.* Another flood of telegrams necessitated our

having a Saturday C.O.S. meeting. The telegrams were mainly concerned with Alexander's difficulties with Tito about Trieste, etc. Also masses about the negotiations for surrender. Envoys to come to Monty's H.Q. and to be sent on to Ike, possibilities of final surrender to-day or on Sunday. Difficulty of carrying the Russians along with us, combined with great reluctance on the part of the Germans to surrender to the Russians, of whom they are terrified."

" Monty faced with difficult problem of surrender of Denmark Occupation troops, over a million German soldiers, 400,000 Russian prisoners, two million excess German population in Schleswig-Holstein, etc."

" *May 6th*. A quiet Sunday; during the afternoon went over to meet Bertie Fisher and to put up hides for nightingale, bullfinch and black-cap nests."

" *May 7th*. Returned early as usual, to find state of uncertainty about the announcement of the surrender of the Germans. Although all documents had been signed, and hostilities were to cease from to-day, the Russians made difficulties, saying that the negotiations should be signed in Berlin and repudiating those documents which their representatives had accepted."

" P.M. had invited Chiefs of Staff with ' Pug ' Ismay and Hollis to lunch at 10 Downing Street to celebrate the culmination of our efforts. It was a disturbed lunch. Winston was expecting a telephone call from the President which only came through after lunch. Meanwhile he received a telegram from Ike stating that it was likely he would have to fly to Berlin for the required Russian final negotiations. This necessitated a call being put through to Ike, which got through during the pudding period! In the intervals Winston discussed the pros and cons of elections in June. We stressed the cons from the military point of view, stating that it could lead only to dispersal of effort which would be better devoted to the war."

" After lunch we went out into the Downing Street

garden to be photographed with Winston. There was no Cabinet meeting, but we were warned for a visit to the Palace for 6.30 p.m. However, this did not materialize, as after the P.M.'s conversation with the President he decided to postpone his announcement till to-morrow afternoon at 3 p.m. The King is also to speak at 9 p.m."

"So this is at last the end of the war! It is hard to realise. I can't feel thrilled; my sensation is one of infinite mental weariness. And yet at the back of it all there is a feeling of only partially-digested wonderful restfulness, a realisation of something I have been endlessly striving for, with hardly any hope of realisation, for months after months."

"*May 8th. V.E. Day.* A day disorganized by victory. A form of disorganization that I can put up with."

"Started with our usual C.O.S. meeting which took most of the morning. Then I had Auchinleck to lunch. He was in a charming mood and we had a most satisfactory talk."

"At 4.10 p.m. left War Office for Buckingham Palace where I was due at 4.30 p.m. A meeting of War Cabinet and Chiefs of Staff with the King. I crossed Whitehall with difficulty, through Horse Guards, battled my way down the Mall and came into an impenetrable crowd outside the Palace. However, with much honking and patience we gradually got through and arrived in good time."

"P.M. was very late and insisted in coming in an open car!"

"At last P.M., Bevin, Woolton, Lyttelton, Morrison, Sinclair and Anderson were gathered, in addition Cunningham, Portal, Ismay and Bridges. The King made a very nice little speech of congratulation, finishing up with a reference to the Chiefs of Staff as that organization of whose real part in securing the success of the war probably only those present in the room had any idea."

" We were then photographed, first all together, and then only the King, P.M., and Chiefs of Staff."

" We then left for the Home Office where a balcony had been prepared on which the P.M., Cabinet and Chiefs of Staff were to come to see the crowd in Whitehall and to be cheered by them. A vast crowd stretching from the War Office to Parliament Square. Then back to War Office to finish off work."

" I had to go and see P.J., and, on coming out, Lady Grigg collared me and brought me out into the passage. She said:—' I watched you getting into your car this morning from the window with a crowd looking at you and none of them realising that beside them was the man who had probably done most to win the war against Germany. It is all wrong that they should not realise it. I do, and lots of people do; tell Lady Brookie from me.' "

" There is no doubt that the public has never understood what the Chiefs of Staff have been doing in the running of this war. On the whole the P.M. has never enlightened them much. It may be inevitable, but I do feel that it is time the country was educated as to how wars are run and strategy controlled. The whole world has now become one large theatre of war, and the Chiefs of Staff represent the Supreme Commander running the war in all its many theatres, regulating the allocation of forces, shipping and munitions, relating plans, resources available, approving or rejecting plans, and issuing the Directives to the various theatres. And most difficult of all, handling the political aspect of the military actions and their co-ordination with our allies."

" It is all far less spectacular than the winning of battles by commanders in the field, and yet, if the Chiefs of Staff make any errors, the commanders in the field will never be in a position to win battles. Their actions are not in the limelight, indeed most of the time they are covered by secrecy. We, therefore, of the C.O.S. were working and working incessantly, shouldering vast responsibilities and incurring great risks without the country ever realising that we were at work."

" It has been a wonderful experience, of never-ending interest. At times the work and the difficulties to be faced have been almost beyond the powers of endurance and I have felt that I could not face a single other day. And yet I would not have missed the last three and a half years of struggle and endeavour for anything on earth."

" I remember the night Winston offered me the job of C.I.G.S. in the large smoking-room at Chequers, and when he went out of the room shortly afterwards I was so overcome that my natural impulse was, when left alone, to kneel and pray God for his assistance in my new task. I have often looked back, during the last three and a half years, to that prayer. I am not a highly religious individual according to many people's outlook. I am, however, convinced that there is a God, all-powerful, looking after the destiny of this world. I had little doubt about this before the war started, but this war has convinced me more than ever of this truth. Again and again during the last six years I have seen His guiding hand guiding and controlling the destiny of this world towards that final and definite destiny which He has ordained."

" The suffering and agony of war must exist gradually to educate us up to the fundamental law of 'loving our neighbour as ourselves'. When that lesson has been learned, then war will cease to exist. We are, however, many centuries from such a state of affairs. Many more wars and much suffering is still required before we finally learn our lesson. Humanity on this world is, however, still young; there are many millions of years to run during which perfection will be attained. For the present we can do no more than go on striving to improve more friendly relations towards those that surround us."

" With these reflections I must leave behind me the German war and now turn my energies, during my few remaining days as C.I.G.S., towards the final defeat of Japan."

" *May 9th.   V.E. 2 Day.* I started my diary well by taking a day off and going home! The day was a national holiday. I found you busy putting up wonderful flagstaffs and decorations, and incidentally cutting your hand badly. We had a very happy and peaceful afternoon together looking after goats, chickens."

Chapter Fourteen

AFTERMATH

His helmet now shall make a hive for bees.

GEORGE PEELE

WITH GERMANY's defeat Brooke's work as a chief designer of the Western Allies' strategy was done. Britain had gone to war in September 1939 to halt the Nazi bid for world dominion, and her objective had been achieved with the total collapse of the German Army and Hitler's suicide in the ruins of the German capital. The war in the Far East, though it had brought America into the fight and so ensured ultimate victory, had been for Britain only a consequential, though agonizing, incident in the long German war, and, with the elimination of Italy and Germany, Japan was now isolated and doomed. The only question was how long she could survive.

The pattern of that Far Eastern War, fought in the immense spaces of the Pacific, had been set, since the American victory of Midway in 1942, by the steadily growing maritime and air power of the United States. It had been directed by the Joint Chiefs of Staff in Washington, in particular, by Admiral King, and, in the South-West Pacific, by General MacArthur, who for three years had exercised a semi-independent American-Australian command from Australia. Except in Burma, where she had fought and won the biggest land-campaign of the war against the Japanese, Britain's part in it had been a comparatively minor one; once the tide of Japanese naval conquest had been halted, her main concern had been to persuade her American ally to allot no greater resources to the Pacific than

460

were compatible with the prior defeat of Germany. Caught in 1941 with her Eastern dominions almost defenceless owing to the committal of all her available resources in Europe, Great Britain had had to wage a humiliating, and at first losing, defensive action in the jungles and swamps of South-East Asia to prevent India from going the way of Malaya and Burma. Now, with the tentacles of Japan's over-stretched power cut by America's swift westward advance across the Pacific, the British, operating from North-East India, had been able to re-conquer Burma whose capital they had liberated five days before the German surrender.

The long drawn-out controversy between Churchill and the British Chiefs of Staff over the Commonwealth's and, in particular, the Royal Navy's role in the Far East had ended as the Chiefs of Staff had always wanted. ' It need never have arisen,' Brooke wrote, ' had Fate allowed us to look into the future and to realise that Japan would collapse as early as she did. Not being able to crystal-gaze, we had to plan a strategy for the British part in the final operation against Japan as soon as the defeat of Germany made it possible to deploy forces in this theatre. Two major alternative strategies were open to us. The first consisted of operations based on India, carried out in the Indian Ocean by South-East Asia Command with the object of liberating Burma, Singapore and possibly Java, Sumatra or Borneo. The second alternative consisted of operations based on Australia, carried out by naval, land and air forces co-operating closely with American and Australian forces in the Pacific. The first of these alternatives was limited to the recapture of British possessions without any direct participation in the final defeat of Japan. I felt that at this stage of the war it was vital that British forces should participate in direct action in the Pacific. I therefore considered that our strategy should aim both at the liberation of Burma by South-East Asia Command based on India and the deployment of new sea, land and air forces to operate with bases in Australia alongside of American forces in the Pacific.'

Brooke's view, repeated in innumerable arguments with the

Prime Minister, had been set out in the Memorandum of March 8th, 1944, with which he and his fellow Chiefs of Staff countered Churchill's attempt to impose on them a purely Indian Ocean strategy.

" Whatever strategy we follow, the major credit for the defeat of Japan is likely to go to the Americans. Their resources and their geographical position must make them the predominant partner in Japan's defeat. The first mortal thrust will be the Pacific thrust, upon which the Americans have already embarked. We should not be excluded from a part in this thrust."[1]

Approved at the Second Quebec Conference in the autumn of 1944, this strategy had now been implemented by the arrival in Australian waters of a British contingent of two of the latest battleships, four fleet-carriers, three cruisers and eleven destroyers[2] and its participation in the early spring of 1945 in operations which the American Navy was carrying out against the Ryukyu Islands preparatory to the invasion of Okinawa— the island on which the attack on the Japanese mainland was to be based. Three more British battleships, five aircraft-carriers and seven cruisers, with two destroyer flotillas and a submarine flotilla were also engaged in the Indian Ocean.

The size of Britain's naval contribution to Admiral Nimitz's forces was dictated by the country's ability to maintain and supply a fleet fifteen thousand miles from home, and for that fleet, built for short hauls in the North Atlantic and Mediterranean, to operate in the huge spaces of the Pacific. Her capacity to carry out the other half of the Chiefs of Staff's Far Eastern strategy and follow up her reconquest of Burma by expelling the Japanese from Malaya and Singapore depended on how quickly she could reinforce her limited land and air forces in South-East Asia from Europe. The difficulties that faced Brooke and his colleagues of the C.O.S. Committee were not so much military as geographical and political. With a

[1] *Ehrman* V, 446.
[2] By the summer of 1945 it was to consist of four battleships, ten aircraft-carriers, sixteen cruisers, forty destroyers and ninety escorts. *Ehrman VI*, 222.

large part of her pre-war Merchant Marine at the bottom of the sea and with the need to feed her population and that of the liberated countries, maintain and re-deploy her overseas forces and import raw materials for her industries, Britain was now faced with the further problem of repatriating the bulk of her four and a half million Service men abroad. For, with the end of the war in Europe, the incompatibility of military requirements with the demands for reconstruction at home became quickly apparent.

To make matters harder Churchill, like a good parliamentarian, had decided to implement an earlier promise and hold an immediate General Election. Parliament had already lasted nearly twice its normal term and, as his Labour colleagues refused to maintain the Coalition beyond the autumn, he felt a new mandate was essential to determine the course of post-war reconstruction. This necessitated, and while the war in the Far East had still to be won, an auction by rival Parties for the suffrages of the people. And as what the British people wanted above everything else was an end to wartime restrictions and shortages and an early demobilization and repatriation of the millions still serving abroad, this posed a conundrum for a C.I.G.S. whose duty it was to deploy and throw the largest possible British striking force against Japan.

Brooke's diary during the early summer of 1945 refers repeatedly to this problem.

" *May 24th*. A long C.O.S. meeting with the Joint Planners in. We were discussing future operations in the Pacific after the capture of Singapore. We want, if possible, to participate with all three Services in the attacks against Japan. It is, however, not easy to make plans as the Americans seem unable to decide between a policy of invasion as opposed to one of encirclement. It also remains to be seen what attitude Winston may take. For the present he is absorbed in his election and for the next few months will be unable to devote much attention to war plans. . . ."

" *June 11th*. Had a difficult time in the C.O.S. meeting owing to P. J. Grigg's statement in the House last week in which he shortened the tour abroad before repatriation. This has raised an outcry from Dickie Mountbatten saying he cannot now stage his offensive on the fixed date owing to the loss of personnel. I am afraid that there is something in what he says and this may be a case of elections affecting operations. Both Portal and Cunningham are inclined to take Dickie's part."

" *June 19th*. The elections continue to have a fatal effect on operations. The Secretary of State's statement in the House reducing service abroad in India from 3 years and 8 months to 3 years and 4 months has had a most pernicious effect on prospects for the recapture of the Malay peninsula. We are now releasing more men than we have shipping to bring home. We therefore lose them from the fighting Forces and disgruntle them by failing to bring them home. . . ."

" *June 20th*. Slim attended our C.O.S. meeting and gave us an outline of the proposed operations for the capture of Malaya. I am still very worried about P. J.'s statement shortening the period of service in South-East Asia Command by four months. I do not see any way out of the muddle this has got us into. Heaven help democracies if they must have elections in wars! "

" *June 21st*. We had a long struggle this morning with the Planners trying to tidy up our policy for the prosecution of the war after the capture of Singapore. It is essential in my mind that we should provide some sort of land force for operations against Japan proper and yet the difficulties produced by the Principal Administrative Officers make it almost impossible. It is exhausting driving people on to make them overcome difficulties. . . ."

" *June 27th*. Long interview with P.J. in which I think we have got him to agree to make a further statement as regards the repatriation of men of 3 years and 4 months being held up owing to transport difficulties."

"*June 28th.* We had both the Principal Administrative Officers and the Planners in our C.O.S. meeting to discuss our plans for operations after Singapore. We are now putting up a paper to the P.M. for discussion next Monday in which we suggest that we should put forward a proposal to the Americans for a small land force of some three to five divisions to participate in the main attack against Japan."

"*July 4th.* We started with our usual C.O.S. meeting and from there went on to a meeting with the P.M. at 12 noon to get him to approve our proposed policy for the war after the capture of Singapore. Winston very tired after all his electioneering tours. He said he had never been so tired physically since the days of his escape during the Boer War.[1] At last we got on to our problem and he confessed that he had not even read the paper which we had prepared for him with such care. I, therefore, proposed that I should run over the suggestions on the map for him. He was delighted with this idea. How much he understood, and really understood, in his exhausted state it is hard to tell. However, I got him to accept the plan in principle, to authorize our sending the paper to the Americans and to pass the telegrams to the Dominion Prime Ministers for their co-operation."

"*July 5th.* Polling Day.[2] Thank Heaven we are getting on with the election, and I hope we shall soon have a Government prepared to govern the country. . . ."

The Japanese war and its incompatibility with the country's desire for a speedy return to peace-time conditions were not Brooke's only worry. Victory over Germany had put an end to the fighting in Europe but not to Britain's responsibilities there. Having been allowed to march into the heart of the

[1] In his *Triumph and Tragedy*, Churchill described himself as being so physically feeble at this time that he had to be carried upstairs in a chair from the Cabinet meetings under the Annexe. *Churchill* VI, 512.

[2] Though the country went to the poll on July 5th, owing to the problem of counting the votes of Service electors the results were not to be known until July 26th.

Continent as a result of America's and Britain's scrupulous adherence to their agreements, the Russians were now making it plain that they not only intended to stay there permanently but, in defiance of those agreements, to deny their Allies any say in the future of the vast areas and national populations—Polish, Balt, Czech, Slav, Croat, Hungarian, Bulgarian, Rumanian, Austrian and German—which they had overrun. Everywhere, under cover of the Red Army, Communist satellite governments were being set up and a ruthless proscription instituted by the massacre and deportation of all elements capable of giving leadership to the helpless peoples now being incorporated into the empire of the Hammer and Sickle. Meanwhile the Communist Yugoslav leader, " Marshal Tito ", marched his partisans into Italy and tried to take possession of the provinces of Venezia Giulia and Istria and the ports of Trieste and Pola. Only the Prime Minister's firmness and Alexander's swift action prevented Britain and America from being presented with a *fait accompli* there.

Yet, though they might protest at their ally's aggression, the British and American leaders were at a hopeless disadvantage. Unlike Stalin and the Communist puppets whom the Red Army had set in the saddle, they could only do what was likely to be endorsed by the electors on whom their power depended and to whom for the past few years they had presented the Russian Communist leaders as champions of democracy. They were prisoners of their own propaganda; to resist the breaches of faith of the Kremlin imperialists by force was out of the question. Those who constituted their own fighting forces were themselves electors, whose one desire now that they had beaten the Nazis was to get home and leave the peoples of Europe to settle their own destinies. Churchill, with his historic sense of Christendom's unity and his far-ranging and prophetic imagination, saw the peril of the European situation; "I moved," he wrote, " amid cheering crowds or sat at a table adorned with congratulations and blessings from every part of the Grand Alliance, with an aching heart and a mind oppressed with forebodings." His former Labour and Liberal colleagues, now aligned against him in electoral battle, and, still more, his American allies failed to share his vision or, if they did so, felt it to be of small importance compared with the immediate practical problem of meeting the electors' demands for peace and disengagement.

The new American President, Truman, a modest man devoted to his former chief's memory, held himself bound to carry out Roosevelt's policy of trusting the Soviet leaders. He was surrounded by advisers, both civil and military, who looked with the utmost suspicion on Churchill's wish to halt the Russians until they had honoured their agreements and while the democracies still possessed the forces in Europe with which to do so.[1] Despite the change in the Soviet attitude since the demarcation lines for the Occupying Armies had been agreed in 1944, Washington now insisted on withdrawing its troops from the Elbe to the west of Leipzig and Erfurt, thus handing over to the Russians a further large slice of Christendom at the very moment when they were extinguishing the last remnants of Polish independence three hundred miles to the east. To the Prime Minister this retreat, which was carried out at the beginning of July, established Soviet tyranny permanently in the centre of Europe, bringing down, as he put it, " an iron curtain between us and everything to the eastward ". But the only American reaction, expressed by the dead President's confidential adviser, Harry Hopkins, was that it was of vital importance that the United States should not be manœuvred into a position where she would be aligned with Great Britain " as a bloc against Russia to implement England's European policy ".[2]

[1] " If the situation is handled firmly before our strength is dispersed, Europe may be saved another blood bath." Prime Minister to President, 12 May, 1945. *Churchill* VI, 484.

[2] *Feis*, 650. " The Prime Minister," the former U.S. Ambassador to Moscow, Joseph Davies, reported to Washington, " is a very great man, but there is no doubt that he is, 'first, last, and all the time', a great Englishman. I could not escape the impression that he was basically more concerned over preserving England's position in Europe than on preserving peace." On this, the Chairman of the American Joint Chiefs of Staff, Admiral Leahy, commented, " This was consistent with our Staff estimate of Churchill's attitude throughout the war." *Idem*, 650-2.

Brooke's diary reflects that summer's troubled European landscape seen by a soldier only indirectly concerned with politics. Five days after VE-Day, after attending the Victory Thanksgiving Service at St. Paul's, he referred to the situation in Venezia Giulia and Istria, where British troops and Yugoslav partisans were uneasily confronting one another while Alexander tried to argue Tito into a more accommodating frame of mind.

" *May 13th*. After the Service Winston had a War Cabinet to discuss the Yugoslav situation. He had received a telegram from Truman full of bellicose views and ready to be rough with Tito. Winston delighted. . . ."

Simultaneously another of Britain's war-time protégés, General de Gaulle, was disturbing the peace in the Levant by seeking to reimpose French suzerainty in Syria and the Lebanon, whose people had been granted independence after the British expulsion of their Vichy rulers in 1941.

" *May 14th*. Fairly full C.O.S. meeting with Tito and Russian troubles, plus de Gaulle brewing up mischief in Syria. Monty came to see me in the afternoon and then a long drawn-out Cabinet . . . . Escaped at 8 p.m. with the Cabinet still in full swing."

" *May 15th*. A C.O.S. meeting full of petty worries. Tito still refuses to withdraw out of Istria. Truman, after adopting a strong attitude towards turning Yugoslavs out of Venezia Giulia last week, now states that he could not dream of asking America to start hostilities unless the Yugoslavs attacked us first. Meanwhile de Gaulle insists on stirring up trouble in Syria by sending French reinforcements there. He also infuriates the Italians by refusing to withdraw his troops from North-West Italy. In fact, the vultures of Europe are now crowding round and quarrelling over bits of the Austro-German-Italian carcass which they are endeavouring to tear off. Meanwhile they gather round a table in San Francisco to discuss how to establish universal peace! "

"*May 16th.* A very rushed C.O.S. meeting between 10.45 and 11.30 a.m. when we went for a meeting with the P.M. and Eisenhower. We were there from 11.30 to 1.30 p.m. and did absolutely nothing! Winston wandered from the number of calories required by German prisoners to Clemmie's experiences in Russia, back to Tito's aspirations in Venezia Giulia, to dash rapidly off into questions of Inter-Allied Control of Germany, back to Clemmie's lunch party in Moscow when all the Moscow ladies had to be provided with dresses by the State, etc., etc."

" A series of good catch words such as:—' When the eagles are silent the parrots begin to jabber.' ' Let the Germans find all the mines they have buried and dig them up. Why should they not? Pigs are used to find olives.' We had to remind him that truffles were what pigs hunted for! We were then told that the children in Russia were taught a creed:—

' I love Lenin,
Lenin was poor, therefore I love poverty.
Lenin went hungry, therefore I can go hungry.
Lenin was often cold, therefore I shall not ask for warmth.'

' Christianity with a tomahawk,' said Winston! "

" *May 23rd.* A long and difficult C.O.S. meeting connected with the Foreign Office proposals for starting the Allied Commission in Germany. Meanwhile Winston insists in retaining that portion of the Russian Zone which we have been able to occupy in our advance, as a bargaining counter with the Russians. Considering that we have already agreed with the Russians as to the Zones of Occupation in Germany, I consider that Winston is fundamentally wrong in using this as a bargaining counter.

" *May 24th.* This evening I went carefully through the Planners' report on the possibility of taking on Russia should trouble arise in our future discussions with her. We were instructed to carry out this investigation. The idea is, of course, fantastic and the chances of success quite impossible. There is no doubt that from now onwards Russia is all-powerful in Europe."

" *May 28th.* Sent for by P.M. for an interview with him, Anthony Eden and Orme Sargent.[1] Evidently Eden wishes the military to step in once the French and Syrians have started a proper row. Winston holds a different view and considers we should stand aside, watch our own interest and let the French and Syrians cut each others' throats. Personally I feel Winston is in this case right. If we step in now, we shall have to shoot up both sides to stop the fight and shall increase our unpopularity with both. There is only one spot to stop the trouble and that is in Paris, by putting it across de Gaulle in no measured terms."

" *May 30th.* Situation in Syria is deteriorating rapidly and will probably result in our having to settle the quarrel at the expense of the friendship of both sides. Meanwhile Paget has wired about situation and Winston convened a Cabinet at 6.30 p.m. Decided to step in and stop the trouble, but first of all to ensure American participation or at any rate approval of our actions."

" *May 31st.* Paget has been ordered to take action to stop any further bloodshed in Syria and Lebanon. Goodness knows where this may end if the Foreign Office does not unite with U.S. State Department and set about de Gaulle in the way he deserves."

" *June 5th.* We were puzzled as to how to deal with the *Jeanne d'Arc* which has started with further reinforcements from Oran for Syria. If she arrives there it can only result in a flare-up of all the trouble we have damped down with such difficulty. In addition de Gaulle is also going mad in North-West Italy, issuing orders to General Doyen to fight sooner than retire."

" *June 11th.* Winston gave a long and very gloomy review of the situation in Europe. The Russians were farther west than they had ever been except once. They

[1] Sir Orme Sargent, Permanent Under-Secretary of State for Foreign Affairs.

were all-powerful in Europe. At any time that it took their fancy they could march across the rest of Europe and drive us back into our island. They had a two-to-one superiority over our forces, and the Americans were returning home. The quicker they went home, the sooner they would be required back here again. He finished up by saying that never in his life had he been more worried by the European situation than he was at present."

Even the home front was not free from violence. " Had to attend a meeting," wrote the harassed C.I.G.S. on July 6th,

" to give details about the Canadian riots in Aldershot during the two last nights. Winston had already called me up at 9 a.m. and been abusive on the telephone. At the meeting he again started being abusive:—' Why could we not keep better order? Had we no British troops to call in to restore order? Where was our military police? Were we going to let these wild Canadians break up the homes of these poor inoffensive shopkeepers? ' etc."

" In most of his suggestions he was drastically wrong. It is only as a very last resort that I should order British troops to rough-handle Canadians who are giving trouble. It would be the very best way of starting real bad troubles. In such cases Canadians must deal with their own nationals. Even British and Red Cap police must be kept out of it. I was very annoyed and I hope he realised it from my answers."

To Brooke all this seemed an infinite weariness; he had done his work and wished to go. When on June 6th he gave one of his celebrated talks on the world situation at the Headquarters of Home Forces, he wrote:

" This is probably the last talk I shall give them before they are all dissolved. I am going back in my mind to all the previous talks I had given them during the difficult days when I never hoped for such a situation as we are in now. But I feel very, very weary."

Three weeks later, on the 29th, he noted in his diary:

" Whilst I was with Winston and we were discussing the necessary changes in senior Army officers I told him that I considered I should go at the end of the year. He said that if, as a result of the election, he got in again he would not hear of my going and that I was quite young(!) and was required to carry out the reorganization of the Army. He said that he considered that Alex should be brought into the War Office in some form or other—Inspector-General or Commander-in-Chief—to assist in the work. I did not argue it out with him but I cannot see how this is to work. The only capacity in which Alex could come in is that of V.C.I.G.S. and he is too senior for that. It would be far better for him to replace me."[1]

About this time a friend passed on to Brooke a rumour that his name was being considered for the Governor-Generalship of Canada. Though he could not believe it—and in view of the part he had so reluctantly had to play in the reorganization of the Canadian Forces it would have been clearly out of the question—he could not repress a wild hope that it might be true. With his happy memories of that land of great lakes and forests and of his days with the Canadians in the First World War, no reward for his services could have given him such satisfaction.

For the rest, it was the hours of bird-watching or helping his wife and children with household tasks that gave Brooke release and happiness in those weeks of weariness and reaction after the end of the German war. " I spent the morning in complete peace," he wrote on the first Saturday after VE-Day, " mending an old rabbit hutch." It was one Sunday afternoon at this time that the great bird photographer, Eric Hosking, then a stranger, called at his house to ask his help in obtaining leave from the local Water Board to put up a hide to photograph a hobby's nest. When permission had been secured Hosking offered him the use of the hide; ' this,' Brooke recalled after-

[1] *Diary,* 29 June, 1945.

wards, ' was the beginning of many happy days bird-photo-graphing with Eric Hosking to whom I owe a great debt.'[1] As always he found renewal in his love of nature. " No good with the trout," he wrote of a May evening's fishing with Rollie Charrington, " but we had dinner out of doors and saw three kingfishers, which was a pleasant change from Whitehall."

.   .   .   .

In July Brooke set out on his travels again—for the seventeenth time in three years. This time it was to Germany. Having failed to persuade the Americans to join in halting the Red tide, the Prime Minister with some difficulty had induced Stalin and President Truman to meet him in Berlin for a last Inter-Allied Conference—" Terminal "—in the hope of either salvaging by international settlement what was left of European independence or of proving to the Americans that the Russians were not to be trusted. The Chiefs of Staff accompanied him to work out a Basic Agreement on Allied shipping priorities with their American colleagues and agree final plans for the *coup de grâce* to Japan and for the Russian entry into the Far Eastern War. Here, in a lakeside villa at Babelsberg and in the royal palace at Potsdam, Brooke spent from July 15th to July 25th, living two doors away from the Prime Minister and next to Mr. Attlee who, though no longer Deputy Prime Minister, attended the Conference at Churchill's invitation as his adviser and possible successor.

" *July 16th. Potsdam.* Started the day with a C.O.S. meeting at which we discussed our Agenda for this after-noon's meeting with the Americans. At breakfast I was told that the P.M. had sent for me last night after I had gone to bed. In the morning he sent for me again before our C.O.S. meeting. This was to tell me that he had heard from Lascelles that the King wanted Alex to replace Athlone as Governor General of Canada. I agree

[1] *Notes on My Life* XVII 6.

that Alex is ideally suited for it and told the P.M. so. Consequently it is pretty well settled that he goes there, and I remain with a few heartburns which I think Kipling's *If* has taught me by now to overcome."

" Monty came to see me at 12.30 and remained till after lunch. At 2.30 we had our first meeting with the Americans. Leahy, Marshall, King and Arnold were all there. An easy meeting with no controversial points."

" After the meeting Marshall and Arnold came to tea, and we then went on to Berlin for a tour round. I was very impressed by the degree of destruction. We went to the Reichstag and from there to the Chancellery. It was possible to imagine the tragedies that had occurred there only some two and a half months ago: Hitler's study in ruins, with his marble top writing-table upside down, the Gestapo H.Q. opposite and the scene of all their last struggles. In one part of the apartments masses of Iron Crosses on the floor and also medal ribbons. On the way up I was handed a German decoration in its box by a Russian private soldier. In fact the whole afternoon seemed like a dream and I found it hard to believe that after all these years I was driving through Berlin. The population did not look too thin but on the whole pathetic and surly. I saw many refugees returning to Berlin, which brought back to me vividly the picture of French refugees rushing back to Lille as we arrived from Brussels."

" *July 17th.* C.O.S. meeting to discuss new papers from the Americans. The first was the reply to our desire to participate in the direct attack on Japan. It was far better than we had hoped for and the offer is accepted in principle. The second was a question of Command in the Pacific. There I foresee more trouble ahead. We want a greater share in the control of the strategy in the Pacific and they are apparently reluctant to provide this share."

" Alexander came to lunch and I had a chance of asking him afterwards how he liked the idea of the Canadian

Governorship. He was delighted with the thought of it, and well he might be."

" We met the Americans at 2.30 p.m. and had a very successful meeting with them. We discussed further questions of our participation in the attack on Japan and decided to accept the plan in principle and to appoint a Corps Commander and Staff as our representatives to discuss plans with MacArthur and Nimitz."

" *July 18th.* A long discussion on Basic Agreements. Leathers had been to the P.M. reporting that our paper did not adequately cover our import programme, and the fat was in the fire! . . ."

" At 2.30 we had a Combined Chiefs of Staff meeting, and one that turned out more successful than I had hoped for. Our first few items were connected with Allied co-operation in the shape of Dutch and French requests to send contingents to the Far East. These points were fairly easily disposed of. We then turned to the question of Command in the Pacific and we were on much thinner ice. We had asked for a quarter share in the control of operations, and the Americans showed every sign of reluctance to afford us such facilities. However, Marshall made a very nice speech, pointing out the difficulties of control in the Pacific and the desirability to simplify the control and avoid delays. They would be prepared to discuss strategy but final decisions must rest with them. If the plan for the invasion of the Tokyo plain did not suit us, we could withhold our forces but they would still carry on. On the whole, I think that the discussion cleared the air a good deal and that the secretaries should now be able to draft out some form of agreement."

" On conclusion of the meeting we were invited by Marshall to visit the 2nd American Armoured Division. The division was formed up on one of the big *autobahns* facing inwards, with all tanks, armoured cars, self-propelled A.A. equipment, and infantry. A most impressive sight. The efficiency of the equipment left a greater mark on one than the physique or turn-out of the men."

" *July 19th*. Leathers attended our C.O.S. meeting. He has been working into the Basic Agreements, which form the foundation of all our transactions with the Americans, certain clauses connected with our import programme. These clauses reduce to a minimum any chances of our ever getting any agreement with the Americans. We finally suggested that the only way to get the matter settled was for him to interview the American General Somervell this afternoon. He agreed to do this. After lunch we had another meeting with the American C.O.S. which went off well and has considerably reduced the points remaining for discussion. . . ."

" *July 20th*. Another troublesome C.O.S. meeting concerning Basic Agreements and the sharing out of Personnel Shipping. It is not easy to reconcile the requirements of Cabinet Ministers and P.M. with the outlook of American Chiefs of Staff. We are expected at times to argue out impossibilities."

" *July 21st*. To Monty's Victory Parade with the 7th Armoured Division in the Charlotten Strasse in Berlin. We arrived opposite the stand where we transferred to trucks to tour round the troops. In leading truck P.M., Anthony Eden, Commander of 7th Armoured Division and myself. Then the Division marched past. I suppose I ought to have been gripped by what this all meant. Here were British troops who had come from Egypt, through North Africa and Italy, to France—a real example of the strategy I had been working for—parading where masses of German forces had goose-stepped in the past. Somehow it left me cold."

" A C.O.S. meeting at which we considered a new bombshell by Americans on Lend-Lease and our suggested Basic Agreement. We then met the American C.O.S. at 3.30 p.m. and were unable to do much owing to this latest paper which they had tabled."

That night, forgetting the logistical conundrums set by the cessation of American Lend-Lease and its effect on the Basic Shipping Agreements, Brooke and his colleague, Portal, flew to a village inn in the American Zone near Oberammergau. Here, rising at 5 a.m., they spent a happy Sunday beside a Bavarian trout stream, though as the river had been recently fished by S.S. guards with hand grenades and later by American G.I.s with worms, they caught little. But they saw " brown-coloured cattle with lovely sounding bells ", roe deer and a stag crossing the stream, and returned to Potsdam, with its Russian guards and depressed population, on Sunday evening greatly refreshed.

Next morning the Conference was resumed.

" *July 23rd.* First of all a C.O.S. meeting at 10.30 with some new amendments by American Chiefs of Staff concerning allotment of captured shipping. Then we went on to a meeting with the American C.O.S. where we squared up most of our outstanding problems and only left over the ' Basic Agreements ', which are dependent on the P.M. fixing up ' Lend-Lease ' and ' Import Programme to U.K.' with the President."

" At 1.30 p.m. we went round to lunch with the P.M. He had seen the American reports of results of the new ' Tube Alloys ' secret explosive which had just been carried out in the States. He had absorbed all the minor American exaggerations and, as a result, was completely carried away. It was now no longer necessary for the Russians to come into the Japanese war; the new explosive alone was sufficient to settle the matter. Furthermore, we now had something in our hands which would redress the balance with the Russians. The secret of this explosive and the power to use it would completely alter the diplomatic equilibrium which was adrift since the defeat of Germany. Now we had a new value which redressed our position (pushing out his chin and scowling);

now we could say, ' If you insist on doing this or that, well. . . . And then where are the Russians!' "

" I tried to crush his over-optimism, based on the result of one experiment, and was asked with contempt what reason I had for minimizing the results of these discoveries. I was trying to dispel his dreams and as usual he did not like it."

' It is interesting to note Winston's reactions and my counter-reactions to the Atomic Bomb news.[1] Winston's appreciation of its value in the future international balance of power was far more accurate than mine. But what was worrying me was that, with his usual enthusiasm for anything new, he was letting himself be carried away by the very first and rather scanty reports of the first atomic explosion. He was already seeing himself capable of eliminating all the Russian centres of industry and population without taking into account any of the connected problems, such as delivery of the bomb, production of bombs, possibility of Russians also possessing such bombs, etc. He had at once painted a wonderful picture of himself as the sole possessor of these bombs and capable of dumping them where he wished, thus all-powerful and capable of dictating to Stalin!'

" During lunch Anthony Eden came in hot from his discussion with Molotov and Byrnes. Delightful as he is, I am afraid that he added to my gloom."

" Spent the afternoon reading up the Minutes of the meetings of the Big Three, and they are very interesting reading. One fact that stands out more clearly than any other is that nothing is ever settled!"

" The day finished with a big dinner by Winston attended by Stalin, Truman, Eden, Molotov, Portal, Ismay, Alexander, Monty, Attlee, Bridges, Zhukov, Antonov, etc.

---

[1] Brooke had long been aware of its possible effects. " I had some nasty moments," he wrote to an old friend that August, " wondering whether the Boche would forestall us with the Atomic Bomb and snatch victory from under our noses." To Major Nigel Aitken, 26 Aug., 1945.

It was a good dinner with the R.A.F. band, rather spoilt by continuous speeches. Truman proposed my health coupled with Antonov. I had to reply and in doing so reminded Stalin of his Yalta toast to ' those men who are always wanted in war and forgotten in peace '. I said that I had studied Antonov's face with care to find whether he was forgotten and was glad to see that he was not. I reminded the politicians and diplomats that even in peace there might be a use for soldiers. And finally proposed the toast to the hope, perhaps a pious hope, that soldiers might not be forgotten in peace! "

" This went down well with Stalin, who replied at once that soldiers would never be forgotten. After dinner we had the menus signed and I went round to ask Stalin for his signature. He turned round, looked at me, smiled very kindly and shook me warmly by the hand before signing. After the band playing all the National Anthems we went off to bed."

" *July 24th*. Plenary meeting at the President's house with him and the P.M. present. I was very interested in this first meeting with Truman after the many we had had with Roosevelt. On the whole, I liked him; not the same personality as his predecessor, but a quick brain, a feeling of honesty, a good business man and a pleasant personality. Last night in one of his quick remarks Stalin had said about him, 'Honesty adorns the man ', and he was not far wrong."

" We went through our final Report and got it all settled up. Leathers and Cherwell had mixed themselves up in the ' Basic Undertaking ' and had as a result made the Americans thoroughly suspicious; consequently the final terms secured by the P.M. were not as favourable as if we had been left to our own devices."

" At 2.30 p.m., we had a meeting with the Russian Chiefs of Staff on a tripartite basis. The meeting was quite cordial. Antonov informed us that the Russians were coming into the war in August. What could we do to hold the Japanese forces to prevent them from concentrating in Manchuria? Marshall and King replied from the American point of view, and I followed on with Cunningham and Portal as regards our own operations."

" Thus finished our Combined Chiefs of Staff meeting in Berlin, where we had never hoped to meet in our wildest dreams of the early stages of the war. And now that we are here I feel too weary and cooked even to get a kick out of it. It all feels flat and empty. I am feeling very, very tired and worn out."

" *July 25th. Return from Potsdam.* The flight back took us three hours and ten minutes, but as the clock went back two hours it left me still with plenty of time to put in some work in the War Office before lunch. I then spent the afternoon working up back papers and getting level with the work here. I find my brain quite exhausted nowadays and have to read each paper two or three times to make any sense out of it."

·   ·   ·   ·   ·   ·   ·   ·

Next day, when the results of the General Election became known, the world in which Brooke had lived and worked for the past five years came to a sudden end. Ever since his return from France in 1940 it had been dominated by one gigantic figure:

" *July 26th.* The Conservative Government has experienced a complete landslide and is out for good and all! If only Winston had followed my advice he would have been in at any rate till the end of the year. Now he is gone, and also P.J. Whom shall I be dealing with in the future? Attlee as P.M. and who as Secretary of State? I feel too old and weary to start off any new experiments."

" It is probably all for the good of England in the long run; any Government in power during the next few years is not likely to last long. But what a ghastly mistake to start elections at this period of the world's history! May God forgive England for it."[1]

"*July 27th.* A day of partings! I had a long interview with the Secretary of State. It was a sad one, and I hate to see him go. We have worked wonderfully together and I have grown to know him well and to appreciate his high qualities. I am very sad at our parting."[2]

"Then at 6.30 p.m. had to go and see Winston at 10 Downing Street with the other Chiefs of Staff. It was a very sad and very moving little meeting at which I found myself unable to say much for fear of breaking down. He was standing the blow wonderfully well."

For when it came to the point, Brooke, who for the past eighteen months had found his daily attendance on Churchill almost intolerable, was overwhelmed with the sense of loss. Only a short while before he had written, " I feel that I can't stick another moment with him and would give almost anything never to see him again."[3] Now, in retrospect, he felt ashamed of the pent-up feelings he had given vent to so often in his diary—' feelings,' he wrote, ' engendered through friction generated from the prolonged contacts of two very tired individuals. Winston had been a very sick man with repeated

---

[1] " Party conflict and party government should not be disparaged. It is in time of peace, and when national safety is not threatened, one of those conditions of a free Parliamentary democracy for which no permanent substitute is known." *Churchill* VI, 509. Brooke's point, however, was that it was not yet " time of peace", and the Japanese war, when the decision to dissolve Parliament was taken, looked like lasting at least another year or eighteen months.

[2] " It would have been hard to find a man with whom I would sooner have worked. The position of a C.I.G.S. in war is a difficult one; he has to serve two masters. In early days I did sense some degree of suspicion on the part of P. J. concerning my activities on the C.O.S. Committee and in my direct contacts with the P.M. However, from the moment that I had gained his confidence and assured him that he would always be kept informed of all my activities in the service of my second master, I received his unstinted help. Gifted with one of the quickest brains I have met, it was an easy task to keep him in the picture even when time was short. The more one saw of him the more one realised his sterling qualities of unflinching straightness." *Notes on My Life*, XVII, 23. A few weeks later, when Sir James Grigg and his wife dined with Brooke, he wrote in his diary, " The more intimately I get to know old P.J., the fonder I become of him. He is one in a thousand, and so is she." *Diary*, 4 Sept., 1945.

[3] *Diary*, 29 March, 1945.

attacks of pneumonia and frequent bouts of temperature; this physical condition together with his mental fatigue accounted for many of the difficulties I had with him, a fact for which I failed to make adequate allowance.' For, now that his long association with his old chief was over, he could see him again in perspective as he had first seen him when it began in 1940— " as the greatest war leader of our times, who guided this country from the very brink of the abyss of destruction to one of the most complete victories ever known in history." And he himself had been placed " in a unique position to assess the magnitude of the task that confronted him, the courage with which he had tackled it and the abounding ability and energy with which he had surmounted all obstacles and difficulties ".

'There are few things that can bind two individuals more closely than to be intimately connected in a vast struggle against overwhelming odds and to emerge on top of all. There were times when I felt I could not stand a single more day, but running through all our difficulties a bond of steel had been formed uniting us. We had been so closely linked in this vast struggle that it would have been impossible for us to go on striving together unless a deep bond of friendship had existed ; had this not been the case there would have been only one alternative, that of parting. No doubt Winston must frequently have felt that he could stand me no longer, and I marvel even now that as a result of some of our differences he did not decide to replace me. I shall always look back on the years I worked with him as some of the most difficult and trying ones in my life. For all that I thank God that I was given an opportunity of working alongside of such a man, and of having my eyes opened to the fact that occasionally such supermen exist on this earth.'

That night Brooke realised that the supreme experience of his career was over and that life would never be the same again. ' The Election,' he wrote, ' was facing me with a double blow.

The loss of these two old friends gave me a desolate and lonely feeling and a disinclination to continue with the struggle.'[1]

. . . .

Little more than a week later, on the first Monday in August, Brooke and his colleagues attended their first Cabinet meeting under the new régime.

" We were asked to deal with the strategic situation. I had to go all round the world, starting with the Occupied Zone. I was asked many questions by Bevan, Miss Wilkinson, etc., all of them mainly concerned with political as opposed to military motives. A wonderful transformation of the Cabinet with a lot of new faces. However, some of the old ones were still there, such as Attlee, Bevin, Stafford Cripps, Morrison and Alexander."

' I remember being very impressed by the efficiency with which Attlee ran his Cabinet. There was not the same touch of genius as with Winston, but there were more business-like methods. We kept to the agenda and he maintained complete order with a somewhat difficult crowd. Our work was quickly and efficiently completed.'

On the day before Brooke gave his strategic Survey to the Labour Government the first atom bomb was dropped by the Americans at Hiroshima. Three days later, on August 9th, the second fell on Nagasaki. The decision to use them had been taken by the President with Churchill's assent, and the British Chiefs of Staff had not been consulted. When a month earlier, before setting out for Potsdam, they had considered a Report of the Joint Intelligence Committee on Japan's ability to carry on the war, it had seemed certain, after the desperate stand by the defenders of Iwo Jima and Okinawa, that a major invasion of the Japanese homeland, preceded by massive conventional bombing, would be necessary before the enemy's resistance could be broken. The initial landing on the southernmost tip of Kyushu island, as planned by the Americans, was to take place in November, and the main one on the Tokyo plain, carried out by twenty-five divisions, in the spring of 1946. Despite their helplessness at sea and in the air, the six or seven million armed defenders of Japan and the Japanese garrisons of the co-prosperity sphere were expected to give a desperate account of themselves, though it had been suggested that there might be some chance of shortening the struggle if a formula for " Unconditional Surrender " could be found that preserved the Mikado's right to reign and the religious basis of Japanese society.[1] Now the whole picture had been transformed in a night.

The sequel to President Truman's momentous decision followed at once.

" *August 10th*. Just before lunch B.B.C. intercepts of Japanese Peace offers were received in the shape of an acceptance of the Potsdam offer. There was, however, one rather obscure clause concerning the prerogatives of the Emperor being retained. P.M. convened a Cabinet for 3 p.m. when the message was examined. Stafford Cripps and Jowitt expressed their legal opinions. Cabinet were unanimous that Americans must assume major share and that, if they were of the opinion that the clause affecting the Emperor was acceptable, we should agree. I had to give a statement of the various measures that would become necessary in order to put the surrender into effect."

" The Chiefs of Staff were liberated from the Cabinet at 4 p.m., and we convened a C.O.S. meeting for 5 p.m. to be attended by the Joint Planners. I told the Planners the general outline of what was required and instructed them to prepare a paper, to be ready by Sunday evening and considered on Monday morning, covering the various actions required. Telegrams to Mountbatten, to Dominions, information for Foreign Office, Dominion Office, etc. One

[1] *Diary*, 10 July, 1945. See also *Idem* 21 June, 1945, when Brooke recorded a visit from the American Director of Military Intelligence who considered that the Japanese defeat could only be achieved by invasion and that encirclement by itself was unlikely to be effective.

of the main points of urgency is that of providing a force for the rapid occupation of Hong Kong. We finished about 6 p.m. I then returned to War Office to deal with urgent papers."

" *August 12th.* Busy dealing with correspondence, telegrams and the Planners' paper. All going well; reply has been sent to Japan and we now await their final acceptance. Meanwhile our plans for the Japanese surrender are progressing. MacArthur as Supreme Commander to work through the Emperor and Fraser to be our representative with him. Force for Hong Kong progressing, also details for a Commonwealth Occupation Force. It is hard to realise that by the end of the coming week the war with Japan may be over."

" *August 15th.* The end of the war for certain! Six very, very long years of continuous struggle, nerve-racking anxieties, dashed hopes, bleak horizons, endless difficulties all finished with! One thing above all others predominates over all other thoughts, namely boundless gratitude to God and to His guiding hand which has brought us where we are."

" In the morning I had to attend the opening of Parliament in the capacity of A.D.C. General to the King. After lunch to Storey's Gate to join P.M., Bevin and Herbert Morrison to proceed to the Palace. The other Chiefs of Staff, ' Pug ' Ismay and Bridges were also there. We were shown in to the King and had a short interview rather similar to the VE-Day one, and subsequently had a photograph taken of the War Cabinet with the King, and one of the King with the Chiefs of Staff."

" *August 19th.* At 1 p.m. motored to Buckingham Palace. Cunningham, Portal and I took our seats in a landau pulled by four bays in the King's procession to St. Paul's. It was an interesting experience to go through, and to look at the crowd instead of being one of them! Subsequently drove back in the procession, which consisted of three landaus, one for the King and Queen, one for Lascelles

and Ladies-in-Waiting, one for us. On arrival at the
Palace the King and Queen sent for us and were, as usual,
kindness itself."

' It had been the King's own idea that the three Chiefs of
Staff should accompany him on his way to and from St. Paul's
Cathedral when he attended the Thanksgiving Service for
Victory. This kind thought was typical of his usual
thoughtfulness.'

"*August 22nd.* A short C.O.S. meeting at which we
decided that Mountbatten must conform to MacArthur's
wishes as regards the dates for the process of surrenders.
Namely, to await the surrenders in Tokyo before attempting surrenders in outlying districts."

With the Japanese war over, there seemed little left to
prevent Brooke's early release. On the 23rd he and his
colleagues, after their morning meeting, held a private discussion
on their possible successors and the dates of their retirement.
But a fortnight later the new Secretary for War, the Rt. Hon.
J. J. Lawson, sent for him and asked him to remain another
year.

"He told me that Attlee had again tackled him about it
and insisted that I should stop on to see them through their
troubles, and if necessary that I should be given a good
leave. It is all very difficult. Lawson was pathetically
insistent on my stopping on and made me feel that I should
be letting him down if I did not. I rather weakly said I
should do my best to help him out, and then came back
to my office and repented it bitterly, as I feel I am cooked
and played out."

For Brooke found it hard to resist Lawson—an ex-coalminer
whose experience of and capacity for military administration
were negligible compared to Grigg's but whose charm, deep
religious conviction and fine character compelled his admiration.
' I had no wish to carry on, but Lawson had put it as a personal
matter and I hated to let him down and it was evident that he

would require a great deal of support.' Yet next day he wrote in his diary:

> " I am still very worried as to whether I really ought to try and knock another six months' work out of myself or not and am very doubtful whether I can stick it out! I should say the odds are against me."

But the Prime Minister reinforced Lawson's request and, though the C.I.G.S. again expressed his wish to be released at the earliest possible moment, it was agreed that he should stay on till the following year.

There was much for him to do. The world was moving into a new age when the scientific discoveries fostered by the war were about to revolutionize all established military and strategic thinking. Many of Brooke's diary-entries that autumn were taken up with the subject.

> " *August 21st.* This afternoon I attended for the first time the new committee which I form part of, with John Anderson as Chairman, to study the future of the atomic bomb. We have got a queer party of scientists, but it promises to be an intensely interesting committee."
>
> " *September 18th.* A long discussion with Professor Ellis on the atomic bomb and atomic energy."
>
> " *September 20th.* Professor Tizard[1] attended our C.O.S. meeting, and I had to try and induce him to carry out another review of the implications of science on strategy in the next few years. He would not take it on but pressed for the formation of a scientific organization under the Committee of Imperial Defence or Defence Ministry to keep scientific development continually under review and to direct research and development to the best advantage of the country. I asked him to submit a paper on his proposals, which he will do. I think he is quite right and that a development of this kind is highly desirable. But we always return to the need to settle the organization at

[1] Sir Henry Tizard, Chairman Advisory Council on Scientific Policy and Defence Research Policy Committee.

the head, namely, to settle on the organization of a Defence Ministry. I doubt, however, whether the present Government would feel sufficiently firmly established to start such drastic changes."

" After lunch attended John Anderson's committee on the atomic bomb. We started by deciding fairly easily on the necessity of starting an experimental plant in this country, but when we went on to discuss what international steps were required to produce the desired security we were on far more dangerous ground. Scientists are unfortunately for the greater part idealists and visionaries. We must realise that by the splitting of the atom the security of this country has been fundamentally undermined. Russia realises this fully and will be very loath to tie her hands to prevent her from taking advantage of a means of obtaining complete control of the Western hemisphere, if not of the whole world. And who can blame her, judging matters on past international standards! "

" *September 26th.* Another long interview with Ellis on the atomic bomb and succeeded in understanding a little more about it."

" *September 27th.* Another of John Anderson's atomic committees; we got a little bit further. I think I succeeded in getting the committee to realise that any international agreement that was not thoroughly efficient was, on the whole, worse than no agreement at all."

" *October 2nd.* To War Office to find Air Vice-Marshal Collier waiting to see me in connection with ' Jumbo ' Wilson's anxiety about our being frozen out of the atomic bomb by our American friends."

" *October 4th.* Started with an Atomic Committee meeting from 10.15 to 11.45. All most unintelligible and connected with details of construction of the experimental factory. Cockcroft[1] was back from U.S.A. and gave his views."

[1] Professor (now Sir John) Cockcroft of Cambridge University, at that time Director Atomic Energy Division.

" *October 9th.* A very long and weary day with Atomic Committee meeting at which we decided on site for the experimental establishment."

While Brooke was helping to lay the foundations of the future Harwell he was also engaged with his colleagues and the Government on the problem of reorganizing the Army's supply services. There is an entry on this subject for October 2nd:

" At 11 a.m. a Cabinet meeting on the amalgamation of the Ministry of Supply and Ministry of Aircraft Production under one new Ministry of Supply. I went into the Cabinet meeting opposed to the new set-up; I argued against it but came out with my convictions altered. I believe we have got more to gain by a Combined Ministry than by Service Ministries and this conclusion is based on the aircraft and Radar supply situations. If aircraft are allotted entirely to the Air Ministry there is no doubt that the Navy, Army and Civil Aviation will suffer. If Radar is split between two Ministries of Supply it will not make the same progress as if handled by one. It was a well-run debate and did much credit to the Labour Cabinet. It was far the best Cabinet debate that I have attended."

The C.I.G.S.'s main concern, however, continued to be the responsibilities of Britain's forces overseas.

" *July 31st.* C.O.S. meeting. We had the Combined Intelligence Committee in and they warned us of the gathering clouds on the northern Greek frontier. Seven Yugoslav divisions close to the frontier, many more behind, seventeen Bulgarian divisions and 350,000 to 400,000 Russians all in Bulgaria. It looks too much like power-politics to be pleasant. Having originally sent troops into Greece to restore law and order internally, we are informed that these forces are required to also defend the frontiers. We are on a slippery slope, with one task leading to another, all requiring more and more forces which we have not got. And at the same time we receive orders to accelerate our demobilization. . . ."

"*August 28th*. This morning I struggled with the C.O.S. trying to get the other two to realise the dangers of the Foreign Office policy in Greece, where they now suggest that we should take on frontier defence as well as our internal task of supporting the Greek Government in maintaining law and order and distributing food."

"*August 30th*. This morning we had representatives from the Dominion Office in whilst we discussed Australia's latest claim to run an Occupation Force quite separate from ours in Japan. We were recommending another attempt to try to get Australia to join in our Commonwealth United Force. They are trying to run out on their own."

"*September 27th*. A long C.O.S. meeting with the Planners in attendance at which we finished the final stage of the composition and organization of command of the Occupation Force for Japan. Australia has at last fallen in with the idea of a Commonwealth Force and unified Imperial control under an Australian commander. Thank Heaven, for if they had been allowed to refuse our last offer of an Australian Command and a Combined Chief of Staff organization on similar lines to the one we have had with the Americans, it would have been the end of all Imperial co-operation."

Two problems at this time, in particular, were causing the C.O.S. concern, especially the C.I.G.S. on whom, as the military member of the Committee, the responsibility for their solution mainly fell. One was the demand by allies whose Far Eastern colonies Britain had helped to liberate for help in suppressing nationalist movements which had sprung up during the Japanese occupation. On October 2nd Brooke recorded that he had been chased all day by the Dutch Ambassador imploring him to send more troops to Java. The British forces there and in Sumatra, who had been entrusted with the task of rounding up the Japanese garrisons and repatriating them to Japan, were now being asked by the Dutch authorities to put down native risings and restore the islands to their pre-war condition. As the only troops available were Indian and the Viceroy was already under heavy fire from Congress for using them to crush national aspirations, this was highly embarrassing. " The Dutch," Brooke wrote on October 9th, " do not realise the strength of the Indonesian movement and rely on us tidying up Java for them. This is also rather the case in French Indo-China." " Java," he noted a week later,

> " has spoilt the day. First we met it at the C.O.S. meeting, then at a meeting with the P.M. at 12.30, and finally at a Defence Committee meeting at 4.15 p.m. We decided that Dickie should send an additional division; also that Van Mook[1] should be instructed by the Dutch that he was to meet the Indonesian quisling."

Brooke was even more gravely embarrassed by the Labour Government's plan for staking Britain's interests in the Middle East on regional pacts within the framework of the United Nations organization. " We were shaken," he wrote on September 3rd, " by Attlee's new Cabinet paper in which apparently the security of the Middle East must rest on the power of the United Nations; we have had enough experience in the League of Nations to be quite clear that, whilst backing this essential and idealistic organization, something more practical is also required." But later that month he had a meeting with the Foreign Secretary, Ernest Bevin—a man he profoundly respected—which led to his being entrusted with a mission to the Middle East to discuss with its rulers a defensive federation or pact for the whole area under which Britain would supply military equipment and material as well as naval, land and air forces with the necessary base organizations, while the Middle East countries would provide additional troops and accommodation, airfields and ports.

This mission was to be carried out as part of a 40,000 mile

[1] Governor-General of the Dutch East Indies.

air-tour which Alanbrooke, as he had become, had arranged to make in the early winter[1] to study at first-hand the situation in all those areas where Britain had post-war or peace-time military commitments. Before setting out he paid a farewell visit to Winston Churchill, calling on him on October 24th before driving to Oxford to receive an Honorary Degree[2] with Eisenhower, Montgomery and his old friend, Winant, the American Ambassador.

" Dashed off to see Winston in his new flat as I felt he might be hurt if I started for Far East without visiting him. I found him very bitter against the Labour Party. He said I was to refer to him if I wanted any help towards a Governorship."

There was another and much harder parting to face before Alanbrooke left. On the evening of October 26th, after finishing his work at the War Office, his diary records,

" Started for home to spend my last evening with you before my departure. How I hate those last hours! Overwhelmed by thoughts that one may not return, wondering whether any of these are rising to the surface, trying to be cheerful and retain usual manners. Inwardly racked by the thought that similar thoughts are going through your brain and tightening your heart-strings as they do

[1] He had been created a baron, taking the title of Lord Alanbrooke of Brookeborough, in October. There is no mention of it in the diary beyond a reference to a discussion with his colleagues about the cost of becoming a baron; " apparently," he wrote, " I can't get out of it under £200 which appals me." Among the honours conferred on him at this time was the Freedom of the City of Belfast, which he and Field-Marshal Alexander received together on October 17th.
[2] The citation for Alanbrooke's D.C.L. ran: " Just as there are forms of life connected with each of the three Elements, so in warfare the Services are three. . . . Each has its Chief of Staff; and over and above these Chiefs is one who sustains, in his solitary eminence, a burden as heavy as Atlas ever bore. The debt we owe to his courage, his knowledge and his guidance is immense. . . . It was to him that we entrusted the safeguarding of our country in its hour of mortal peril and it was he, with his team of Chiefs of Staff in closest sympathy, who worked undismayed, even in the worst of times, to win over those allies, prepare those forces and devise those plans which have enabled us, after five years, to conquer no less than three hostile Powers in a war co-extensive with the globe."

mine. It is agony when two souls closely linked together live through such hours! I hope that our partings of this kind will now come to an end."

.   .   .   .

Next morning, at dawn, the C.I.G.S. was off.

" *October 27th.* With your miraculous efficiency you succeeded in calling us at 5.30 a.m. and dressing and cooking simultaneously! Accompanied by you and Rollie we left Ferney Close about 6.45 a.m. for Hartfordbridge Flats. We started shortly after 7 a.m. Within half an hour we were crossing the French coast at Avranches and looking down on the old Mulberry harbour. It brought back floods of memories of preparations, plans, conferences, anxieties, landing with Winston, etc. From there we headed south before swinging east to Toulouse and crossed the coast near Perpignan. On the way we had a glorious view of the Pyrenees standing out over a blanket of clouds."

" We crossed the toe of Italy just above the Straits of Messina and headed straight for the Bay of Corinth; lovely scenery all the way down the Canal where we were able to see the damage done by the German demolitions prior to their departure. At 3 p.m. we sailed on to the aerodrome east of Athens where we found Morgan, Scobie[1] and two Greek generals to meet us."

" *October 28th. Athens.* A most interesting day in Athens. Started by driving down to Scobie's H.Q. to see his Sunday morning Guard-changing, as the entry of Greece into the war was being celebrated. Streets were crowded, roofs and windows packed. Tremendous cheering for Scobie who is exceptionally popular. Continual cries of ' Scobie, Scobie, Scobie! ' "

" We then went on to the Unknown Soldier's Grave,

[1] General Sir William Morgan, now Supreme Commander, Mediterranean, and Lt.-Gen. Sir Ronald Scobie, G.O.C. British Forces in Greece.

near the Old Palace, for the great celebration of the day. All the Greek Cabinet, Foreign Ambassadors, etc., turned up. Also very picturesque Greek women dressed in national dresses some two hundred years old, Greek body-guard dressed in white stockings and white skirts, bishops and archbishops with crowns on their heads. I would not have missed it for anything."

" I was very much impressed by the progress that the Greek Army had made in the six months which we have been working at it. The men have got a distinct look of being proud of being soldiers. I was also impressed by the young officers; there is however a great deal of dead wood that requires to be cut out."

" *October 29th.* Started the day by accompanying Scobie to his H.Q. where we absorbed all the latest news. From there we went to the Embassy where I had half an hour with the Ambassador and Financial Adviser. The Financial Adviser was very interesting; he considers that monetary troubles are inevitable, entailing a devaluation of currency, but, as these conditions will be more or less universal throughout Europe, they do not constitute the main danger. According to him the real danger lies in the fact that Greece cannot live without UNRRA assistance. Should UNRRA be cut off in two years, as might well be the case, Greece would collapse. We must therefore examine the long-term aspect of the problem. What is Greece going to cost us in treasure and men? Can we afford to meet this liability? Will America take a share? Are the assets to be derived worth the liabilities to be incurred? If not what are the alternatives? It is essential that these questions should be answered."

" From the Embassy we went to the Old Palace to have an interview with the Minister for War and the members of the Army Council. I got the Minister to explain his proposed organization, and then laid special stress on keeping the military members clear of politics. Their position, I pressed, must not be affected by any change of

494

Government. The Army was the servant of the State, and so was the Government; the loyalty of the Army remained always for the State and consequently for the Government selected by the country. I think the remarks went home."

" I then went on to pay my official visit to His Beatitude, the Regent.[1] I was received by a band which played the General Salute and by a guard of honour of those lovely Greek soldiers with white skirts. Morgan, Scobie and I were shown straight into his presence, and spent about half an hour with him. He is a most imposing man to look at and has great charm and, I should say, both courage and ability."

That afternoon Alanbrooke flew from Athens to Egypt.

" We sailed over those lovely little islands leading up to Crete and passed over the east end of the island. We had a wonderful view of the whole island and were able to conjure up what the German airborne attack must have been like."

During the flight he prepared his report on the experiences and impressions of the last two days.

' One of the main difficulties of a trip such as I was now engaged in was to absorb all the information from every port of call. I had spent two days soaking in all the Greek problems and difficulties; just as I was beginning to feel familiar with them my plane had picked me up and, in just over three hours, was transplanting me nearly seven hundred miles to an entirely new set of problems handled by a different set of people. It was clear that unless I disposed of all the data connected with one locality before landing in the next, my mind would be in a state of utter confusion before we had finished even half the trip. I had therefore decided to fly by day and finish off all my notes connected with one locality whilst in the air and before reaching the next. This was fatiguing but worked admirably.'

[1] Archbishop Damaskinos.

" *October 30th. Cairo.* Started at 9 a.m. for Paget's office where I met John Cunningham and had about an hour with him on the future of the Navy in the Middle East. From there to call on Prince Mohammed Ali, uncle of King Farouk. He received us in his slippers as he was just preparing for prayer, and while we were talking came the distant chanting from his private Mosque calling him away. However, he refused to respond and gave us a long discourse on the evils of the world due to the lack of despotic power! "

" We then returned for lunch where I met the Prime Minister, Mohammed Nokrashy Pasha. During lunch we carried out a general conversation, and afterwards I tackled him on the necessity for some form of Confederation of Defence in the Middle East, namely a partnership between all those Powers who had an interest in its defence, each Power providing its quota either of troops, aerodromes, bases, facilities for transit or locations for troops. I pointed out how the world had shrunk owing to mechanization, aviation, wireless, etc.; that war in any one sphere was bound to spread to others; that modern war called for a vast industrial power to back it; that the rapidity with which action could be taken before any declaration of war all rendered it most desirable that some such defensive confederation should be formed. The only reply I could get out of him was that until Egypt obtained complete freedom and the removal of British forces, the defence would be weakened by lack of true bonds of friendship. Once freedom was gained, an alliance could be formed with Great Britain. Egypt would raise three Armoured divisions and two Infantry divisions; she could certainly finance such a force and at the same time raise air and naval forces, etc. I pressed that this was not leading to a concerted defence of the Middle East and that it was courting the individual defeat of each separate State. No arguments were of any avail; he always returned to his theme of independence before anything else."

" After a good hour with him we proceeded to King Farouk's palace. We were kept waiting a little time and finally Sir Ahmed Hassanein Pasha, Chef du Cabinet, came to us and had a long talk. He assured us of the King's loyalty and friendship to the British in spite of the bad treatment he had received from Killearn. He stated that when Rommel was at the gates of Cairo, the late Prime Minister had come wishing to prepare to welcome the Germans and that the King had opposed it himself. (I believe Killearn's account of this episode is just the reverse!) "

" Finally Paget and I were shown into the King's presence. He had evidently been studying records of my career, as he started by referring to my having speared a wolf, to my being reported as being a good shot, to my having children in the Service, etc. When this was over I was able to start in on the same lines as with the Prime Minister. But here I met with a great response. He was in full agreement that such a course was desirable but he foresaw political difficulties. Nevertheless, he would be prepared to co-operate. He is definitely frightened of Russia and considers another war only a matter of a few years. He referred to his desire for the friendliest of relations with us, in spite of the many slights to which he had been subjected by us."

" The interview was most friendly and most promising; if handled right I feel certain we can make a strong ally of him. There are, however, certain essentials. . . . We must start moving soon and not let too much grass grow under our feet."

' In spite of Farouk's undignified end as King of Egypt, I still believe that he was badly handled in the early days. Had he been properly taken in hand in his youth he might have been prevented from descending to the tendencies which overshadowed the latter part of his reign. He was certainly far from being a fool; his intelligence might well have been

directed into better channels and his influence increased
throughout Egypt. He might have used his influence to
counter the anglophobia which resulted in our final departure. Whilst talking to him he said to me, " I have sufficient
intelligence to see that there are now only two Powers left
in Europe, and I am not so foolish as not to know which of
these nations to turn to, in spite of the treatment I have
received at the hands of this nation ".

' As far as Nokrashy was concerned, it was clear from my
conversation with him that there was little hope of making
any headway in a Federation of Defence as long as British
troops remained on Egyptian soil.'

' I should like at this juncture to pay a special tribute to
Paget. He had suffered a bitter disappointment in being
superseded by Monty in command of troops he had trained
for the liberation of France. Although I am certain that our
decision was right, and that the experience and confidence
of Monty made it essential to use him, nevertheless I have
always realised what a desperately bitter pill this must have
been for Paget to swallow. He had put his whole soul into the
training of Home Forces and it must have been heartbreaking for him to hand over the sword he had forged and sharp-
ened to another. As I now visited him in Egypt I had
every reason to admire the way in which he faced his new
task with an enthusiasm that never showed any sign of being
tarnished by the disappointments he had suffered.'

. . . .

Next day, October 31st, the C.I.G.S. flew to Transjordan,
landing at Jericho and motoring to Amman.

" We went straight to the British Resident's House.
After a short talk we went on to the Emir Abdullah Ibn
Hussein's Palace. We were met there by the Guard of
Honour and a band playing ' God Save the King '. We
started with a talk lasting close on an hour with the Emir.
Fear of Russia dominated his views; he could not see

how we could expect more than a few more months of peace before the next war! He was not happy with conditions in Iraq; Russian penetration was apparent in the north. Lebanon and Syria were in an unhappy condition and required strong leadership; the French should be speedily evacuated and British rule established. Egypt suffered from an ulcer, and ulcers should at once be treated by lancing them! American attitude or manners he had little use for. He had supported the British in the past and would go on doing so, but Britain was like a man who kept on divorcing his wife and taking on a new one and in this process found no real happiness. As for Russia, if she came he would fight with his Army till they were all killed. He would not change his religion nor would he work as a slave."

" From all this talk some points were clear. First, he was very frightened of Russia. Secondly, he had aspirations towards ruling part of Syria. Thirdly, an invitation to England to express his views to the P.M. would be very welcome. He left on me the impression of a true friend of this country well worth a little encouragement."

After spending the night of the 31st at Jerusalem and discussing the Palestine question with his old Commander-in-Chief of Dunkirk days, Lord Gort—the High Commissioner—Alanbrooke set off on the morning of November 1st for Iraq.

" Came down to breakfast to find that the Jews had started being troublesome during the night. They had attacked the railway at eighty different spots and had a large-scale attack on Lydda station, with a total of some five or six fatal casualties amongst troops and police. As a result it was decided that it would be inadvisable for us to drive down to Lydda aerodrome through the defiles in the hills; we were therefore to fly in an Anson aircraft to Lydda where we were to pick up the Dakota."

" I wrote out a message for the Foreign Secretary on the result of my meetings in Cairo and then had a walk with

499

Gort in his garden. At noon we left and flew to Lydda. From there we had a very pleasant flight to Baghdad."

Next day, after spending the night at the Embassy, the C.I.G.S. had his official meeting with the rulers of Iraq.

"*November 2nd.* At 10 a.m. I drove off with the ambassador for our meeting with the Prince Regent and Cabinet. We went to the King's palace where we were introduced to the King—a nice little boy of ten, very well brought up but who does not look at all well. He suffers from asthma and apparently was given half an aspirin yesterday which made all his face swell up. Doctors came to the conclusion that he must be allergic to aspirin! "

" We then moved into the conference room. We began by discussing shortages of equipment in the Iraq army and steps we are taking to put this right. I then started in on the theme of a Partnership of Defence or Defensive Confederation and found that it went down very well indeed. The Regent said they would welcome such a plan; the Prime Minister said that the sooner we got down to it the better."

' There was no doubt that the nearer you got to Russia the greater was the desire for some form of co-operation in defence. Both Trans-Jordania and Iraq were all for some such plan; it was only Egypt that was so intent on the removal of Occupation Forces that she refused to look at the advantages to be derived from a federation.'

That afternoon, after a State luncheon with the Regent, Alanbrooke was off again, to visit the oil refinery at Abadan and discuss measures for its security now that the British garrison was being withdrawn from Persia. Leaving at 3.30 p.m. he flew down the Tigris, passing " over those wonderful marshes at the juncture of this river with the Euphrates " and landing after dark. The Chairman and the General Manager of the Anglo-Iranian Oil Company were there and he had a long talk with them that night about the Company's problems.

Next morning at eight he began his tour of the refinery " to get a general idea of the processes involved, the size of the installation and its vulnerability to sabotage or to air attack ". Then he did a three hundred-mile air tour of the port installations and the Company's wells, listened to a lecture by its geological expert, and saw a film on oil production.

By 8.40 next morning he was off to Karachi.

> " *November 4th.* I have changed planes and am now in Winston's old York with a very comfortable cabin all to myself in the tail. It is the machine I flew out to Cairo in when Winston went out by sea."

> " *Later.* We passed over Bahrein, a desolate and sun-baked spot, and cut across the mountainous isthmus just south of the Strait of Hormuz. We then crossed over to the north coast of the Gulf and followed this coast-line for the rest of the way. On reaching the Hingol I got the pilot to do a circle round, as I was nearly drowned at the bar of this river some thirty-four years ago when returning from shooting Sind ibex. We had struck the forerunner of the monsoon and come in for a tremendous sea which nearly swamped us as we came out of the river. It kept us in a state of the worst anxiety throughout the night as we battled with a raging sea in an open boat with three men bailing for their lives to keep our boat from swamping."

> " At 3.15 p.m. we landed at Karachi. I had the joy of recognizing the old Artillery Barracks where I served thirty-four years ago, also my old bungalow and the Mess. Those glances back into one's earlier days always give me great joy. I like lapsing back into the past and recalling my thoughts, interests, ideals and ambitions, and then comparing them with the course of events that Fate decided my life should take."

On the afternoon of November 5th, after completing two thousand miles since leaving Abadan on the previous morning, the C.I.G.S. reached Delhi. He found the Viceroy depressed about the state of India and expecting serious trouble within the next six months. Though Wavell felt that the Army would probably remain loyal—a belief subsequently confirmed by the Commander-in-Chief, General Auchinleck—he repeatedly referred to " the inclination of the Indian to worship the rising sun in preference to the setting sun ". ' As we sat on the terrace outside the Viceroy's House,' Alanbrooke recalled, ' surrounded by Viceregal pomp, I was reminded of my weeks with my brother Victor when he was Military Secretary to Minto. In those days there was a feeling of permanency about British control of India; now the whole atmosphere was entirely changed and one felt that the British days in India were numbered. I could not help wondering what kind of festivities, if any, would take place on these verandas.'

During the four days he spent at Delhi—interspersed by a visit by air to the Punjab and the military training establishments at Lahore where he was much impressed by the keenness and enthusiasm of the young Indian recruits—the C.I.G.S. held a number of discussions with the Viceroy and the Supreme Commander, South-East Asia, and his principal officers about the independence movements in Burma and the Dutch East Indies. It was decided to try to reach a working understanding with the Indonesian leader Sukarno[1] so that, if Imperial forces had to be used, it would be in support of Sukarno's Government against the extremists he was unable to control. For the same reason—the inadvisability of using Indian troops to suppress Asian nationalist movements—it was felt best to avoid all provocation in Burma. As regards the future Alanbrooke put forward proposals for establishing Imperial strategic defence zones similar to the one he had been advocating in the Middle East. He proposed an Indian Zone to include Ceylon, Baluchistan and Burma with links with Persia and Afghanistan; a Far East Zone comprising Singapore, Malaya, Borneo and Hong Kong and linked with French Indo-China and the Dutch East Indies; and an Australian Zone to include New Zealand, New Guinea and the Solomons.

[1] To-day President of Indonesia.

" I leave India," Alanbrooke wrote at the end of his stay

" with feelings of the gravest uncertainty as to the future. What seems certain is that trouble is brewing fast, but what shape this trouble will take is much harder to define. The ultimate fate will depend on the attitude of the Army. For the present there seems no doubt that the Army is entirely uncontaminated, but that does not mean that some form of rot might not set in. If some parts were affected and constituted themselves as the nucleus of the future Indian National Army, how far could the remainder be counted on to restore the situation? Would Indian be prepared to fight Indian under such conditions? What attitude would the police take? All these factors seem ill-defined, but from the slight clarification that I have arrived at I feel very uneasy. I am, however, surprised that Nehru is not taking more active steps to get at the loyalty of the Army, as without its support his plans can have little hope of success."

" The present Indian National Army trials are not doing us much good. The Opposition Press is making the most of them to further its cause and in doing so is not beyond twisting facts to suit itself. We, on the other hand, are remaining dumb lest we should be accused of influencing the trials by offering pre-judged opinion. I doubt whether the Indian Army understands such fine points of law."

During these days in India Alanbrooke was constantly being reminded of his past. Flying over the Ambala-Delhi road he recalled how he had marched the Eagle Troop along it on his way to the Delhi Durbar in 1911. ' I could not help feeling,' he wrote, ' how surprised I would have been if I had been told whilst trotting down the Grand Trunk Road that thirty-two years later I should fly over the same road. I should have laughed, refused to believe it and gone trotting on! ' So, at Government House, Calcutta, where he stopped two nights with the Caseys on his way to Burma, he remembered standing in the reception hall as a very shy subaltern waiting to make his bow to the Viceroy and shivering in his boots. But his chief memories of his eight years in India before the first War were of great happiness—'memories,' he wrote, 'of a life when responsibilities were light and the incentive to get the maximum out of life predominated '.

.   .   .   .

On the morning of November 12th the C.I.G.S. left Calcutta for Rangoon. " Have just passed Chittagong," he wrote, " and turned south along the Arakan coast. I am looking out over a lovely view of jungle-covered Burma mountain ranges with blankets of white clouds interposed between them."

" *Later.* We flew on past Akyab where we did a ring round and had an excellent view of the whole island and were able to picture all the operations. It was fascinating to be able to see at last in its true form the country I had been studying for weeks, months and years on maps. We passed over Ramree island and on to Tangup and saw clearly the road to Prome. Finally we crossed over the jungle-covered hills and dropped down into the valley of the Irrawaddy and by 12.30 p.m. were taxi-ing down the runway of the Rangoon airport."

That night the C.I.G.S. dined with the Governor of Burma,[1] who had returned to the country a month earlier to find, as everywhere else, great changes after three and a half years of Japanese occupation.

" The only troops at his disposal are Indians. Archie Wavell is not looking on with much pleasure at any situation where Indian troops have to be used to suppress Burmese Independence movements. There is an appalling amount of work required to replace Rangoon on its legs. Roads are in a bad state, houses want repairing, new power wanted for lighting, etc., in fact most public services want restoring. Unfortunately the Burmese are born so idle that they are not raising a finger to restore the situation. They

[1] The Rt. Hon. Sir Reginald Dorman-Smith.

won't repair the roads, they won't attend to their sanitation, and they won't grow more than one crop! They have been used to an Indian native coolie population to do all their dirty work and hard work and without them won't function. And yet politically they, of course, have the highest aspirations towards independence. They are going to present us with one more of our many headaches. In fact, the more I travel round the more appalled I become at the problems that face us. Would to God that we had a more enterprising youth at home, once more prepared to accept responsibilities throughout the Empire and to seek them out, instead of shackling themselves to picture houses and other comforts of civilization."

At Mandalay, where he climbed a thousand steps in the midday sun to visit the pagodas and called on the Head Lama, Alanbrooke met the same story. He left for Hong Kong on the 15th, feeling that the problem of governing Burma was far greater than was realised.

At Hong Kong where he spent two nights the situation seemed much more promising. " Most of the Chinese labour employed by us before the war has come back again, some of them having marched a hundred miles to return here," he wrote in his diary for the 16th. " The main impression that I have gathered is that the Chinese in Hong Kong do not appear to resent our return and that it should not take long to restore normal life here." Even the Japanese civilian prisoners seemed content; when the C.I.G.S. visited them in their camp " they all bowed in correct fashion as we motored past in the old pre-war Governor's car driven by the old pre-war chauffeur, both of which were found intact! "

Yet haunting Alanbrooke's mind all the time he toured the island, attended conferences and inspected Service establishments and guards of honour, was the memory of the day four years before.

" when the Secretary of State for War came to collect me in the middle of lunch at the ' Rag ' to go off to see the

Colonial Secretary who was wanting to instruct the Governor to surrender before having put up much resistance; he was obsessed with the thought that the Japanese would put the whole garrison to the sword. We had to convince him that the moment had not yet arrived. The memory of those awful days was vividly brought back by seeing the scene of the disaster."

On November 17th, after flying over Formosa, the C.I.G.S. stopped a night at Okinawa, which the Americans had captured after fierce fighting that summer—" a desperate scene of desolation " that reminded him of the Somme in the first War. What impressed him most there was the vast amount of work put in by the Americans.

"Everywhere bulldozers had been at work. The main road could take four cars abreast easily, twenty-two aerodromes had been built, a quarter of a million men were at work on the island and all the small bays were crammed with shipping. Okinawa was truly a wonderful sight; hill-tops had been removed and pushed into valleys, one trunk arterial road ran the whole length of the island with excellent side-roads distributed like ribs along its length. The island had become one vast aerodrome fringed with small ports and harbours in the various bays."

" The sight of all this work reminded me of a story I had heard whilst in Burma. Some Americans asked some of the captured Japanese who they considered were the best jungle fighters. The Japanese replied the Australians; when pressed as to who came next they said the Indians, followed by the British. The Americans, somewhat hurt by these replies, asked what about the Americans as jungle fighters. Whereupon the Japanese replied:—' Oh! the Americans! They are not jungle fighters, they remove the jungle first! ' "

On the 18th the C.I.G.S. reached the farthest point of his

journey, Japan. Leaving Okinawa before it was light his aircraft crossed the Japanese coast near Hiroshima that morning.

" Now-we are approaching the Tokyo plain and the snow-covered mountains are looking glorious as they show up clear cut against a blue sky. Fujiyama is just coming into sight."

" *Later*. Shortly after writing the above we passed close to Fujiyama and level with the belt of clouds round its middle. The snow was shining in the sun and stood outlined sharply against the blue sky. Below the cloud-belt could be seen the base, free from snow and in the shadow of the clouds, making a wonderful contrast with the vivid white of the summit."

" We were due to arrive at 11 a.m. sharp as MacArthur was coming to meet me. We were, however, about fifteen minutes late owing to head winds. As we landed MacArthur came forward and I had my first meeting with him. He lived well up to all my expectations and gives one at once the feeling of a big man."

" We drove off together in his car and went for miles through Yokohama and Tokyo; our drive must have taken us well over the hour. Everywhere the same desolation; it must be seen to be believed. The bulk of both these towns consisted of wooden houses, and they have been entirely consumed. All that there is to be seen are the corrugated shacks put up by the inhabitants."

" I had a long and interesting talk with MacArthur. According to him the abject surrender of the Japanese was almost repulsive but they gave no trouble and ran their own disarming and demobilization quite exceptionally efficiently. Food they had till about February; after that food would have to be imported. Trains were running efficiently but coastal sea traffic was badly disrupted. Casualties in Tokyo and Yokohama probably about 80,000 killed and two and a half times as many casualties."

" He became most interesting about the Russians. According to him they were at present interested in converting Manchuria, and Korea if possible, into Communist States with some form of allegiance to the Soviet Union, as has already been done to Mongolia. He felt certain that they would also attempt to convert Japan into a similar subject country so as to be able to use Japanese man-power at a later date for operations in the Pacific."

" He considered the Russians a greater menace than the Nazis had ever been—complete barbarians—as exemplified by one commander who had issued orders that every woman, between the ages of 16 and 60, was to be raped twice by Russian soldiery as an example of the superiority of the Russian race. MacArthur considers that they should be met by force, if necessary, and not by conciliatory methods which would only be interpreted as weakness by the Russians. He is not at all happy about the situation; his own force is only about one-third of its original strength, whilst there is no diminution in the Russian strength."

" Talking about the Japanese he told me that what surprised him was that they had only put about 40% of industrial effort into the war compared to the effort put in by British and Americans."

" We finished up our drive at the American Embassy, where MacArthur was living. Then I met Mrs. MacArthur whom I sat next to at lunch, quite easy to talk to as she ripples on the whole time. MacArthur rather silent at lunch and, according to Gairdner,[1] never has people to lunch nor lunches out if he can help it. Apparently a very great compliment his coming to meet me at the aerodrome, as he had not been known to do so before."

" In the evening we went to dine with General Eichelberger who commands the 8th Army and is eventually to command the whole of the Forces in Japan. He and his staff were quite charming, and before leaving he presented

[1] Gen. Sir Charles Gairdner, British Liaison Officer to MacArthur.

me with two Japanese swords, one Japanese pistol and a beautiful pair of Japanese field-glasses."

' I had kept a very careful watch on MacArthur's strategy in the Pacific, and the more I saw of it the more impressed had I become. The masterly way in which he had jumped from point to point leaving masses of Japs to decay behind him had filled me with admiration, whereas any ordinary general might have eaten up penny packets of Japs till he had such indigestion that he could proceed no farther. The points he selected for his jumps were always those best suited for the efficient use of the three Services. In addition I had heard a great deal about MacArthur from our excellent Liaison Officers, Lumsden and Gairdner.'

' From everything I saw of him that day he confirmed the admiration I already had. A very striking personality, with perhaps a tinge of the actor, but any failing in this direction was certainly not offensive. On the contrary, he assumed the attitude of the " grand seigneur " and did so with great dignity.'

Next day Alanbrooke flew to Korea, once more passing over Hiroshima.

"We dropped down low and circled round several times and were able to have an excellent view of the effects of the bomb. I was very much struck by its local effect. There is a definite central area where all wooden huts have disappeared, but on the outskirts the houses undamaged and the few large concrete buildings appeared very little damaged. The impression I had was that the effect of such a bomb on London would have been to set fire to wooden roofs and demolish the poorer houses. I do not believe that the well-built steel and concrete houses would have suffered much. No doubt, as the bomb is further developed the results will be infinitely greater, but for the present my impression is that the effect has been exaggerated."

Of Korea, where he spent the night of the 19th and was entertained by General Hodges of the U.S. XXIV Corps, the C.I.G.S. carried away an impression of

> " old students of Confucianism in their white gowns and black witches' top-hats smoking long pipes; women dressed with much more colour than in Japan; small brown bulls pulling carts; ordinary electric trams crammed with humanity; small girls in black evidently returning from some convent school; native boys dressed as Boy Scouts; fine wide roads, modern large imposing buildings mixed with small Korean wooden houses, untidy policemen, and a mass of humanity of all sizes and shapes."

Otherwise he could see little to distinguish Koreans from the Japanese.

Already, General Hodges told him, an iron curtain had fallen along the frontiers of North and South Korea; relations with the U.S.S.R. were proving no easier in Asia than in Europe. " There is an impenetrable wall on the 36th parallel behind which the Russians are, and nothing is known of them." When, two days later, after a visit to General Kreuger, Commander of the 6th U.S. Army at Kioto—" a most attractive person, a disciplinarian and first-class fighting general, full of good common sense "—the C.I.G.S. returned to Tokyo, he had the impressions gathered in Korea confirmed in a farewell interview with MacArthur.

> " He began by asking me my impressions of my visit to Korea. I told him that I had been interested to find there the same lack of co-operation on the part of the Russians in this Eastern Theatre as in the Western. This started him off on the threat of Russia to the future peace of the world. In his opinion we should be prepared for trouble and assemble at least a thousand atomic bombs in England and in the States. We must prepare safe aerodromes by tunnelling into the sides of mountains so that we shall be able to go on operating from England even when attacked. In the Pacific, with the new super-bomber

now on the slips in America, we should be able to attack Russia from America after refuelling at Okinawa. With such a combined attack from east and west Russia could be brought to her senses if she started giving trouble. But we must prepare at once."

" I pointed out that as long as we had armies of occupation in Europe we should have a land front with Russia and that, after the gradual reduction of these forces which is at present taking place, we should not be in a position to hold the Russians back, and that with the Russians on the Channel we should be in a very difficult position. He agreed that this would present a very serious problem, but I do not think that he fully appreciates the situation in Europe."

" We then discussed China and he gave me a long message he had just received from Wedemeyer. The gist of it was that Chiang Kai-shek was being hindered by American assistance and influence. The aspirations of China were to shake loose from foreign clutches and this made it desirable to withdraw American help; he even went so far as to suggest that China's future should be placed under the trusteeship of the United Nations. As regards Northern China he had little hope that Chiang Kai-shek would be able to restore his power. He felt that Russia, making use of Chinese Communists, would endeavour, and would probably succeed, in organizing Northern China on the basis of some form or other of Soviet Republic such as Mongolia. MacArthur did not agree with Wedemeyer's suggestion of a trusteeship."

" He then informed me that China had now said that she was too heavily engaged on the mainland to take any part in the occupation of Japan. Russia had also said that she could not join in the occupation unless we established a Control Commission in Japan to consist of Russia, America and Britain but not China. This is a new move on the part of Russia. MacArthur had not yet heard from America as to what the next steps would be, but he considered it would probably result in a temporary stalemate."

Alanbrooke then raised the question of the Commonwealth Occupation Force which he was anxious to see established in Japan and which was the purpose of his visit, and to which, according to Australian sources, MacArthur was objecting.

" I asked him what his views were. He said that Australia had put forward a plan which he was not in agreement with, as it was unsound. They had suggested a Commonwealth Force including all three Services as one entity. This would not work; he already had three Service representatives working under him, and a small Supreme Commander in the middle would upset the whole organization. He said he was delighted to have Commonwealth Forces but they must fit into his organization, namely Land forces under his Land commander, Naval forces under his admiral, and Air forces under his airman. This seems quite a legitimate request."

" He then told me that Marshall was now definitely retiring, that Eisenhower would replace him. MacArthur said he had told the Government that he was prepared to remain on at his present job for another three or even five years if he was wanted; on the other hand, he was prepared to retire at any moment. In any case he said that this was the last appointment he would hold. So I presume that he no longer has any aspirations to the Presidency."

" He finished by presenting me with a signed photograph of himself. When I thanked him for all his hospitality and great kindness and told him how much I had enjoyed meeting him, he said that it was he who was grateful for my visit which he had greatly appreciated, especially as it was the first time during the war that he had ever been visited by any of the Chiefs of Staff. I am certain he was referring to the fact that the American Chiefs of Staff had not visited him."

" I came away with the impression that he is a very big

man and the biggest general I have yet seen during this war. He is head and shoulders bigger than Marshall, and if he had been in the latter's place during the last four years I feel certain that my task in the Combined Chiefs of Staff would have been far easier."

' MacArthur was the greatest general and best strategist that the war produced. He certainly outshone Marshall, Eisenhower and all other American and British generals including Montgomery. As a fighter of battles and as a leader of men Monty was hard to beat, but I doubt whether he would have shown the same strategic genius had he been in MacArthur's position. After his liberation from Corregidor MacArthur showed considerable political ability in the handling of the Australian Prime Minister, Curtin, and the Australians themselves. He rapidly gained their confidence in the organization of Australia as a base for operations in the Pacific. He directed the employment of Australian forces in the early days, and before adequate American forces were available, in the overland operations through New Guinea. Subsequently with masterly genius he proceeded to leap-frog his way up to the Philippines.'

' In all these operations I never felt he had the full support of the American Chiefs of Staff. Certainly Ernie King bore him no friendly feelings, but this may have been part of the normal friction between the Navy and the Army in the U.S.. I never felt that Marshall had any great affection for MacArthur; I may, of course, have been mistaken but always felt that some slight friction existed there.'

' It must be remembered that he had spent a large part of his life in the Pacific and had acquired a Pacific as opposed to a global aspect. The decisions he finally arrived at as regards the war in Korea were, I think, based on a Pacific outlook and, as such, in my opinion were right. He has been accused of taking actions without previous political approval, but he had been unable to obtain the political policy and the guidance he had sought. To my mind a general who is not prepared to assume some responsibility on his own, when unable to obtain political direction, is of little value.'

' I am convinced that, with the lapse of years and as the war can be viewed in better perspective, it will be agreed that the strategic ability shown by MacArthur was in a class of its own.'

.   .   .   .

Alanbrooke left Tokyo at five o'clock on the morning of November 22nd in cold, pelting rain and landed that evening at Manila in semi-tropical heat. He spent the 23rd visiting Corregidor and the principal scenes of the Philippine fighting. On the 24th, rising at 2 a.m., he made the long flight to Australia, crossing the Equator just before noon and landing at Port Darwin, 2200 miles away, soon after 3 p.m. Here to his joy he found his second mail since leaving England. " It is exactly four weeks," he wrote,

> " since we took off from Hartfordbridge Flats, and it is almost unbelievable the number of countries we have seen, people we have met and problems we have studied and examined. I only wish I had a younger and more retentive brain to store all these treasures without allowing time to blur and dim the sharpness of these impressions."

From Port Darwin, where he asked if there were any aborigines and was taken out to see a settlement of them playing rugger,[1] he flew on the 25th a further two thousand miles to Melbourne, crossing the deserts and salt lakes of the Australian interior—" it would be hard to imagine a more lonely and desolate area." After ten hours' flying he reached Melbourne, delighted to find himself in a city with all its houses intact. Here on the 26th he conferred with the Australian Chiefs of Staff and, being able to report MacArthur's views, made some progress with the settlement of the Commonwealth Occupation Force which was the principal object of the visit. Then, despite

[1] " They had their referee, an interested crowd of spectators and appeared to be conforming to all the rules of the game." *Diary*, 24 Nov., 1945.

a sore throat, heavy cold and splitting headache—after a day in which he made an impromptu speech at a mayoral reception, visited a Bird Sanctuary and dined at Government House, sitting up till midnight talking to the Duke of Gloucester—he rose at 3.15 a.m. on November 27th and flew a further 1700 miles to New Zealand—

> " an interesting country very like England, very green, lovely yellow lupins, golden gorse, sheep everywhere and large herds of Jersey cattle with the bulls feeding with them."

Alanbrooke spent three days in New Zealand, visiting Palmerston, Auckland and Wellington, where he gave an address to the Cabinet, and struggling with his cold which threatened to turn into influenza. " It is a wonderful island," he wrote in his diary, " and the nearest approach to England that I have seen yet. We covered some five hundred miles by car during our short stay and drove right across the Northern Island. I found it all especially interesting as I had made plans to go out and settle in New Zealand some twenty years ago when promotion in the Army seemed hopeless. I kept wondering what my life might have been like if I had come out. I am quite certain of one thing, that no matter what happiness might have been found in this country, it could never have ever compared with the happiness I found with you in England."

On December 1st he started on his homeward journey, reaching Sydney that afternoon. Here he spent two days, flying on one of them to Canberra for an interview with the Commonwealth Prime Minister and enjoying everywhere boundless hospitality. " They were all kindness itself," he wrote, " but Country Clubs are not in my line at all! I am too old to go on talking nonsense to people I am unlikely ever to meet again; I find it very exhausting." Then on the 4th he set off again over the Australian desert, with its vast empty spaces and small scattered homesteads,[1] crossing the continent from east

---

[1] " Looking down one realises what a hard life some of those people must be living, the thinness of the Australians on the ground and their essential need for an increase in their population." *Diary*, 4th Dec. 1945

to west to spend a last few hours in Perth before flying out seventeen hundred miles into the Indian Ocean to Cocos.

" After dinner at 10 p.m. (Perth time) we took off again for our next flight to Cocos. Frankly I dislike this flight. It is a rotten small island to find in a vast ocean, and I pray to God that we may be fortunate in finding it all right! We have a flight of eight hours and fifty minutes. I always have rather a lonely depressed feeling when I take off in a plane, wondering under what conditions I shall again regain touch with the ground! This feeling has never worn off in spite of over 100,000 miles flying; this evening it was stronger than ever."

" I leave Australia with many regrets and wish I could have spent more time here, and at the same time I thank God that I came even for these few days. I have now at least a very hazy outline picture of both Australia and New Zealand, an impression of vast expanses of blotting paper capable of just soaking up humanity. Countries full of problems, and I carry away uneasy feelings from Sydney and Melbourne of too much luxury when there is still a rough and rocky road to follow in the development of the country."

" I saw wonderful specimens of humanity, but not that hardness and love of enterprise and self-sacrifice of the pioneers of a young country. Is this perhaps another sign of the decline of the British Empire? Frankly, I expected to find a hardier and less luxury-loving breed of men than I have seen. I have, however, only visited the large cities and not the back-country, and yet is it not a fact that one of the worst problems of this country is that the luxury of the towns draws the population away from the country which is badly in need of the pioneering hard-bitten type?"

" Must now go and sleep while we fly out into oceanic space in the hope of finding the minute Cocos islands! "

" *December 5th.* Absolutely according to schedule we arrived off Cocos island at dawn after a flight of over eight hours. I did not sleep much owing to the roar of the engines but had quite a comfortable night. Cocos runway is cut straight out of a long strip of an island covered with coconut palms. It has only recently been finished, first to provide a base from which Singapore could be bombed, and secondly for the air-transport route as a stepping-stone between Ceylon and Australia."

" After some three hours' rest for the crew and to refuel with petrol, we started off for Singapore. Before leaving I photographed the crew round the plane and also the Cocos control tower, with the notice on it that the height is only three feet above sea level! "

That evening, after flying close on five thousand miles since leaving Sydney, the C.I.G.S.'s York sighted the Malayan coast.

" We had a wonderful approach to Singapore. Small fleecy clouds and a pearly grey sky with the mass of small islands looking like ink stains on a silvery plate. When I suddenly saw Singapore loom out in front of us my heart almost stood still. Memories of those awful last days of Singapore surged so fast on me that they almost stifled me. Those ghastly days of the loss of Hong Kong, Singapore and Burma just after I had taken over C.I.G.S. cut a deep groove in my mind that can never be obliterated. And there in front of me was Singapore. Somehow all the anxiety, all the anguish, all the shame came flooding in like one great tidal wave, and I found it hard to recover my mental balance in time to step out of the plane to meet Dickie Mountbatten."

" He had got a three-Service guard of honour for me, Navy on the right, Airborne Division in the centre, Air Force parachutists on the left, with a Marine Band playing a General Salute. As I walked round that guard of honour I experienced a feeling which I find impossible to express. Somehow this guard of honour seemed to be an outward and visible sign of the culmination of all my work. Germany beaten, Japan beaten, and all the lost bits of the

Empire restored. I felt, 'Well, now I can return quite peacefully after having seen this.'"

.   .   .   .

During a day and two nights at Singapore the C.I.G.S. settled in conference with Mountbatten, the latter's Chief of Staff, General Browning, and the Army Commander, Sir Miles Dempsey, and with the Dutch and French civil and military authorities, the lines of his recommendations to the Cabinet for dealing with the problems of the Dutch East Indies, Indo-China and Siam. The last two presented no particular difficulty, for General Leclerc, whom Alanbrooke thought the best type of French soldier—" hard bitten, capable and with great charm "—was bringing in two French divisions from Europe to establish order and wanted little now from the British except landing-craft. It was otherwise with Java and Sumatra where the Dutch were still expecting Great Britain to pull their chestnuts out of the fire. Beyond agreeing that Sourabaya should be held for the present and that additional troops should be moved into the Batavia area to create a peaceful zone from which negotiations for a settlement could be carried out, Alanbrooke in his discussions with the Dutch stood firmly by the three principles he and his fellow British commanders had agreed in a midnight conference on the night of his arrival and which he had set down afterwards in his diary:

" (*a*) The problem of using Indian troops in Java, owing to impending trouble in India and the fact that there are no British troops available, does not admit of our contemplating any extensive operations to restore Dutch rule.

" (*b*) Therefore the Dutch must be told that unless they are prepared to grant Dominion Status to the Netherlands East Indies of a nature acceptable to the Indonesians we are not in a position to support them.

" (c) Should they disagree, then we should inform them that we have no alternative but to disassociate ourselves entirely from them and to deal with the Netherlands East Indies purely from the aspect of concluding the war by disarming the Japanese, returning them to Japan and freeing the prisoners they had made. Should the Indonesians interfere with this policy we should inform them that any resistance they offered could only be classified as co-operation with the Japanese and treated accordingly. They all agreed that this was the line to take and the one I should represent to the Government."

"I think," the C.I.G.S. wrote of the meeting with the Dutch on the 6th, "the Conference did good and that Dickie ran it very well. There is no doubt that during the last few years he has come on in a most astonishing way."

Alanbrooke had hoped to continue his journey by way of Ceylon, but owing to the weather he was forced on December 7th to fly to Calcutta instead of Colombo. He spent that night there and reached Bombay on the afternoon of the 8th—a place he had not visited since before the first War.

" I saw myself landing here when twenty-five years old and all the old thrills of that moment came back. I saw myself arriving at the Taj Mahal Hotel on my leaves, with all life coloured at its brightest. I saw myself returning again after periods of leave full of thrills at what lay in front of me. Finally I saw myself with my elbows on the rail of the stern of the P. & O. going home in June 1914 to be married, with grave doubts as to what married life would be like in India without enough money to support a wife and graver doubts as to how I would face the loss of bachelor freedom to wander through jungles and over the Himalayas which had been my one great happiness of the past eight years. As if it had been yesterday, I remember looking back at the Malabar Point as it faded into the mist and feeling that it would be a very sad day when I looked at the same point fading into the distance for the last time. Little did I know then that it would be thirty-one years before I should see the Malabar Point again and that I should then approach it from the air to spend the night on it in Government House! All these thoughts brought with them an overpowering longing to be back landing on the quay in Bombay at the age of twenty-five with all life in front of me. I would willingly go back and start it all again and wish to God that I had the option to do so."

Next day, December 9th, he flew to Aden.

" After five hours we struck the south coast of Arabia just west of Masira island and then skirted along the coast. I had often longed to see what that coast was like. It would be hard to describe the utter desolation, scarcely any signs of life, and it is only here and there that a small cluster of houses is to be seen close to the coast and the white sail of some dhow. In places the coastline is far more mountainous than I had expected. With a tail wind driving us along we made better time than we had expected and arrived half an hour earlier than schedule time. We were met on the aerodrome by a guard of honour of the 1st Patiala Lancers."

Having no business to transact other than to meet the local commanders at a Government House dinner party, Alanbrooke characteristically spent what remained of the day sea-fishing in a motor launch. He caught a 15-lb. albacore and saw " an osprey, some flamingoes and several Red Sea terns ". Then, on the 10th, after breakfasting on the fish he had caught, he flew over Abyssinia and Northern Kenya to Nairobi. Here, in the intervals of inspecting troops and sites for prospective military bases, he spent a night and the best part of two days in the Masai Game Preserve where he saw eighteen major species of wild animal, including elephants, rhinoceroses, giraffes and zebra, and more than thirty different kinds of birds. The rhinoceroses proved particularly agreeable:

" *December 12th.* We got up early and by 6.30 a.m. had started off in our cars to look for rhino. Before long we found a family of three. At first we thought it was Pa, Ma and the baby. However, it turned out to look more like the eternal triangle, because the two larger ones began to fight! We drove up within about a hundred yards of them, and I was busy taking photographs out of the car window when Ritchie[1] suddenly shouted, ' Look out! ' and I saw a huge fourth rhino charging down on the car. I just had time to snap him as he charged before Ritchie swung the car round and tore off. The old rhino did not follow us far."

" Later we found a solitary one and stalked him with the car, but he winded us and started making off. We followed him to try and get a photograph, and I had just asked Ritchie to stop so as to snap him when he turned and came for the car like an express train! I just had time to take one snapshot close to Ritchie's nose before he swung the car away from the rhino. I looked out of the opposite window and found the native tracker sitting on the back seat with the rifle getting ready to shoot, but could see no rhino. I then looked through the back window and in the middle of a cloud of dust of the car saw the old rhino's head closing fast on to the back of the car. It was a thrilling moment! Luckily the going was very good and the car gained momentum rapidly and was doing a good 40 m.p.h., bumping and crashing in all directions. When the rhino found that the car was gaining on him he chucked the pursuit after chasing us for two hundred to three hundred yards. It was most exciting and I would not have missed it for anything."

" We also found another bull elephant which I stalked on foot with Ritchie. We got within seventy to eighty yards, but Ritchie would not go nearer as he said that he gave every sign of being bad-tempered and likely to charge."

[1] The Game Warden.

" After seeing masses of other game we finally returned very ready for breakfast at 10 a.m. Afterwards we went to another small pond where I saw a stilt and several other waders. We went to hunt for the feather-eared oryx which we found and photographed, also some ostriches. We saw many lion tracks but, unfortunately, could not see any lions."

" Returned to camp at 2 p.m. after which we were flown back to Nairobi. Thus finished two of the happiest days I had had for a long time."

The purpose of Alanbrooke's visit to Nairobi was to examine the possibility of locating the British strategic reserve for the Mediterranean and Middle East in Kenya in the event of Egypt being evacuated. During a further day spent flying round the country, in the course of which he saw hundreds of thousands of startled flamingoes over Lake Elmonteita—" a lovely sight never to be forgotten "—he collected the data he required and reached the conclusion that, though a full division could easily be located in the country under ideal health and training conditions, the distances involved were too great and the transport and port facilities too inadequate to make it practicable as a suitable base for a strategic reserve.

On December 14th he flew on to Khartoum, passing over Lake Victoria.

" As I write I am looking out over the lake and its northern shores, a vast expanse of water. How I should love to come down and study the birds that live on its shores. The span of a man's life is too short to be able even to begin to absorb some of the marvels of the world we live in. The more one sees its marvels the more one realises the greatness of God."

" It will be very hard sitting at an office desk in the War Office after being to these wild places. How I wish I could be young again to wander off into the untrodden regions of the world where civilization has not yet succeeded in forcing in its unwelcome face. It is very sad to feel that this interesting trip is coming to an end."

The C.I.G.S. stayed two nights there with the Governor of the Sudan, Sir Hubert Huddleston, and General Paget who had flown from Cairo to meet him. Then on the 16th he crossed back to Asia to visit King Ibn Saud of Saudi Arabia at his capital, Jedda—

"a strange city of miniature Arabic skyscrapers, four to five stories high with much wood carving on the front and very attractive grey houses with their carved windows and verandas. To the Palace for a banquet with the King. The clothes of all the attendants and guests were past description. Everywhere state swords, daggers, pistols, bandoliers of cartridges, rifles and on the top of it all some wonderful wild faces. The King's bodyguard were the most impressive of the lot, dressed in a sort of coloured dressing-gown and covered with weapons of all descriptions."

"I was shown into a large reception room with the King seated on his Throne at the far end. A most impressive-looking figure well over six foot with a refined Arab face. I sat on his right and we spoke about general subjects, mainly connected with my journey. He also introduced me to some of his many sons (forty I believe in all). The youngest is his special pet and the one he drew my attention to repeatedly."

"After talking for about a quarter of an hour we processed in to the banqueting hall. We must have sat down close on sixty to eighty. He had invited the whole of our party including the crew of the aeroplane. The table was groaning with food of every description. Behind me was a footman who kept piling food on to my plate and then removing it while I was talking to the King and then starting again with a new plate and other dishes!"

"It was not long before he started referring to the Russians and his distaste for them. He said that their doctrines in this world were like a cancer in a man's stomach. He told me the story of a hunter who met a snake. The snake said it was being pursued by a wolf and asked for shelter. The hunter put him in his clothes. The snake said it was not enough and that the hunter must put it into his mouth, which the hunter did. Shortly afterwards the snake looked out and said, ' Where is the wolf.' The hunter then told him that the wolf was dead. The snake then said, ' And now you are in my power shall I bite you in the tongue or in the palate? ' "

" After dinner we washed our hands and mouth in a basin handed to us as we rose. The King then rubbed my hands with special scent put on with a stick, and of an oily nature, which we rubbed into our hands. We then sat in a ring on a terrace in the moonlight. First rose-water was brought round and put on our hands,[1] then incense burners swung under our noses. This was followed by much coffee drinking, a bitter brew of coffee with no sugar and a good deal of cinnamon mixed with it. We sat for about half an hour and then excused ourselves."

' The Banquet with Ibn Saud had been a wonderful experience. I had been terrified lest he should press a sheep's eye on me, and wondered what on earth I should do with it; I knew I could not swallow it! Luckily I escaped without having to solve this problem. As we sat at dinner he said to me, " I suppose you know your countryman opposite you? " I looked across the table and saw nothing but a row of bearded Arabs in their native kit. Then amongst them he pointed out Harry St. John Bridger Philby—one of those interesting specimens who has practically made Arabia his home.'

Next day, at the Palace, Alanbrooke had a formal conference with the King and his chief sons and Ministers.

" I started with a dissertation on the mobility of modern war and the difficulty of localizing it. I then passed on to

---

[1] " He said that once equipped in this way it was no longer possible to remain alone in bed. However, he did not provide me with any companion!" Lord Alanbrooke to Lady Brookeborough, 25 Dec., 1945. Lord Alanbrooke, *Personal Files*.

my conversations with the Middle East States on the question of partnership in defence. I told him that I thoroughly realised that his Holy country must always be kept out of war, but that his great influence amongst Arab States would be a great asset if he would give his general support to some form of Confederation of Defence in the Middle East. He was most receptive and said that in his recent visit to Farouk he had recommended partnership with us and the maintenance of friendly relations between all Arab races and the British."

" After that we worked round again to his fear of Russia upsetting the peace of the world and its methods. Finally he came to what was predominant in his mind at present, his difference of opinion with Iraq concerning the surrender of Rashid Ali who has taken refuge with him. According to the Bedouin code he does not like to return him to be hanged; however, he is seeking some diplomatic cover for this action in the shape of existing treaties. Morally his case may be good as an Arab, but politically it struck me as being rather shaky. I then asked him whether he would wish me to convey any message to the King, which he said he would be very grateful for and gave me the usual form of message."

" To finish up the meeting I presented him with a walking stick I had brought out for him with a gold band and an inscription. I then took leave of him and of the Prince Regent and we left for the aerodrome. There again I found one of those marvellous guards of honour of wild men."

" On the whole, I think that my visit to King Ibn Saud may have been of some use; at any rate, it has been of the greatest interest. There is no doubt that he is a genuine friend of the British and a most useful one at that."

After breaking his journey for a few hours at Cairo the C.I.G.S. flew on that night to Naples to stay with the Supreme Commander, Mediterranean, General Sir William Morgan.

Here he discussed the latter's problems and met the new American Theatre Commander, General Ridgway,[1] who impressed him deeply both as a soldier and a man. He should have left for England on the 19th, but for the first time on his tour the weather ahead closed down completely and he was air-bound at Naples for a day. He spent it giving a lecture on the world situation to the officers of Morgan's Headquarters and in discussing war experiences with Ridgway. Then, as the weather in Northern Europe still made his flight home impossible, he flew to Rome on the 20th in " torrents of rain and howling wind ". Here he spent an afternoon sightseeing and secured an Audience with the Pope for that evening.

But as he was being taken round the newly-excavated Pagan tombs in the foundations of St. Peter's he met with an accident.

" As we were finishing our inspection I stepped into an open drain in the dark with a two-foot drop. At the bottom there was an iron pipe which caught my toes and bent my foot up, giving my Achilles tendon and calf a fearful wrench. It was real agony for a few minutes and I nearly passed out; the whole place began to swim round and I had to sit down for a bit. I succeeded then in hobbling out in great pain and went to the hotel where I fomented the leg in hot water and sent for the doctor. He said he did not think anything was broken, but the sinews were torn; he nevertheless wanted to take an X-ray photograph."

" I had, however, an appointment with the Pope for 6 p.m. which I did not want to miss. I therefore left the hotel at 5.30 p.m. to pick up Osborne, our Representative at the Vatican, and we went on together. After a long and very painful walk through many chambers with Swiss Guards, we were finally shown in to His Holiness's Presence. He was dressed in white with a little white skull-cap, a very pleasant face and very easy to talk to. I told him about my journeys and impressions and he was very interested.

---

[1] He afterwards commanded in Korea and became Chief of Staff in Washington.

It was apparently a great privilege that he had agreed to see me at 6 p.m. which is not one of his reception hours. We discussed Russia mainly and its threat to the peace of the world. He finally gave me a silver medal of himself as a souvenir. I then introduced Rollie and Brian."[1]

' I am afraid that I must have created a very poor impression on the Pope! My leg was hurting very badly and I did not know how I would ever manage the visit, so Lockwood, my invaluable batman, took the matter in hand and gave me the largest brandy I have ever drunk! It had a marvellous effect as regards restoring my morale, and with the help of two sticks I felt like facing anything. But when I entered the room swaying on two sticks and breathing brandy I am certain that the Pope wrote me off as one of those drunken Orangemen from the North of Ireland that are beyond praying for! Perhaps he hoped that the silver medal with his face on one side and the Good Samaritan on the other might do something towards reforming me from my wicked ways. In any case he was certainly quite charming and never disclosed his feelings.'

After an agonizing two days with his foot, in the course of which he had a conference with the Italian Prime Minister, de Gasperi, the weather cleared sufficiently to make the flight to England possible and in the early afternoon of December 23rd Alanbrooke landed at Blackbushe aerodrome. In eight weeks he had covered 42,404 miles, bringing his total flying distance since the beginning of the war to 157,700 miles or more than six times the circumference of the globe. During his tour he had visited sixteen countries and met eight Sovereign Rulers or Regents, five Prime Ministers, eleven Governors and the Pope. And he had obtained the necessary information and prepared the ground for the three major tasks which lay before him: the making of a C.O.S. key-plan for Bevin's mutual defence Confederation for the Middle East, the

[1] Colonels Charrington and Boyle, his Personal and Military Assistants, to both of whom Brooke paid a glowing tribute in his diary of the trip.

dispatch of a Commonwealth Occupation Force to Japan under Australian Command, and the organization of regional Zones of Defence for the Empire."

.   .   .   .

Alanbrooke spent Christmas Day at home with his wife and children but, despite having to have his leg put in plaster of Paris, he was not allowed much peace. On December 27th he was summoned to Chequers by the Prime Minister for a conference with the Dutch Prime Minister, Foreign Secretary and Minister of Overseas Territories and the Governor-General of the East Indies to discuss a settlement of the Indonesian problem on the lines he had recommended.

> " We met with them during the whole afternoon and went on after tea and dinner only finishing up about 11 p.m. We did, however, make some progress and arrived at a general statement for the Press. The most important part was the new concessions which the Dutch are prepared to make and which may go a long way towards settling matters in Java."

> ' This was my first visit to Chequers under the Attlee régime. Somehow it was all very different from the Winston days, but there was perhaps a homely atmosphere which did not exist in the former days. The period was just after Christmas, and the decorations showed that the Attlee family had just spent a very happy quiet Christmas at Chequers.'

On New Year's Day, 1946, Alanbrooke was made a Viscount. A few weeks later he took his seat in the House of Lords, feeling, he wrote after the ceremony, rather like Alice in Wonderland. Other honours conferred on him at this time were a D.C.L. at Cambridge, the Freedom of the City of London, the American Distinguished Service Medal, the Grand Cross of the Legion of Honour and the Grand Cordon of Leopold, during the presentation of which in Brussels he again wrenched his injured leg and all but fainted on the Palace stairs. He was also given three Czech awards by President Benes at a ceremony in

Prague to which he flew through fog and snow in February, subsequently going on to Vienna to inspect the British Occupation Forces in Austria and stay with their commander, Dick McCreery, whom he had made Chief of Staff to Alexander in 1942 and whose part in the great Tunis victory had never, he felt, been sufficiently recognized.

Three weeks after the end of his Commonwealth tour the C.I.G.S., to his intense relief, settled the date of his retirement —at midsummer—and the appointment of Montgomery as his successor. His leg was continuing to give him a good deal of pain which increased his general exhaustion; in March, as the medical authorities at Millbank considered him too old for a successful operation, he was fitted with iron leg-supports and told—wrongly, as it turned out—that he would never have a sound foot again. " I am feeling," he confided to his diary, " abominably weary." He had by now lost the last of the colleagues with whom in the dark days of 1942 he had planned the turn of the tide. " I shall miss him badly," he had written on December 31st, when the Chief of Air Staff attended his final C.O.S. meeting.

' We understood each other well, were prepared to have the most heated professional discussions, but these were never allowed to affect our personal relations. I had the greatest admiration for Peter's ability, not only in connection with the air where he was superb but in all the other matters we had to deal with. In debate with the Americans he was invaluable and had a wonderful way of clarifying complicated problems. The country was indeed fortunate to have had a man of such ability and character at the head of the Air Force throughout the war.'

Portal's place was filled by Tedder, while about the same time Alanbrooke's other colleague on the C.O.S., Andrew Cunningham, was temporarily forced to go sick owing to heart strain.

All this increased the C.I.G.S.'s burden and the Government's dependence on his experience and judgment. The policies it was pursuing did not always meet with his approval.

Its demand for the rapid reduction of the Armed Forces was incompatible, as he pointed out, with the commitments they had to meet. " We have now," he wrote after a Defence Committee meeting on January 21st,

> " provided estimates of the man-power situation in June, '46, December '46 and March '47. These later dates consist of mere crystal-gazing, and yet we are asked to cut another 350,000 out of our December figure. I said we would convert this new figure into the corresponding loss of security for the Cabinet to decide whether they are prepared to take this risk. In any case it is for them to decide."

" Dalton," he added three weeks later, " is wanting another 10% cut on the estimates."

> " We discussed further cuts in our Army strength; we had produced a paper showing that cuts must seriously affect the efficiency of the three Fighting Services, would necessitate serious risks in Germany and could only be achieved on the assumption that both Italy and Greece would be evacuated before the end of the year. Apparently Defence Committee were prepared to accept these conditions. . . ."

None the less, though he did not share their faith in the ability of the United Nations organization to keep the peace, Alanbrooke was far from being critical of his new political masters. " I wish to record," he wrote after his last day as C.I.G.S., " that I found this Labour Government most co-operative to work with: Bevin a tower of strength, Addison always ready to help if possible, and Attlee a good business man who certainly got through a Cabinet meeting far quicker and more efficiently than his predecessor." When he made his report on his Commonwealth tour to the Prime Minister he found him a charming and most attentive listener who asked many shrewd questions and obviously took a real interest in everything he had to relate. As for the Foreign Secretary,

Alanbrooke's admiration for him grew steadily. " The more I see of Bevin," he wrote on January 4th, " the more impressed I am by him and by his great qualities. He approaches all his problems from the simplest of points of view and arrives at clear-cut solutions." " He is a most wonderful helpful individual always full of ideas," he added two months later. " It is astonishing the ease with which he absorbs international situations and the soundness of his judgment."[1]

Among the problems the Foreign Secretary had to solve were those which had faced the C.I.G.S. on his Commonwealth tour. The most intractable from Alanbrooke's point of view were Egypt and the security of the Middle East. The Government felt that evacuation to the Canal Zone and ultimately to Kenya was the only solution; but for Bevin and the Chiefs of Staff Committee a complete withdrawal from the Eastern Mediterranean would probably have taken place. Yet though the inadequacy of its rail, road and port facilities, which Alanbrooke had seen to be the insuperable obstacle to the use of Kenya as the main base for Britain's overseas reserve, was accepted as such by the Government, as a result of a mission by Lord Stansgate to Cairo in the spring the demands of the Egyptian " anti-imperialists " were conceded almost *in toto*, regardless of security requirements. Alanbrooke recognized, though with reluctance, the inevitability of evacuation from a country which had been given full sovereignty and independence by the 1936 Anglo-Egyptian Treaty; at a conference on April 28th, he supported Bevin against Smuts whose views for once he considered to be unrealistic.

" Smuts does not agree that we should clear out. On the whole he is inclined to take a rather diehard attitude,

[1] *Diary*, 18 Mar., 1946. " Cabinet from 11 to 12.30 to discuss Estimates and White Paper. . . . Thanks to Bevin we finally got it all through." *Idem*, 18 Feb. " Bevin as usual very wise and clear in his vision." *Idem*, 28 March. " Bevin in tremendous form telling stories after dinner such as the following:—' Lady at the Zoo talking to Zoo keeper,' ' And what might this animal be, my man? ' ' That, my lady, is a hippopotamus.' ' Indeed! how very interesting, my man, and is this a gentleman or lady hippopotamus? ' ' That, my lady, can only be a matter of interest to another hippopotamus.' " *Idem*, 12 April.

prepared to run all the risks but not to provide the resources to meet these risks. Also he had not clearly realised that we should be in a very awkward position when Egypt appealed to U.N.O. to clear us out after we had been shooting them up in an attempt to enforce our stay in the country. It is an unpleasant business, but I think we have chosen the right course."

But the C.I.G.S. also felt, in view of the vital strategic importance of the Suez Canal, that the British negotiators were showing a lack of backbone in not obtaining an adequate *quid pro quo* from the Egyptian politicians. " To my mind," he wrote " we are on a slippery slope and are gracefully sliding out of Egypt without getting anything in the way of security."[1] He told the Cabinet so bluntly and when, a few days before his retirement, the Prime Minister asked him whether he would go out to Cairo to join the negotiators, he refused. " I do not like the whole business at all," he wrote. " I am anxious not to be connected with that Treaty more than I can help, as I am not in sympathy with it and do not agree with Stansgate's handling of it."

There was another and still graver threat to the Commonwealth's strategic future but one against which, though he saw it clearly, Alanbrooke felt there could be no contending. During the six months that remained to him after his return from the Far East, he was busy trying to put into practice his project for basing the future security of the Empire on Zones of Interest, each centred round a Commonwealth nation under the strategic control of its own inter-Service Chiefs of Staff Committee and linked with one another by an Imperial Chiefs of Staff Committee. Under this scheme every member of the Commonwealth would accept responsibility for a mutual defence Zone and within it, and, in conjunction with its smaller neighbours and dependencies, prepare and put into execution plans to meet any hostile eventuality.

But the Government's decision to withdraw from India and

Diary, 6 June, 1946.

allow the country to be partitioned was to cause a fatal gap in Alanbrooke's proposed chain of inter-linked Defence Zones encircling the globe. At the beginning of April the Defence Committee had formally approved his plan for making the Middle East, India, Burma and Ceylon, and Australasia the main Zones of Defence for the Eastern hemisphere. But a week later, on April 12th, the C.O.S. Committee met to consider

> " the Cabinet's decision to accept the partition of India into Pakistan and Hindustan sooner than plunge India into chaos by failure of negotiations and requiring from the Chiefs of Staff a Strategic Appreciation showing the effects of such a partition on Defence. We pointed out the weaknesses and the fact that in such a case defensive security should be sought in a Defensive Committee covering Pakistan, Hindustan, Native States, Burma and Ceylon."

' With the loss of India and Burma, the keystone of the arch of our Commonwealth Defence was lost, and our Imperial Defence crashed. Without the central strategic reserve of Indian troops ready to operate either east or west we were left impotent and even the smallest of nations were at liberty to twist the lion's tail.'[1]

' And yet,' Alanbrooke added, ' I do not see how we could have remained in India and I think we were right in withdrawing when we did; but few realised what the strategic loss would amount to.'

One farewell legacy the C.I.G.S. bequeathed to the national defence system before he relinquished office. On February 18th, at a meeting of senior Ministers at Downing Street, the C.O.S. Committee's proposals were approved for the appointment of a Defence Minister and the correlation of the three Service Ministers under him. In an Address which he gave to the Royal Empire Society shortly after his retirement Alanbrooke defined the principles underlying this change in the

[1] *Notes on My Life*, XVII, 68.

traditional peacetime system of controlling the nation's Fighting Forces.

" The actions of the three Fighting Services must in the first place be closely integrated. It is not sufficient only to rely on such integration once hostilities are forced on us. The development of the three Services in times of peace must be co-ordinated and correlated to ensure that we have a closely-knit and well-balanced fighting machine at our disposal. This in itself is not sufficient. Our fighting machine must be closely enmeshed into the gear wheels of Government. Modern defence embraces questions intimately connected with foreign policy, home security, man-power labour, transportation, supply, food, and most of the other matters of Government concern. Defensive plans at all times must be closely interlocked with the activities of all the various Government Departments so as to ensure that from their very inception they are built on the rocks of close co-operation and not on the sands of isolation. Furthermore, the defensive organization must be so closely integrated with the Government executive as to provide responsible statesmen with that true appreciation of the country's strength and weakness so essential in ensuring a relation between selected policy and the strength required to support it."

" We have built up in this country during the last couple of decades the organization of the Chiefs of Staff Committee, constituting probably the best system that history has produced up to date. This organization started between the two World Wars and functioned for the first time during the last War. It worked admirably and stood up to all the stresses and strains of six years of war, emerging finally in a more mature form. As a result of experience gained in war, it has now been amplified by the formation of a Defence Ministry."[1]

.   .   .   .

[1] *Address to Royal Empire Society*, 4 Nov., 1946. Lord Alanbrooke, *Personal Files.*

At the end of March Alanbrooke opened a three days' Commander-in-Chiefs' Conference at Camberley. At its close he bade farewell to those who had been his principal lieutenants during the war. ' It had been a very long association and through momentous days, and it was all I could do to prevent myself breaking down and my good-bye had consequently to be shortened.' One of those present was soon to succeed him, and one of his minor problems that winter was that of " drilling into Monty how he is to behave when he takes over C.I.G.S." For fame and victory had not dimmed his brilliant protégé's talent for making the sparks fly, as one exasperated diary entry reveals.

" At 5 p.m. interview with Secretary of State concerning Monty's most recent statements to the Press! As usual he has been stirring matters up by making unnecessary state-ments such as ' Occupation must last another ten years at least '; ' You need have no fear, we shall export no food to Germany ' (when Cabinet had just decided to do so) and other such statements. As a result we shall have to wire him to come and see Secretary of State."[1]

For, despite the far more placid tone of his entries since Churchill's departure, the diarist could still on occasion be caustic. " He does not improve on acquaintance," he wrote of one statesman, " but no doubt possesses all the necessary qualities for a successful political career," and of another—of the opposite Party—" He is not at his best when he is frightened and it does not require a great deal to frighten him! "

Yet, on the whole, though a tired, it was a relaxed and equable recorder whom the diary—hitherto so anxious and troubled—mirrored in its last year. " As you say," he wrote to his niece, " things have changed, and I am no longer pulled out after dinner to see Winston; work goes much quicker and easier and I am no longer bombarded by Minutes."[2] It made his pages seem almost as unruffled and calm as he him-

---

[1] *Diary*, 9 April, 1946. ' Poor Monty! he should have known by then the dangers of talking to the Press. I cannot, however, see any great sin in his prediction that the Occupation would last another ten years.' *Notes on My Life* XVII, 69.

[2] To Lady Brookeborough, 27 August, 1945.

self had always appeared to his colleagues at desk or conference table. And its judgments now were nearly always kindly. When Eisenhower, whose strategy he had criticized so severely, was given the Freedom of the City of London, he was full of praise.

> " Ike made a *wonderful* speech and impressed all hearers in the Guildhall including all the Cabinet. He then made an equally good speech of a different kind outside the Mansion House, and a first-class speech at the Mansion House lunch. I had never realized that Ike was as big a man until I heard his performance to-day."

And when the Labour Ministers, after their decision to grant immediate independence to India, showed unexpected firmness towards unreasonable Indian demands that threatened a breakdown, he gave them full credit.

> " I was interested in the general attitude of the Cabinet which showed considerable backbone and no inclination towards a hasty exodus out of India[1]. . . . After we left the Cabinet, opinion went even further towards not letting Congress dictate to us."

.   .   .   .

Though the ceaseless anxiety of the war years was over and no longer reflected in his diary, Alanbrooke had worries of his own. With two families to provide for and more obligations to meet than his retirement gratuity of £311 and his future pay as an unemployed Field-Marshal would cover, he was trying to sell his home and to find some employment for the future. When one of his senior assistants left the Army to return to Industry, he remarked, half in earnest, half in jest, " Can you give me some sort of job when I get out, for I can't afford not to work and goodness knows who will have me when all this is over." He confided his troubles to his niece, telling her that he was looking for " some means of making money,"

---

[1] *Diary,* 5 June, 1946. " We put up a C.O.S. paper to the Cabinet showing that should the Indian Army not remain reliable our commitment might be a very heavy one. Cabinet prepared to face the music." *Idem,* 17 June.

" I am broke and forced to sell my bird books. I hope to find something in the line of a directorship which will help me along. I had hoped to settle down and enjoy the few remaining years fishing and photographing birds but no doubt will find some time for that too."[1]

For having as yet been unable to sell his house—a problem aggravated by a fire which destroyed the stables—and having no money to buy a smaller, he was now forced to dispose of his most prized possession:

" *April 11th.* After lunch with a very heavy heart went to Francis Edwards, the bookseller, to discuss the sale of my Gould collection. It looks as if I should make a profit on it but it is a frightful wrench."

' I had the whole complete collection of Gould's works, 45 volumes. It nearly broke my heart having to part with them. But, as I had to buy my house to live in, I could not afford to keep this capital locked up in books.'

He had compensations of another kind. Before he retired Alanbrooke received the greatest honour of his career. " Received a letter from Lascelles," he wrote on April 10th,

" stating that the King wished to confer the Order of Merit on me in his Birthday Honours List."

' My remarks in my diary,' he commented afterwards,

' are surprisingly laconic and certainly fail to give any idea of the intense satisfaction I felt. Of all the orders and decorations that I received none of them have ever seemed in the same category. I felt intense gratitude that my services should have been recognized in such a manner.'

He probably obtained an almost equal satisfaction from two letters which he received about this time from the men who had been his principal lieutenants. When the announcement

---

[1] To Lady Brookeborough, 16 Jan., 1946.

of Brooke's impending retirement was made, Montgomery, who was to be his successor, wrote

" During the late war you have given me many tasks to carry out; each one has been more difficult than the last, and each one has somehow been brought to a successful conclusion. But there have been moments when I have gone " off the rails ": due to impetuosity, irritation, or some such reason. You always pulled me back on to the rails, and I started off down the course again. I know very well that when I used to go " off the rails " it increased your own work and anxieties 100 per cent. But you never complained. In the goodness of your heart you lent me a helping hand and asked nothing in return: not that I could have done anything for you.

I want to say two things.
First. I am terribly grateful for all you have done for me.
Second. I could never have achieved anything if you had not
    been there to help me; it has been your wise guidance,
    and your firm handling of a very difficult subordinate,
    that really did the business. I could have done
    nothing alone."[1]

From Archie Nye, who as V.C.I.G.S. had been his assistant for four and a half years of ceaseless strain and responsibility, Brooke received a further letter:

" I felt far too deeply and was much too affected to say all I wanted to say to you—and I can't even in a letter—it would need an essay! And indeed, I hope to write one so that those coming on will know what sort of problems you had to face and how you mastered them. I was in a better position than anyone else to know all you had to cope with; and could therefore know better than others not only your great gifts but your singleness of purpose, your incorruptibility and your absolute integrity—and a combination of these qualities has made you a gigantic figure which no one could fail to admire.

[1] Printed in *The Turn of the Tide*, 32-33.

" But above all this, you gave me your confidence and your friendship, and you gave with both hands and unreservedly. I shall always remember the warmth of your affection and will treasure your friendship as one of the most rare and precious things I possess."[1]

It was a time of partings. At the end of April the C.I.G.S. attended the Foreign Secretary's farewell dinner to Winant, the American Ambassador, a friend for whom he had come to feel deep affection. A few days later, on May 2nd, he spent his last night in the familiar flat in Westminster Gardens. " The walls," he wrote,

> " are stripped of their pictures, most of the chairs are gone, the writing-table removed, and memories of the last four and a half years surge round me. The unpleasant nights with bombs crashing round, the late telephone calls from Winston to come to 10 Downing Street, the return home at 3 a.m. worn to a shred, those horrible wakeful moments in the early hours when all life looks at its worst and doubts swamp one's confidence, those lovely spells when you came to share the flat, quiet restful evenings after long trying days, and many solitary hours when I communed with myself and wondered how correct I was in the policies I was pursuing."

For the rest of May Alanbrooke was on leave, taking a fishing holiday in Scotland, by far the longest spell of absence he had enjoyed since he crossed to France in September 1939. He returned on June 3rd for his last three weeks as C.I.G.S. and for the critical Cabinet and Defence Committee debates over the evacuation of Egypt and India. On the 8th, with his two war-time colleagues, he took part in the Victory Parade.

> " Shortly after 8 a.m. motored to Regent's Park where all Commanders were being assembled. After waiting about for some time Cunningham, Portal and I got into

[1] Gen. Sir Archibald Nye to C.I.G.S., 3 Feb., 1945. Lord Alanbrooke, *Personal Files*.

the leading car. It was a tight fit, but we all three got into the one seat. We had insisted on travelling in the same car. They had first of all offered one car for First Sea Lord and C.I.G.S. and a separate one for the Chief of Air Staff. But we refused and said we had been united as a trinity throughout the War and could not be separated on such an occasion! "

" We went the whole course of the Mechanised Column and finally fetched up at the Grand Stand on the Mall. There the Royal Family and Attlee and Winston gradually collected, with finally the King."

" The Parade ran like clockwork and was most impressive. When it was over you and I motored off to 10 Downing Street for lunch. In the evening we went to the House of Commons and left the children on the terrace whilst we went to the Lord Chamberlain's room to see the fireworks. We found there the King, Queen, Queen Mary, the Princesses, the Duchess of Kent, Crown Prince of Norway, Athlones, Churchill family, Attlee family. Did not get home till after midnight."

' I did not attempt that evening to commit to paper what my feelings had been during that Victory Parade. Nor could I do so now. All I remember distinctly now is sniffing hard and hoping nobody saw me wiping my eyes.'

Three days later the First Sea Lord—now Lord Cunningham of Hyndhope—attended the Chiefs of Staff meeting for the last time. It was for Brooke the passing of a tried comrade—the first seaman of the age—whom he had not only learnt to rely on implicitly but to love. His own departure followed a fortnight later.

" *June 24th.* My last full day as C.I.G.S. During the morning said goodbye to Adjutant-General, Director Royal Artillery and Permanent Under-Secretary. After lunch my last C.O.S. meeting at which ' Pug ' said a few nice remarks. The meeting brought back vividly our first that I attended when I succeeded Dill and was welcomed by Pound and Portal. I shudder to think of all the meetings I have attended since! "

" At 5 p.m. went to a meeting of Attlee, Stansgate and Orme Sargent on the Egyptian Treaty. I was there for 1½ hours and finally had to dash off to the Palace to receive my O.M. in company with dear old Andrew Cunningham."

" After dinner at 9.30 p.m. sent for again by P.M. who wanted to know whether I would go out to Cairo to assist with the negotiations. I refused on the grounds of being too tired and not fresh enough. . . ."

" *June 25th.* My last day as C.I.G.S.! My four and a half years to a day will have been completed, plus an additional month which I did for Dill while he was still officially in the Chair. There have been moments when I wondered whether I should last the course—times of intense fatigue when work had become an unbearable burden, when responsibility weighed heavier than ever and when it became more and more difficult to make decisions. My feelings were so mixed that I found it hard to disentangle them. But above everything the longing for rest predominated over all other feelings. The last day was necessarily a trying one. Good-byes to Kirkman, Simpson, Eric Speed, Jack Lawson, Miss Wolf, all the clerks, hall porters, etc."

" Thus ended my active military career."

After that Alanbrooke went back to his temporary flat, packed his clothes and drove down to Norfolk where he had arranged to stay with his friend and fellow ornithologist, Sir Archibald Jamieson, at Thornham. He spent what he described as " two lovely days, one on Scolt Head Island and one on Hickling Marshes " making a film of a roseate tern which had just hatched off her family; " my two days in Norfolk," he wrote, " softened the break." And with that his diary ended.

ACKNOWLEDGMENTS

IN WRITING this volume, covering the last two years of a world-wide war, I have been indebted to many, only a few of whom there is space to mention by name. First I have to thank Field-Marshal Lord Montgomery, who with great kindness and generosity has again allowed me to use his unpublished letters; Field-Marshal Lord Alexander has also generously given me leave to quote from his wartime letters to Lord Alanbrooke; and Nancy Lady Dill who has allowed me to quote from those of her husband, the late Field-Marshal Sir John Dill. I am also indebted to Lady Brookeborough for permission to use letters written to her by her uncle, Lord Alanbrooke, and to Major Nigel Aitken for the use of letters written to him. For their great kindness in reading and criticising the book in manuscript and proof and for making many invaluable suggestions I have to thank the Rt. Hon. Sir James Grigg who, as Secretary of State for War, was Lord Alanbrooke's political chief during the greater part of his term of office; General Sir Archibald Nye who was his Assistant Vice-C.I.G.S. from 1941 to 1946; General Sir Bernard Paget who was his Chief of Staff in 1940 and later succeeded him as Commander-in-Chief, Home Forces; Lieut.-General Sir Ian Jacob, formerly Military Assistant Secretary to the War Cabinet; Field-Marshal Lord Montgomery; General Sir William Morgan; Mr. C. D. Hamilton; Captain Bertram Brooke, Tuan Muda of Sarawak; Mr. Herbert van Thal; Mr. Adrian House; Mr. Mark Bonham Carter, M.P.; and Mr. Ronald Politzer. Even more am I indebted to Mr. Milton Waldman who has given me the benefit of his wise advice and constructive criticism at every stage of my labours, and to Mrs. M. C. Long for her invaluable work in research and in checking facts and figures, as well as to my secretary, Miss Elizabeth Black, who must have typed every sentence in the book, in one form or another, at least half a dozen times. My gratitude, too, is due to the Librarian of the War Office, Mr. King, and his staff, and to Mrs. Astley, formerly Miss Joan Bright and secretary during the war to General Lord Ismay. Last but certainly not least, I must thank Lord Alanbrooke, whose diary and autobiographical notes are the foundation of this book and form so large a part of it, and whose help and advice have been at my disposal throughout its preparation and writing.

I am grateful to the authors and publishers for permission to quote important extracts from the following works: *The Second World War*, by Sir Winston Churchill, Cassell, and Houghton Mifflin; *History of The Second World War, Grand Strategy*, Vols. V and VI. by J. Ehrman, H.M.S.O.; *The White House Papers of Harry L. Hopkins*, Vol. II, by Robert E. Sherwood, Eyre & Spottiswoode, and Harper & Bros.; *Fleet Admiral King* by Whitehill & King, Eyre & Spottiswoode, and Norton; *Three Years with Eisenhower* by H. C. Butcher, Wm. Heinemann, and Simon & Schuster; *The Goebbels Diaries*, Ed. Louis Lochner, Hamish Hamilton, and Doubleday; *Top Secret* by Ralph Ingersoll, Frederick Muller, and Harcourt Brace.

The photograph from which the frontispiece is taken is by Lieutenant Maurice Constant, United States Naval Reserve, and the maps were drawn by Mr. Charles Green.

LIST OF ABBREVIATIONS USED IN
FOOTNOTES

ARNOLD.—H. H. Arnold, *Global Mission*, 1951.

BEHRENS.—C. B. A. Behrens, *Merchant Shipping and the Demands of War* (H.M.S.O.), 1955.

BRADLEY.—O. Bradley, *A Soldier's Story*, 1951.

BUTCHER.—H. C. Butcher, *Three Years with Eisenhower*, 1946.

CHURCHILL.—W. S. Churchill, *The Second World War*, Vols. V and VI, 1952 and 1954.

CROSS-CHANNEL ATTACK.—*United States Army in World War II: European Theatre of Operations*—G. A. Harrison, *Cross-Channel Attack*, 1951.

DEFEAT INTO VICTORY.—Field-Marshal Sir William Slim, *Defeat into Victory*, 1956.

DE GUINGAND.—F. de Guingand, *Operation Victory*, 1947.

DIARY.—Field-Marshal Lord Alanbrooke, MS. *Diaries*, 1939-46.

EHRMAN.—John Ehrman, *History of the Second World War, Grand Strategy*, (H.M.S.O.) Vols. V and VI, 1956.

EISENHOWER.—D. Eisenhower, *Crusade in Europe*, 1948.

FEIS.—Herbert Feis, *Churchill, Roosevelt, Stalin*, 1957.

GILBERT.—P. Gilbert, *Hitler Directs His War*, 1950.

GOEBBELS.—*The Goebbels Diaries* (ed. L. P. Lochner), 1948.

LEAHY.—Fleet Admiral W. D. Leahy, *I Was There*, 1950.

MONTGOMERY, MEMOIRS.—Field-Marshal Lord Montgomery, *The Memoirs of Field-Marshal Montgomery*, 1958.

MORISON.—Samuel Eliot Morison, *U.S. Naval Operations in World War II*, 1948-57.

NORMANDY TO THE BALTIC.—Field-Marshal Lord Montgomery, *Normandy to the Baltic*, 1947.

NOTES ON MY LIFE.—Field-Marshal Lord Alanbrooke, MS. *Autobiographical Notes*.

PERSONAL FILES.—Field-Marshal Lord Alanbrooke, MS. *Files of Personal Correspondence*.

POGUE.—Forrest C. Pogue, *United States Army in World War II—The Supreme Command*, 1954.

SPEIDEL.—General Speidel, *We Defended Normandy*, 1951.

STILWELL PAPERS.—*The Stilwell Papers* (ed. T. H. White), 1949.

WHITE HOUSE PAPERS.—Robert E. Sherwood, *The White House Papers of Harry L. Hopkins*, Vol. II, 1949.

WHITEHILL.—E. J. King and W. M. Whitehill, *Fleet Admiral King*, 1953.

WILMOT.—Chester Wilmot, *The Struggle for Europe*, 1952.

INDEX

Aachen, 283, 317, 422, 423
Abadan, 500
Aberdeen, 185
Abdul-Ilah, Crown Prince (Regent of Irak), 500
Abyssinia, 520
Accolade, Operation, 50, 52
Adam, Gen. Sir R., 73, 126, 163, 251, 376, 419, 540
Addison, Rt. Hon. Viscount, 530
Addu Attol, 168
Aden, 520
Adige, R., 374, 380
Admiralty Islands, 166
Adriatic, 47, 120, 215, 216, 221, 267, 283, 318, 340
Aegean, 47, 49, 50, 68, 70, 76, 79, 82, 84, 103, 107, 297
Afghanistan, 502
Africa, *see under* North, West, East and South Africa
Aitken, Major Nigel, 451, 478, 543
Akyab, 43, 504
Alamein, El, battle of, 138, 228, 442, 454
Alam Halfa, battle of, 28, 35
Alanbrooke, Field-Marshal Viscount (*see* Brooke, Field-Marshal Sir Alan)
Albania, 30, 66, 67, 404
Aldershot, 471
Alençon, 251
Alexander, Rt. Hon. A. V., 483
Alexander, Field-Marshal Sir Harold (Earl)
  Brooke's regard for, 117, 231, 258, 396, 474
  " a soldier of the very highest principles ", 117, 426
  conduct of Italian campaign, 47, 48, 55, 56, 57, 69, 78, 105, 106, 118-24, 138-9, 148-9, 159, 165, 172, 174, 181, 183, 184, 189, 193, 194-5, 197, 200, 205, 209, 212, 213, 221, 222, 224, 226, 227, 229, 230, 253-8, 272, 275, 283, 287, 294-5, 314, 318, 373, 375, 395, 399, 440, 452

wanted by Eisenhower for *Overlord*, 114-5
high opinion of German troops, 174
criticized by Churchill, 229, 230
plan for advance on Vienna, 222, 223-4, 226, 227, 254-6, 287, 294, 295, 374
relations with Gen. Maitland Wilson, 258
promotion to Field-Marshal, 267
made Supreme Commander, Mediterranean, 320-2, 332-3, 347
suggested as Deputy Supreme Commander to Eisenhower, 341, 374, 390, 392, 396, 401, 416, 425-6
commits forces to Greece, 351, 376, 380-1, 382, 388, 396
at Yalta, 403, 411
receives peace proposals, 427-8
receives surrender of nearly a million Germans, 452-3
difficulties over Trieste, 455, 466, 468
proposed by Churchill for War Office, 472
made Governor-General of Canada, 473, 474-5
given Freedom of Belfast, 492
letters from, 174, 213, 255, 287, 543
Brooke's letters to, 159, 189, 255, 287, 381
other references, 111, 130, 163, 261, 418, 419, 478, 529
Alexandria, 72, 74
Algiers, 69, 116, 181n, 205, 326
Allfrey, Lt.-Gen. Sir C., 148
Alsace, 262, 363, 374, 376
Alsos, 333
Alurka, 402
Alushta, 402
Ambala, 503
Amboina, 217, 232, 266
Amery, Rt. Hon. L. S., 131, 188, 252
Amiens, 375
Amman, 498
Ancona, 209, 255, 258
Andaman Is., 76, 77, 88, 91, 95, 104, 106, 108

547